ecpr classics

ies Editors:
Alan Ware (University of Oxford) and
Vincent Hoffmann-Martinot (Sciences Po Bordeaux)

people, states & fear

second edition

an agenda for international security studies in the post-cold war era

Barry Buzan

with a new introduction by the author

© Barry Buzan

First published in 1991
by Harvester Wheatsheaf

First published by the ECPR Press in 2007

The ECPR Press is the publishing imprint of the European Consortium for
Political Research (ECPR), a scholarly association, which supports and encourages the training, research and cross-national cooperation of political scientists in
institutions throughout Europe and beyond. The ECPR's Central Services are
located at the University of Essex, Wivenhoe Park,
Colchester, CO4 3SQ, UK

Typeset in Times 10pt by the ECPR Press
Printed and bound in the UK by the University of Essex Print Centre

British Library Cataloguing in Publication Data
A catalogue record for this book is available from the British Library

ISBN13 978-0-9552488-1-8

The ECPR Classics series is published by the ECPR Press, the publishing imprint of the European Consortium for Political Research (ECPR).

As an independent, scholarly institution, one of the ECPR's objectives is to facilitate research in political science among European universities. To that end, the ECPR has developed a strong publishing portfolio since the 1970s.

The policy to extend that portfolio by launching its own publishing imprint was discussed by the Executive Committee of the ECPR in 2002, and the decision to proceed was taken in early 2003.

It was decided that the first two series to be published under the imprint should be complementary. The ECPR Monographs series publishes major new research in all sub-disciplines of political science. The ECPR Classics series facilitates scholarly access to significant works from earlier eras of political science by re-publishing books that have been out of print. It believes this will enable contemporary students and researchers to develop their own work more effectively.

While every effort has been made to reproduce faithfully the original text, the pagination of this ECPR Classics edition differs slightly from the pagination in the original edition of the work; this follows from the decision to keep the size of page and font consistent across all titles in the series. To enable scholars to locate cited page references to the earlier edition, the original chapter pagination is stated at the beginning of the corresponding chapter in this ECPR Classics edition. The Index of this edition also includes both the original and the ECPR Classics edition page numbers for each entry. References to other pages within the main body of text are to this edition.

contents

new introduction by the author

This edition of *People, States and Fear* (*PSF*) is, apart from this preface, identical to that published in 1991. The purpose of this preface is therefore partly to explain why there was no revised third edition, but mainly to reflect on how *PSF* relates to both the Copenhagen school and the writings of myself and others that followed it, and what my perspective on the book is now looking back at it through the lens of that subsequent work. What was abandoned and what was retained in the follow-on work? What else would I change and what would I leave the same? How do I understand, and react to, the impact of *PSF*?

WHY NO REVISED THIRD EDITION?

The simple answer to this question is that I was never asked to do one. If the book had stayed with a publisher interested in International Relations (IR), I think I probably would have been asked. The book had steady sales for many years, and unlike other books in this ECPR Classics series never went out of print. But in the great welter of mergers in the publishing industry it ended up with Pearson, a large educational text publisher with no noticeable interest in IR.

A second reason is that I was lucky with the timing of the 1991 revision. Through no foresight of mine, the revision process caught the ending of the Cold War. This made the second edition a post-Cold War book meaning that it did not date as quickly as it would otherwise have done. In addition, the revision from first (1983) to second edition was very substantial. The second edition is much more fully worked out than the first, meaning that I had said most of what I wanted to say.

The third and most substantial reason is that from the late 1980s I embarked on a series of publications with colleagues at COPRI (The Copenhagen Peace Research Institute), where in 1988 I had taken on the job of project leader for the group on non-military aspects of European security. Work on the first of these books was done in parallel with my revision of *PSF*.[1] The COPRI connection influenced the *PSF* revision in many ways, not least by making me more aware of what impact the first edition had made. Part of this influence can be seen in the references to the work of Ole Wæver, who quickly became my principal collaborator there. Subsequent works had some of their roots in *PSF*, and in building on it occupied the space that a third edition would have moved into. They also reflected other sources, particularly in Ole Wæver's post-structuralist realist thinking about security which eventually matured into his *securitization* theory: the idea that the social construction of threats needed to be understood separately from traditional 'objective' materialist threat analysis.[2] He and I shared roots in realism, but post-structuralist and constructivist epistemologies were quite alien to my earlier ways of thinking, and this co-mingling meant that the series of books that came out of what was later labelled the Copenhagen school, moved increasingly away from some aspects of the thinking that underpinned *PSF*. Basically, I bought into Wæver's constructivist approach to security, and loosened my attachment to the materialist ways of thinking on which *PSF* was based. As these developments matured through the 1990s and into the twenty-first century, they amplified the difficulty of undertaking a third edition. Not only was the intellectual space for it largely occupied by other books, but the change of epistemological direction would have required a very radical reworking. So by the time an engaged publisher might have asked me to do a third edition, it would have been too late. By 1998 there were two follow-on books from COPRI, and by 2006 three with a fourth in prospect.[3]

In saying this I am certainly not relegating *PSF* to the intellectual dustbin. I think there is still much of interest in it, as I hope to show. In part because it helped to give rise to a lot of subsequent work, mine and others', it remains in some ways what it was always intended to be: an entry point to thinking about security. It is just that when it was first written there was rather little thinking about the concept of security, and now there is rather a lot.

WHAT ARE THE KEY CONTINUITES WITH, AND THE KEY CHANGES FROM, *PSF* IN MY SUBSEQUENT WRITINGS?

The most remarkable discovery for me on re-reading *PSF* for the first time in fifteen years was the extent to which it shaped most of my subsequent thinking and writing. I had been generally aware that this was the case, but the depth and detail of it was a considerable surprise. Ken Booth said of *PSF* that it 'remains the most comprehensive theoretical analysis of the concept [of security] in international relations literature to date, and since its publication the rest of us have been writing footnotes to it.'[4] 'The rest of us' here clearly includes me, and not just in relation to security, but also including my subsequent writing on IR theory more broadly. There are, in other words, many continuities. I think the explanation for this can be found in Ole Wæver's observation that *PSF* 'showed that it was possible to take the concept of security serious and use it as an analytical perspective on a large part of international relations subjects. He managed to organise general IR theory around it.'[5] It was not my intention to do that, but that was how the book turned out, and it therefore provided directions forward for both further thinking about security, and a variety of more general work on IR theory.

Perhaps the most striking continuity is the central role that levels and sectors of analysis have played in nearly all of my subsequent work. Both are clearly set out in *PSF* (pp. 34, 38, 42–3, 107–19) and provide the main structuring principles for the book. Levels of analysis (the idea of structuring theory in terms of spatial scale from individual through state to system) is an old staple of IR thinking, and my use of it was and is largely derivative from Waltz.[6] Sectors (views of the system through the lens of a particular type of relationship and activity: military, political, economic, social, etc.) was always implicit in IR theorizing, and indeed in the division of the social sciences generally into disciplines. But it was neither discussed nor labelled in the same way as levels. Making sectors explicit, and combining them with levels in a matrix, was an original move.[7]

In relation to subsequent Copenhagen school (CS) writing about security, both levels and sectors have continued to play strongly. There have been three main CS positions based on levels. The first has carried on the argument from *PSF* (ch. 1) that international security cannot and should not be reduced to individual security. Subsequent works have stuck with the idea that there is something important and distinctive about the security of human collectivities, whether states, nations, or some other kind. That position puts the CS at odds with some Peace Researchers, Critical Security Studies people, and normative political theorists who want to privilege the individual as the ultimate referent object of security. It also puts it partly in line with state-centric approaches to both IR and International Security, most obviously realism, but only partly, because the CS position opens up for collectivities other than states.

The second, and in many ways most conspicuous, CS position on levels has been strong advocacy for the importance of the regional level in security analysis. Regional security complex theory (RSCT) is set out in Chapter 5 of *PSF*.[8] It rests on the idea that because most types of threats travel more easily over short distances than over long ones, security interdependencies tend to cluster in regional formations, and these formations have ontological and analytical standing distinct from the system or state levels. RSCT was developed further in *Security: A New Framework from Analysis*, most notably in the change of definition of security interdependence to incorporate the securitisation approach.[9] Finally, *Regions and Power: The Structure of International Security* gave it an exhaustive theoretical and empirical presentation, filling in the gaps and modifying some of the ideas and empirical analyses from *PSF*.[10]

The work on RSCT relates closely to the third CS position on levels, which continues the arguments in *PSF* (pp. 138–42, 172–3) about the limitations of polarity theory (the idea that the number of great powers in a system is a crucial variable) for security analysis. RSCT makes use of polarity both as a structural variable within security complexes and as a way of thinking about the interplay between the regional and global levels, where the latter is defined by great powers and superpowers. But polarity is not held to determine amity/enmity which is seen as an independent variable alongside it at both the regional and global levels. This is set out in some detail in *Regions and Powers*, which also makes considerable play of unipolarity at the regional level as one form of 'centred' security complex.[11] In subsequent work of my own that builds on the 2003 book I extend the critique of polarity theory by arguing that the distinction between great powers and superpowers is so substantial that it undermines the central assumption of polarity theory that there need be only one distinction between great powers and all other (lesser) states.[12]

Sectors have also remained prominent in all subsequent CS collective books as well as in my individual work. Here there has been a marked division of labour. I have by and large stuck with interests in the military and economic sectors, and up to a point the political one, which are the main focus in *PSF*. In *Security: A New Framework for Analysis*, which unlike *PSF* is primarily structured around sectors, I took the lead on the military and economic chapters. My engagement with the whole discussion of economic security has been a long one, steadily evolving since the 1983 edition of *PSF*.[13] The societal sector was certainly raised in *PSF*, particularly in relation to the distinction between state and nation as referent objects (pp. 37, 74–100, 111–12). There is discussion of the malleability of identity in the idea of the state (pp. 74–83) and about migration (pp. 90–92) both of which anticipated later discussions about identity in societal security. From the early 1990s Ole Wæver became the principal researcher on this sector, resulting in the book on *Identity, Migration and the New Security Agenda in Europe*.[14] He also took the lead on the societal (and political) sector chapters in the 1998 book. The environmental sector gets only a brief mention in *PSF* (pp. 117–19), and I made only one brief excursion into it.[15] For the 1998 book Jaap de Wilde took the lead on that chapter.

The 1998 book with Eric Herring, *The Arms Dynamic in World Politics*, is sometimes seen as an anomaly in my opus.[16] To understand its position (other than as an extension of my ongoing interest in things military), it helps to know that the first (1983) edition of *PSF* was a failed attempt to write what later became *An Introduction to Strategic Studies*.[17] It started out as the first chapter of that book, intending to introduce the concept of security as the central idea of Strategic Studies. But it quickly took on a life of its own and became a separate book. So like the 1987 book, *The Arms Dynamic in World Politics* was a follow-on to an edition of *PSF*. Its purpose was to update *An Introduction to Strategic Studies* for the post-Cold War market.

As noted above, there is also much continuity between what appears in *PSF* and my subsequent writings about IR theory. Here too, levels and sectors are prominent throughout, and one can trace increasing sophistication in how both are conceptualised. My contribution to *The Logic of Anarchy* (*LoA*)[18] is structured around levels and sectors, adding to them the idea of sources of explanation (variables that explain behaviour on any level of analysis and in any sector: structure, process, interaction capacity). In *PSF*, sectors had simply been set out empirically, but in *LoA* they were specifically presented in terms of the lens metaphor

(30–33) (comparing the sectoral concepts to the analytical instruments of the natural sciences from visible light lenses through infra-red to X-rays). The idea of lenses is present in *PSF*, but only as a general characteristic of concepts: each type of lens makes some features stand out more clearly but obscures others. This formulation of sectors in terms of lenses carried forward into the Copenhagen school work.[19] I wrote a separate paper on levels,[20] and these two threads were combined strongly into the project with Richard Little that resulted in *International Systems in World History* (*ISWH*).[21] That book took up and refined the levels, sectors and sources of explanation scheme from *LoA*, and used it as a framework for thinking about IR in terms of world history. Plenty of other ideas that featured in these general IR theory works are also foreshadowed in *PSF*. The idea of interaction capacity (the amount and type of transportation, communication and organisation capability in the unit/system that determine what types and degrees of interaction are possible) that plays a big role in both *LoA* and *ISWH* is there (pp.128–33). The identification of Waltz's confusion between the system level and structure, which played a major role in *LoA* is also there (p. 133). The idea of weak states (defined as those with low socio-political cohesion) in strong systems (p. 134) is taken up in *ISWH*, as is the idea of national identity as independently durable (p. 78), which later became part of both societal security and the *ISWH* theme of parochialism in the societal sector.

PSF also provided surprisingly many threads leading into the development of my interest in the English school (ES). At the time of rewriting *PSF* in 1989–90 I doubt that I had actually registered the term 'English school', though I was familiar with the work of Hedley Bull and the idea of international society. On a deeper level I may have been predisposed in this direction by the influential teaching of Kal Holsti, whose own work was in the ES tradition even though he didn't use that label. Perhaps the key bridge to the ES was the concern with logics of anarchy already quite strongly present in *PSF*. The idea of a spectrum from immature (conflictual, disorderly) to mature (peaceful, rule-governed) anarchies developed in Chapters 4 and 6 is quite firmly set up in conjunction with international society ideas. Had I been better versed in the ES, I might have framed this discussion in its language of pluralism and solidarism, as I would come to do in subsequent writings. Nevertheless, this interest in the multiple logics of anarchy set up in *PSF* quickly carried forward both into critiques of neorealism,[22] and into specific work on linking ES thinking into mainstream IR theory[23] and Security Studies.[24] It also provided the basis for some useful exchanges with Alex Wendt, whose thinking was going in the same direction, and this set up links to my more recent attempt to recast ES theory into social structural terms drawing on Wendtian style constructivism.[25] Although I was hardly, if at all, aware of constructivism as such at the time of writing *PSF*, there are references to the 'mutually constitutive' conception of both state and system (p. 67–8) and sovereignty and anarchy (p. 129), and a strong general argument throughout on the malleability of anarchy (e.g. pp. 128–33). Once constructivism had established itself on the epistemological spectrum in IR, *PSF* had set me up to be receptive to it.

The thinking in terms of levels and sectors begun in *PSF* also plays strongly into my subsequent thinking about the ES. Sectors provided a way of conceptualising international and world society in terms of their societal, economic and political characteristics. Nationalism is presented in terms very close to what I would later call a primary institution of international society (p. 80), and the work on economic security in *PSF* enabled me to more easily see the deficiency of the ES in this sector. In Chapter 8 on the power-security dilemma I failed to see the linkage between Status Quo and Revisionist states and the nature of international society despite the now obvious parallel between my three types of revisionist – orthodox, reformist, revolutionary, and Wight's three R's of realism, rationalism and revolutionism. A similar echo of form can be found in my staging of security as a *via media* between power and peace,[26] which suggests a disposition towards the similar ES staging of international society (Grotius) as the *via media* between Hobbes and Kant. Along these lines, my hard questioning in Chapter 2 of the analogy between anarchy at the individual level, and international anarchies where states are the members, parallels Bull's similar exercise. This move opens the pathway to later thinking[27] about second order societies (those with collective entities as the members) as the key ES and IR departure from reductionist sociological and political theory thinking which ties the concept of society exclusively to individuals as members. Just as anarchies based on individuals are profoundly different from those based on states, so are societies.

The links between *PSF* and my work on the ES also stretch into the future. There is a quite detailed argument in Chapter 4 (pp. 142–7) against the pessimism of Bull and Watson's historical interpretation of the expansion of international society.[28] I began to develop this in *From International to World Society?*, but have a larger plan, with Richard Little, to retell the whole story from the perspective of the rise, evolution, sometime decline, and interplay among, primary institutions (those that are deep, evolved and constitutive of society, in contrast to the 'secondary' institutions most often studied in IR which are recent and instrumental, mainly regimes and intergovernmental organisations). Putting back what the classical ES writers left out (most obviously the international economy and regions) should produce a more solidarist, and more positive account of this crucially important story.

Amidst all this continuity, the major change, already noted above, was my taking on board of Wæver's securitisation theory, with the consequent shift from neorealist/materialist foundations in the discussion of threats to constructivist ones. But even here there is some continuity. Wæver's ideas were already penetrating my thinking during the rewriting of *PSF*, as can be seen from acknowledgement of his speech act approach (pp. 36, 106–7, 288). And although I was not particularly conscious of it at the time, the staging of amity/enmity in security complexes as a variable distinct from the balance of power (p. 159–60), is already a big step towards a Wendtian-style constructivism focusing on relationships of friends, rivals and enemies.[29]

IF I WAS REVISING *PSF*,
WHAT WOULD I KEEP AND WHAT CHANGE?

Part of the answer to this question is already clear from the discussion above about what did change and what did not, but it is worth focusing here on some specific points.

In a new revision I would certainly retain two arguments that feature strongly in *PSF*. The first is the position on individual security and opposition to the reduction of international security to human security. As I have argued, human security is largely redundant in analytical terms, adding almost nothing to the concept of human rights.[30] The motive for its deployment is largely political, and in my view often mistaken and counterproductive even in those terms. I still broadly accept the argument in Chapter 1, and think that focusing on the enduring tensions between the levels of analysis and the referent objects of security is a better way of incorporating the individual level than trying to stage it as the ultimate referent object. Because it is primarily about the security of collective entities, international security is about much more than human security, and to lose sight of this is, in my view, not only an analytical error, but also one likely to put further out of reach the normative goals of many of those who promote human security.

The second argument I would retain is that from Chapter 10, that International Security Studies should incorporate Strategic Studies, and not the other way around. This position is inherent in the securitisation approach which in principle allows any appropriate construction of threat, and not just military or military-related ones, to count as 'security'. It has been carried forward strongly in subsequent CS work.[31]

I would probably also keep the main lines of argument in Chapter 9 on policy problems. It seems to me a quite nice setting out of all of the cross pressures, though I would now set up the concluding discussion about convergence and mature anarchy in terms of the ES framing in *From International to World Society?*.

The most obvious change would be to weave the securitisation argument much more deeply throughout the text, though doing so would make the book look increasingly like *Security: A New Framework for Analysis* and its successor *The Politics of Security*. In this perspective, the whole of Chapter 3 on threats is a kind of wrong turn, even though the discussion within it is perfectly sensible in materialist terms. It is the place in *PSF* where sectors get a major airing, but the discussion of threats is wholly materialist and not at all open to securitisation thinking. Neither are sectors seen as sources of referent objects. Indeed, the whole approach of *PSF* is much more conditioned by levels than by sectors, and from my present perspective, that makes it much too state centric. The argument for state as key referent object is made (pp. 42–4) almost entirely on the basis of subordinating the other two main levels, individual and system, to it. For the reasons given above, I would mainly stick with subordinating the individual level, but later work has opened up scope for system level referent objects in their own right.[32] Some of these system-level referent objects (e.g. the rules of the global economy, or some of the larger patterns of identity) only become clearly visible in sectors other than the military and political. In *PSF* I never really considered sectors as sources of referent objects, not even in the quite extensive economic sector discussion in Chapter 6. I got caught up in a mainly levels framing for thinking about referent objects. In this state-centrism, Wæver and I were, at that time, in the same boat, as shown by the framing of the policy discussion in Chapter 9 in terms of his state-centric 'hourglass' model of security. But it was not long before the emerging Copenhagen school abandoned this position, first in the book on societal security,[33] which allowed in identity groups such as nations and religions as referent objects, and then to the general opening up to referent objects in all sectors driven by the move to securitisation theory.[34]

The second general change would be to build an English school perspective much more widely and deeply into the argument along the lines suggested by the subsequent works reviewed above.

In addition to these two general changes, there are a number of other specific arguments that would not stand in their current form.

In the discussion of types of state in Chapter 2 (pp. 74–83) the category of nation-state should be scrapped. I have read a lot of history and historical sociology and constructivist theory in the meantime, and it is clear that all contemporary nation-states are in one form or another the products of a state-nation process.

Partly because of the focus on weak/strong states there is no real mention of the democratic peace idea as part of the argument about the variability of anarchy/states. This would need correcting.

In *PSF* I seem totally committed to the idea that the post-Cold War world would be multipolar, and seemingly sold on the declinist view of the US. I never even consider the unipolar possibility. This blindness is systematic, and is evident in the discussion of great powers and regional security complexes (pp. 172–3); of IPE and mature anarchy (pp. 210–13); and of the defence dilemma (pp. 228–30), where I miss not only that but the imminent demise of the Soviet Union. This latter is particularly galling given that in the Preface to the second edition (p. 21) I crow about having correctly identified the Soviet Union as a weakish state in the first edition (1983: 66).

Regional Security Complex Theory as presented in Chapter 5 is still generally OK, though it would need to be brought into line with the turn to securitisation as was done in later works.[35] Again, there would be the problem of how to revise without running into later work, especially the massive treatment of regional security complex theory in *Regions and Powers*. One obvious change to note from the *PSF* treatment is the abandonment of the distinction between 'higher' and 'lower' level complexes (p. 163) in favour of global and regional levels, great power complexes and supercomplexes. Another is that the Horn of Africa is no longer seen as being part of the Middle Eastern complex (p. 166), but understood as being part of sub-Saharan Africa. Also I would now give more prominence to boundaries and boundary change as part of essential structure (pp. 173–6), as is done in *Regions and Powers*.

CONCLUSION: THE SUCCESSES AND FAILURES OF *PSF*

Judging by such measures as the social science citation index and the number of links one gets returned in a Google search, *PSF* is by a large distance my most successful publication, though it is beginning to be challenged by two Copenhagen school books: *Security: A New Framework for Analysis*, and *Regions and Powers*. The three stated aims of the book were (p. 38) to:
- 'raise the conceptual sophistication with which people discuss security'
- 'reduce the political potency of national security by exposing its limits and contradictions' and
- 'lead to a new synthesis of understanding about international relations as a whole'.

The first of these aims has been substantially achieved, though much more among academics and their students than within the public policy discourse. Security is no longer an underdeveloped concept, and there are many schools of thought now in play.[36] It does not seem unreasonable to claim that *PSF* played a useful role in this development, though as Wæver argues, the development itself is much more obvious within Europe (and up to a point Asia) than the US.[37] The mainstream debates about security in Europe often take the concept itself, as well as policy issues, as what needs to be investigated, and this is broadly in line with what *PSF* tried to encourage. Mainstream debates about security in the US mostly take the concept itself as given, and focus on policy and strategy, sometimes pausing along the way to take a position on whether security should be confined just to the military and political sectors, and the use of force, or whether it should cover a wider range of sectors. *PSF* is quite widely cited in the US security literature, but made little impact there on thinking about the concept of security itself. One spinoff from the raised conceptual sophistication about security has been the substantial convergence on security as a shared ground between Peace Research and Security Studies, which was a campaigning point of *PSF* in both the 1983 and 1991 editions.

The second aim was probably always rather utopian, and especially in the post 9/11 world it is difficult to see much progress. The public policy discourse in many countries, most obviously in Israel and much of the Middle East, the US, Russia, China, and authoritarian states in many places, still use security unreflectively as a trump card to justify and legitimise harsh policies and regimes.

The third aim has in some ways seen considerable progress inasmuch as over the last decade IR has become conceptually much more sophisticated. As Wæver notes, some of that sophistication results from spillovers from Security Studies into the wider IR debates.[38] It would, however, be hard to claim that *PSF* played more than a <u>very</u> tiny role in that turn.

More specifically, a number of arguments, positions and concepts from *PSF* have filtered their way into the literature quite successfully. The sectoral framework begun there has influenced not only subsequent Copenhagen school work, but is now prominent in Security Studies texts.[39] This in part reflects the substantial success of the move to widen the agenda of International Security Studies, and to see security more in terms of interdependence. Both of these themes are strong in *PSF*, though their overall success results from the impact of many works and a wide array of developments in the real world, not least the dramatic surge of globalisation, both in fact and as a defining concept. At best, *PSF* can claim to have caught the *Zeitgeist* at an early stage and pointed in the right direction. Interest in the security dilemma has grown, but to the extent that I can tell, the approach to this developed in *PSF* (ch. 8) has had only a marginal impact. I still think there are some good ideas in that chapter: e.g. tracking the path of China from revolutionary to almost orthodox revisionist. Were I revising that chapter, as noted above, framing the discussion in English school terms, with Status Quo and Revisionism set explicitly in the context of international society, would be very useful.

One measure of career success (or not) in IR is whether one can invent terms that become established in the general usage of the discipline: think of polarity, interdependence, clash of civilisations. *PSF* can make modest claims in that regard in relation to *sectors* and *referent objects*, both of which are used so freely that their source has been forgotten. It is also worth noting that Wæver's term *securitisation*, which is prominent in both his own work and that of the Copenhagen school, has also been a considerable success in this way. There are two other terms within *PSF* that, to my ongoing disappointment and frustration, failed to make the leap into general usage despite the fact that they capture important points not covered by other terms. The first of these is the distinction between *weak and strong states* (rooted in the socio-political cohesion of the state, and therefore its ability to claim stateness) versus *weak and strong powers* (rooted mainly in material capability) (pp. 92–100). In a world in which failed and failing states, and identity politics, rank high on the international agenda, this distinction is absolutely central. Yet the literature struggles on in terminal confusion, with these two terms being used as synonyms, and sometimes covering one meaning, sometimes the other, and at its nadir sometimes both. Among other things, this distinction can serve as a basis both for countering the neorealist commitment to 'like units' and as a questioning of the sovereignty/anarchy framing of both international system and international society thinking.

The second failure is of the term *defence dilemma* (ch. 7) which is about the tension between fear of war and fear of defeat. This is not at all the same as the security dilemma, which is about the interplay of actors around fear of defeat. The defence dilemma occurs within individual actors, the most obvious examples being Japan and Germany which suffered heavy defeats and which throughout the Cold War were on the front lines of any nuclear engagement. Had such an engagement occurred, both would have been obliterated. Ole Wæver's arguments about securitisation in the EU being based on Europe's fear of returning to its own pre-1945 past are also rooted in the defence dilemma. This seems an extremely useful term, not just for theory discussions but also in relation to the actual condition of important parts of the world. As both the cost and the destructive power of weapons grows, what this term represents can only become more important in international relations, a theme picked up most tellingly in Dan Deudney's work.[40]

One final reflection is on the question raised in *PSF* (p. 124) about whether states need to be, or feel, threatened in order both to maintain their claim to Hobbesian functions (and thus their political legitimacy), and to facilitate the process of government within them (by generating a centripetal force to counter whatever centrifugal forces tend to fragment the polity). Do states, or rather their leaderships, not only respond to threats, but generate and manipulate them in order to increase their control over their citizens? This rather fundamental question gets no answer in *PSF* and seems a ripe candidate for further work. Its theoretical implications point right to the heart of securitisation theory. Empirically, one can think of the horrible saga around the break-up of Yugoslavia; the curious casting about of the US for an enemy during the 1990s (first Japan, then China, then Islam, then rogue states, the problem finally being solved by 9/11); and the seeming dependence of Pakistan on its rivalry with India to justify its own sense of being. All of these suggest the validity of the question and the importance of acquiring some general understanding of the nature of the state in this respect. With questions such as this still pressing for attention, it seems that *PSF* will continue to be a powerful influence on my research agenda. It seems that much of my work over the past quarter century, and much of what I still plan to do, has been shaped by the thoughts of a young lecturer in his thirties struggling to write his second book. Whether I should feel more inspired or more daunted by this is difficult to decide. It should, however, inspire the current crop of ambitious thirty-somethings to believe that their work might really be of durable interest.

NOTES

1. Buzan, Barry (1990) Morten Kelstrup, Pierre Lemaitre, Elzbieta Tromer and Ole Wæver, *The European Security Order Recast: Scenarios for the Post-Cold War Era*, London, Pinter.
2. Wæver, Ole (1995) 'Securitization and Desecuritization', in Ronnie D. Lipschutz (ed.) *On Security*, New York: Columbia University Press, 46–86.
3. Wæver, Ole, Barry Buzan, Morten Kelstrup, Pierre Lemaitre, *et al.* (1993) *Identity, Migration and the New Security Agenda in Europe*, London, Pinter; Buzan, Barry, Ole Wæver and Jaap de Wilde (1998) *Security: A New Framework for Analysis*, Boulder Co., Lynne Rienner; Buzan, Barry and Ole Wæver (2003) *Regions and Powers: The Structure of International Security*, Cambridge: Cambridge University Press; Wæver, Ole, Barry Buzan, and Jaap de Wilde (2007) *The Politics of Security*, Boulder Co., Lynne Rienner.
4. Booth, Ken (1991) 'Security and Emancipation', *Review of International Studies*, 17:4, 313–26.
5. Wæver, Ole (2005), 'Ole Wæver's 10', Politik Tidsskriftet Politik, 4:7, http://www.tidsskriftetpolitik.dk/index.php?id=125 (accessed 18 June 2006)
6. Waltz, Kenneth N. (1959) *Man, The State and War*, New York: Columbia University Press; Waltz, Kenneth N. (1979) *Theory of International Politics*, Reading, Mass.: Addison-Wesley.
7. See later, Buzan, Barry, Charles Jones and Richard Little (1993) *The Logic of Anarchy:*

Neorealism to Structural Realism, New York: Columbia University Press.

8. See also, Buzan, Kelstrup, Lemaitre, Tromer and Wæver, *op. cit.*

9. Buzan, Barry, Ole Wæver and Jaap de Wilde (1998) *Security: A New Framework for Analysis*, Boulder Co., Lynne Rienner.

10. Buzan and Wæver, *op.cit.*

11. Buzan and Wæver, *op. cit.*

12. Buzan, Barry (2004b) *The United States and the Great Powers: World Politics in the Twenty-First Century*, Oxford: Polity.

13. Buzan, Barry 'Economic Structure and International Security: the Limits of the Liberal Case', *International Organization*, 38:4 (1984) 597–24; Buzan, Barry, 'Economic Security', in Richard Stubbs and Geoffrey Underhill (eds.), *Political Economy and the International System: Global Issues, Regional Dynamics and Political Conflict*, Toronto, McLelland and Stewart (London, Macmillan), 1994.

14. Wæver, Buzan, Kelstrup, Lemaitre, *et al.*, *op.cit.*

15. Buzan, Barry (1992) 'Environment as a Security Issue', in Paul Painchaud (ed)., *Geopolitical Perspectives on Environmental Security*, Cahiers du GERPE, Laval University, Quebec, May.

16. Buzan, Barry and Eric Herring (1998) *The Arms Dynamic in World Politics*, Boulder Co., Lynne Rienner.

17. Buzan, Barry (1987) *An Introduction to Strategic Studies: Military Technology and International Relations*, London: Macmillan.

18. Buzan, Jones and Little, *op.cit.*

19. Buzan, Wæver and de Wilde, *op.cit.*

20. Buzan, Barry (1995) 'The level of analysis problem in international relations reconsidered' in Ken Booth and Steve Smith (eds.), *International Political Theory Today*, London, Polity Press, 198–216.

21. Buzan, Barry and Richard Little (2000) *International Systems and World History: Remaking the Study of International Relations*, New York: Oxford University Press

22. Buzan, Jones and Little, *op. cit.*

23. Buzan, Barry (1993) 'From International System to International Society: Structural Realism and Regime Theory Meet the English School', *International Organization*, 47:3, 327–52.

24. Buzan, Barry (1996) 'International Security and International Society', in Rick Fawn, Jeremy Larkin and Robert Newman (eds.), *International Society After the Cold War*, London, Macmillan, 261–87.

25. Buzan, Barry (2004a) *From International to World Society? English School Theory and the Social Structure of Globalisation*, Cambridge: Cambridge University Press.

26. In *PSF*, but more explicitly in Buzan, *op. cit.*, 109–25.

27. Buzan, *op. cit.*

28. Bull, Hedley, and Adam Watson (eds.) (1984) *The Expansion of International Society*, Oxford: Oxford University Press.

29. Wendt, Alexander (1999): *Social Theory of International Politics*, Cambridge: Cambridge University Press.

30. Buzan, Barry (2004c) 'A Reductionist, Idealistic Notion that Adds Little Analytical Value' in 'Special Section: What is "Human Security"?', *Security Dialogue*, 35:3, 369–70.

31. Buzan, Wæver and de Wilde, *op. cit.*; Wæver, Buzan, and de Wilde, *op. cit.*

32. Buzan, Wæver and de Wilde, *op. cit.*; Wæver, Buzan, and de Wilde, *op. cit.*

33. Wæver, Buzan, Kelstrup, Lemaitre, *et al.*, *op. cit.*

34. Buzan, Wæver and de Wilde, *op. cit.*; Wæver, Buzan, and de Wilde, *op. cit.*

35. Buzan, Wæver and de Wilde, *op. cit.*; Buzan and Wæver, *op. cit.*

36. Smith, Steve (1999) 'The Increasing Insecurity of Security Studies: Conceptualizing Security in the Last Twenty Years', *Contemporary Security Policy*, 20:3, 72–101; Wæver, Ole (2004): 'Aberystwyth, Paris, Copenhagen: New "Schools" in Security Theory and their Origins between Core and Periphery', paper for ISA in Montreal, March 2004. http://zope.polforsk1.dk/securitytheory/waevermontreal/

37. Wæver, Ole, and Barry Buzan 'After the Return to Theory: The Past, Present, and Future of Security Studies, in Alan Collins (ed.) *Contemporary Security Studies*, Oxford University Press, 2006.

38. *Ibid.*

39. Hough, Peter (2004) *Understanding Global Security*, London: Routledge; Sheehan, Michael (2005) *International Security: An Analytical Survey*, Boulder Co.: Lynne Rienner; Collins, Alan (ed.) *Contemporary Security Studies*, Oxford: Oxford University Press, 2006.

40. Deudney, Daniel H. (1995) 'The Philadelphian System: Sovereignty, Arms Control, and Balance of Power in the American States-Union, Circa 1787–1861', *International Organization*, 49: 2, 191–228; Deudney, Daniel (2000) 'Regrounding Realism: Anarchy, Security and Changing Material Contexts' , *Security Studies* 10:1, 1–45; Deudney, Dan (2006) *Bounding Power: Republican Security Theory from the Polis to the Global Village*, Princeton: Princeton University Press.

SOME ADDITIONAL COPENHAGEN SCHOOL AND OTHER BUZAN PUBLICATIONS EVOLVING WITH AND AFTER *PSF* (IN CHRONOLOGICAL ORDER):

Jahn, Egbert, Pierre Lemaitre, Ole Wæver (1987) *European Security – Problems of Research on Non-Military Aspects*, Copenhagen Papers 1, Centre for Peace and Conflict Research (later Copenhagen Peace Research Institute), August.

Buzan, Barry (1989) 'The Future of European Security', in Pierre Lemaitre, Ole Wæver and Elzbieta Tromer (eds.), *The European Polyphony*, London, Macmillan.

Buzan, Barry (1991) 'New patterns of global security in the twenty-first century', *International Affairs*, 67:3, 431–51.

Buzan, Barry (1991) 'Is International Security Possible?', in Ken Booth (ed.), *New Thinking About Strategy and International Security*, London, Unwin-Hyman, 1991.

Buzan, Barry (1992) 'Third World Regional Security in Historical and Structural Perspective', in Brian Job (ed.) *The Insecurity Dilemma: National Security of Third World States*, Boulder: Lynne Rienner, 167–98.

Buzan, Barry and Ole Wæver (1992) 'Framing Nordic Security – European Scenarios for the 1990s and Beyond', in Jan Øberg (ed.), *Nordic Security in the 1990s: Options in the Changing Europe*, London, Pinter, 85–104.

Buzan, Barry (1994) 'Does NOD have a future in the post-Cold War world?' in Bjørn Møller and Håkan Wiberg (eds.), *Non-Offensive Defence for the 21st Century*, Westview Press, 11–24.

Buzan, Barry (1994) 'The Post-Cold War Asia-Pacific Security Order: Conflict or Cooperation', in Andrew Mack and John Ravenhill, (eds), *Pacific Cooperation: Building Economic and Security Regimes in the Asia-Pacific Region*, St. Leonards: Allen and Unwin Australia; Boulder Co.: Westview Press, 130–51.

Buzan, Barry (1995) 'Security, the State and the New World Order, and Beyond' in Ronnie Lipschutz (ed.), *On Security*, New York, Columbia University Press, 187–211.

Buzan, Barry (1996) 'Changing Paradigms of National and International Security and Their Implications for the Security Planning of Middle Powers', in Byong-Moo Hwang and Yong-Sup Han (eds), *Korean Security Policies Toward Peace and Unification*, Korea, Korean Association of International Studies, 3–30.

Barry Buzan and Ole Wæver (1996–7) 'Slippery? contradictory? sociologically untenable?: the Copenhagen School replies', *Review of International Studies*, 23:2, 143–52.

Buzan, Barry (1997) 'Regions and Regionalism in a Global Perspective', in Gavin Cawthra and Bjørn Møller (eds), *Defensive Restucturing of the Armed Forces in Southern Africa*, Aldershot: Ashgate, 21–31.

Buzan, Barry (1997) 'Rethinking Security After the Cold War', *Cooperation and Conflict*, 32:1, 5–28.

Buzan, Barry (1998) 'The Asia Pacific: What Sort of Region in What Sort of World?' in Anthony McGrew and Christopher Brook (eds.) *Asia- Pacific in the New World Order*, London: Routledge, 68–87.

Buzan, Barry (1998) 'Conclusions: System Versus Units in Theorizing about the Third World' in Stephanie Neuman (ed), *International Relations Theory and the Third World*, New York, St. Martin's Press, 213–34.

Buzan, Barry (1999–2000) 'The Logic of Regional Security in the Post-Cold War World', in Bjorn Hettne *et al.* (eds) *The New Regionalism and the Future of Security and Development*, London, Macmillan, as Volume 4 of *New Regionalism*, 1–28. Revised version in Fredrik Söderbaum and Timothy Shaw (eds.) (2002) *Approaches to the New Regionalism*, Palgrave.

Wæver, Ole and Barry Buzan (2000) 'Europe and the Middle East – an inter-regional analysis: NATO's New Strategic Concept and the Theory of Security Complexes', in Sven Behrendt and Christian-Peter Hanelt (eds), *Bound to Cooperate: Europe and the Middle East*, Bertelsmann Foundation Publishers, Guetersloh, 55–106.

Buzan, Barry (2001) 'Human Security in International Perspective', in Mely Anthony and Mohamed Jawhar Hassan (eds), *The Asia Pacific in the New*

Millennium: Political and Security Challenges, ISIS Malaysia, 583–596.

Buzan, Barry (2003) 'Security architecture in Asia: the interplay of regional and global levels', *The Pacific Review*, 16:2, 143–73.

Buzan, Barry (2006) 'The Changing Agenda of Military Security' in Hans Günter Brauch, John Grin, Czeslaw Mesjasz, Navnita Chadha Behera, Béchir Chourou, Ursula Oswald Spring, P. H. Liotta, Patricia Kameri-Mbote (eds) *Globalisation and Environmental Challenges*, Berlin: Springer-Verlag.

Buzan, Barry and Lene Hansen (forthcoming 2008) *The Evolution of International Security Studies*, Cambridge: Cambridge University Press.

preface to the first edition

This book has had a long gestation. The idea of it took root in my mind during 1976, and in the intervening period the work of many people has influenced its development. As the idea grew, it increasingly conditioned my reading, pushing me into unfamiliar areas and establishing the relevance of literatures which previously lay at the periphery of my thinking. Partly because the sources became so diverse, I have used bibliographical footnotes rather than a single bibliography to acknowledge my debts. Since the references do not constitute a coherent literature, it seemed more useful to concentrate them at their point of relevance in the text rather than to cluster them at the end.

Many people have helped in ways more direct than my encounters with their writing. The late Fred Hirsch told me I would have to learn some political economy, and on that point, as on many others, he proved correct. My participation in the colloquium organized by John Ruggie on 'alternative conceptions of international order' provided an ideal context in which to pursue Fred's advice, and set me to thinking on a scale appropriate to this book. Dialogues with H. O. Nazareth have enriched my mind more than he might suspect, and although they have been in a completely different context from this project, the cross-fertilization has been considerable. The International Relations Group chaired by R. J. Barry Jones has stimulated me to think about several questions which I would otherwise probably have ignored, and important parts of this book have grown from seeds planted during its discussions.

I am deeply grateful to following friends and colleagues for their comments on the penultimate draft: Ken Booth, Hedley Bull, Deborah Buzan, Tony Buzan, Joseph Frankel, Roger Harrison, Kal Holsti, Peter Mangold, Peter Murray, Gonzalo Ramos, Gowher Rizvi, John Ruggie and Kenneth Waltz. Richard Little did me the immense service of commenting on a first draft, and Charles Jones and Robert Skidelsky contributed detailed criticisms of Chapter 5. The book would not be what it is without their assistance, and even where I have not agreed with them, they have prodded me to express my own views more clearly. The published result is, of course, my responsibility, but I can carry that responsibility more confidently for having taken some of my beatings in earlier rounds of criticism.

I would like also to thank the University of Warwick for allowing me two terms of sabbatical leave during 1981. Without that uninterrupted stretch of time I could not have written the complete first draft which was the distant ancestor of this book. Finally, I take pleasure in acknowledging the very able assistance of Mrs Joy Gardner, who does more than her share to make our Department an efficient and pleasant place in which to work, and who produced all the typescripts neatly and on time.

Barry Buzan
London
August 1982

preface to the second edition

Welcome to those reading this book for the second time. This Preface will tell you how and why the second edition differs from the first.

The suggestion from the publishers that I prepare a second edition of this book posed the problem of whether merely to update the old version, or to reconsider the whole agenda. In favour of a light revision was the 'leave well enough alone' argument of preserving the identity of the book. In favour of a more thorough rewrite was the opportunity to reconsider what still defines my own research agenda in the light not only of much new work, but also the deeply heartening changes in the international system that began during the later 1980s. I decided to use the opportunity to rethink the whole agenda, as well as bringing it up to date with the work that I and others have done in the meantime. This is therefore a post-1989 book. It addresses the same questions as its predecessor, and uses the same general framework, but has a quite different tone and a substantially revised content.

One overall change is hinted at in the new subtitle. Instead of seeing this book as part of the lobby to open up Strategic Studies, I now see it as an agenda for a new field of International Security Studies. Some of you were puzzled by my 1987 book *An Introduction to Strategic Studies: Military technology and international relations* and the question arose as to how such a narrowly conceived book could be a follow-on to *People, States and Fear*. You will find the answer to this question, as I see it, in the last section of the Introduction chapter, and in Chapter 10.

My impression is that this edition is more positive in tone, clearer in explanation and less long-winded (though longer overall) than the earlier one. It also puts more emphasis on the economic, societal and environmental aspects of security, while still keeping the strong political emphasis. The military dimension is of course still firmly present, but I have cut its detail sharply by referencing out to fuller discussions in *An Introduction to Strategic Studies*. I still put the focus on understanding ideas rather than proposing policies, but I hope that those of you who find this approach incomplete will at least see some narrowing of the gap between theoretical discussion and policy analysis.

Most of the chapters have been thoroughly reworked even where the section headings remain the same. In the Introduction, there is a new section on developments during the 1980s. Chapter 1 is updated, but has no major changes. Chapter 2 has the same arrangement, but contains longer discussions on the theory of the state, and on weak and strong states. Chapter 3 is extensively rewritten around the same idea as before, but I hope much more clearly and with more detail on types of threat. Chapter 4 is also extensively rewritten; the opening material on anarchy is similar, but the approach to system structure analysis is quite different, reflecting my engagement with Neorealist theory over the last few years. The section on international society is wholly new. The discussion on regional security complexes has been upgraded into a new Chapter 5, which builds on the first crack at a fully operational framework for regional security analysis made in Buzan and Rizvi *et al.*, *South Asian Insecurity and the Great Powers* (London: Macmillan, 1986). Chapter 6 is a complete rewrite of old Chapter 5, using some of the previous material, but as the new title suggests, refocused specifically on the knotty question of economic security; the last few pages build on the idea of mature anarchy sketched in Chapter 4. Chapters 7 and 8 are updates of the old Chapters 6 and 7. The major change is the deletion of much of the arms dynamic detail, and a more constructive attempt to think about what might be done to mute the power-security dilemma. Chapter 9 is an update of old Chapter 8 and Chapter 10 is a substantially revised version of old Chapter 9, picking up the arguments for a new field of International Security Studies.

My hope is that this revision will both extend the life of the book for its existing audience, and perhaps open a new market among those interested in International Security Studies. I am aware that the greater clarity of this work may alienate some, particularly those eager to promote the reduction of security issues down to the individual level. It may also be that the newly begun formation of the post-Cold War era will make International Security Studies unfashionable, though I doubt it.

I owe thanks to many people who have given me feedback on the book over the years and to several people who helped me specifically with this revision. Bengt Sundelius, Bob McKinlay and Svante Karlsson, all of whom have used it as a teaching text, provided me with thoughtful comments on the first edition. Ole Wæver and Chris Smith read and commented on the first draft of the second edition, and Stephen Gill, Jeffrey Golden and Gautam Sen gave particular help on Chapter 6. Ken Booth made me think harder about the subtitle (and therefore about the book as a whole) than I otherwise would have done, and also challenged me at just the right time to try to answer the question: 'Is international security possible?'. My wife Deborah saved me from the problem caused by the fact that the first edition was written before word processing became widespread. She bore the agonies and ecstasies of the writing time with her usual good nature. The Centre for Peace and Conflict Research in Copenhagen helped in several ways. It provided me with stimulating colleagues, opened my eyes to the way in which the first edition had been received, invited me to test myself on some more practical security questions and circulated drafts of Chapters 5 and 10 as working papers. The University of Warwick gave me a study leave in the spring of 1990. Without that release from the increasing stresses and strains of British academic life under

Thatcherism the whole process would have taken much longer.

I would like finally to register a debating point against the not inconsiderable numbers of people who poured scorn on my 1983 classification of the Soviet Union as having a mixture of weak and strong state characteristics!

Barry Buzan
London
April 1990

figures and tables

introduction

THE NATIONAL SECURITY PROBLEM IN
INTERNATIONAL RELATIONS

Few people would deny that security, whether individual, national, or international, ranks prominently among the problems facing humanity. National security is particularly central because states dominate many of the conditions that determine security at the other two levels, and states seem unable to coexist with each other in harmony. Throughout the history of states, each has been made insecure by the existence of others. The military and economic actions of each in pursuit of its own national security have frequently combined with those of others to produce economic dislocation and war. The intensity and character of the national security problem vary dramatically over time – sometimes exceedingly confrontational, sometimes, as in the nineteenth century and as at the time of writing, moving into periods of lower tension and increased cooperation. But despite these fluctuations, the general problem remains, along with all the uncertainties and fears that it generates.

In order to have a proper understanding of the national security problem one must first understand the concept of security. In much of its prevailing usage, especially by those associated with state policy-making, this concept is so weakly developed as to be inadequate for the task. I seek to demonstrate that a simple-minded concept of security constitutes such a substantial barrier to progress that it might almost be counted as part of the problem. By simple-minded I mean an understanding of national security that is inadequately aware of the contradictions latent within the concept itself, and/or inadequately aware of the fact that the logic of security almost always involves high levels of interdependence among the actors trying to make themselves secure. I shall try to show how a more fully developed and broadly based concept can lead to constructive redefinitions of the national security problem.

Security is not the only concept through which the national security problem can be approached. Traditionally, most of the literature that attempted analysis or prescription was, and to some extent still is, based on the concepts of power and peace. Those who favour the approach through power derive their thinking from the Realist school of International Relations represented by writers such as E. H. Carr and Hans

Morgenthau.[1] It can be argued that power not only reveals the basic pattern of capabilities in the international system but also highlights a prime motive for the behaviour of actors. Those who favour the approach through peace are more loosely associated into the Idealist school. Idealists argue that their concept leads them not only to see the problem in holistic terms, as opposed to the necessarily fragmented view of the Realists, but also that it focuses attention directly on the essential issue of war. Since war is the major threat arising from the national security problem, a solution to it would largely eliminate the problem from the international agenda.

Until the 1980s, these two approaches dominated thinking about the national security problem. They usually led, as I have argued in more detail elsewhere[2], to highly polarized and conflicting prescriptions. Within this universe of debate the concept of security played a subsidiary role. Realists tended to see security as a derivative of power: an actor with enough power to reach a dominating position would acquire security as a result. This view was easy to take when power was defined in the very broad terms sketched by Morgenthau.[3] Although security was rightly placed as the goal, the understanding that power was the route to it was inherently self-defeating. Idealists tended to see security as a consequence of peace: a lasting peace would provide security for all.

In this book I argue that the concept of security is, in itself, a more versatile, penetrating and useful way to approach the study of international relations than either power or peace. It points to a prime motive for behaviour which is different from, but no less significant than, that provided by power. It also leads to a comprehensive perspective which is likewise different from, but no less useful than, that provided by peace. In combination, these add up to an analytical framework which stands comparison with anything available from the more established concepts. A more fully developed concept of security can be seen to lie between the extremes of power and peace, incorporating most of their insights, and adding more of its own. It provides many ideas which link the established conventions of the other two schools and help to bridge the political and intellectual gulf which normally, and to their mutual detriment, separates them.

The task is to habilitate the concept of security – it cannot be rehabilitated because it has never been properly developed. Work on this project has been seriously underway since the early 1980s, but it is useful to begin the discussion by considering the reasons for the long-standing underdevelopment of security.

SECURITY AS AN UNDERDEVELOPED CONCEPT

The principal evidence for the underdevelopment of security as a concept in International Relations is to be found in its use in the literature. The literature on power contains not only a mass of empirical work, but also a well-developed body of theoretical writing. One might reasonably expect to find a similar balance for any widely used academic concept, but until very recently, this was not the case for security.

The term itself is in general use in International Relations and other disciplines, and appears to be accepted as a central organizing concept by both practitioners and academics. But the literature on it is very unbalanced. A large and flourishing body of work exists on the empirical side dealing with contemporary national security problems and issues. Most of this comes out of the sub-field of Strategic Studies, for which security is a central normative focus. The foreign, military and economic policies of states, the intersections of these policies in areas of change or dispute and the general structure of relations which they create, are all analysed in terms of aspirations to achieve national and/or international security. But until the rise of economic and environmental concerns during the 1970s the concept of security was seldom addressed in terms other than the policy interests of particular actors, and right up to the end of the 1980s the discussion still had a heavy military emphasis.

When one searches for a matching conceptual literature on security relatively little comes to hand before 1980, and there is still no coherent school of thought. The enthusiasm for collective security after the First World War had some promise in this direction, but the failure of both the League of Nations and the United Nations to measure up to the task truncated interest in this whole approach.[4] What might have been a major breakthrough was John Herz's idea of the 'security dilemma' in the early 1950s,[5] a structural notion in which the self-help attempts of states to look after their security needs tend, regardless of intention, to lead to rising insecurity for others as each interprets its own measures as defensive, and the measures of others as potentially threatening. The security dilemma idea is widely acknowledged in the literature, but the Cold War environment proved to be infertile soil for such a liberal seed, restricting most people's view to the action-reaction dynamics of rival powers. Not until the later 1970s, most notably in work by Robert Jervis, was there an attempt to build on it by shifting attention back to the unintentional and interdependence elements of security relations.[6] This is surprising, because the idea offers a weighty and sophisticated alternative to the power struggle model as a way of interpreting the basic dynamics of international politics.

Probably the best known conceptual piece on security is Arnold Wolfers' article on national security.[7] Wolfers' emphasis on *national* security certainly reflected the dominant orientation in the empirical literature, and his essay is a masterly introduction to the many-dimensioned complexities of the concept. His characterization of security as an 'ambiguous symbol' – at one point he argues that it 'may not have any precise meaning at all' – would seem, unfortunately, to have discouraged further interest in developing security as a major approach to understanding international relations. This was almost certainly not his intention, since the principal burden of the essay was to point out the potential mischief of ambiguity in a national symbol of such great political potency.

Aside from these core works, one finds only a few other conceptual discussions of security that predate the relative boom starting in the early 1980s. Hedley Bull, Bernard Brodie, Frank Trager and Frank Simonie made brief but useful contributions on the difficulties of applying it.[8] Hugh Macdonald attempted to tackle the ambiguity of the concept, but ended up defeated by his own categories and withdrew from the struggle by dismissing security as an 'inadequate' concept – a view also arrived at for quite different reasons by Hans Mouritzen.[9] Robert Jervis introduced the interesting idea of security regimes, which draws attention from the state to the system level of analysis.[10] And Gert Krell attempted a broad critique of excessively military conceptions of security from a peace research perspective.[11] More peripherally, one finds general discussions of security in the context of American policy choices.[12] The large and well-known critical literature on Strategic Studies also contains comments relevant to the use of security as a concept.[13] But these works, despite their individual merits, did not begin to add up to a coherent investigation of the concept. At best, like those by Herz, Jervis and Bull, they generated useful ways of looking at particular problems, but they did not tap the full potential of the concept as a lens through which to view the subject as a whole.

The hazards of a weakly conceptualized but politically powerful concept like security did not go unnoticed. The domination of the concept by the idea of national security, and the militarized interpretation of security to which this approach easily, though not necessarily, gave rise, was criticized by several authors as excessively narrow and hollow. Wolfers' article cited above, written during the thick of the Cold War, pointed in this direction. Richard Ashley mounted an extensive critique of reductionist, actor-oriented, narrowly focused approaches to security analysis (what he calls 'technical rationality'), urging instead a more holistic, linkage-orientated, systematic view ('rationality proper').[14] He argued that technical rationality is itself a principal factor exacerbating the security dilemma. Ken Booth argued convincingly that state-bound, ethnocentric confines within which Strategic Studies pursues its analysis are not only seriously deficient in relation to the character of the problem, but also dangerous in that the resultant skewed diagnosis, as applied through state policy, makes the problem worse. Despite their wholly different starting points, both Ashley and Booth came to similar conclusions, in Booth's words: 'those strategists who do not attempt to be part of the solution will undoubtedly become an increasingly important part of the problem.'[15]

Leonard Beaton similarly argued for the need to expand conceptions of security outward from the limits of parochial national security to include a range of systemic considerations.[16] Likewise, but again from a different perspective, Stanley Hoffmann argued for the need to begin 'turning national security into an aspect of world order policy'.[17] Hedley Bull argued against excessive self-interest in approaches to national security, and for a broader view in which common interests and linkage among national securities receive greater attention.[18] More generally, L. B. Krause and Joseph Nye observed that 'neither economists nor political scientists have paid enough attention to the complexity of the concept of security, including its *instrumental role* in the enhancement of other values.'[19] The Brandt Commission called for a new concept of security that would transcend the narrow notions of military defence and look more towards the logic of a broader interdependence.[20]

The common theme underlying these voices was that a notion of security bound to the level of individual states and military issues is inherently inadequate. At best, such a notion produced the dangerously ambiguous symbol outlined by Wolfers which 'while appearing to offer guidance and a basis for broad consensus...may be permitting everyone to label whatever policy he favours with an attractive and possibly deceptive name'.[21] At worst, it drives the security dilemma to such a pitch of intensity that it begins to resemble the model of those who see international relations as an unending struggle for power. *National* security, these authors argue, might well be so self-defeating as almost to amount to a contradiction in terms.

Because security was seen primarily in terms of national power by both policy-makers and strategists, an unhelpful uniformity dominated. That section of academia which was most concerned with security was largely locked into a power view of it. National policy-makers were, and are, required by their position, and by the nature of their powers and responsibilities to take a predominantly national view. Almost no independent policy-makers exist above the national level. Thus, a situation prevailed in which the primary thrusts of both policy analysis were pushing in a counterproductive direction, and in which the main actors, both academics and practitioners, were locked into their roles by deeply rooted and heavily institutionalized traditions.

The persistent underdevelopment of thinking about security, despite the fact that disputes at the empirical level often arose from the lack of any deeper and more general understanding of the concept, can be explained in at least five different ways.

The first possible explanation is simply that the idea has proved too complex to attract analysts, and has therefore been neglected in favour of more tractable concepts. This argument has some weight, for security is, as those of you who make it through this book will discover, a difficult concept. But it is no more difficult than other core concepts in the social sciences. Like power, justice, peace, equality, love and freedom, all of which have inspired large literatures, it is what W. B. Gallie has called an 'essentially contested concept'.[22] Such concepts necessarily generate unsolvable debates about their meaning and application because, as Richard Little points out, they 'contain an ideological element which renders empirical evidence irrelevant as a means of resolving the dispute'.[23] Even an apparently concrete concept like the state virtually defies precise, generally accepted definition because of its essentially contested nature.[24] Paradoxically, the utility of these concepts stems in part from whatever it is that makes them inherently ambiguous, not least because ambiguity stimulates theoretical discussion about them. Within the landscape of social science they encompass a whole domain, rather than just a fixed point, and for this reason cannot be defined in any general sense, but only in relation to specific cases. Essentially contested concepts delineate an area of concern rather than specifying a precise condition. They require theoretical analysis in order to identify the boundaries of their application, the contradictions which occur within them and the significance for them of new developments. The domain and contradictions of security have not been adequately explored, and as this book hopes to demonstrate, the reason cannot be found in the inherent difficulty of the task.

A second, and more convincing explanation for the neglect of security lies in the real scope for overlap between it and the concept of power under conditions of acute confrontation. Even a very crude Realist model of international politics as a pure struggle for power had obvious relevance in the highly polarized environment of the Second World War, and almost immediately thereafter of the Cold War. States were seen as locked into a power struggle, and security was easily seen as a derivative of power, especially military power. Security shrank conceptually to being a way of saying either how well any particular state or allied group of states was doing in the struggle for power, or how stable the balance of power overall appeared to be. Reduced to little more than a synonym for power, security had little independent relevance in wider systemic terms, and therefore the security dilemma approach could function at best as a minor adjunct to the power struggle model of international relations. The point here is not that power and security *are* interchangeable, but merely that they *appeared* to be so at the time. That appearance was sufficiently convincing to stifle further enquiry into security as a separate concept. Power may become the essence of security in situations of intense confrontation or conflict, but to assume that such an identity always holds creates the risk of a self-fulfiling prophecy. From this point of view, the counterpoint to Cold War of the two periods of detente, one during the 1970s, and even more so that starting in the mid-1980s, has played an important role in stimulating a reconsideration of security as an alternative concept to power.

A third reason for the underdevelopment of security lies in the nature of the various revolts against Realist orthodoxy up to the end of the 1970s. Those of an Idealist bent rejected the Realist model as dangerously self-fulfiling, and far too war-prone for a nuclear-armed world. They could have organized themselves around the concept of security, as many of like mind did during the interwar years, but because the idea of collective security had been so emasculated by the experiences of the 1930s they did not. Idealists turned instead to the even grander, essentially contested concept of peace. The policies for peace – arms control and disarmament, and international cooperation – echoed those of the interwar years, and in the shadow of nuclear obliteration clearly provided a more inspirational base than the complexities of security, which played only a marginal role in Peace Research. Security was, in any case, already sullied by its association with the power model.

A later reaction against Realism centred on the concept of interdependence. This reflected concerns as diverse as the environment and human rights, and potentially offered an intellectual orientation highly appropriate to the development of security along the paths opened by Herz. But the primary motivation for this movement stemmed from the deepening of America's economic troubles in the early 1970s, and most of its non-Marxist practitioners understandably concerned themselves mainly with the impact of economic issues on world politics. Their inclination was to push the traditional, military power-oriented Realist model into the background, seeing its competitive, fragmented, force-based approach as increasingly irrelevant to the interwoven network world of international political economy. This attitude tended to produce a two-tiered framework. Military considerations were seen as marginal to outcomes involving interdependence issues. They were left as an almost separate sector, important as an underlying condition for interdependence, but operating in a more or less self-contained fashion. Because great power military relations were largely paralyzed by the nuclear stalemate, military power no longer stood as the undisputed centre of high politics. Economic issues crept into Strategic Studies in the form of worries over supplies of strategic resources, and power models infiltrated interdependence thinking as it became apparent that interdependence was distributed unevenly.[25] But despite the useful lead given by deterrence theory, in which the interdependence of threats of mutually assured destruction was clearly understood,[26] little attempt was made to integrate the two by applying interdependence logic, via the more connective concept of security, to the problem of military power in an international anarchy. During the 1980s both of these barriers broke down.

Security also suffered neglect because of the methodological upheaval which consumed the field of International Relations from the late 1950s through to the mid-1970s. Behaviouralism, with its scientific, value-free, and quantitative concerns, was by definition not suited to the universe of essentially contested concepts. Indeed, it was an explicit revolt against the dominance of such an ambiguous and non-cumulative mode of thought. Behaviouralists had to deal with power because it represented the dominant orthodoxy. The prospect of yet another operational quagmire like security could hardly be expected to arouse them to enthusiasm. This obstacle has also dwindled as behaviouralism shed many of its initial pretensions in coming to terms with a complex reality.

A fourth reason for the conceptual underdevelopment of security can be found in the nature of Strategic Studies, which as a sub-field produced a large volume of empirical literature on problems of military policy. Why then has this not served as a base for development of security's more conceptual side? As I have argued at length elsewhere, there are two reasons.[27] First is that Strategic Studies has to spend a very high proportion of its energies on keeping up with new developments. The shifting patterns of international amity and enmity, plus the ceaseless interplay of developments in weapons technology and deployment, require constant monitoring and evaluation. The vastness of this task has largely confined Strategic Studies to short-term perspectives, leaving neither much capacity nor much inclination to move beyond empirical and policy-oriented horizons.

Second, Strategic Studies is for the most part an offspring of Anglo-American, and more broadly Western, defence policy needs, and as such it bears conspicuous signs of its parentage. Its attachment to security is heavily conditioned by the status quo orientations of hegemonic countries safely removed from the pressure of large attached neighbours. Strategic Studies is policy-oriented, and therefore both empirically bound and constrained not to wander much beyond the imperatives of the national policy level. In this sense, and despite extensive use of the term security within Strategic Studies, the field still exists largely within the confines of the Realist model of the struggle for power.[28] As will be made clear below, drawing the distinction between Strategic Studies and Security Studies is one purpose of this revised edition, especially when seen in relation to the definition of Strategic Studies in my 1987 book, *An Introduction to Strategic Studies: Military technology and international relations*, as being about 'the effects of the instruments of force on international relations'.[29]

A fifth, final, and enduring cause of the neglect of security hinges on the argument that, for the practitioners of state policy, compelling reasons exist for maintaining its symbolic ambiguity. The appeal to national security as a justification for actions and policies which would otherwise have to be explained is a political tool of immense convenience for a large variety of sectional interests in all types of state. Because of the leakage over domestic affairs which can be obtained by invoking it, an undefined notion of national security offers scope for power-maximizing strategies to political and military elites. While such leverage may sometimes be justified, as in periods such as the late 1930s, when there is acute danger of attack from expansionist powers, the natural ambiguity of foreign threats during peacetime makes it easy to disguise more sinister intentions in the cloak of national security.

It hardly needs to be pointed out, for example, that many interests in the United States and the Soviet Union benefited from exaggerating the level of threat which each posed to the other. Cultivation of hostile images abroad can justify intensified political surveillance, shifts of resources to the military, economic protectionism, and other such policies with deep implications for the conduct of domestic political life. Threats in the international system are nearly always real enough to make their exaggeration credible. At an extreme, the need for national security can even be evoked as a reason for not discussing it. One has only to think of the dying days of the Nixon Administration, or the Chinese government's behaviour after the June 1989 massacre of demonstrators in Tiananmen Square, to feel the implications of this state of affairs. This reasoning points back to the notion of essentially contested concepts, whose ideological cores take us to the heart of politics. Security is an intensely political concept, and exploration of this aspect will be a recurrent theme of subsequent chapters.

DEVELOPMENTS DURING THE 1980s

Since I first wrote this book in 1981 the concept of security has become much more prominent, and in some ways better developed, than the portrait I then painted of it. In noting this timing, I claim no more than a small role in a process that has many larger causes. Perhaps most fundamentally, it reflects the relentless pressure of interdependence on the older ways of thinking of both Realists and Idealists.

For Realists, interdependence raised the profile of economic, environmental and societal issues in the international system, as against the narrower, and often more nationalist, agenda of power politics. Both traditional Realism and Strategic Studies were vulnerable to the interdependence critique, Realism because it no longer reflected the preoccupations of much of the international agenda and Strategic Studies because after three decades of development and implementation its central doctrine of deterrence provided neither intellectual nor practical security.[30] In response, the Neorealists, most notably Kenneth Waltz with his influential structural theory of power politics, put the security motive at the centre of state behaviour in an anarchic system: 'In anarchy, security is the highest end...The goal the system encourages them [states] to seek is security.'[31] Strategists, with the new journal *International Security*, and millions of dollars of MacArthur Foundation funding to encourage them, responded by seeking to broaden their debate. Calls to use security logic to add economic, political, societal and environmental issues to the strategic agenda became commonplace.[32] Some writers argued that 'international security' should become the central concept of the field,[33] and others even began to refer to the field as 'international security studies'.[34]

For peace researchers, the pressures of interdependence meant that neither isolationist (unilateral disarmament, small-is-beautiful anti-statism) nor globalist (world disarmament, world government) approaches to peace could offer credible policies. Like the strategists, the peace movements were suffering from doctrinal malaise and a practical failure to deliver the goods. The idea of interdependence was in many ways already congenial to Idealist perspectives. What it forced them to take on board was the inescapable fact that the whole structure of interdependence involved intense, often competitive, interactions among many different, and firmly established states. The outcome of this synthesis between the logic of anarchy and the imperatives of Idealism was the idea of *common security*, first given prominence by the Palme Commission in 1982, and subsequently the subject of a wide-ranging debate.[35] Common security emphasized the interdependence of security relations as opposed to the national security priorities of traditional strategy. It coincided with, and helped to justify the movement of an increasing body of peace researchers into the debates about defence policy (rather than just criticizing them from the outside), most notably through the operational idea of non-provocative defence.[36]

In this way, and also because increasing numbers of people wanted a real change from a status quo made dangerous by the return of Cold War and recession, the foundations were laid (no more than that) for a convergence in the Realist and Idealist agendas. Significant sections on both sides had adopted security as their preferred conceptual tool. In policy terms, both strategists and peace researchers faced an expanded agenda, part of which was the need to think about defence policies compatible with the realities of both durable anarchic political organization and intensifying interdependence.[37] The intellectual development of security was taken up by a new generation of writers such as Ole Wæver and Rob Walker, who began to explore the concept of security in terms of its historical, philosophical and politico-linguistic aspects.[38] The concept was also adopted by increasing numbers of East Europeans as a preferred way of talking about the remarkable transformations in East-East and East-West relations that followed Gorbachev's accession to power in the Soviet Union.[39]

As the Cold War and bipolar structures of the post-war international system began to unravel during the late 1980s, there were grounds for thinking that security was developing into the preferred concept for dealing with high politics in the emerging post-post-war international system.

THE APPROACH OF THIS BOOK

It is almost no longer controversial to say that traditional conceptions of security were (and in many minds still are) too narrowly founded. That advance does not, however, mean that a consensus exists on what a more broadly constructed conception should look like. It is still a useful exercise to survey the ground on which any broader view must be built. In other words, it is necessary to map the domain of security as an essentially contested concept. This cartographic exercise is inevitably more abstract than empirical because its purpose is to define the conceptual sub-structures on which the mass of empirical studies by strategists and others rests. In trying to transcend criticisms aimed at too narrow a focus on national security, analysts must detach themselves from the pressures of day-to-day policy issues and the conventional modes of thought that have grown up around them. The approach in this book will thus be in complete, though complementary, contrast to that taken by Neville Brown in *The Future Global Challenge: A predictive study of world security 1977–1990*.[40] Both books aim to encourage a wider perspective on security than that encompassed by the traditional focus on national military policy. Operating somewhat in the tradition of the International Institute for Strategic Studies' annual *Strategic Survey*, Brown argues specifically from the multifaceted trends and developments in world affairs. He surveys these exhaustively, and concludes that the changing character of the international environment necessitates a broader view of security. The limits to his highly empirical approach come from the rapidly decreasing reliability of linear projections into the future as they move away from the known facts of any specified present. Anyone predicting the actual state of affairs in Eastern Europe in 1989 from the perspective of 1983, would have been thought hopelessly unrealistic.

What follows will look more at the idea of security itself than at the contemporary empirical conditions in which security policy has to be formulated. What does security mean, in a general sense? How is this general meaning transferred to the specific entities such as people and states that must be the objects of security policy? What exactly is the referent object of security when one refers to national security? If it is the state, what does that mean? Is one to take the state as meaning the sum of the individuals within it, or is it in some sense more than the sum of its parts? In either case, how do individuals relate to an idea like national security in terms of their own interests? At the other extreme, what does international security mean? Does it apply to some entity higher than states, or is there some sense in which security among states is an indivisible phenomenon?

The character of this exercise is as much philosophical as empirical. Because security is an essentially contested concept it naturally generates questions as well as answers. It encompasses several important contradictions and a host of nuances all of which can cause confusion if not understood. Major contradictions include that between defence and security, that between individual security and national security, that between national security and international security, and that between violent means and peaceful ends. Add to these the difficulties of determining the referent object of security (i.e. what is it that is to be made secure) and the pitfalls of applying the idea across a range of sectors (military, political, economic, environmental and societal), and the scope of the task becomes clear.

The object of the exercise is not to try to resolve these conundrums, but rather to explore them, and thereby clarify the difficulties – and the opportunities – that they pose for any attempt to apply the concept to real problems. The easy part of the exercise is using these insights to demolish the logic of simple-minded applications of security which ignore some of the contradictions they contain. For example, defence policies that raise threats by provoking the fears of other states may decrease security more than they increase it. The German naval challenge to Britain before the First World War is a case in point. The harder part of the exercise is finding derived concepts which enable the concept of security to be applied to practical situations in the full knowledge of the contradictions involved. The great merit of ideas like non-provocative defence is that they start from a solid understanding of both the necessity of, and the contradictions inherent within, the pursuit of military security.

As argued above, the nature of security defies pursuit of an agreed general definition. Because this is so, the formulation of such a definition is *not* one of the aims of this book. But both the desire for intellectual neatness and the attempt to clarify the ends of security policy naturally create a demand for definition, and it is instructive to survey the results. Wolfers warned about the ambiguity of security, and Charles Schultze argues explicitly that: 'The concept of national security does not lend itself to neat and precise formulation. It deals with a wide variety of risks about whose probabilities we have little knowledge and of contingencies whose nature we can only dimly perceive.'[41] Despite these warnings, quite a number of writers have been unable to resist the temptation to try:

József Balázs: International security is determined basically by the internal and external security of the various social systems, by the extent, in general, to which system identity depends on external circumstances. Experts generally define social security as internal security. Its essential function is to ensure the political and economic power of a given ruling class, or the survival of the social system and an adequate degree of public security.[42]

Ian Bellany: Security itself is a relative freedom from war, coupled with a relatively high expectation that defeat will not be a consequence of any war that should occur.[43]

Penelope Hartland-Thunberg: [National security is] the ability of a nation to pursue successfully its national interests, as it sees them, any place in the world.[44]

Walter Lippmann: a nation is secure to the extent to which it is not in danger of having to sacrifice core values if it wishes to avoid war, and is able, if challenged, to maintain them by victory in such a war.[45]

Michael H. H. Louw: [National security includes traditional defence policy and also] the non-military actions of a state to ensure its total capacity to survive as a political entity in order to exert influence and to carry out its internal and international objectives.[46]

Giacomo Luciani: National security may be defined as the ability to withstand aggression from abroad.[47]

Laurence Martin: [Security is the] assurance of future well being.[48]

John E. Mroz: [Security is] the *relative freedom* from harmful threats.[49]

National Defence College (Canada): [National Security is] the preservation of a way of life acceptable to the...people and compatible with the needs and legitimate aspirations of others. It includes freedom from military attack or coercion, freedom from internal subversion and freedom from the erosion of the political, economic and social values which are essential to the quality of life.[50]

Frank N. Trager and F. N. Simonie: National security is that part of government policy having as its objective the creation of national and international political conditions favourable to the protection or extension of vital national values against existing and potential adversaries.[51]

Richard Ullman: a threat to national security is an action or sequence of events that (1) threatens drastically and over a relatively brief span of time to degrade the quality of life for the inhabitants of a state, or (2) threatens significantly to narrow the range of policy choices available to the government of a state or to private, nongovernmental entities (persons, groups, corporations) within the state.[52]

Ole Wæver: One can view 'security' as that which is in language theory called a speech act:...it is the utterance itself that is the actæ...By saying 'security' a state-representative moves the particular case into a specific area; claiming a special right to use the means necessary to block this development.[53]

Arnold Wolfers: Security, in any objective sense, measures the absence of threats to acquired values, in a subjective sense, the absence of fear that such values will be attacked.[54]

These definitions do a useful service in pointing out some of the criteria for national security, particularly the centrality of values, the timing and intensity of threats and the political nature of security as an objective of the state. But they can do a disservice by giving the concept an appearance of firmness which it does not merit. For purely semantic reasons, it is difficult to avoid the absolute sense of security. The word itself implies an absolute condition – something is either secure or insecure – and does not lend itself to the idea of a graded spectrum like that which fills the space between hot and cold. Most definitions avoid one or more crucial questions. What are 'core values'? Are they a fixed or a floating reference point? Are they in themselves free from contradictions? What sources of change are acceptable and what are not? Does 'victory' mean anything under contemporary conditions of warfare? Are subjective and objective aspects of security separable in any meaningful way? Is war the only form of threat relevant to national security? How can relative security goals be adequately defined? Is national security really national, or merely an expression of dominant groups? What right does a state have to define its security values in terms which require it to have influence beyond its own territory, with the almost inevitable infringement of others' security interests that this implies? How are terms like 'threat' and 'aggression' defined in relation to normal activity? The inadequacy of these definitions should be neither surprising nor discouraging. Years of effort have also failed to produce a generally accepted definition or measure for power. The concept of justice requires legions of lawyers to service its ambiguities. There is no reason to think that security will be any easier to crack, and as with power and justice, the absence of a universal definition does not prevent constructive discussion. Although precise definitions will always be controversial, the general sense of what one is talking about is nevertheless clear: the political effects of physical capabilities in the case of power; the pursuit of fair outcomes when behaviour is contested in the case of justice.

In the case of security, the discussion is about the pursuit of freedom from threat. When this discussion is in the context of the international system, security is about the ability of states and societies to maintain their independent identity and their functional integrity. In seeking security, state and society are sometimes in harmony with each other, sometimes opposed. Its bottom line is about survival, but it also reasonably includes a substantial range of concerns about the conditions of existence. Quite where this range of concerns ceases to merit the urgency of the 'security' label and becomes part of the everyday uncertainties of life, is one of the difficulties of the concept. Security is primarily about the fate of human collectivities, and only secondarily about the personal security of individual human beings. In the contemporary international system, the standard unit of security is thus the sovereign territorial state. The ideal type is the nation-state, where ethnic and cultural boundaries line up with political ones, as in Japan and Denmark. But since nations and states do not fit neatly together in many places, non-state collectivities, particularly nations, are also important units of analysis. Because the structure of the international system is anarchic (without central authority) in all of its major organizational dimensions (political, economic, societal), the natural focus of security concerns is the units. Since states are the dominant units, 'national security' is the central issue, both in its normal, but ambiguous, reference to the state and in its more direct application to ethno-cultural units. Since some military and ecological threats affect the conditions of survival on the entire planet, there is also an important sense in which security applies to the collectivity of mankind as a whole.

The security of human collectivities is affected by factors in five major sectors: military, political, economic, societal and environmental. Generally speaking, military security concerns the two-level interplay of the armed offensive and defensive capabilities of states, and states' perceptions of each other's intentions. Political security concerns the organizational stability of states, systems of government and the ideologies that give them legitimacy. Economic security concerns access to the resources, finance and markets necessary to sustain acceptable levels of welfare and state power. Societal security concerns the sustainability, within acceptable conditions for evolution, of traditional patterns of language, culture and religious and national identity and custom. Environmental security concerns the maintenance of the local and the planetary biosphere as the essential support system on which all other human enterprises depend. These five sectors do not operate in isolation from each other. Each defines a focal point within the security problematique, and a way of ordering priorities, but all are woven together in a strong web of linkages.

Given this reasonably clear sense of what security is about, the lack of an overall definition does not block progress. Attempts at precise definition are much more suitably directed towards empirical cases where the particular factors in play can be identified. Since I shall not be working at the level of case studies in this book, the task here is to develop a broader framework of security that will help those wishing to apply the concept to particular cases. Such an understanding encompasses the contradictions in the concept rather than attempting to resolve them. My purpose is to map the terrain of the concept, identifying both its general features and its conspicuous hazards. Such a map will reveal not only the costs of working with a narrow conception of security, but also the advantages to be gained by attempting to apply a broader view.

The objective of this intellectual trek is not to arrive somewhere new, but 'to arrive where we started and know the place for the first time'.[55] As Michael Howard pointed out in comment not yet entirely out of date, discussion about security affairs is frequently marked by appallingly crude conceptual standards: 'pronouncements about military power and disarmament are still made by public figures of apparent intelligence and considerable authority with a naïve dogmatism of a kind such as one finds in virtually no other area of social studies or public affairs.'[56] The result of the present exercise might serve to raise the conceptual sophistication with which people discuss security. It might also reduce the political potency of national security by exposing its limits and contradictions, thereby mitigating some of the dangers pointed out three decades ago by Wolfers. At best, it might lead to a new synthesis of understanding about international relations as a whole, a possibility with implications both for the field of International Studies and for the narrower debate about the scope of Strategic Studies.

For International Studies, the security approach both opens up a new perspective on the field, and confirms the centrality of Neorealist insights to any understanding of the international system. Because security is such a fundamental concept, the process of mapping it inevitably takes one on a grand tour of the field.

One visits much familiar ground, but sees it through the perceptual lens of security rather than through more familiar lenses like power, wealth and peace. As a result, in the same way that derived concepts like the balance of power emerge from looking at international relations through the power lens, newly derived concepts emerge to fit the patterns that the security lens reveals. New light is cast on old concepts like system structure and arms racing, and new concepts are addressed to the old problem of national security policy-making.[57]

The centrality of Neorealist insights is confirmed by the powerful logic that makes the anarchic structure of the international system the primary political context for international security.[58] In this usage anarchy means the absence of central government. In the international system, anarchy does not mean the absence of government per se, but rather that government resides in the units of the system. If those units are states, then they will claim sovereignty, which is the right to treat themselves as the ultimate source of governing authority within the territorial limits of their jurisdiction. Since the claim of sovereignty automatically denies recognition of any higher political authority, a system of sovereign states is by definition politically structured as an anarchy.

International anarchy is thus a decentralized form of political order. It does not necessarily, or even probably, merit the Hobbesian implications of disorder and chaos that attach to it when the subject is relations among individual human beings. On the individual level, anarchy means the absence of *all* government. A political system structured in that way could only avoid chaos if human society had evolved to far higher levels of cohesion and responsibility than any yet attained. Indeed, no greater indication of the difference between anarchy at the individual and international levels is possible than the fact that the former requires the abolition of the state, whereas the latter finds its most perfect expression in the state.

The anarchic context sets the elemental political conditions in which all meanings of national and international security have to be constructed. Anarchy can be seen fatalistically as a product of history, representing either the current limit of the ongoing human attempt to create stable political units on an ever larger scale, or the natural political expression of a geographically, ethnically and culturally diverse population. It can also be seen as a preferred form of political order, representing values of ideological and cultural diversity, economic decentralization and political independence and self-reliance. In either perspective, the structure of anarchy is highly durable, because the actions states take to preserve their independence and sovereignty automatically perpetuate the anarchic system. In turn, that structure generates system-wide effects on relations among states. An anarchic structure imposes competitive, self-help conditions of existence on the states within the system. To say this, is not to say either that relations between states are inevitably, or even probably, violent under anarchy. Neither is it to say that international anarchy makes cooperation unlikely or impossible.[59] Violent conflict is always possible under anarchy, and in some circumstances likely. Competition, however, is pervasive, and takes political, economic, and societal forms as well as military ones.

The context of anarchy thus imposes three major conditions on the concept of security:

1. States are the principal referent object of security because they are both the framework of order and the highest source of governing authority. This explains the dominating policy concern with 'national' security.
2. Although states are the principal objects of security, the dynamics of national security are highly relational and interdependent between states. Domestic insecurities may or may not dominate the national security agenda, but external threats will almost always comprise a major element of the national security problem. The idea of 'international security' is therefore best used to refer to the systemic conditions that influence the ways in which states make each other feel more or less secure. Individual national securities can only be fully understood when considered in relation both to each other and to larger patterns of relations in the system as a whole.
3. Given the durability of anarchy, the practical meaning of security can only be constructed sensibly if it can be made operational within an environment in which competitive relations are inescapable. If security depends on either harmony or hegemony, then it cannot be lastingly achieved within anarchy. Among other things, this means that under anarchy, security can only be relative, never absolute. So long as anarchy holds, these conditions will obtain. If there is ever a structural shift out of anarchy, then the entire framework of the security problematique would have to be redefined.

The second academic purpose served by raising the profile of security is to help clarify the proper scope of Strategic Studies as a sub-field within International Studies. My own view on this much debated question is strong, and almost certainly not representative of majority opinion.[60] Put baldly, I think that International Security Studies should not, and probably cannot be incorporated within Strategic Studies. It should not be because Strategic Studies is, and should remain, a body of experts on the military aspects of international relations. Although that expertise is certainly relevant to Security Studies, trying to locate the broad agenda of the newer field within the narrow one of the old, would stunt and skew the development of Security Studies. It would be like giving responsibility for designing a national transportation system to the makers of automobiles. Their expertise would enable them to do the job, but their specialization would bias and restrict the nature of the outcome in all sorts of undesirable ways. Strategic Studies probably could not adequately absorb Security Studies without large-scale retraining in areas such as political economy, system theory, sociology and philosophy. Aside from the impracticality of such retraining, it would have no point, since it would simply reproduce the wider expertise already available in International Studies.

Thus I fully agree with those such as Brown, Ullman, Nye and Lynn-Jones, and Mathews who argue that International Security Studies needs an agenda that is substantially wider than military security.[61] I also fully agree with those such as Nye, Freedman and Booth who argue that there needs to be a revival of thinking in the manner of 'grand strategy'.[62] But I disagree strongly with them that the right place for this development is within Strategic Studies. If International Security Studies is to develop as a distinct sub-field in its own right, it should do so within the wider multidisciplinary framework of International Studies as a whole. Only there can be found the scope and expertise necessary for the full development of security thinking. In return, Security Studies could provide the field as a whole with an integrating framework that would help to tie together sub-fields such as Strategic Studies, Human Rights, Environmental and Development Studies and International Political Economy that are now too isolated from each other.

Strategic Studies already has both a clear identity and a well-established presence as a sub-field of International Studies. Its military focus gives it not only intellectual and social coherence, but also a useful – indeed vital – role in the division of labour within the field as a whole. Military strategists have a well-defined specialist expertise that gives them a role in the field somewhat analogous to that which accountants or lawyers have in a company. No major decision can sensibly be taken without their participation and advice. But neither would it be fruitful for the company always to subordinate its decisions to such specialists at the expense of inputs from experts in other relevant areas such as marketing, personnel and research and development.

A division of labour works best when two conditions are met. First, the specialization of tasks has to be both sensible in relation to the work overall, and congenial to those whose jobs it defines. Secondly, everyone within the project must be kept aware that they are part of a division of labour, and care must be taken to ensure that the different specialisms communicate with each other sufficiently to coordinate their work overall. This idea underlies the entire human ascent to civilization. In relation to the rather more parochial issue of the place of Strategic Studies within International Studies the most conspicuous room for improvement is in communication with other specialisms, in both directions. In my view, the rewards from addressing this issue would be greater than those from an attempt to reform Strategic Studies.

I conclude that while there is a very strong case for developing International Security Studies, and for establishing its identity as a source of insight on policy, there is no good case for doing so within Strategic Studies. My own sense of how the two should relate is clear from the way in which the contents of *An Introduction to Strategic Studies: Military technology and international relations* fit with the agenda for International Security Studies reflected in the contents of this book. Strategic Studies is much the narrower subject. Its agenda (or at least its agenda as I see it) is largely confined to Chapters 7 and 8, with additional bits from Chapters 3, 5 and 9. Security Studies has a much more wide-ranging agenda. Strategic Studies is certainly part of it, but in my view it would be quite counterproductive to try to force the larger subject into the mould shaped by the smaller. The natural home of grand strategy is the field of International Studies as a whole. For these reasons, I cannot agree with Ken Booth's view, cited above, that 'those strategists who do not attempt to be part of the solution will undoubtedly become an increasingly important part of the problem.' Strategists have a legitimate and useful specialist perspective, which they should stick to. Many of them would, I think, welcome a division of labour that clarified their position, removed them from the taint of being accomplices to militarism and freed them to pursue their expertise within a broader framework. The problem is not to force strategic specialists to become security experts. It is to develop a corps of grand strategists, firmly and consciously based in International Studies, whose broad expertise will enable the fruits of Strategic Studies to be used, and to develop, within the full context of the Security perspective.

THE STRUCTURE OF THIS BOOK

For reasons that should now be clear the reader will find that what follows is not organized around the conventional subject categories of Strategic Studies. While topics such as deterrence, arms control and disarmament, crisis management, alliances, military technology, strategy, arms racing and contemporary national security problems and policies will play an illustrative part in the discussion, they do not constitute its principal focus. Instead, enquiry centres on two questions: What is the referent object for security? What are the necessary conditions for security? These questions are pursued across the political and economic, and to some extent also the societal and environmental, landscapes, as well as the military one. They are accompanied by a persistent attention to the dialectic of threats and vulnerabilities, the policy consequences of overemphasizing one or the other and the existence of contradictions within and between ideas about security.

Security as a concept clearly requires a referent object, for without an answer to the question 'The security of what?' the idea makes no sense. To answer simply 'The state', does not solve the problem. Not only is the state an amorphous, multifaceted, collective object to which security could be applied in many different ways, but also there are many states, and the security of one cannot be discussed without reference to the others. The search for a referent object of security goes hand-in-hand with that for its necessary conditions. One soon discovers that security has many potential referent objects. These objects of security multiply not only as the membership of the society of states increases, but also as one moves down through the state to the level of individuals, and up beyond it to the level of the international system as a whole. Since the security of any one referent object or level cannot be achieved in isolation from the others, the security of each becomes, in part, a condition for the security of all.

The need to explore the referent objects of security on several different levels is what determines the structure of this book. I have taken from Waltz the idea of three levels of analysis centred on individuals, states and the international system,[63] and they provide the framework around which the chapters are organized.

These levels should be treated only as a convenient sorting device, and not as strict categorizations. Extensive grey areas exist, and although the levels form the major ordering principle of the book, no inference should be drawn that security can be isolated for treatment at any single level. Rationalizations for single-level security policies are quite common, as in the case of individuals who arm themselves before going out onto the streets and states that pursue policies of national security by cultivating military power. The burden of the argument here is precisely to refute such notions. As already argued, however, in the security context of the international system the state level, with its focus on human collectivities as units in the system, has primacy. The use of the three levels here will thus follow Wæver's scheme (see Chapter 9), in which the referent objects for security are found primarily on the state level, with the individual and system levels contributing major elements to the conditions for security. The reasons for the primacy of the state level as the location of referent objects for security will be developed by examining the consequences of trying to base Security Studies on referent objects located at the other levels. This academic disaggregation is undertaken only in order to make the reassembled whole easier to understand.

Chapter 1 begins by looking at individuals and security. To what extent are individuals the basic referent object of security, and how does individual security relate to the state? Chapter 2 follows this line of enquiry up to the state level, concentrating on the nature of the state as an object of security. Extensive investigation is made into the different components of the state to which security might apply, and attention is focused on the socio-political cohesion of the state as a major factor in any attempt to think about national security. Conclusions are drawn about the centrality of state-society relations, and about the limitations of the concept of national security. These first two chapters introduce the contradiction between individual and national security. Chapter 3 is a survey of the threats and vulnerabilities which define national insecurity across all five sectors. Part of security as a policy problem is revealed here in the unresolvable ambiguity of threats.

Chapter 4 takes up the question of state-society relations on the system level. It looks at the anarchic political structure of the international system as a major foundation for the whole security problematique. Having established the nature of anarchic security conditions, it begins to look at other factors that mediate and shape the consequences of anarchy. The socio-political cohesion of states is considered again, as is the idea of international society. First conclusions are drawn around the idea that different configurations of factors within anarchic structure lead toward or away from anarchies that are mature or immature in terms of the range and intensity of threats and vulnerabilities that they generate among their component parts. Chapter 5 continues the focus on the political and societal sectors, but on the regional level, presenting a fully-developed framework for regional security analysis using the idea of security complexes.

Chapter 6 moves into the economic sector. It starts by considering the relationship between the international economy and anarchic political structure, goes on to discuss the intense contradictions in the idea of economic security and then surveys the political economy of security in the light of a range of referent objects from the individual through the state to the system level. Chapters 7 and 8 concentrate on the military and power dynamics of security interactions among states and the contradictions they produce between national and international security. Two dilemmas are explored: the defence dilemma, which stems from the contradiction between defence and security; and the power-security dilemma, basic to anarchic structure, which is generated both by the tension between status quo and revisionist actors and by relentless advances in military technology. Conclusions are drawn about what mediating factors can reduce the tendency of anarchic structures to generate a power-security dilemma.

Chapter 9 draws the arguments from the three levels together in the context of national security policy-making, and addresses the contradiction between ends and means. The logical, perceptual and political problems facing national security policy-makers are explored, and the domestic policy process is identified as an independent factor in the national security problem. Chapter 10 offers a summary of how the different levels and sectors of the security problem interact with each other and where their contradictions lie. It draws conclusions about the folly of trying to separate individual, national and international security as approaches to the problem, and looks at the arguments for, and institutional consequences of, adopting a broad interpretation of security. It finishes by exploring the implications for policy of a broad security agenda.

NOTES

1. E. H. Carr, *The Twenty Years Crisis* (London, Macmillan: 1946, 2nd edn); Hans Morgenthau, *Politics Among Nations* (New York: Knopf, 1973, 5th edn). See also, for a more recent Neorealist view, Kenneth N. Waltz, *Theory of International Politics* (Reading, Mass.: Addison-Wesley, 1979). Realism in this context should not be confused with the philosophical school of the same name.

2. Buzan, 'Peace, power, and security: contending concepts in the study of international relations', *Journal of Peace Research*, 21:2 1984).

3. Peter Gellman, 'Hans J, Morgenthau and the legacy of political realism', *Review of International Studies*, 14:4 (1988), pp. 50–8.

4. See, for example, Otto Pick and Julian Critchley, *Collective Security* (London: Macmillan, 1974); Roland N, Stromberg, *Collective Security and American Foreign Policy* (New York: Praeger, 1963); M. V. Naidu, *Collective Security and the United Nations* (Delhi: Macmillan 1974); and Barry Buzan, 'Common security, non-provocative defence, and the future of Western Europe', *Review of International Studies*, 13:4 (1987), pp. 265–7.

5. John H. Herz, 'Idealist internationalism and the security dilemma', *World Politics*, 2 (1950), pp. 157–80; John H. Herz, *Political Realism and Political Idealism* (Chicago: University of Chicago Press, 1951); and John H. Herz, *International Politics in the Atomic Age* (New York: Columbia University Press, 1959), pp. 231– 43.

6. Robert Jervis, *Perception and Misperception in International Politics* (Princeton, NJ:

Princeton University Press, 1976) esp. ch. 3; 'Security regimes', *International Organization*, 36:2 (1982) and 'Cooperation under the security dilemma', *World Politics*, 30:2 (1978), pp. 167–214. See also Richard K. Ashley, *The Political Economy of War and Peace: The Sino-Soviet-American triangle and the modern security problematique* (London: Pinter, 1980).

7. Arnold Wolfers, 'National security as an ambiguous symbol', *Discord and Collaboration 7* (Baltimore: Johns Hopkins University Press, 1962), ch. 10.

8. Hedley Bull, *The Control of the Arms Race* (London: Weidenfeld & Nicolson, 1961), pp. 25–9; Bernard Brodie, *War and Politics* (London: Cassell, 1973), ch. 8; Frank N. Trager and Frank L. Simonie, 'An introduction to the study of national security', in F. N. Trager and P. S. Kronenberg (eds), *National Security and American Society* (Lawrence: University Press of Kansas, 1973).

9. Hugh Macdonald, 'The place of strategy and the idea of security', *Millennium*, 10: 3 (1981); Hans Mouritzen, *Finlandization: Towards a general theory of adaptive politics* (Aldershot: Avebury, 1988), pp. 46–7.

10. Jervis, *op. cit.* (note 6, 1982).

11. Gert Krell, 'The development of the concept of security' *Arbeitspapier* 3/1979, Peace Research Institute, Frankfurt.

12. For example, Richard J. Barnet, 'The illusion of security', in Charles R. Beitz and Theodore Herman (eds), *Peace and War* (San Francisco: W. H. Freeman, 1973); and Maxwell D. Taylor, 'The legitimate claims of national security', *Foreign Affairs*, 52:3 (1974).

13. See Barry Buzan, *An Introduction to Strategic Studies: Military technology and international relations* (London: Macmillan, 1987), pp. 12–13.

14. Ashley, *op cit.* (note 6), esp. ch. 10.

15. Ken Booth, *Strategy and Ethnocentrism* (London: Croom Helm, 1979), p. 133.

16. Leonard Beaton, *The Reform of Power: A proposal for an international security system* (London: Chatto & Windus, 1972).

17. Stanley Hoffmann, *Primacy or World Order* (New York: McGraw-Hill, 1978), p. 252.

18. Bull, *op. cit.* (note 8), pp. 28–9.

19. L. B. Krause and J. S. Nye, 'Reflections on the economics and politics of international economic organizations', in C. F. Bergsten and L. B. Krause (eds), *World Politics and International Economics* (Washington, DC: Brookings Institution, 1975), p. 329 (emphasis in original).

20. *North-South: A programme for survival*, Report of the Brandt Commission (London: Pan, 1980) pp. 124–5.

21. Wolfers, *op cit.* (note 7), p. 147.

22. W. B. Gallie, 'Essentially contested concepts', in Max Black (ed.), *The Importance of Language* (Englewood Cliffs, NJ: Prentice Hall, 1962), pp. 121–46. See also T. D. Weldon, *The Vocabulary of Politics* (Harmondsworth: Penguin, 1953), esp. ch. 2.

23. Richard Little, 'Ideology and change', in Barry Buzan and R. J. Barry Jones (eds), *Change and the Study of International Relations* (London: Pinter, 1981), p. 35.

24. Kenneth H. F. Dyson, *The State Tradition in Western Europe* (Oxford: Martin Robertson, 1980), pp. 205–6.

25. For the latter phenomenon, see Robert O. Keohane and Joseph S. Nye, *Power and*

Interdependence (Boston: Little Brown, 1977). Chapter 2 makes the case for pushing military factors into the background, thereby throwing out the security baby with the Realist bathwater.

26. Buzan, *op. cit.* (note 13), chs 11–12.

27. Barry Buzan, 'Change and insecurity: a critique of strategic studies, in Buzan and Jones, *op. cit.* (note 23), ch. 9; and Buzan, *op. cit.* (note 13), esp. ch.1.

28. For an excellent critique of Strategic Studies from this perspective, see Booth, *op. cit.* (note 15), ch. 9.

29. Buzan, *op. cit.* (note 13), p. 8.

30. Buzan, *op. cit.* (note 13), pp. 199–202.

31. Waltz, *op. cit.* (note 1), p. 126.

32. Joseph S. Nye Jr and Sean M. Lynn-Jones, 'International security studies', *International Security*, 12:4 (1988); Jessica Tuchman Mathews, 'Redefining security', *Foreign Affairs*, 68:2 (1989); Richard , H. Ullman, 'Redefining security' *International Security*, 8: 1 (1983); Joseph S. Nye Jr. 'The contribution of strategic studies: future challenges', *Adelphi Papers*, No. 235 (London: IISS, 1989).

33. Nye, *ibid.* (1989), p. 25.

34. Nye and Lynn-Jones, *op. cit.* (note 32); Helge Haftendorn, 'The state of the field: a German view', *International Security*, 13:2 (1988).

35. Report of the Independent Commission on Disarmament and Security Issues, *Common Security: A programme for disarmament* (London: Pan Books, 1982); Barry Buzan, *op. cit.* (note 4); Josephine O'Connor Howe (ed.), *Armed Peace: The search for world security* (London: Macmillan, 1984); Stockholm International Peace Research Institute (SIPRI), Policies for Common Security (London: Taylor and Francis, 1985); Stan Windass (ed.), *Avoiding Nuclear War: Common security as a strategy for the defence of the West* (London: Brassey's, 1985); Reinhard Mutz, *Common Security: Elements of an alternative to deterrence peace* (Hamburg: Institut für Friedensforschung and Sicherheitspolitik, 1986); Raimo Väyrynen, 'Common security and the state system', unpublished paper, Helsinki, 1988.

36. Buzan, *op. cit.* (note 13), ch. 17; W. Agrell, 'Offensive versus defensive: military strategy and alternative defence', *Journal of Peace Research*, 24:1 (1987); Johan Galtung, 'Transarmament: from offensive to defensive defence', *Journal of Peace Research*, 21:2 (1984); David Gates, *Non-Offensive Defence: A strategic contradiction?*, Occasional Paper 29 (London: Institute for European Defence and Strategic Studies, 1987); Björn Möller, *Resolving the Security Dilemma in Europe* (London: Brassey's, 1990). Generally, see the *Non-Offensive Defence (NOD)* Newsletter, Centre for Peace and Conflict Research, Copenhagen.

37. Barry Buzan, 'Is international security possible?', in Ken Booth (ed.), *New Thinking about Strategy and International Security* (London: Unwin Hyman, 1990).

38. Ole Wæver, 'Security, the speech act: analysing the politics of a word', unpublished second draft, Centre for Peace and Conflict Research, Copenhagen, 1989; R. B. J. Walker, 'The concept of security and international relations theory', unpublished paper, University of Victoria, 1987.

39. Ole Wæver, Pierre Lemaitre, Elzbieta Tromer (eds), *European Polyphony* (London: Macmillan, 1989); Pierre Lemaitre, 'Krise und reform in den socialistischen staaten und das

Sicherheitssystem Europas', in C. Wellmann (ed.), *Frieden in und mit Osteuropa*, (forthcoming, Suhrkamp Verlag); 'International security' *Külpolitika: a special edition*, 1988; József Balázs, 'A note on the interpretation of security', *Development and Peace*, 6 (1985), pp. 143–50.

40. Neville Brown, *The Future Global Challenge: A predictive study of world security 1977–1990* (London: RUSI, 1977).

41. Charles L. Schultze, 'The economic content of national security policy', *Foreign Affairs*, 51:3 (1973) pp. 529–30.

42. Balázs, *op. cit.* (note 39), p. 146.

43. Ian Bellany, 'Towards a theory of international security', *Political Studies*, 29:1 (1981), p. 102.

44. Penelope Hartland-Thunberg, 'National economic security: inter dependence and vulnerability', in Frans A.M. Alting von Geusau and Jacques Pelkmans (eds), *National Economic Security* (Tilburg: John F. Kennedy Institute, 1982), p. 50.

45. Cited in Arnold Wolfers, *Discord and Collaboration* (Baltimore: Johns Hopkins University Press, 1962), p. 150.

46. Michael H. H. Louw, *National Security* (Pretoria: ISS–University of Pretoria, 1978), the quote is from the introductory note titled 'The purpose of the symposium'.

47. Giacomo Luciani, 'The economic content of security', *Journal of Public Policy*, 8:2 (1989), p. 151.

48. Laurence Martin, 'Can there be national security in an insecure age?', *Encounter*, 60:3 (1983) p. 12.

49. John E. Mroz, *Beyond Security: Private perceptions among Arabs and Israelis* (New York: International Peace Academy, 1980), p. 105 (emphasis in original).

50. Course documents, National Defence College of Canada, Kingston, 1989.

51. Frank N. Trager and Frank L. Simonie, 'An introduction to the study of national security', in F. N. Trager and P. S. Kronenberg, *National Security and American Society* (Lawrence: University Press of Kansas, 1973), p. 36.

52. Ullman, *op. cit.* (note 32) p. 133.

53. Wæver, *op. cit.* (note 38), pp. 5–6.

54. Wolfers, *op. cit.* (note 45), p. 150.

55. T. S. Eliot, *Collected Poems 1902–1962* (London: Faber and Faber, 1963), 'Little Gidding', p. 222.

56. Michael Howard, 'Military power and international order', *International Affairs*, 40:3 (1964), pp. 407–8.

57. Although the tour will touch on most aspects of international relations I will not go into the subject of war. Under conditions of war, security assumes a largely military identity which bears little relation to its character in the absence of war. In war, security hinges on a much narrower, and on the whole better understood, set of factors than is the case during peace. The whole issue of security during war has declined in salience because of deterrence and the nuclear stalemate, but at the same time the general concern about security has not diminished. The national security problem is a constant feature of international relations regardless of war: it could exist, for example, within the framework of a political economy struggle such as that envisaged within the Soviet idea of peaceful coexistence. For these reasons, and for considerations of space, I shall treat war as part of the national security problem

without examining in any depth the special case of security in war conditions.

58. Waltz, *op. cit.* (note 1), chs 5 and 6; Barry Buzan, 'Rethinking structure', in Barry Buzan, Charles Jones and Richard Little, *The Logic of Anarchy* (forthcoming).

59. R. Axelrod and R. Keohane, 'Achieving cooperation under anarchy', Robert Jervis, 'From balance to concert: a study of international security cooperation', K. Oye, 'Explaining cooperation under anarchy', all in *World Politics* 38:1 (1985); Robert Keohane, *After Hegemony: Cooperation and discord in the world political economy* (Princeton, NJ: Princeton University Press, 1984).

60. See the discussion in Gerald Segal (ed.), *New Directions in Strategic Studies: A Chatham House debate*, RIIA Discussion Papers 17 (1989).

61. Brown, *op. cit.* (note 40); Ullman, Mathews and Nye and Lynn-Jones, *op. cit.* (note 32).

62. *op. cit.* (note 60); Nye, *op. cit.* (note 32).

63. Kenneth N. Waltz, *Man, the State, and War* (New York: Columbia University Press, 1959). For other approaches using variations on the idea of a three-level analysis, see: J. David Singer, 'The level of analysis problem in international relations', in Klaus Knorr and Sidney Verba (eds), *The International System* (Princeton, NJ: Princeton University Press, 1961); Arnold Wolfers, 'Nation-state', in F. A. Sonderman, W. C. Olson and D. S. McLellan (eds), *The Theory and Practice of International Relations* (Englewood Cliffs, NJ, Prentice Hall, 1970), pp. 16–22; R. W. Cox, 'Social forces, and world orders', *Millennium*, 10:2 (1981); and Andrew Linklater, 'Men and citizens in international relations', *Review of International Studies*, 7:1 (1981).

chapter | individual security and national
one | security

The individual represents the irreducible basic unit to which the concept of security can be applied. This fact makes individual security a good starting point for a more wide-ranging analysis, in part because it provides a clear basis from which to demolish the reductionist illusion that national and international security are simply extensions to a concern with the fate of individual human beings. To pursue individual security as a subject in its own right would take one deeply into the realms of politics, psychology and sociology. Such a study is beyond the scope of this book, and has been done elsewhere.[1] The relevance of individual security to this enquiry lies in the network of connections and contradictions between personal security and the security of the state. The state is a major source of both threats to and security for individuals. Individuals provide much of the reason for, and some of the limits to, the security-seeking activities of the state. Given that human beings are the prime source of each other's insecurity, the question of individual security quickly takes on broader societal and political dimensions.[2] It leads directly to questions about the basic nature of the state, and this chapter consequently serves as a foundation for Chapter 2, in which the question of the state is the central focus.

INDIVIDUAL SECURITY AS A SOCIETAL PROBLEM

The idea of security is easier to apply to things than to people. The security of money in a bank, for example, is amenable to calculation in relation to specified threats of unauthorized removal or the likelihood of *in situ* deflation in value. Since material goods are often replaceable with like items, their security (that is, the owner's security in possession of them) can usually be enhanced further by insuring them against loss, the insurance itself being based on actuarial statistics of risk. Security for individuals cannot be defined so easily. The factors involved – life, health, status, wealth, freedom – are far more complicated, and many of them cannot be replaced if lost (life, limbs, status). Different aspects of individual security are frequently contradictory (protection from crime versus erosion of civil liberties), and plagued by the difficulty of distinguishing between objective and subjective evaluation (are threats real or imagined?). Cause-effect relationships with regard to threats are often obscure and controversial (individual versus social explanations for crime).

Dictionary definitions of security give the flavour of these difficulties with their reference to being protected from danger (objective security) feeling safe (subjective security), and being free from doubt (confidence in one's knowledge). The referent threats (danger and doubt) are very vague, and the subjective feeling of safety or confidence has no necessary connections with actually being safe or right. Even if one takes as an illustration a well-off individual in a well-off country, the resultant image of day-to-day life leaves no doubt that security in any comprehensive sense is beyond reasonable possibility of attainment. An enormous array of threats, dangers and doubts loom over everyone, and although the better-off can distance themselves from some of these (starvation, preventable/curable disease, physical exposure, criminal violence, economic exploitation, and such like), they share others equally with the poor (incurable disease, natural disasters, nuclear war), and create some new ones for themselves because of their advantages (air crashes, sporting accidents, kidnapping, diseases of excessive consumption). Security cannot be complete for any individual: few would relish for more than a short time the flatness and predictability of a life in which it was so.

The impossibility of general security drives analysis towards specific threats. Against some threats, such as preventable diseases or poverty, some individuals can achieve very high levels of security. Against others, especially where cause-effect relationships are obscure (cancer, crime, unemployment), security measures may be chancy at best. Given limits on resources, decisions have to be made as to where to allocate them in relation to a large number of possible threats. Efforts to achieve security can become self-defeating, even if objectively successful, if their effect is to raise awareness of threats to such a pitch that felt insecurity is greater than before the measures were undertaken. Urban householders' efforts to burglar-proof their houses can have this effect. As locks, alarms and bars proliferate, their daily presence amplifies the magnitude of the threat by advertising to burglars the presence of valuable possessions, thereby leading to a net loss of tranquillity for the fortified householders. Paranoia is the logical endpoint of obsession with security. There is a cruel irony in that meaning of secure which is 'unable to escape'.

Most threats to individuals arise from the fact that people find themselves embedded in a human environment which generates unavoidable social, economic and political pressures. Societal threats come in a wide variety of forms, but there are four obvious basic types: physical threats (pain, injury, death), economic threats (seizure or destruction of property, denial of access to work or resources), threats to rights (imprisonment, denial of normal civil liberties) and threats to position or status (demotion, public humiliation). These types of threat are not mutually exclusive in that the application of one (injury) may well carry penalties in another (loss of job). The existence of these threats to individuals within society points to the great dilemma which lies at the root of much political philosophy: how to balance freedom of action for the individual against the potential and actual threats which such freedom poses to others. Put another way, this dilemma can be formulated as how to enhance the liberation of community without amplifying oppression by authority. The great potency of Hobbes's image of the state of nature derives precisely from the fact that it expresses this dilemma with such clarity. Individuals (or collective human behavioural units such as states and nations) existing with others of their kind in an anarchical relationship, find their freedom increased only at the expense of their security. As Waltz puts it: 'States, like people, are insecure in proportion to the extent of their freedom. If freedom is wanted, insecurity must be accepted.'[3]

The state of nature image postulates a primal anarchy in which the living conditions for the individuals involved are marked by unacceptably high levels of societal threat, in a word, chaos. Unacceptable chaos becomes the motive for sacrificing some freedom in order to improve levels of security, and in this process, government and the state are born. In the words of Hobbes, people found states in order to 'defend them from the invasion of foreigners and the injuries of one another, and thereby to secure them in such sort as that by their own industry, and by the fruits of the earth, they may nourish themselves and live contentedly'.[4] Similarly John Locke: 'The great and chief end…of men's…putting themselves under government is the preservation of their property' (meaning here their 'lives, liberties and estates') which in the state of nature is 'very unsafe, very unsecure'.[5] The state becomes the mechanism by which people seek to achieve adequate levels of security against societal threats, a phenomenon that R. N. Berki sees as: 'the most important distinguishing mark of our modern Western civilization'.[6]

The paradox, of course, is that as state power grows the state also becomes a source of threat against the individual. The stability of the state derives not only from its centralizing power, but also from the understanding by its citizens that it is the lesser of two evils (that is, that whatever threats come from the state will be of a lower order of magnitude than those which would arise in its absence). This assumption grows in force as society develops around the state, becoming increasingly dependent on it as a lynchpin for social and economic structures. As the symbiosis of society and state develops along more complex, sophisticated and economically productive lines, the state of nature image becomes more and more unappealing. The enormous costs of the reversion have to be added to the dubious benefits of existence in a state of nature. Examples of stateless anarchy, such as that in Lebanon since 1976, starkly underline the value of the state as the lesser evil. If the state of nature was unacceptable to thinly scattered and primitive peoples, how much more unacceptable would it be to the huge, densely-packed and interdependent populations of today?

On this logic, the state is irreversible. There is no real option of going back, and therefore the security of individuals is inseparably entangled with that of the state.

INDIVIDUAL SECURITY AND THE TWO FACES OF THE STATE

If the security of individuals is irreversibly connected to the state, so, as state and society become increasingly indistinguishable, is their insecurity. This is not only a question of the efficiency, or lack thereof, with which the state performs its internal (social order) and external (group defence) functions, but also a matter of the state itself becoming a source of controversy and threat. If the state becomes a major source of threat to its citizens, does it not thereby undermine the prime justification for its existence? How does one deal with the alleged quip of a Brazilian president that: 'Brazil's doing fine, but the people are doing badly.'?[7] To deal with this paradox, it is necessary to consider the basic relationship between citizens state. One can divide views on this issue into two general models: the *minimal* and the *maximal* conceptions of the state.

The minimal state arises out of John Locke's concept of a social contract which provides a view of the state very much oriented towards the individuals who make it up. The foundations of the state rest on the consent of its citizens to be governed, and therefore the actions of the state can be judged according to their impact on the interests of its citizens. In this view, the state should not be much more than the sum of its parts, and serious clashes between citizens and state should be avoided. P. A. Reynolds argues explicitly that individual values are, or should be, the prime referent by which state behaviour is judged, and similar sentiments underlie Robert Tucker's thoughtful essay on this subject. Robert Nozick offers a deep and wide-ranging defence of the minimal state in which the acknowledged need for collective structures is subordinated to the prime value of individual rights.[8] If one accepts this view, it necessarily leads to an interpretation of national security which places great emphasis on values derived directly from the interests of individual citizens. It also requires a form of government in which the consent of the governed plays such an active part that clashes of interest between state and citizens do not assume major proportions.

The maximal state view grows from the assumption that the state is, or should be, considerably more than the sum of its parts, and that it therefore has interests of its own. These interests might derive from a number of sources. Marxists interpret them as the interests of a dominant elite who use the state to advance their own cause.[9] Realists construct the state as a necessary unit for the well-being and survival of any human group within the anarchic international environment. They thus have the makings of a transcendent state purpose in the imperative of the struggle for power and security. One extreme version of this is the position taken by Heinrich von Treitschke. Building on Hegel's 'deification' of the state, he argues forcefully that the state is 'primordial and necessary', that it exists as 'an independent force' and that 'it does not ask primarily for opinion, but demands obedience'.[10] In his view, the state as a collective entity encompassing the nation stands above the individuals comprising it. The state cannot be seen as something created by individuals, as implied in notions of social contract.

One can, ironically, also reach the maximalist conclusion by extending the social contract view. Here the argument is that the state acquires independent standing above its citizens because of the essential role it plays in the realization of individual interests. In the state of nature, chaotic conditions prevent the effective pursuit of individual values, which therefore cannot be said to have meaning outside the framework of the state. Since the state has to be viewed either as the source of all value, or, at a minimum, as the necessary condition for the realization of any value, the preservation of the state, and the consequent pursuit of state interest, supersede the individual values from which they notionally derive.[11] In either version, the maximal view results in a quite different interpretation of the relationship between individual security and national security from the minimal one. To the extent that the state is more than the sum of its parts, then it can be detached from, and legitimately unresponsive to, individual security needs.[12]

The minimal view of the state tries to collapse the contradiction between individual and national security by arguing that the state is, or should be, merely the sum of its parts, and instrumental to their ends. It opens the way for a reductionist logic that interprets national and international security in terms of individual security. The maximal view blocks the possibility of reductionism by interposing the state as an independent variable. This theoretically clear distinction, however, is not so easy to make in practice. The difficulty arises from another traditional puzzle of political philosophy, the linked problems of how to determine the general will, and how to calculate what level of state intervention in the lives of the citizens will be necessary to fulfil even the minimal tasks of defending them from the 'invasion of foreigners and the injuries of one another'. If one assumes the citizens to be naturally fractious, and the international environment to be unremittingly hostile, then even a minimal state will be a large intervening force in the lives of its citizens. This uncertainty makes it impossible in practice to draw a clear empirical boundary between minimal and maximal states. How far can maintenance of civil order and provision for external defence go before the immensity of the task creates in the state an overriding purpose and momentum of its own?

Two factors suggest themselves as possible boundary-markers between minimal and maximal states. First is the existence of extensive civil disorder such as that in Russia in 1905, in Hungary in 1956, in Lebanon after 1976, in Nicaragua during the late 1970s, in Iran after 1979, in El Salvador and South Africa during the 1980s, in parts of the Soviet Union and Eastern Europe during the late 1980s and in numerous other places where popular unrest has dominated the news over the years. Such disorder could indicate a degree of falling out between citizens and government arising where a maximal state has pursued its own interests to the excessive detriment of the mass of individual interests within it. Unfortunately, disorder could also indicate the failure of a minimal state to contain the contradictions among its citizens, and thus cannot reliably be used to distinguish the two types.

The second possible indicator is the existence of a disproportionate internal security apparatus, though again considerable difficulties occur in finding a measure for this. The argument is that a minimal state should not require a massive police force, and that the presence of one is symptomatic of the distance between a maximal state and its people. A minimal police state might just be possible in conditions of severe external threats of penetration, as in Israel, or even Korea. But the kind of police machinery associated with totalitarian states, or the kind of independent police powers exemplified by the apartheid regime in South Africa, might normally be taken to indicate a maximal state. One problem here is that opinions differ markedly on where normal policing ends and the police state begins. Britain would be far removed from most lists of police states, but many black citizens in Bristol, Brixton and Notting Hill cite excessive policing as a major grievance underlying riots there. Similar views could easily be found in many American cities. In both the United States and Britain there are, in addition, recurrent bouts of concern about the domestic activities of intelligence agencies.

Thus even the level of policing does not, in the end, provide one with a reliable distinction between minimal and maximal states. It can plausibly be argued that both domestic disorder and heavy policing might reflect the difficulty of maintaining a minimal state given the nature of particular historical circumstances. If the Russians and Chinese have too many police, and the Philippines and Central Americans too much disorder, that could simply indicate the severe domestic problems of establishing a minimal state in these areas.

This line of argument pushes increasingly towards the conclusion that in practice the maximal state, or something very like it, rules. As Berki concludes, there is no escape from the paradoxes of individual security without the state.[13] With the state, there is no escape from contradictions between individual and national security. Since the maximal state model seems to offer a better correspondence with what one actually finds in the real world, the main utility of the minimal state view is to set a standard for judgement and criticism. This conclusion has important implications for thinking about the relationship between individual security and the state. In the minimal state model, one assumes a low level of disharmony between state and individual interests. The state structure should be responsive to individual interests except for the restraints imposed in pursuit of civil order and external defence. Although one would expect to find some tension between state and citizen in such an arrangement, one would expect there to be neither a major domestic side to state security, nor a substantial individual security problem stemming from the state.

In the maximal state model, by contrast, internal security becomes a natural and expected dimension, and there is no necessary striving to harmonize state and individual interests. Limits to the disharmony between state and citizen do, of course, exist, and constraints of efficiency require that even extreme maximal states pay some attention to the needs of their people. Those that fail to do so risk either or both of two fates: collapse into civil war, or loss of international power and status in relation to those states able to mobilize their human resources more efficiently. These limits, however, are wide enough to give governments quite a lot of latitude in how they relate to their citizens. States of all types benefit from the widespread feeling among individuals that anything is better than reversion to the state of nature. So long as the state performs its Hobbesian tasks of keeping chaos at bay, this service will be seen by many to offset the costs of other state purposes, whatever they may be. Thus what might be judged appalling regimes by outside observers (the Duvaliers in Haiti, Boukassa in Central Africa, Pol Pot in Cambodia, Stalin, Hitler, Ceaucescu and many others) keep themselves in power by a combination of heavy, but by no means cripplingly expensive, police presence, and a reliance on the formidable ballast of political inertia in the population. Under these conditions, the clash between individual and state interests might normally be quite extensive. When the maximal state rules, it is neither unusual nor paradoxical to find individuals dependent on the state for maintenance of their general security environment, while at the same time seeing the state as a significant source of threats to their personal security.

THE STATE AS A SOURCE OF THREAT

If one expects to find a two-edged relationship between state and individual security as the normal human condition, then it is useful to set out the character of the contradiction in more detail. The individual citizen faces many threats which emanate either directly or indirectly from the state. These can occupy an important place in the person's life. Such threats can be grouped into four general categories: those arising from domestic law-making and enforcement; those arising from direct administrative or political action by the state against individuals or groups; those arising from struggles over control of the state machinery; and those arising from the state's external security policies.

Threats to the individual from the process of domestic law can occur as a result of inadequate or excessive policing and prosecution practices. Miscarried or deficient justice can have an immense impact on the lives of the individuals concerned, either by exposing them to criminal activity or by inflicting unjustified penalties on them. In the United States for example, 440,000 citizens were killed, 1. 7 million wounded and 2.7 million robbed by people using guns between 1963 and 1982.[14] Cases of both types are an inevitable cost of any attempt to balance effective law enforcement with protection of broad civil liberties. This problem, however, is not generally relevant to national security unless disaffection with law enforcement becomes very widespread and politicized. A variant on this type of threat arises with environmental issues. Contemporary concern over chemical and nuclear pollution reflects individual fears of both inadequacies in state regulation and misplaced priorities in what activities the state promotes. Impacts at the individual level can be catastrophic in terms of probabilities of cancer, birth defects and other threats to health. Given the magnitude of pollution, this issue has now acquired an international security dimension.

A rather more directly political threat can come to individuals specifically targeted by the institutions of the state. The late-night knock on the door of police states is still the most striking image of this threat, but it comes in many lesser forms as well. The modern bureaucratic administration possesses an enormous range of legal powers which it can exercise against its citizens in the name of the common good. Property owners can be expropriated to make way for motorways, the children of unstable families can be taken into care, manipulations of the economy can throw millions out of work. All of this has to be balanced against the services and social security provided by the state, but it is clear that the powers and actions of the state constitute significant threats to many individuals.

Some of this is what Galtung has characterized as 'structural violence', where damage is inflicted on individuals not by other individuals but by the operation of impersonal structural forces.[15] Much of it is still straightforward direct violence. The ruining of people's careers in the McCarthy hearings in the United States, the incarceration of Soviet dissidents in psychiatric hospitals in the pre-Gorbachev era, the removal of the right to worship for Huguenots in France by the revocation of the Edict of Nantes in 1685, the persecution of Jews in Nazi Germany, legal discrimination against blacks in South Africa, maiming of suspects by police in India, assassinations by police 'death squads' in Latin America, ruthless relocation, liquidation and enforced labour in Pol Pot's Kampuchea and an endless catalogue of similar items, are all examples of the kinds of threat which the state can pose to its citizens. These threats can arise as part of explicit state policy against certain groups, such as the purges against leftists in Chile after the fall of Allende in 1973 or Stalin's purges against a wide variety of opponents during the 1930s. Or they can arise simply as a matter of normal policy procedure in which the state sacrifices the interests of some for what is seen to be a higher collective interest, as in the case of those condemned to unemployment because of the need to control the money supply. For perhaps a majority of the world's people threats from the state are among the major sources of insecurity in their lives. This is certainly true in many parts of the Third World where, as Migdal argues, the state is frequently in opposition to much of the society it contains.[16] Perhaps the ultimate embodiment of this type of threat is the theory that the rights, comforts and welfare of the present generation must be sacrificed for the development of a better life for those to come, a thesis critically examined by Peter Berger in *Pyramids of Sacrifice: Political ethics and social change* in both its capitalist and socialist variants.[17]

The other side of the coin of threat from the state is threat arising from political disorder: the struggle for control over the state's institutions. Only a minority of states have developed stable mechanisms for the transfer of political power. In the rest, violent conflicts over the reins of office pose an intermittent and frequently serious threat to sections of the population. The archetypes for this situation are countries like Argentina and Bolivia where until very recently military factions played a seemingly endless game of push-and-shove around the high offices of the state, while at the same time fighting an interminable, and often savage internal war against a variety of mostly left-wing revolutionary groups. The state is sufficiently durable to withstand quite astonishing amounts of disarray in domestic political life, but on the individual level such disarray becomes a central source of personal insecurity for many.

In many states, participation in what passes for the national political process can bring threats of imprisonment, death or worse, and even opting for the role of innocent bystander is no guarantee of safety. Society as a whole stands in fear of political violence, and those (temporarily) in control of the state apparatus use it in the ways outlined in the previous paragraph to support their own political ends. Political violence can become endemic, as it did in Turkey in the late 1970s, with factional gun battles and assassinations producing casualties on a war-like scale, and eventually leading in 1978 to extensive imposition of martial law. It can lead to the nightmare of civil war, as in Spain during the early and mid-1930s, or to the political limbo and institutionalized violence of a state in dissolution, as in the Lebanon since 1976. Domestic political violence frequently opens the door to the further threat of external intervention, either as participant on one side or the other (the Syrians and the Israelis in Lebanon, the Indians in Sri Lanka), or as invaders taking advantage of a state weakened by internal dispute (the Japanese in China during the 1930s). One has only to recall the catastrophic effects of American intervention on the people of Vietnam and Cambodia to sense the full dimension of this threat.

Political terrorism also fits under this heading, regardless of whether or not the terrorists see themselves as contending for political power. The use of terror, such as bombings, shootings or hijackings, to pressure, weaken or discredit a government explicitly poses threats to the citizens who are obliged to play the role of victim. Individuals face random risks of victimization because of others' disputes about the nature or control of state policy. Those varieties of terrorism which take the state apparatus as their direct target also threaten individuals although, innocent bystanders excepted, these come from a much more select group than the mass victims of hijackers and public bombings. Terrorism, like other forms of political violence, not only undermines the individual's security directly, it is likely also to increase the threats to individual security offered by the state itself, as well as those coming from other states. By undermining trust in the state's capacity to provide domestic security, terrorists can force the state to make its security measures more obtrusive. This process has been much enhanced by the actual and potential danger of terrorists acquiring high technology weapons. The extreme fear here is that of terrorists armed with a nuclear weapon. The combination of ruthless or mindless determination, and a capacity for mass destruction, would pose an unprecedented challenge to the balance between individual rights and public order. In responding to such threats, even a minimal state would necessarily begin to adopt maximal forms.

The final dimension in which state policy and individual security clash is foreign policy. Just as there is a very mixed set of costs and benefits to individual security in relation to the state's civil order functions, so is there for its external security functions. The state is supposed to provide a measure of protection to its citizens from foreign interference, attack and invasion. But it cannot do so without imposing risks and costs on them. In essence, this arrangement does not normally raise extensive controversy. As with the risks of a certain level of miscarried justice and unpunished crime, the risk of war service is usually accepted by citizens as a fair trade-off for the broader measure of security provided by the state. While the principle may be firmly rooted, however, the practice which develops around it can easily become an intense source of dispute on the grounds of individual versus national security. This process is much stronger and more visible in democracies, because the expression and mobilization of public opinion is easier and more influential in the democratic context. Modern war is known to produce high risks and high casualties, and this makes decisions about what constitutes a threat to the security of the state a matter of considerable public concern.

The state can usually count on mass support in an obvious and imminent crisis, as in Britain after 1938. But more remote and ambiguous entanglements can easily run the risk of being seen as insufficient cause for placing citizens at risk, as the United States discovered during the Vietnam War. Especially where armed forces are raised by conscription, policies requiring citizens to place themselves at risk in the service of the state will naturally tend to raise political questions about the value of the trade-offs involved between individual and national security. This is not nearly so much the case where professional soldiers are involved, as in the 1982 Falklands War between Britain and Argentina, because they are seen as having already made a free decision to place other values higher than their own lives.

Indeed, it is a point too easily forgotten that individuals frequently choose to place their lives at risk in pursuit of other values. The early American pioneers accepted substantial risks on the frontier in order to pursue freedom and wealth. Enthusiasts for dangerous sports like hang-gliding and potholing balance the risks against the thrills of achievement. American teenagers, playing 'chicken' in their cars (to take one of the famous metaphors of Strategic Studies), gamble injury or death against status in the eyes of their group. Policemen, soldiers and mercenaries accept the risk of injury and death for a great variety of reasons, among which, for some, is the pleasure of being authorized to inflict injury and death on others. Life for its own sake is often not ranked first among individual values, and it is useful to keep this in mind when trying to judge the morality of state policies against values derived from the interests of the citizens (that is, when using standards based on the minimal model of the state). Maximal states do not have this problem to the same extent because they are by definition less bound, or not bound at all in some cases, to the notion that individual values have any relation to state policy in the short term.

A different, but no less interesting, variant of the conflict potential between individual and national security arises in relation to nuclear weapons and the kinds of national security policies based on them. The whole idea of a national security policy based on threats of exchanged nuclear salvoes strikes many people as being the *reductio ad absurdum* of arguments for collective defence. If the minimal state point of view is taken, then any policy which envisages the possibility of the population being obliterated is unacceptable almost by definition. Even with a maximal state view, it becomes hard to find ends which justify such risks. The fine logic of deterrence theory appears to be an exceedingly thin thread on which to hang security. It adds insult to prospective injury by the notion of mutually assured destruction, which aims to ensure deterrence stability by deliberately keeping populations vulnerable to nuclear attack. The merits of nuclear deterrence have been powerfully argued both ways, and there is no need to repeat the exercise in these pages.[18] The point of interest here is that deterrence policy displays the divorce between individual and national security at the highest and most visible level. The apparent end of a long tradition of national defence is a situation in which states seek to preserve themselves by offering each other their citizens as hostages. Obviously, there is a strong logic in deterrence which connects the interests of the individual to those of the state. But no matter how impeccable this logic is, it remains a political fact that large numbers of people think that a threat of societal extinction is too high a price to pay for national security. This theme is the subject of Chapter 7.

Contradictions between individual security and national security lead not only to specific policy issues of defence and deterrence, but also to broader policy questions such as human rights. The whole issue of human rights rose to international prominence during the 1970s and 1980s.[19] It did so precisely in order to address the relationship between state and citizen, and the place that individual security considerations should have in the way states relate to each other. Because individual security became an international issue, it also became part of the national security problem for many states that would not otherwise have seen it as such. The linkage between individual, national and international security has even been used, albeit in a now somewhat dated way, to attempt a grand synthesis of political understanding.[20] Harold Lasswell's ambitious, though not always convincing (or clear!) book tries to link individual and mass psychology to both the machinery of state control and the pressures of the international anarchy. His holistic analysis functions both ways, tying the murkier aspects of Freudian insecurity to the structural insecurities of a threatening international system. He sees these two levels mediated through the political processes of the state, with particular emphasis on the linking role of symbols and identities. State and nation offer symbols and identities which both attract individuals seeking expression and outlet for their insecurities, and reproduce the political conditions that are one of the major sources of personal insecurity.

CONCLUSIONS: INDIVIDUAL SECURITY AND NATIONAL SECURITY

There is no necessary harmony between individual and national security. A gruesome symbol of this contradiction was provided by 'Baby Doc' Duvalier, who renamed as the 'Volunteers for National Security' his father's notorious private police, the Ton Ton Macoutes.[21] A quite different indicator of it is the facility for individuals to appeal against their governments under the European Convention on Human Rights. While the state provides some security to the individual, it can only do so by imposing threats. These threats, whether direct or indirect, and whether intended or unanticipated side-effects, are frequently serious enough to dominate the relatively small and fragile universe of individual security. Although they are powerfully balanced by the domestic and external security which the state provides, these threats, and therefore the contradiction between individual and national security, are unavoidable. Consequently, it is mistaken to assume, as John Herz did, that political authority will only accrue to states able to provide both pacification of and control over internal relations, and protection from outside interference.[22] The record indicates that viable states need only provide some security in these directions, and that they can get away with being a considerable source of threat themselves. The state enjoys a wide tolerance for its inefficiencies and perversities in relation to domestic security. The decline in its defensive impermeability brought about by the development of strategic bombing and nuclear weapons is unlikely to undercut its authority significantly. The link between individual and national security is anyway so partial that variations in the latter should not be expected to produce immediate or drastic variations in the political stability of the state as a whole.

The unavoidability of this contradiction between individual and national security must be emphasized. The contradiction is rooted in the nature of political collectives. In the real world, it can be neither resolved nor evaded. Consequently, the task in the chapters that follow will not be to reduce the other levels down to some basic common denominator of individual security. To attempt this, would in my view simply avoid the reality of a permanent tension between the individual and the collective. Instead, the task will be to register this contradiction as a central dilemma in the concept of security, and to observe its effects on the other levels of the problem. This is not to dismiss the political importance of individual security. Rather, it is to assert the independent importance of the state and system levels of security analysis, and to make them the main focus of analysis.

One further question remains: how might the actions of individuals motivated by their own security needs have feedback effects up to the national security level? Individuals can do many things to enhance their security both against threats from the state and against threats which the state has failed to alleviate, though their range of options will be much narrower in a tightly run maximal state than in a relatively open democracy. Much can be done by way of self-help in terms of individual security strategies for both person and property. In many countries a considerable industry caters to this demand.

Beyond the personal level, it is possible for individuals to set up or join organizations of many kinds aimed at improving their security. These can be of a direct defence kind, such as the Catholic and Protestant militant groups in Northern Ireland, vigilante groups set up by Asians in British cities to defend themselves against 'Paki-bashing' racists, militant nationalist pups in Spain (Basques), Sri-Lanka (Tamils), Iran and Iraq (Kurds), and elsewhere. They can be militant political groups such as the Ku Klux Klan in the United States, the Red Army factions in Europe and Japan, or the Chinese secret societies of pre-communist days. Or they can be more indirect and political in nature, working as pressure groups on governments and trying to turn state policy in directions more conducive to the security needs of the individuals involved. These organizations include minority rights groups, peace organizations like END, or the various campaigns against the Vietnam War, political parties, local community groups, human rights organizations, environmental organizations, indeed almost the whole array of sub-state organizations encompassed by the notion of pluralist politics. In states where the structure of government is weak, and the state itself is not pervasive in society, pre-state social structures such as families, clans, tribes and religious organizations also play a central role in relation to individual security needs. When the organizational approach to individual security is taken, of course, an additional level of collective interest is likely to interpose itself between individual and state, making the domestic model of security richer and more complex than the simple polarization between individual and state.

This considerable range of individually oriented security concerns and policies can have very substantial implications for national security in at least four ways. First, individuals or sub-state groups can become a national security problem in their own right. Assassins, terrorists, separatists, coup-makers and revolutionaries all pose threats to the state. The United States has to weigh the safety of its leaders against the right of its citizens to bear arms. Western European states have to weigh anti-terrorist police measures against civil liberties. Military resources have to be allocated against separatist movements in Britain, Spain, Pakistan, Iran, Yugoslavia, Indonesia, Nigeria, Sri Lanka and elsewhere. Spanish, Latin American and many other governments must guard themselves against coup-makers. Governments everywhere devote resources to preventing revolutions against their authority, sometimes covertly, as in most Western states, sometimes with more obvious repression, a under Stalinist regimes, and sometimes by all-out internal warfare, as in China before 1949, and Indonesia in 1965–6. A highly divided state with rather narrow political views of legitimate activity might have to treat virtually its whole population as a security problem, largely determining its own character and pattern of resource allocation in the process. Post-1989 revelations about East Germany, for example, show that the state security police (Stasi) had computer files on nearly one-third of the population.[23] The problem of domestic security raised by conflict between citizens and their state raises difficult questions about the very meaning of national security, and these will be taken up in Chapter 2.

Second, and related to the direct domestic security problem, is the role that citizens can play as a fifth column in support of some other state's interests. Nazis in France during the 1930s, Moscow-oriented communists in many countries during the Cold War, Japanese in the United States and Canada during the Second World War, Western-oriented dissidents in the Soviet Union, Chinese in Malaya during the 1950s, Palestinians in Israel and such-like, have all either played, or been cast in, this role. The permeability of states to both ideas and peoples associated with other states blurs the boundary between domestic and national security. Where this happens, neat distinctions between citizens and foreigners, state and government and domestic and international policy, begin to break down, and the meaning of national security becomes even more ambiguous than usual.

The third implication of individual security for national security lies in the broad political pressures and constraints which bear upwards from citizens to the state. The essence of these pressures stems not from direct threats to the state or government, but from the influence that public opinion exerts on state policy, or from the limits to the state's ability to mould public opinion to its own ends. Examples of the phenomenon include: Woodrow Wilson's and Franklin Roosevelt's struggles against isolationist opinion in the United States respectively after the First World War and before the Second World War; the Jewish lobby's influence on American Middle-East policy; French-Canadian objections to conscription in Canada; electorally significant anti-nuclear weapons sentiments in Britain, the Netherlands, Japan and elsewhere; nationalist and religious movements in the Soviet Union; and popular opposition to particular wars or actions, as in Britain over Suez, America over Vietnam and France over Algeria. Such influence may also come from élite groups such as the armed forces, in countries like Pakistan, South Korea, Egypt, Nigeria, Chile, Japan before 1945 and others; landowners, as in much of the Spanish-speaking Third World; or business élites, as in Japan, the United States and Brazil.

Fourth is the role that individuals play as leaders of the state. The abstract distinction between individual and state dissolves at the level at which individuals make a reality of the concept we refer to as the state. Each of these individuals has his or her own universe of security concerns and perceptions, and it is part of the work of historians, journalists and pundits to assess the influence of this on state policy. Chamberlain and Churchill demonstrated markedly different styles and degrees of security consciousness, and the gulf between them indicates the potential impact of this variable on national security policy-making. At the extreme of centralized dictatorship, as in Germany under Hitler, or the Soviet Union under Stalin, individual and state merge to the point of indistinguishability. At the extremes of pluralist democracy, as in the United States, the Netherlands and Denmark, the intricate divisions of power make it difficult for any individual to have much impact on the totality of national policy.

The whole subject of the relationship between individuals, whether as leaders, or aggregated as interest groups or public opinion, has been well explored in the literature on foreign policy analysis, and there is no need to repeat that effort here.[24] The purpose of this chapter is served by the following conclusions:

1. Although individual security does represent a distinct and important level of analysis, it is essentially subordinate to the higher-level political structures of state and international system. Because this is so, national and international security cannot be reduced to individual security.

2. Individual security is affected both positively and negatively by the state, and the grounds for disharmony between individual and national security represent a permanent contradiction.

3. Individual pursuit of security has a variety of influences on national security. Where state and citizens are severely at odds, domestic disarray may threaten the coherence of the state in ways that make the concept of national security difficult to apply.

NOTES

1. R. N. Berki, *Security and Society: Reflections on law, order and politics* (London: J. M. Dent, 1986); Harold Lasswell, *World Politics and Personal Insecurity* (New York: Free Press, 1965/1935).
2. Berki, *ibid.*, pp. 24–40.
3. Kenneth N. Waltz, *Theory of International Politics* (Reading, Mass.: Addison-Wesley, 1979), p. 112.
4. Thomas Hobbes, *Leviathan*, reprinted in Carl Cohen (ed.), *Communism, Fascism and Democracy: The theoretical foundations* (New York: Random House, 1972, 2nd edn.), p. 275.
5. John Locke, *Second Treatise of Government*, reprinted in Cohen, *ibid.*, pp. 406–7.
6. Berki, *op. cit.* (note I), pp. 27–8.
7. *The Guardian Weekly* (15 August 1982), p. 14.
8. P. A. Reynolds, *An Introduction to International Relations* (London: Longman, 1980), pp. 47–8; Part II, 'The rationale of force', in Robert E. Osgood and Robert W. Tucker, *Force, Order and Justice* (Baltimore: Johns Hopkins University Press, 1967); and Robert Nozick, *Anarchy State and Utopia* (Oxford: Blackwell, 1974). For a critique of the liberal view of the relationship between individual and state, see Vernon Van Dyke, 'The individual, the state and ethnic communities in political theory', *World Politics*, 29:3 (1977).
9. See, for example, Fred Block, 'Marxist theories of the state in world systems analysis', in Barbara H. Kaplan (ed.), *Social Change in the Capitalist World Economy* (Beverly Hills: Sage, 1978), p. 27; and Ralph Miliband, *The State in Capitalist Society* (London: Quartet Books, 1973).
10. Heinrich von Treitschke, *Politics*, reprinted in Cohen (ed.), *op. cit.* (note 4), pp. 289–96.
11. This line of argument is explored in more depth by Tucker, *op. cit.* (note 8), pp. 282–4.
12. See Ralph Pettman, *State and Class: A sociology of international affairs* (London: Croom Helm, 1979), ch. 4, for a useful review and assessment of theories of the state. This view of the primacy of state over individual interests can reflect two lines of thought: one in the mould of Treitschke, that state interests in some holistic sense are transcendent over individual ones; the other, in the Marxist mould, that sectional interests dominate the state and use it to serve their own ends. An interesting contemporary manifestation of the former view is explained and attacked in Roberto Calvo, 'The church and the doctrine of national security', *Journal of Inter-American Studies and World Affairs*, 21:1 (1979).
13. Berki, *op. cit.* (note 1), pp. 238–40.
14. *The Guardian Weekly* (28 November 1982).
15. Johan Galtung, 'Violence, peace and peace research', *Journal of Peace Research*, vol. 2 (1969), pp. 166–91.
16. Joel S. Migdal, *Strong Societies and Weak States: State-society relations and state capabilities in the Third World* (Princeton, NJ: Princeton University Press, 1988).

17. Peter L. Berger, *Pyramids of Sacrifice: Political ethics and social change* (Harmondsworth: Penguin, 1974).

18. For an overview, see Barry Buzan, *An Introduction to Strategic Studies: Military technology and international relations* (London: Macmillan, 1987), chs 10–13.

19. See R. J. Vincent, *Human Rights and International Relations*, and (ed.), *Foreign Policy and Human Rights: Issues and responses*, (both Cambridge: Cambridge University Press, 1986).

20. Lasswell, *op. cit.* (note 1).

21. *The Guardian Weekly* (24 January 1982), p. 17.

22. John Herz, *International Politics in the Atomic Age* (New York: Columbia University Press, 1959), pp. 40–2; and 'The rise and demise of the territorial state', *World Politics*, 9 (1957). Herz later qualified his view when it became apparent that nuclear weapons had created a substantial paralysis of large-scale use of force: 'The territorial state revisited', *Polity*, 1:1 (1968).

23. *International Herald Tribune* (26 March 1990), p. 5.

24. See, for example Kenneth N. Waltz, *Foreign Policy and Democratic Politics* (Boston: Little Brown, 1967); J. N. Rosenau (ed.), *Domestic Sources of Foreign Policy* (New York: Free Press, 1967); J. N. Rosenau, 'Pre-theories and theories of foreign policy', in R. Barry Farrell (ed.), *Approaches to Comparative and International Politics*, (Evanston: Northwestern University Press, 1966); Henry Kissinger, 'Domestic structure and foreign policy', *Daedalus*, 95 (1966); Steve Smith and Michael Clarke (eds.), *Foreign Policy Implementation* (London: Allen and Unwin, 1985); Walter Carlsnaes, *Ideology and Foreign Policy*, (Oxford: Blackwell, 1986); Steven G. Walker, *Role Theory and Foreign Policy Analysis* (Durham: Duke University Press, 1987); Charles F, Hermann, Charles W. Kegley Jr. and James N. Rosenau, *New Directions in the Study of Foreign Policy* (Boston: Allen and Unwin, 1987); Christopher Clapham, *Foreign Policy Making in Developing States* (Farnborough: Saxon House, 1977).

chapter two | national security and the nature of the state

If, as argued above, the state is central to the whole concept of security, then one needs to examine the state as a referent object of the term. Since the state is composed of individuals bound together into a collective political unit, one might expect the difficulties encountered in the previous chapter to be compounded when trying to make sense of security on the state level. What is it that policymakers are trying to make secure within the multifaceted phenomenon that we call a state? What does 'national security' refer to and what does it mean? This chapter will attempt to answer these questions by unpacking the notion of the state. One aim is to see how both its contents and its totality relate to the idea of national security. Another is to prepare the ground for considering the idea of international security. At the system level the state is also central to security, and its domestic characteristics cannot be disentangled from the character of the security problem in the international system as a whole.

IDENTIFYING THE STATE AS AN OBJECT OF SECURITY

States are larger and more complicated entities than individuals, and they are more amorphous in character. While one can identify individuals with ease, and be fairly certain about the meaning of threats and injuries to them, the same exercise cannot as easily be applied to collective units like nations and states. Can such units die or go bankrupt, and what are the criteria for these conditions? Austria-Hungary no longer exists, but its component parts live on in a way that has no analogue for individuals. Did Poland, France, Germany and Japan cease to exist in some sense during periods of foreign occupation? How does one reconcile such discontinuities with obvious continuities which those units have in historical terms? If death is ambiguous, what constitutes a threat to the state? Where are its physical boundaries so that one may observe when it is touched by the actions of other units? That states do have boundaries other than their territorial ones can be seen from the way they define threats in the ideological realm. Republicanism did not in itself threaten state territorial boundaries in the eighteenth and nineteenth centuries. Communism (or capitalism) did not threaten them during the Cold War except in the unusual circumstances of previously united nations such as Germany and Korea that were divided into ideologically defined states. Was the outcome of the Second World War good or bad for Japan in national security terms? What is the time-scale by which the actions, reactions, injuries and advances of collective units should be assessed?

These questions reveal some of the difficulties that arise in identifying the state as a referent object of security. Simple answers to them do not take one far in the real world of international relations. Whereas individuals are physically coherent systems whose behaviour, welfare and survival can be analysed in fairly precise terms, states are a much looser type of system, offering less scope for analytical rigour. No agreement exists as to what the state is as a behavioural unit, let alone whether or not such anthropomorphic notions as life-cycle, growth, development, purpose, progress, will and suchlike are relevant to it.

Despite the elusive character of the state as a behavioural unit, both International Relations and Strategic Studies make it the central focus of their analyses. Sound reasons justify this priority. States are by far the most powerful type of unit in the international system. As a form of political organization, the state has transcended, and often crushed, all other political units to the extent that it has become the universal standard of political legitimacy. In theory, the state dominates both in terms of political allegiance and authority, and in terms of its command over instruments of force, particularly the major military machines required for modern warfare. This theory is close to reality in a large minority of states, and enables the biggest and best organized of them to exert powerful system-wide influence. Even among the majority, where theory and reality are more widely separated, the state still dominates local political life. Most of the non-state units that command political military power see themselves either as aspirant state-makers or as seeking more control over a political space within an existing state. These are mostly nationalist organizations such as those representing Palestinians, Irish, Kurds, Eritreans, Zulus, Sikhs and many others. Socio-political centrality and military power make the state the dominant type of unit in the international system despite its lack of anthropomorphic coherence. Consequently, one cannot avoid the difficult task of unravelling the interplay between the ambiguous symbol of security and the ambiguous structure of the state.

The first difficulty facing this enterprise is that there is an academic dispute about what the term 'state' should refer to. On one hand, much of the literature discussing the state does so from the rather inward-looking perspectives of Political Science and Sociology. Both perspectives emphasize the domestic realm over the international one. Much of the analysis in this literature rests on distinguishing 'state' from 'society' within the domestic realm, and trying to understand how they interact. This distinction leads directly to definition of the state in Weberian terms, where state and society are viewed as separate phenomena, and the state is seen almost entirely in politico-institutional terms.[1] In this conception, 'state' means nearly the same thing as 'central government'. As Migdal puts it, an ideal-type definition of the state is: 'an organization composed of numerous agencies led and coordinated by the state's leadership (executive authority) that has the ability or authority to make and implement the binding rules for all the people as well as the parameters of rule making for other social organizations in a given territory, using force if necessary to have its way'.[2] This narrow definition of the state is reinforced by Marxian thinking, which also stresses the separation of government and society. Although this perspective has its uses, it is much too narrow to serve as a basis for thinking about security. Among other things, it can lead to arguments that Britain and America are 'stateless societies',[3] a position that looks absurd when seen from an international perspective. The reduction of 'state' to mean simply the institutions of central government does not work at the international level.

On the other hand, the traditional International Relations view of the state as a politico-territorial billiard ball is also too restrictive.[4] While it captures an important aspect of reality at the system level, it has tended to discourage enquiry into the domestic structure of states. Security issues within an international anarchy are highly conditioned not only by the structure of the system and by the interactions of states, but also by the domestic characteristics of states. Consequently, security analysis requires a comprehensive definition of the state that combines both of these perspectives. Fortunately, there is nothing other than the momentum of habit and argument to prevent the merger of these two views. As enshrined by the United Nations Charter, the territorial-political view of the state is now a universal norm governing the way states relate to each other. Within this framework, nothing prevents one from looking inside to investigate the relationship between governing institutions and their societies. Indeed, much evidence suggests that such questions should occupy a prominent place on the security agenda.

From the systemic perspective, one is almost compelled to see states as territorially defined socio-political entities. They represent human collectivities in which governing institutions and societies are interwoven within a bounded territory. For many, though not all, of the major purposes of interaction within the system this nexus of territory, government and society is what constitutes the state. In international perspective, the linkages that bind this package together are central to understanding security, and thus the merger of the two views of the state is a key to effective analysis. For the purposes of security analysis, 'state' has to be conceptualized broadly enough to encompass not only the relationship between the internal dynamics of individual territory-government-society packages, but also the larger systemic dynamics of the way in which these packages relate to each other.

This systemic concept of the state provides the framework for the discussion that follows. Security analysis requires a view that places state and system into a mutually constitutive relationship.[5] States are partly self-constructed, from their own internal dynamics, and partly products of the competitive and sometimes fierce anarchic environment. The domestic and the international dynamics are both essential to security analysis, as is the complex relationship between them. The mutually constitutive conception of state and system is easiest to grasp when state is understood in the broad sense of territorial-political-societal nexus. International Relations theory often conspires to make the mutually constructing relationship of state and system difficult to understand.[6] Historians make it more obvious, particularly those such as William H. McNeill who leave their readers in no doubt about the power of this massive dialectic over the whole 5,000 years of recorded human history.[7]

Joel Migdal captures this understanding well (even though in doing so he departs markedly from his narrow Weberian definition of the state towards the broader conception outlined above):

> When the new state entered into the tumble of history's events, it did not do so in splendid isolation. It appeared with a handful of other similar political entities that together constituted a new state system. They formed a system because, as one would move up the scale of the attributes of 'stateness', it would precipitate changes in the others, stemming from the fear leaders had of the growing strength of their neighbours.... The state's fantastic advantage over other political entities in mobilizing and organizing resources for war, as well as for other purposes, brought the survival of the other political forms into question.... There was a driving compulsion to establish state social control within society, for that was the key that could unlock the doors to increased capabilities in the international arena.[8]

This broader meaning of 'state' requires some clash with well-established terminology. The confusion that this involves is tedious, but unavoidable: without the more comprehensive view one simply cannot make sense of the security problematique. I shall flag the places where pursuit of the logic generated by the framework used here creates clashes with other usages.

It is this fuller, almost organic, conception of the state in terms of territory/population (body) and socio-political character (mind) that creates the temptation to draw analogies between individuals and states as a way of understanding state behaviour. But this analogy is often profoundly misleading. As argued in the previous chapter, the state is not the same sort object as an individual, and therefore analogies between the two in relation to security must be undertaken with extreme caution. The tendency to draw analogies is supported by a number of similarities between individuals and states. Both are sentient, self-regarding, behavioural units with definable physical attributes. Both exist in a social environment with units of the same type, and therefore face similar sets of problems in working out satisfactory conditions for coexistence. And both share what might be called a human essence, the individual by definition, and the state because it is composed of, and run by, individuals. These similarities must be balanced against some formidable differences. Physical dissimilarities are particularly striking. States are much larger. Their territorial 'bodies' bear little resemblance to the human organism. They are largely fixed in one position. Their demise does not necessarily, or even usually, result in the death of their component parts, and vice versa. They have neither a standard life-cycle which progresses from birth to death, nor a reproductive (as opposed to self-maintenance) requirement.

The great size of states compared to individuals correlates with a much looser structure. For all their mental confusion and imprecise physical control, individuals are simply on a different plane of coherence than are states. This makes them far swifter, more agile, and more oriented towards detail in their behaviour than are states, but it also leaves them less powerful, and much more physically fragile and vulnerable. The state may be lumbering, incoherent and generally brontosaurus-like in its behaviour, but it has no fear of certain death, can defend itself much more efficiently than a sleep-betrayed and easily killed individual, and can command an enormous range of resources to its support.[9] Furthermore, while the state may reflect its human components to some extent, it quickly becomes more than the sum of its parts, and therefore develops non-human modes of behaviour. This phenomenon underlies the 'idiosyncratic' versus 'role' variables used in analysing the actions of individuals holding state offices. Do the people concerned do what they do because of factors unique to them as individuals, or because of factors stemming from their position as office-holders?[10] Taken together, these factors make the state a significantly different type of actor, within a quite different kind of society, from the individual.

If the analogy between individual and state carries too many flaws to be used safely, particularly in regard to the central questions of death and injury, how can we best approach the question of what is being referred to when we talk of national security? What is the essence of the state to which the idea of security applies? There is no easy answer to this question. Ralph Miliband suggests that '"the state" is not a thing... it does not, as such, exist.'[11] Those who have experienced the sting of state power in forms varying from tax demands and conscription notices, to bombardments and destabilization campaigns might argue that whether it is ephemeral or not, the state certainly manifests itself in concrete terms. The view of the state as a package of territory, polity and society suggests that it is both metaphysical and concrete.

The contrast between individual and state provides an interesting lead as to why the abstract side of the state is so important to the understanding of national security. States are vulnerable to physical damage and deprivation, but the state appears to be much less intimately connected with its 'body' than is the case for an individual. A population and its associated territory comprise the physical foundations of a state, and yet both of these can exist without the state, or at least without any particular state. Conversely, damage to territory and population does not affect the survival of the state nearly so directly as damage to the human body affects individual survival. States can even survive the temporary loss of their 'bodies' as when governments in exile continue to command widespread international and domestic support.

One can infer from these points that the state exists, or has its essence, primarily on the socio-political rather than on the physical plane. In some important senses, the state is more an idea held in common by a group of people, than it is a physical organism. To be sure, the state depends on a physical base, and past a certain point cannot exist without it. Armenians, Palestinians and other exiled nations, keep alive the idea of a state, but cannot give it physical expression without command of the appropriate territory. The state also generates physical expressions of itself in the familiar institutions of law and government. These are a vital part of its being, but they do not constitute – though they may express – its essence. Without a widespread and quite deeply rooted idea of the state among the population, the state institutions themselves have difficulty functioning and surviving, though, as dictatorships like that of Ceausescu in Romania and Pinochet in Chile indicate, strongly held state institutions can prevail for long periods against majority disapproval. The centrality of a binding idea is particularly important to the broad conception of the state that is necessary for security analysis. It is the idea of the state that both provides the major bindings holding the territorial-polity-society package together, and defines much of its character and power as an actor in the international system.

Tracing the essence of the state to the socio-political level gives us a major clue about how to approach the idea of national security. If the heart of the state resides in the idea of it held in the minds of the population, then that idea itself becomes a major object of national security. Since the idea of the state might take many forms, and might even be quite different among those who could reasonably be said to share common loyalty to a particular state, this notion raises security problems of a very different nature from those normally associated with individual security. Although it would not be impossible, individuals are not usually described in terms of some essential idea. If idea implies purpose, then one tends to think along the physical lines of individual survival and reproduction, which are so closely connected to biological imperatives as scarcely to count as independently existing ideas. Grander ideas of human purpose are not in short supply, ranging from religious and philosophical perfections of the spirit to the conquest of material knowledge and the founding of galactic civilization. But these ideas are not as central to the existence of individuals as similar ones are to the existence of states. Humans may sacrifice their lives for these ideas, but they do not cease to exist without them. A state without a binding idea might be so disadvantaged as to be unable to sustain its existence in a competitive international system. Because of this difference between the nature of individuals and states, one must expect national security to be much more varied and complex than individual security. Not only is there huge scope for diversity of ideas about the state, but also the distinction between the idea, the institutional expression, and the physical base of the state provides a more numerous, fragmented and potentially contradictory range of security objects than does the more integrated structure of the individual.

This line of analysis suggests a simple descriptive model that can be used to guide exploration into the nature of the state and national security. The model is given in Figure 2.1,[12] and represents the three components of the state discussed above. There is no suggestion that the three components stand separately, for they are obviously interlinked in myriad ways. Rather, the model is meant to emphasize two things: first, that these three elements are distinguishable from each other to a sufficient extent to allow them to be discussed as objects of security in their own right, and second, that examination of the linkages between them is a fruitful source of insight into the national security problematique.

Figure 2.1 The component parts of the state

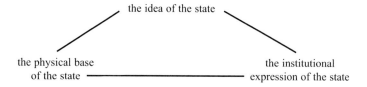

The model suggests that units must meet certain criteria before they can be considered as states. Whereas individuals define themselves in strict biological terms – problems of soul, severe mental retardation and definitions of death aside – states do not make such a self-evident category. What are the defining characteristics of states as a class of objects? They must have a physical base of population and territory; they must have institutions of some sort which govern the physical base; and there must be some idea of the state which establishes its legitimacy in the minds of its people. These three features alone, however, do not add up to statehood. An agricultural commune, a factory, a family household and numerous other social units could meet these criteria. The additional factors which make states a distinctive group of entities are size and sovereignty.

Although no strict bottom limit on size exists, there is unquestionably a strong sense of mass attached to the state which casts doubt on units with small populations. A unit with a population of ten or 100 would never qualify as a state, and even a population between 1,000 and 10,000 would generally be considered inadequate. A population of 100,000 is still considered dangerously small, but begins to approach the level of acceptability. Willetts argues that the United Nations has acted to ease the criteria for statehood, and in evidence there are now many quasi-state units, particularly small islands, recognized by the UN.[13] The full status of many of these as states, however, remains in doubt.

Size counts because states are supposed to be relative permanent constructions fulfiling the wide range of functions necessary for self-government. Without sufficient size, the unit is too fragile in the company of its larger fellows, and lacks the capability to perform all the tasks of self-rule. Traditional micro-states like Andorra and Liechtenstein are incapable of mounting defence and foreign relations establishments, and depend on larger neighbours to perform these functions for them. Many of the new post-colonial micro-states find themselves in the same position. Although exceptions may occur, such as the Vatican, and a variety of quasi-states may persist, the necessities of what might be called critical political mass will continue to draw a fairly high bottom line for the population size of states. Similar arguments might also be made about territorial size, but since the state is primarily a social phenomenon, population takes precedence. There is no question about the statehood of Singapore even though its 2.6 million population occupy a territory of only 232.4 square miles.

Size alone does not allow one to distinguish states from other units because some large units of other types might still meet the criteria – corporations for example. Sovereignty provides the crucial element dividing states from all other social units. It is the glue that binds the territorial-polity-society package together. Much of the argument about size hinges on the need to provide sufficient capability for sovereignty to be exercised. Sovereignty, simply put, means self-government. It requires denial of any higher political authority, and the claiming by the state of supreme decision-making authority both within its territory and over its citizens. The claim to supreme authority is not conterminous with that to power, and has sometimes to be exercised under conditions of relative weakness and severe outside pressure. This is a source of much confusion about the concept. Sovereignty can be divided, as in the case of those micro-states which claim it only over their domestic affairs, but the mark of the true state is that it claims undivided sovereignty in all temporal affairs. Sovereignty is divided among states, but not within them. The claim to sovereignty makes the state the highest form of human collective, and explains its centrality to political analysis.

That said, however, the concept of sovereignty can itself be contested, and harbours a number of practical problems. Can sovereignty exist without being exercised? In other words, is it primarily a legal idea which exists as a right? Or is it primarily a political idea, which comes into being only when exercised? If the latter, what distinguishes it from power? If sovereignty is an attribute of the state, where is it located? Does it reside with the population in some way? Is it vested in a ruler or governing institutions? Or is it somehow diffused throughout all aspects of the state? Who, in practice, exercises the authority it confers? And if that right is concentrated in an individual or an institution, what distinguishes the ruler from the state? Since the planetary supply of sovereignty has been divided up among states, is sovereignty an attribute that derives primarily from within the state? Or is it in some sense conferred externally by the recognition of other states?

These problems, though formidable, do not endanger the present line of analysis. Although conceptually difficult, sovereignty is usually easy to recognize in practice. Social units which claim it must do so openly, and failure to exercise it, or disputes over the right to do so, will usually be evident. Most collective units do not claim it, and signify this by subordinating themselves to one of those that does.

What can one conclude about states as a class of objects? As Waltz points out, categories define groups of things on the basis of their similarity in some respects only.[14] Thus all apples will share a wide range of characteristics, though individual apples will differ somewhat in weight, shape and taste. But the category of fruit describes a considerably looser set of objects, which may display more differences than similarities, as, say, between bananas and oranges. States make a looser category than do individuals. Although states share several types of features, the differences among these features are enormous.[15] If we extend Waltz's analogy, individuals form a category more like that of apples, while states form one more like that of fruit. Differences in size, power, physical geography, relative location, character of population, resources, domestic political economic and social structures, and degree of independence, are so obvious and so great as not to require illustration.

Even sovereignty, which is conventionally assumed to be a key defining characteristic of statehood, and therefore identical across all states, may not, in fact, be equally distributed. If one takes Waltz's definition of sovereign as meaning that a state 'decides for itself how it will cope with its internal and external problems, including whether or not to seek assistance from others and in doing so to limit its freedom by making commitments to them',[16] then one runs into problems with heavily penetrated states such as Lesotho, Laos, Lebanon and the Maldives, not to mention historical examples such as the American clients in Central America before 1960, and the Soviet satellites in Eastern Europe before 1989. One has to question seriously whether such states really had or have much option about seeking assistance from others and limiting their freedom in the process. There is a world of difference between the qualification Waltz offers, which is having the independence to make one's own decision even though one's circumstances are highly constrained, and the situation in which the constraints intrude into the heart of the decision-making process itself. Can such heavily penetrated states really be said to be equally sovereign to Britain, France or the United States in terms of deciding for themselves how they will cope with their internal and external problems? If they cannot, then it has to be conceded that sovereignty, like power and independence, also varies in degree among states, since nearly all such countries enjoy recognition as states by virtually every standard criteria.[17]

One must conclude, then, that states form a category rather like those formed by aircraft, galaxies and mountains. In each case, the category is united by some outstanding feature or features which distinguishes its members from the universe of all other things. But although the link among the members is both unique and strong, it does not prevent enormous diversity in many vital respects among them. Thus, when one compares members of the category with each other, one may well be struck much more by their differences than by their similarities. What has Concorde in common with a child's glider compared with their differences, or Everest in common with Fuji, or the Soviet Union in common with Fiji, compared with their differences? The looser nature of the category of states necessitates a further break in the analogy between them, and the much tighter category of individuals.

Because of the importance of what is different among states in determining their relations with each other, one cannot expect the concept of national security to exhibit much unity of meaning in any general sense. The specific meaning of security will be nearly as diverse as the condition and situation of the different states to which it applies. Because national security is so diverse in application, it cannot be compared with more stable, and more easily defined concepts such as wealth, and it certainly cannot be pegged to any simple indicator like military capability. For this reason, attempts to build theories of security along market economy lines seem unlikely to enjoy much success.[18] Looking at the three components of the state is one way to appreciate the diversity of states as referent objects for security.

THE IDEA OF THE STATE

The idea of the state is the most abstract component of the model, but also the most central. The notion of purpose is what distinguishes the idea of the state from its physical base and its institutions. The physical base simply exists. The institutions govern, and serve as 'a gatekeeper between intrasocietal and extrasocietal flows of action',[19] but their functional logic falls a long way short of defining the totality of the state. Although institutions are closely tied to aspects of the idea of the state, it is, as Dyson points out, a 'category error' to conflate the idea of the state with its apparatus.[20] In a properly constituted state one should expect to find a distinctive idea of some sort which lies at the heart of the state's political identity. What does the state exist to do? Why is it there? What is its relation to the society it contains? Why some particular size and form of state, when a glance at any historical atlas will reveal a variety of possible alternatives?

In defining the idea of the state, reference to the basic governing functions of providing civil order, collective goods and external defence does not take one very far. Although these functional considerations inevitably form part of the idea of the state, they indicate little about what binds the people into a socio-political and territorial entity that requires such services. Something more than a simple desire to escape the state of nature is at work in the creation and maintenance of particular states. Otherwise there would be no barrier to the founding of a universal state which would solve the state of nature problem without causing the troublesome intermediary of a fragmented international system of sovereign states. The two main sources for the idea of the state are to be found in the nation and in organizing ideologies. The rest of this section will examine these in some depth.

The importance of nation to the idea of the state is hinted at by the term *national* security itself. Why national security? National security implies strongly that the object of security is the nation, and raises questions about the links between nation and state. In modern usage a nation is defined as a large group of people sharing the same cultural, and possibly the same ethnic or racial, heritage. Because nations are products of a closely shared history, they normally constitute the majority population of some core territory. If the territories of nation and the state coincide, then one can look for the purpose of the state in the protection and expression of an independently existing cultural entity: nation would define much of the relationship between state and society. This fact would provide some handles on what values might be at stake, and what priorities they might have, in the definition of national security. If the purpose of the state is to protect and express a cultural group, then life and culture must come high on the list of national priorities. A pure model of the nation-state would require that the nation precede the state, and in a sense give rise to it, as in the case of Japan, Germany, Poland, Swaziland and others. But it is obvious from a quick survey of the company of states that very few of them fit this model. Some nations have no state, like the Kurds, the Palestinians, the Armenians and, before 1947, the Jews. Many nations are divided into more than one state, like the Koreans, the Germans, the Irish, the Bengalis and the Chinese. And some states contain several nations, like India, Yugoslavia, the Soviet Union, Nigeria and Britain.

Given this evidence, one must conclude either that *national* security in a strict sense is a concept with only limited application to the state, or that the relationship between state and nation is more complex than that suggested by the simple nation-state model. Grounds for exploring a more complex relationship arise from the fact that the definition of nation poses no condition of permanence. The historical atlas shows that nations, like states, are changeable qualities. Where now are the Sumerians, the Etruscans, the Huns, the Mayas, the Parthians? Since both culture and race are malleable qualities, there is no reason in principle why states cannot create nations as well as be created by them. The United States provides an outstanding example of this process by which diverse territories and peoples can be forged into a self-regarding nation by the conscious action of government. The possibility of state institutions being used to create nations, as well as just expressing them, considerably complicates and enriches the idea of nation. Since nations represent a pattern which covers the whole fabric of humanity, new nations cannot be created without destroying, or at least overlaying, old ones. The only exception to this rule is where new nations can be created on previously uninhabited territory, since the emigration of surplus population need not destroy the contributing nation(s). The United States benefited from this exception, though it largely destroyed the neolithic Indian nations in the process. But most contemporary efforts at nation-building in Africa and Asia must take place in the more difficult context of *in situ* populations, whose ethno-cultural identities often do not line up with the states in which they find themselves.

One obvious implication of this situation is that extensive grounds for conflict exist between natural nations and the attempts of governments to create nations which coincide with state boundaries. The civil wars in Nigeria, Uganda, Burundi, Ethiopia, Sudan and Burma; the struggles of the Kurds in Iran, Iraq and Turkey; and the nationalist unrest around the fringes of the Soviet Union, all illustrate this problem. Because the state quite frequently poses major threats to nations, these struggles point to an ironic level of contradiction in the meaning of national security. Clearly, from the point of view of both efficient domestic government, and the establishment of a firm presence in a challenging international environment, having state and nation coincide provides tremendous advantages. In terms of unifying identities, ease of communication, definition of purpose, and international standing, the nation-state is a powerful ideal if not a widespread reality.[21]

One can conclude that the link between state and nation is not simple, and that the nation as the idea of the state, particularly in national security terms, will not be simple either. Despite this complexity, it is clear that national identity is a central component of the security problematique whether or not it lines up with the state. The continuing power of national identity as a mobilizing force is made evident by events from Tibet and Sri Lanka to Estonia and Yugoslavia. As a determinant of individual behaviour, national identity can either powerfully reinforce, or deeply undermine the state. Michael Howard even goes so far as to argue that international relations is more about relations among nations than it is about inter-state relations.[22] In order to understand the state as a referent object for security it is clearly necessary to understand the links between nation and state.

Four models of possible *nation-state* links suggest themselves. First is the primal nation-state, exemplified by Hungary, Italy and Japan. Here the nation precedes the state, and plays a major role in giving rise to it. The state's purpose is to protect and express the nation, and the bond between the two is deep and profound. The nation provides the state with both a strong identity in the international arena, and a solid base of domestic legitimacy – solid enough to withstand revolutionary upheavals, as in the case of France at the end of the eighteenth century, or defeat and occupation by foreign powers, as in the case of France and Japan during the 1940s. In principle, a nation-state should have a fairly unambiguous territorial identity defined by settlement of the nation, but in practice there may be a host ambiguities around the margins, as strikingly illustrated by the case of 1930s Germany.

The second model has been called the *state-nation*. Here the state plays an instrumental role in creating the nation, rather than the other way around.[23] The model is top-down rather bottom-up. As suggested above, this process is easiest to perform when populations have been largely transplanted from elsewhere to fill an empty, or weakly-held, territory. Thus the United States, Australia and many Latin American countries provide the best examples. The state generates and propagates uniform cultural elements like language, arts, custom and law, so that over time these take root and produce a distinctive, nation-like, cultural entity which identifies with the state. Citizens begin to attach their primary social loyalties to the state-nation, referring to themselves as Americans, Chileans, Australians. Eventually, if all works well, an entity is produced which is similar in all respects except ancient history to a primal nation-state. Although citizens may still retain some dual identity with their original culture, as so-called 'hyphenated Americans' do, this is not territorially organized, and is not incompatible with the newer national identity.

The state-nation model can also be tried in places where the state incorporates a multitude of nationalities, though here it requires the absorption or subordination of the indigenous nations on their own ground, a much tougher task than the incorporation of uprooted and dispersed immigrants. Many post-colonial Asian and African states, faced with complex ethnic, tribal and religious divisions, look to the state-nation process as their salvation. This may involve trying to obliterate existing identities in order to create a single new nationality, or, more likely, adding a new layer of collective identity on top of existing ones. The latter route exploits the human potential to have several layers of identity, and aims at a multi-nation-state like Britain, where it is possible to identify oneself as English, Scottish or Welsh (and for some, Irish), while also accepting the more general identity of British.

A well-established state-nation like the United States will differ little from a nation-state in respect of the security implications of the state-nation link. But newer entrants into this process, especially those like Nigeria that have to deal with a diversity of indigenous national identities, will be highly vulnerable and insecure in this regard. The idea of the state represented by the state-nation will be weakly developed and poorly established, and thus vulnerable to challenge and interference from within and without. Separatists may try to opt out, as the Ibos did in Nigeria. Or one domestic group may try to capture the nation-building process for its own advantage, as the whites have done in South Africa, and as the Serbs are apparently trying to do in Yugoslavia. Or the whole fragile process may be penetrated by stronger external cultures, as symbolized by the 'Coca-colaiza-tion' of many Third World states, and the general complaint about Western cultur-al imperialism. So long as such states fail to solve their nationality problem, they remain vulnerable to dismemberment, intervention, instability and internal con-flict in ways not normally experienced by states in harmony with their nations.

One view of the state-nation process has it that even some apparently primal nation-states are merely long-standing products of the state-nation process. Thus France and Japan could be seen as having been themselves forged into nations by the agency of the state during earlier historical periods. This view implies a spec-trum of development ranging from those states newly embarked on the state-nation building process, to those where the state-nation has long since become a stable and self-sustaining feature of political life.[24]

The third model is the *part nation-state*. This is where a nation is divided up among two or more states, and where the population of each state consists large-ly of people from that nation. Thus the Korean, Chinese, Greek, and until 1973 the Vietnamese nations were divided into two states. During the Cold War the German nation was split among three states, though some would argue that Austria, like Denmark and the Netherlands, is sufficiently distinctive to count as a nation in its own right. This model does not include nations split up among several states, but not dominant in any, such as the Kurds and Palestinians. A variant of it is where a nation-state exists, but a substantial minority of its members fall outside its bound-aries, living as minority groups in neighbouring states. Germany during the 1920s and 1930s, and Somalia and Hungary today, illustrate this case.

The mystique of the unified nation-state frequently exercises a strong hold on part nation-states, and can easily become an obsessive and overriding security issue. Rival part nation-states like East and West Germany, and North and South Korea, almost automatically undermine each other's legitimacy, and the imperative for reunification is widely assumed to be an immutable factor that will re-emerge whenever opportunity beckons. Germany's reunification drive during the 1930s, and Vietnam's epic struggle of nearly three decades, illustrate the force of this drive, and explain the intractable and deeply-felt nature of the German problem in Cold War Europe. Part nation-states frequently commit themselves to an intense version of the state-nation process in an attempt to build up their legitimacy by differentiating their part of the nation from the other parts. The frenzied competition between the two systems in North and South Korea provides perhaps the best contemporary illustration of this strategy, which, given time, has some prospects of success. Part nation-states, then, can represent a severe source of insecurity both to themselves and to others. Their case offers the maximum level of contradiction in the idea of national security as applied to states, for it is precisely the nation that makes the idea of the state insecure.

The fourth model can be called the *multination-state*, and comprises those states which contain two or more substantially complete nations within their boundaries. Two sub-types exist within this model which are sufficiently distinct almost to count as models in their own right, and these can be labelled the *federative state* and the *imperial state*. Federative states, at least in theory, reject the nation-state as the ideal type. By federative, I do not simply mean any state with a federal political structure, but rather states which contain two or more nations without trying to impose an artificial state-nation over them. Separate nations are allowed, even encouraged to pursue their own identities, and attempts are made to structure the state in such a way that no one nationality comes to dominate the whole state structure.

Canada and Yugoslavia offer clear examples of this multicultural model, and countries like Czechoslovakia, Britain, New Zealand and India can be interpreted at least partly along these lines. Obviously, the idea of a federative state cannot be rooted in nationalism, and this fact leaves a dangerous political void at the heart of the state. The federative state has to justify itself by appeal to less emotive ideas like economies of scale – the argument that the component nations are too small by themselves to generate effective nation-states under the geo-political circumstances in which they are located. Such states have no natural unifying principle, and consequently are more vulnerable to dismemberment, separatism and political interference than are nation-states. Nationality issues pose a constant source of insecurity for the state, as illustrated by Yugoslavia, and national security can easily be threatened by purely political action, as in the case of General de Gaulle's famous 1967 'Vive le Quebec libre' speech in Canada.

Imperial states are those in which one of the nations within the state dominates the state structures to its own advantage: the Great Russians within the Tsarist and Soviet states, the Punjabis in Pakistan, the Tutsis in Burundi and the Amharas in Ethiopia are examples. Several kinds of emphasis are possible within an imperial state. The dominant nation may seek to suppress the other nationalities by means ranging from massacre to cultural and racial absorption, with a view to transforming itself into something like a nation-state. It may seek simply to retain its dominance, using the machinery of the state to enforce its position without try-ing to absorb or eliminate other groups, or it may adopt the more subtle approach of cultivating a pervasive non-nationalist ideology, such as Islam or communism, which appears to transcend the national issue while in fact perpetuating the status quo. Imperial states contain possibilities of transformation into all the other types, and, like federative states, are vulnerable to threats aimed at their national divi-sions. Such states may be threatened by separatism, as in Ethiopia, China, Sudan and Gorbachev's Soviet Union; by shifts in the demographic balance of the nations, as often mooted about the Soviet Union; or by dismemberment, as in the cases of Pakistan and Lebanon. The stability of the imperial state depends on the ability of the dominant nation to retain control. If its ability is weakened either by internal developments or external intervention, the state structure stands at risk of complete collapse, like Austria-Hungary and the Ottoman empire after the First World War. Political threats are thus a key element in the national security prob-lem of imperial states.

These models represent ideal types, and as with any such classification, not many real world cases fit smoothly into them. Some minor 'special case' cate-gories can be found. Switzerland, for example, contains fragments of three nations organized along federative lines, but has no distinctive or dominant national group of its own. Most states contain elements of all the models, though one model will usually fit the predominant characteristics. France fits most closely into the nation-state mould, but Breton nationalists might claim with some justice that, from their minority viewpoint, the French state appears more imperial in nature. Similarly, North American Indians might claim that Canada and the United States have imperial elements, just as smaller and weaker groups in Yugoslavia complain about Serbian dominance. Conversely, imperial states like the Stalinist Soviet Union may try to disguise themselves as federative ones. Appearances can also be deceptive in that periods of strength and prosperity may hide domestic rifts and give the appearance of a nation-state, only to give way to separatism when pros-perity or central authority diminishes. The rise of regional nationalism in declin-ing 1970s Britain, and 1980s Soviet Union, illustrate this case.

Despite these difficulties, the models give us a useful framework within which to consider the links between state and nation. They make it clear that national security with regard to the nation/state nexus can be read in several different ways, and that consequently different states will experience very different kinds of inse-curity and security in relation to the nationality question. Some states will derive great strength from their link to the nation, whereas for others the tensions between state and nation will define their weakest and most vulnerable point. The importance of the nation as a vital component in the idea of the state has to be measured externally as well as internally. Unless the idea of the state is firmly planted in the minds of the population, the state as a whole has no secure founda-tion. Equally, unless the idea of the state is firmly planted in the 'minds' of other states, the state has no secure environment. Because the idea of national self-rule has a high legitimacy in the present international system, a firmly established link between state and nation acts as a powerful moderator on the unconstrained operation of the international anarchy. It is therefore one key to the contemporary possibilities for international society, as well as being a vital element of national security. On the system level, the confluence between the nation as a legitimizing idea underpinning the state, and sovereignty, as the principal idea underpinning the anarchical society of the international system as a whole, becomes centrally important to developing a concept of international security.

While the concept of nation provides one with considerable insight into the relationship between the idea of the state, and the problem of national security, it falls short of exhausting the subject. Nationalism adds an element to the functions of the state that can range in richness from the basic survivalism of the Finns and the Poles to the transcendent notions of culture and civilization associated with France. But it still leaves plenty of room for additional notions of purpose in the organizing ideology of the state, among which may be transcending nationalism. These additional notions differ from nationalism in that they tend to be less deeply rooted, and therefore more vulnerable to disruption. A firmly established nation reproduces itself automatically by the transfer of culture to the young, and once established is extremely difficult to remove by measures short of obliteration. The well-founded nation is, in this sense, more stable and more secure than the state. The principles of political organization are fragile by comparison, and thus both more sensitive and more ephemeral as objects of security. For example, fascism as an idea of the state was largely purged out of Germany, Japan and Italy by relatively brief and mild periods of foreign occupation. Similar measures would scarcely have dented the sense of nation in those countries.

The idea of the state can take many forms at this higher level, and it is not necessary to explore these definitively here. An indication of the types and range will suffice to give an adequate sense of their security implications. Organizing ideologies are perhaps the most obvious type of higher idea of the state. These can take the form of identification with some fairly general principle, like Islam, or democracy, or some more specific doctrine, like republicanism or communism. Many varieties of political, economic, religious and social ideology can serve as an idea of the state, and will be closely connected to the state's institutional structures. In some cases, an organizing ideology will be so deeply ingrained into the state that change would have transformational, or perhaps fatal, implications. Pluralist democracy and capitalism, for example, are so basic to the construction of the United States that it is hard to imagine the American state without them. Similarly for Saudi Arabia and Islam, and Israel and Zionism. In other cases, organizing ideologies have only shallow roots, and large changes in official orientation occur frequently. Many Third World states display this tendency, as organizing ideologies come and go with different leaderships, never striking deeper roots among the population. Since these ideologies address the bases of relations between government and society they define the conditions for both harmony and conflict in domestic politics. If the ideas themselves are weak; or if they are weakly held within society; or if strongly held, but opposed, ideas compete within society: then the state stands on fragile political foundations.

Different organizing ideologies may represent different ends, as in the case of the Islamic state which emerged in Iran after the fall of the Shah, in comparison with the monarchist and materialist values which preceded it. But they may also represent different convictions about means, as in the liberal democratic versus communist approaches to achieving material prosperity that fuelled the post-war ideological rivalry. They can also come in both positive and negative forms. The United States, for instance, pursues democracy and capitalism as positive values, but at the same time gives anti-communism almost equal weight as a negative organizing principle. Some organizing ideologies, particularly those with universalizing aspirations, can make contradictory foundations for an idea of the state. Both communism and Islam have been drafted into service by considerable numbers of states, but both contain strong elements of logic that work against the very concept of the territorial nation-state itself.[25] Since organizing ideologies are so closely tied to state institutions, we can deal with much of their security side when we discuss the institutional component of the state.

Other concepts can also serve as, or contribute to, the idea of the state. A sense of national purpose can spring from ideas about racial preservation, as in South Africa, or from ideas relating to a larger civilization, as in pre-1917 Russian images of the Tsarist empire as a third Rome. Even simple fear or hatred of some external group might provide a substantial part of the idea of the state. One would expect to find this in a state occupying a highly exposed position, as, for example, in the Austrian empire and Spain at the heights of the Ottoman and Moorish Islamic expansions.[26] Each state will have its own unique idea, which in reality will be a compilation of many elements. In Japan, for example, the nation, and the values associated with national culture, would constitute a large slice of the idea of the state, but democratic and capitalist ideas would also weigh significantly.

On this basis, it seems uncontroversial to conclude that the idea of the state is a central issue in national security. The problem is how to apply a concept like security to something as ephemeral as an idea. Where the idea is firmly established, like that of an ancient nation, the problem of security is mitigated by the inherent difficulty of instigating change. But for higher ideas, even defining criteria for security is not easy, let alone formulating policies. Most organizing ideologies are themselves essentially contested concepts, and therefore impossible to define with precision, and probably in a constant process of natural evolution. Given this amorphous character, how is one to determine that the idea has been attacked or endangered? The classic illustration here is the old conundrum about democracy and free speech. If free speech is a necessary condition of democracy, but also a licence for anti-democratic propaganda, how does one devise a security policy for democracy? By its own logic, democracy's main defence has to be its superior attractiveness to competing ideas. The component ideas which go to make up a concept like democracy change over time, as any history of Britain or the United States over the last two centuries reveals. Even the cultural ideas which bind the nation do not remain constant, as illustrated by the 'generation gap' phenomena, in which older generations clash with younger ones about a wide range of cultural norms and interpretations.

The natural ambiguity and development of these ideas mean that security cannot successfully be applied to them unless some criteria exist for distinguishing between acceptable and unacceptable sources and forms of change. This task is beyond reasonable hope of complete fulfilment given, among other things, the weakness of our understanding of many of the subtle cause-effect relationships involved in the evolution of ideas. Ideas are, by their very nature, vulnerable to interplay with other ideas, which makes it extraordinarily difficult to apply a conservative concept like security to them. This does not stop some states – notably communist and Islamic ones – from trying to make ideas secure despite the high costs of the attempt. Over-insulated political ideas risk a growing divorce from reality, and so invite the insecurity of collapses in legitimacy like that which overtook orthodox communism during the 1980s.

In part, because of this indeterminate character of ideas, it is possible to see them as potentially threatened from many quarters. Organizing ideologies can be penetrated, distorted, corrupted and eventually undermined by contact with other ideas. They can be attacked through their supporting institutions, and they can be suppressed by force. Even national cultures are vulnerable in this way, as illustrated on a small scale by French sensitivity to the penetration of the national language by English words and usages. Because of this broad spectrum vulnerability, an attempt to apply the concept of security to the idea of the state can lead to exceedingly sweeping criteria being set for attaining acceptable levels of security. This can give rise to a dangerous streak of absolutism in national security policy. Making the idea of the state secure might logically be seen to require either a heavily fortified isolationism aimed at keeping out corrupting influences, or an expansionist imperial policy aimed at eliminating or suppressing threats at their source. Thus one reading of German and Japanese expansionism up to the Second World War is that neither nation could make itself secure without dominating the countries around it. The Wilsonian idea of making the world safe for democracy by eliminating other forms of government has overtones of this theme about it, as does the idea common to many new revolutionary governments – most recently that in Iran – that they can only make their own revolution secure by spreading similar revolutions beyond their borders.

An important undercurrent of the above discussion has been that a strong idea of some sort is a necessary component of a secure state, and the clear implication has been that the idea of the state must not only be coherent in its own right, but also widely held. Unless an idea is widely held, it cannot count as part of the idea of the state, but only as one of the ideas contained within the state, as in the distinction between a nation-state and a federative multination-state. From this perspective, it does not matter if ideas like nationalism and democracy stem from, and serve the interests of, particular groups or classes, so long as they command general support. Indeed, one of the advantages of an ambiguous idea like democracy is that its very looseness and flexibility allow it to attract a broad social consensus. Narrower ideas almost by definition imply greater difficulty in generating a popular base, and thus point to a larger role for institutions in underpinning the structure of the state. If the idea of the state is strong and widely held, then the state can endure periods of weak institutions, as France and Italy have done, without serious threat to its overall integrity. If the idea of the state is weakly held, or strongly contested, however, then a lapse in institutional strength might well bring the whole structure crashing down in revolution, civil war, or the disintegration of the state as a political unit.

THE INSTITUTIONS OF THE STATE

The institutions of the state comprise the entire machinery of government, including its executive, legislative, administrative and judicial bodies, and the laws, procedures and norms by which they operate. In many countries, this machinery represents a very substantial proportion of the national substance, and one that has been growing in proportion to the rest of the state since before the beginning of this century. In Britain, for example, government spending as a percentage of GNP rose from below 10 per cent at the end of the nineteenth century, to around 50 per cent during the 1970s. Governments vary enormously in extent and character. To get the flavour, think of the contrasts among the government machineries of the Soviet Union, Iran, Uganda, the United States and Ireland. One can, however, say something general about the nature of governments as objects of security, and point out some significant criteria for evaluating differences among them.

Perhaps the easiest way to approach this problem is to look at an extreme case. In the previous section, it was argued that ideas were a vital component of the state, essential to its coherence and purpose, and providing a mechanism for persuading citizens to subordinate themselves to the state's authority. Strong and widely held ideas served to bind the state into something like an organic entity. It was also argued that organizing ideologies were closely linked to the machinery of government. The question then arises: is it possible to have a state in which the idea of the state is very weak or non-existent, and in which the institutional component therefore has to take up all its functions? This question raises the image of a maximal state in which an élite commands the machinery of government, particularly its armed enforcement agencies, and uses it to run the state in its own interest. The idea of the state in such a case would amount to little more than the ruling élite's definition of its own self-interest. The coherence of the state would be preserved by unstinting use of the state's coercive powers against its citizens. Fear would replace more positive ideas as the primary unifying element, and the government would command obedience rather than loyalty.

This model has enough of an echo in the real world to give credence to the idea that institutions can, to a very considerable extent, replace ideas in the overall structure of the state. The cases of the Duvalier dynasty in Haiti, Somoza in Nicaragua, Amin in Uganda, Nguema in Equatorial Guinea, Pinochet in Chile and

Ceaucescu in Romania come to mind, and one would not have to go very far back in history to reach a point when most states were of this type. Government by a foreign occupying power also fits this model, such as those set up by the Germans during the Second World War, and those established by European colonial powers in places like India, Vietnam and the Middle East, where a local tradition of central governing structures was already well established. Although some cases approach the pure institutional model of the state quite closely, many more appear to be mixed models, in which the institutions of the state compensate for weaknesses in the idea of the state, rather than replacing it completely. The model of the imperial state from the previous section fits this category, because rule is not just by an élite, but represents a large group within the state which may be a minority of the population, like the Austrians in the Austrian empire, or a majority like Great Russians in the Tsarist and Soviet empires.

Weakness in the idea of the state may be along ideological rather than national lines, as in the case of almost any state captured by a dogmatic political creed. Hitler's Germany, Stalin's Soviet Union, and Khomeini's Iran all had to devote considerable police resources to suppressing dissidents, especially in the early years of their rule. The fact that the government itself represents an enterprise of considerable extent in relation to the total national substance cannot be ignored. Given the total size of government machinery, what might be characterized as self-interested élite rule can encompass a rather large group: in communist states party membership can run to many millions of people constituting several per cent of the population. Since the state machinery disposes of relatively great resources, it can attract and coopt support from large numbers of people without the aid of any idea more potent than greed. If sufficient people can be recruited in this way, perhaps with the aid of a leader cult and negative ideology, then the coercive and administrative arms of the state can be sustained without any general element of popular support. This is especially so if the public attitude is one of indifference, either because the public is not politically mobilized, or because the government has not made its exploitation intolerable, and continues to provide some legitimate basic services such as defence and internal security. A negative ideology might also prove a useful means of attracting external resources, as in the case of Third World regimes that drew aid from the United States by touting an anti-communist line.

On this basis, one might posit something like a sliding-scale, on which ideas and institutions can to a considerable but not complete extent be substituted for each other. Substitutability would decline at either end of the scale, because even a strong idea of the state needs government machinery, and even strong institutions need, or at least prefer, to be supported by some ideas. Ideas are a far more stable and cost-effective means of governing than coercion, and any state that drains off resources merely to sustain itself risks long-term decline in relation to those that are more efficiently organized. In this sense, the long-term evolutionary pressure of life under the competitive conditions of international anarchy, should favour the emergence states with a strong idea of themselves.

Nevertheless, it seems fair to note that institutions can substitute more for ideas than the other way around. An extreme institutional model of the state – rule by pure coercion – has some empirical credibility, whereas a pure idea model – government without institutions – appears not to exist outside the fantasies of a few anarchists. Against this, however, has to be set the strong disposition of governments to create unifying ideas, either by cultivating an ideological orthodoxy, or by embarking on the state-nation process described in the previous section. This line of thought leads to a rather different characterization of the relationship between institutions and ideas, where they are not so much distinct and substitutable elements, as complementary components in the process of government.

Although the nation as an idea does not suggest much about appropriate forms of government – except in the case of multi-nation-states – organizing ideologies are intimately connected with governmental structures. Ideologies have, for the most part, much broader roots than the state in that they exist independently of any particular state. For this reason, government can draw legitimacy from identifying with an ideology because it ties them to ideas and purposes larger than their own self-interest. This link cannot be made without incurring quite stringent obligations, since the institutions of the state will have to be structured so as to express and amplify the ideology. The character of these obligations is fairly obvious, and does not require discussion here. The familiar literatures on fascism, communism, democracy, monarchy and feudalism, all cover the complementary and constraining interaction between ideas and institutions. The main point of interest for this discussion is that the ideas and the institutions are inseparably intertwined. The idea of democracy or communism is useless without institutions to put it into operation, just as the institutions would be pointless, and maybe even impossible, without the idea to give them definition and purpose. This interdependence means that institutions and organizing ideologies tend to stand or fall together in the context of any particular state, and this fact has obvious implications for either, or both, as objects of security.

The institutions of the state are much more tangible than the idea of the state as an object of security. Because they have a physical existence they are more vulnerable to physical threats than are ideas. Institutions can be uprooted and destroyed much more easily than can ideas, and they do not suffer from, or enjoy, the same level of ambiguity that makes ideas so difficult as an object of security. Institutions can be threatened by force, or by political action based on ideas which have different institutional implications. The fascist governments of the Axis powers, for example, were overthrown by external military force, and replaced by institutions reflecting the ideologies of the conquering powers. Communist governments have traditionally tried to defend themselves by restricting the circulation of other political ideas within their domains, just a monarchies earlier felt threatened by the circulation of republican ideas. Minor political reforms might take place with little use of force, as in the change from the Fourth to the Fifth Republic in France; but major transformations usually require either revolutionary violence, as in Russia, China and Iran, or very long periods of incremental reform, as in the transformation of Britain from monarchy to democracy. It is this tendency towards violence that makes Gorbachev's attempt to reconstruct the ideology and institutions of the Soviet Union so breathtakingly bold. Since institutions must adapt themselves to meet changed conditions, some of the ambiguities which apply to ideas also complicate security policy for institutions. How does one judge, for example, whether advocating the abolition of the House of Lords in Britain should be interpreted as a threat to the institutions of the state, or as a wise and timely move to adapt the institutions to the socio-political conditions of the twenty-first century?

When institutions are threatened by force, the danger is that they will be overpowered, and the remedy is defence. When they are threatened by opposing ideas, the danger is that their legitimacy will be eroded, as in Poland after 1980, and that they will collapse for lack of support, as East Germany did in 1989–90. Armed force might sustain them, as argued above, but institutions without mass support are much more precariously positioned than those with it. On this basis, state institutions vary enormously in terms of their domestic stability. For many, the principal threat to security comes from within the state rather than from outside it. These domestic threats may range from small, relatively isolated groups of militants, as in many Western countries; through powerful, centrally located groups of coup-makers, as in many Third World countries, or substantial guerrilla movements, as in Peru, the Philippines and Afghanistan; to widespread popular discontent, as in South Africa, and in Poland during the 1980s, or full scale revolution, as in Cuba and Iran.

The particular security problems of governing institutions constitute only part of the whole national security problematique, existing in a condition of more or less permanent interplay with other parts. Governing institutions can change without interrupting the continuity of the state. This vital fact means that on the domestic level the security of the government can be differentiated from the security of the state in a manner not possible on the international level, where state and government are inseparably bound together. This curious duality in governmental versus national security would be a manageable, if complicated, state of affairs if the domestic and international environments remained isolated from each other. Unfortunately for the analyst, domestic isolation is more the exception than the rule and, consequently, national and international politics spill into each other.

From an international perspective, governments are a perfectly legitimate target in the game of nations. Since governments largely determine the international activity and orientation of states, and since changes in government, even for purely domestic reasons, can result in significant shifts in international behaviour, it is no surprise that states interfere in each other's domestic politics. Think, for example, of consequences for the United States of the change of government in Iran in 1979. The style and effectiveness of such interventions depends on a host of factors, not least of which is the stability of domestic politics in the target state. American and Soviet concern to prevent the establishment of ideologically antagonistic governments in their spheres of influence illustrate the kinds of motives involved in these interventions. The lesson of the 1930s about the failure to inter-vene against Hitler perhaps gives them a lingering aura of legitimacy.

American actions against the government of Fidel Castro in Cuba furnish many illustrations of the range of techniques available.[27] At the lower end of the spectrum come actions such as propaganda against the organizing ideology, pro-vision of funds and facilities to opposition groups, and denial of recognition. In the middle range come actions such as encouragement of armed revolts, assassi-nation attempts, and the mounting of external economic pressures in an attempt to undermine the government's domestic credibility. In the upper range are spon-sored invasions and direct intervention by armed force. Where the intervening state is a great power and the target state a minor one, relatively small resources devoted by the former might have a large impact on the latter. It is not difficult to imagine circumstances in which externally provided funds exceed the resources available from domestic sources in a small state: American aid to Israel and Soviet aid to Cuba both reached levels of several hundred dollars per citizen per year. As these latter examples indicate, intervention can take the form of assistance to a friendly government which is under challenge from domestic, foreign, or some combination of domestic and foreign, opposition. Soviet and Cuban aid to Angola in the late 1970s and British aid to Oman and Mozambique also illustrate this approach.

Because all of these options for intervention exist, and because motives for them are strong and opportunities tempting, the fusion between government and state which properly exists at the international level, frequently gets transferred to domestic politics. If a government is under attack by foreign intervention in the domestic political process, then it can legitimately invoke national security in its own defence. Drawing the line between indirect foreign intervention and legiti-mate internal political struggle, however, is not easy. The position of communists in the United States during the Cold War provides a good illustration of the dilem-ma. Should American communists have been considered as agents for the Union and therefore treated as a national security item? Or should they have been treat-ed as a legitimate manifestation of democratic politics within the domestic domain and therefore not subjected to the repressive machinery of the state? The Soviet Union could not help influencing and encouraging such individuals, whether or not it channelled resources to them. At least up until the ideological crisis of the 1980s, its very existence acted as a stimulant and inspiration to those who shared its ideology. Similarly, the existence of the United States motivated the dissidents within the Soviet Union. In large, politically stable states, the government need not feel unduly threatened by such linkages. But in states where the government institutions have only superficial roots in their societies, this issue can be of great significance.

The problem for national security in all this is that governments can easily exploit the linkage between their own security and that of the state in order to increase their leverage over domestic politics. Governments can be assumed to have their own interests, both organizational and individual, apart from the state interests which they represent. By importing the appeal to national security into the domestic environment, governments can increase their powers against domestic opponents. The main political function of national security is to try the use of force. The use of force is more legitimate in the international than in the domestic arena, but if national security can be invoked, then it acquires greater legitimacy in the domestic context.

If domestic security can be permanently tied into national security, then the government can protect itself with the whole apparatus of a police state, as in Stalin's Soviet Union, Ceausescu's Romania, and apartheid South Africa. This is not to argue that such linkage necessarily indicates nefarious intent on the part of the government (though of course it may). There obviously does exist a significant national security front in the domestic arena of all states, a fact that causes periodic agonizings over the proper role and constitutions of bodies such as MI5 and the CIA even in stable democracies. The cases of political intervention by one state in the domestic affairs of another that justify this concern are too numerous to require illustration. But the general legitimacy of the concern does not justify every case in which it is invoked. A great temptation exists for governments to appeal to national security in their own defence by identifying domestic political opposition with the policies of some foreign state. This temptation must be particularly strong for governments that are weakly founded in their domestic environment, and which consequently face strong, and often politically unsympathetic, opposition.

This problem is inherent to a system of sovereign states, especially so since the decline in the legitimacy of territorial seizures has diverted effort into the management of interdependencies. Such management emphasizes domestic-international linkages, and so gives governments a sustained interest in each other's domestic affairs.[28] Since we have to live with this linkage, one useful approach to reducing its unhelpful impact on security analysis is to formulate a distinction among types of states in terms of their level of domestic institutional stability, or, to put it another way, their level of socio-political cohesion between government and society. On this factor hinges much of the answer as to whether the dominant threat to the government comes from outside or inside the state. I shall return to this question in the final section of this chapter.

THE PHYSICAL BASE OF THE STATE

The physical base of the state comprises its population and territory, including all of the natural resources and man-made wealth contained within its borders. It is much the most concrete of the three components in the model, and consequently the easiest to discuss as an object of security. Because of its relatively concrete character, the physical base is also the area in which states share the most similarities in relation to security. In contrast to the ideas and institutions of the state, the basic quality of territory and population as objects of security does not vary much from state to state. Although population and territory vary enormously among states in terms of extent, configuration, level of development and resources, the threats to the state's physical base are common in type to all states because of the similar physical quality of the objects involved. Threats to physical objects are necessarily more direct and obvious in terms of seizure or damage than are threats to more amorphous objects like ideas and institutions.

Since the state covers a more or less precisely defined territory, threats against the physical base can be determined with considerable precision. A state usually claims a specified territory as its own, and this claim may or may not be recognized by other states. In theory, there is no necessary connection between any given state and a particular territory, the argument being that state boundaries are determined only by the ability of other states to hold their ground. Powerful states like Russia and Germany could and did expand their territories into weakly-held areas like Poland. Even with nation-states, where one might expect to find a home territory defined by the settlement pattern of the national group, no permanent delimitation occurs because of the prospect of migration and conquest. The case of Germany and the *Lebensraum* question between 1870 and 1945 provides the most dramatic contemporary illustration of the fluidity of the relationship between nation-state and territory, but many countries harbour a 'greater' territorial image of themselves. The territory of the state tends to be clearly fixed at any given point in time, though minor ambiguities are quite common, but it is not constrained over the longer run of history.

That said, however, it may well be that the past flexibility of state boundaries no longer serves as a reliable guide to the future. The advent of the United Nations, combined with a situation in which most available territory is claimed by states nearly all of which recognize each other, has produced an appearance of unprecedented territorial stability. Mutual territorial recognition is, indeed, the foundation of contemporary international society. It may well be that territorial instability is characteristic of immature state systems, and that as states acquire longer histories themselves they begin to identify permanently with quite closely defined territories. Long-standing states like France, for example, have a clear and powerful attachment to a specified national territory which is inseparably associated with the history of the French state. Contraction of it would be unacceptable, as demonstrated by the case of Alsace-Lorraine, and no strong indigenous imperative exists to expand it beyond its present borders. This situation contrasts markedly with that of many newer states, like Somalia, Libya, Israel, Bolivia and Iraq, where strong domestic pressures for territorial expansion periodically chafe against the norms of the UN system.

A state's territory can be threatened with seizure both by other states, as in Somali threats to both Ethiopia and Kenya, and by internal secessionist movements, as in the case of the Tamils in Sri Lanka. Secessionists may wish either to establish their own state, like the Ibos in Nigeria, or to join with another state, like the republicans in Northern Ireland. Secessionist movements offer a wealth of opportunity for foreign intervention, and rarely occur without importing some

level of national security into the domestic arena. Territorial losses do not necessarily, or even usually, threaten the state with extinction. Germany, Pakistan,
Mexico and Poland have all lost substantial areas without disrupting the historical
continuity of the state. Although as a rule states will contest all challenges to their
territorial integrity, some pieces of territory are clearly more valuable than others.
This value may arise because of resources, like oil in the areas contested between
Iran and Iraq; because of transportation access, like the Polish Corridor; for rea-
sons arising from historical tradition or the cultural identity of occupants, like
Alsace-Lorraine; for symbolic reasons, like Berlin; for strategic reasons, like
Gibraltar; or for combinations of these, such as the Falklands, Kashmir and
Japan's four northern islands. Such territory will have much higher priority as an
object of security than other areas, and some territory will have very low priority.
India clearly places a much lower priority on the remote mountain areas seized by
China in 1962 than on the dispute with Pakistan over Kashmir. The Russian sale
of Alaska to the United States in 1867 probably illustrates the nadir of national
identification with territory. The value of any territory may rise or fall with
changes in the technological, strategic or economic environment, or with discov-
eries about its resource potential. States possessing a territory with international
strategic significance, such as Turkey, Egypt and Panama, may easily find that it
becomes a source of threat to the state because it promotes intervention or attack.

Territory can also be threatened with damage as well as with seizure. If 'territory' is understood in the broad sense of national property (not including the population), it is clear that policies like deterrence and compellence work in part
through threats to territory. The United States and the Soviet Union constrain each
other's behaviour not through threats of territorial annexation, but by threats to
wreak huge damage on each other's physical property. The American bombing of
North Vietnam was in part an attempt to coerce the North Vietnamese into changing their behaviour by damaging their territory; and Israel has used similar threats
of damage against its Arab foes. Threats to territory tie in at this point to threats
to the population, since the two are normally so closely associated that one cannot
be damaged without damaging the other. While territory can be annexed without
its population, as in the case of mass migrations of Germans westward at the close
of the Second World War, threats of annexation and damage are usually aimed at
both populations and territory. Nuclear deterrence works not only because the
laboriously acquired material wealth of the nation is under threat, but also because
the population itself is held hostage to destruction.

A quite different, and altogether more complex threat to population can arise
from human migrations. This threat works primarily on the societal level, especially when the incoming population is of a different cultural or ethnic stock from
those already resident. It can also work in the economic and environmental sectors if newcomers overburden a fragile environment or compete for scarce
resources as in marginal desert lands. In a long historical view, nearly all nations
are the product of cosmopolitan blending, and occupy their current positions as a
result of earlier migrations. Most of the current states in the western hemisphere

owe much of their form and society to quite recent, and in many cases still continuing, immigration. But immigration can be seen as a threat as well as a boon. In the long run, it has the potential to reshape what 'nation' stands for, and thus to redefine the idea of the state. Even a generally welcoming country such as the United States passed laws restricting Asian immigration in the late nineteenth century (and the Japanese now get their own back by comparing America's polyglot character unfavourably with their own remarkable homogeneity). Proportionately small immigration can raise local fears about cultural and ethnic purity. Racism, as immigrants everywhere have discovered, is a widespread and politically potent sentiment. Ethnic and cultural parochialism is everywhere a stronger political force than cosmopolitanism.

Up to a point, outcries about immigrants of different colour or culture can be dismissed as minority bigotry. The fear of being swamped by foreigners is, however, easy to mobilize onto the political agenda as a security issue, not least because it has happened so often in history. Scenarios vary from the obliteration of the Tasmanians and Hottentots, through suppression of the Indian nations in the Americas, to the steady northward drive of Latin Americans into the United States. Ironically, cultural and ethnic swamping often operates most fiercely within multination-states, often with government backing. Estonians, Latvians and Lithuanians feel threatened by Russian immigration, the Punjabis colonize Baluchistan, the Chinese do the same in Tibet, the Brazilians massacre Indian tribes as they exploit the resources of the Amazon and the Iraqis kill or relocate Kurds. This list could easily be extended at length. Even co-religionists in immigrant-made Israel are divided between Ashkenazis and Sephardis, the balance between them profoundly affecting the character of Israeli society and politics.[29] This kind of migration can be seen as part of the state-nation process, though it can also weaken the government-society-territory nexus and lead towards secessionism.

International migration is in theory controllable by state enforcement of immigration regulations, but in practice few states can seal their borders against determined entrants. The potential for further human movement is large, and the incentives are mounting as huge gaps open up in the quality of life available in different states. The line between political refugees and economic migrants is already a problem between Eastern and Western Europe, and between Vietnam and much of East Asia. The Japanese fear an explosion of Chinese boat people as a consequence of the hard-line communist reassertion after June 1980. India has already experienced huge inflows of Bengalis because of civil war, and may do so again if even rather modest rises in sea level begin to flood Bangladesh. The Americans have not been able to stop the flow of Latinos, which is steadily turning large parts of the country into a bilingual culture. The underlying pressures for migration look set to make this issue an increasing part of the security agenda, especially for the wealthier states. As hope fades for any quick closure of the development gap, more and more people in poor, misgoverned, stagnant and/or repressive states will have incentives to seek a better life in the developed states. Whether they are welcomed as assets to economy and culture, or opposed as threats to national identity, will depend on a whole range of local conditions. It nevertheless seems a safe bet that societal insecurities related to migration will occupy a prominent role on the national security agenda for the foreseeable future.

Since the state ultimately rests on its physical base, the protection of territory and population must count as fundamental national security concerns, though they may sometimes be sacrificed in considerable measure to protect the other two components of the state. The enormous losses of the Soviet Union during the Second World War, and of Iran and Iraq during the Gulf War, illustrate this type of trade-off. They point to the bleak calculus of deterrence with its assumption of 'unacceptable damage'. Given the social nature of the state, progressive destruction of its physical base would, at some point, effectively obliterate all values associated with it. Short of that point, however, very considerable damage to the base can be sustained without endangering either the institutions or the idea of the state. Here the argument links to that in Chapter 1 about disharmonies between individual security and national security. It also links to the arguments above about the idea of the state, which can be threatened either by destroying the individuals who carry it, or by changing their minds about what its content should be.

Before concluding this section it is worth noting some anomalies that arise in relation to the physical base as an object of security. Although the state is normally taken to encompass a specified territory and population, ambiguities frequently exist. Many boundaries are either ill-defined or actively disputed, as between India and China, Japan and the Soviet Union, Argentina and Chile, and numerous others.[30] Recent extensions in maritime boundaries have amplified this problem considerably.[31] Acknowledged sea-boundary disputes tend to have a less inflammable character than violations of land boundaries generally accepted as settled, and can acquire a semi-permanent status of uncertainty, like the Senkaku (Tiao Yu Tai) islands disputed among Taiwan, Japan and China.[32] A more serious anomaly arises in the case of states which define their security in terms of territory and population *not* under their control. This can occur because members of the nation are occupying territory outside the bounds of the nation-state, as in the case of the Sudeten Germans, and both Greeks and Turks in Cyprus; or because the state has been deprived of some territory seen as crucial to the national interest, as in the case of Bolivia's corridor to the sea annexed by Chile in 1880. In such cases, the security dimension of the physical base takes on a quite different quality from the interest in protecting an already acquired domain.

CONCLUSIONS: WEAK AND STRONG STATES

What can one conclude about the state as an object of security from this survey of its three components? The most obvious conclusion refers back to one of the early observations: namely that states, like fruit, are exceedingly varied despite their fundamental similarities. Each of the three components presents itself in a wide variety of options. When combined, these result in an open-ended array of combinations around which a state might be structured. Because of this diversity, the particular nature of the national security problem differs substantially from state to state. All states are vulnerable to military and environmental threats. Nearly all are open to economic threats, and many also suffer from basic political and societal insecurities. The different components of the state appear vulnerable to different kinds of threat, which makes national security a problem in many dimensions rather than just a matter of military defence. The idea of the state, its institutions, and even its territory can all be threatened as much by the manipulation of ideas as by the wielding of military power. Since the ideas underpinning the state are themselves subject to evolution, the problem is not only difficult to solve, but may even be hard to specify with any precision. This diversity of states as referent objects for security underpins the argument in the Introduction about the impossibility of devising a universal definition for national security. The concept of security can be mapped in a general sense, but it can only be given specific substance in relation to concrete cases. Ideally, theoretical and case-study work should inform and complement each other.

If the diversity of national security problems is the most obvious conclusion to arise from this investigation of the state, the most important one is a refinement by which one can transform a universe of unique cases into a spectrum of distinguishable types. Waltz's arguments about states as 'like units' notwithstanding,[33] states vary in more than their status powers. They also vary in terms of their degree of socio-political cohesion, which is the very essence of what qualifies them to stand as members of the category of states. On the basis of the broader definition of state established above, when the idea and institutions of a state are both weak, then that state is in a very real sense less of a state than one in which the idea and institutions are strong. The distinction between weak and strong states is vital to any analysis of national security. In order to facilitate discussion, I shall adopt here the following usage: weak or strong *states* will refer to the degree of socio-political cohesion; weak or strong *powers* will refer to the traditional distinction among states in respect of their military and economic capability in relation to each other. This usage differs from that in the literature discussed above, where 'state' is used to refer to governing institutions, and where 'weak state' refers to governments such as the American that are highly constrained and/or diffusely structured in relation to their societies.[34]

Strength as a state neither depends on, nor correlates with power. Weak powers, like Austria, the Netherlands, Norway and Singapore, are all strong states, while quite substantial powers, like Argentina, Brazil, Nigeria, Indonesia and Pakistan are all rather weak as states. Even major powers, like China and the Soviet Union, have serious weaknesses as states. The Soviet Union has not succeeded in submerging its many nationalities into an overarching ideological identity, and as of the late 1980s, both it and China face an increasing crisis over how to interpret their organizing ideology. Both are obliged to maintain extensive internal security establishments. Many factors explain why some states are stronger than others as states. The existence of a strong state may simply reflect a long history during which the state has had time to consolidate and mature. France and Britain clearly benefit in this way. Strong states may benefit from a good fit with a well-developed nation, such as Japan.

Many, though not all, weak states are found in the Third World, and that fact points to decolonization as one cause. The decolonization process created large numbers of new territorial states in the European image. But for the most part it neither took much account of existing cultural and ethnic boundaries, nor created new nations to fit within them. The apparent surge of nationalism that accompanied decolonization was not the positive unity of a coherent cultural group, but the negative one of common opposition to occupying foreigners. The bond of xenophobia disintegrated as soon as the euphoria of independence died down, leaving arbitrarily defined populations occupying post-colonial states possessing no firm political foundations of their own other than the fact of their existence, and their recognition by the international community. The political legacy of most Third World governments was a state without a nation, or even worse, a state with many nations.[35] This legacy, plus the existence of societies not well suited to the demands of complex economic and political relations, defines much of the problem of weak states in the Third World.

Because they are still in the early stages of the attempt to consolidate themselves as state-nations, domestic violence is endemic in such states. Under these circumstances, violence is as likely to be a sign of the accumulation of central state power as it is to be a symptom of political decay.[36] If these new states follow the consolidation model of the European states, then state-building is likely to generate plenty of violence both internally and externally. Weak states may find themselves trapped by historical patterns of economic development and political power which leave them underdeveloped and politically penetrated, and therefore unable to muster the economic and political resources necessary to build a stronger state. The relationship between Latin American states and the United States is often characterized in these terms, and the *dependencia* school of thought tried to emphasize the role of external factors in the creation and maintenance of weak states.

Whatever the reasons for the existence of weak states, their principal distinguishing feature is their high level of concern with domestically generated threats to the security of the government; in other words, weak states either do not have, or failed to create, a domestic political and societal consensus of sufficient strength to eliminate the large-scale use of force as a major and continuing element in the domestic political life of the nation. This indicator connects back to the internal security dimension of the relationship between the state and its citizens explored in the previous chapter. It raises again the awkward problem of defining a boundary in levels of domestic use of force, because even the strongest states require some level of domestic policing against criminals, violent dissidents and foreign agents.

In trying to apply the variable of socio-political cohesion scientifically, one faces the same problem that arises in trying to apply the concept of power, name-ly, the lack of a quantifiable measure. Both concepts ideally require precise and objective measures not only to differentiate states on the spectrum of high to low, but also to enable hypotheses about differences to be led. The lack of such meas-ures restricts what can be done with both concepts, but does not prevent them from being useful for analysis. Both concepts have common sense applicability. They indicate differences that are large enough to be obvious, and significant enough to be important. Very few people would dispute the statement that there are large and significant differences of both power and socio-political cohesion among states. Widespread agreement could even be obtained for a crude ranking. Who would dispute that the United States is more powerful than France or that France is more cohesive than Sri Lanka? Only when it comes to finer rankings is one unable to proceed. Who can say whether France is more powerful than China, or Italy more cohesive than Spain?

No single indicator adequately defines the difference between weak and strong states. The following list outlines the kinds of conditions one would expect to find in weak states (with some recent examples), and the presence of any of which would make one query whether a state should be classed as strong:

1. High levels of political violence (Afghanistan, Cambodia, Israel, Sri Lanka, South Africa, Ethiopia).
2. A conspicuous role for political police in the everyday lives of citizens (Soviet Union, Romania, China, Iraq, North Korea).
3. Major political conflict over what ideology will be used to organize the state (Peru, El Salvador, Poland, Afghanistan).
4. Lack of a coherent national identity, or the presence of contending national identities within the state (Nigeria, Ethiopia, Sudan, Turkey, South Africa, Yugoslavia, Soviet Union, Sri Lanka).
5. Lack of a clear and observed hierarchy of political authority (Lebanon, Sudan, Chad, Uganda, increasingly Yugoslavia).
6. A high degree of state control over the media (Nicaragua before 1990, China, Iran, East Germany before 1989).

Where the state is strong, national security can be viewed primarily in terms of pro-tecting the components of the state from outside threat and interference. The idea of the state, its institutions and its territory will all be clearly defined and stable in their own right. Approved mechanisms for adjustment, change and transfer of power will exist, and will command sufficient support so that they are not serious-ly threatened from within the state. Where the state is weak, only its physical base, and sometimes not even that, may be sufficiently well defined to constitute a clear object of national security. Because its idea and its institutions are internally con-tested to the point of violence they are not properly national in scope, and do not offer clear referents as objects of national security. Very weak states possess neither a widely accepted and coherent idea of the state among their populations, nor a governing power strong enough to impose unity in the absence of political consensus. The fact that they exist as states at all is largely a result of other states recognizing them as such and/or not disputing their existence. When viewed from the outside they look like states because they have embassies, a flag, boundaries on maps and a seat in the United Nations. But viewed from within they are anarchic, with different armed self-governing groups controlling their own territories and contesting central government, with each other, by force. Such states exist in a condition of effective civil war which mirrors all the worst and none of the best features of anarchic structure at the international system level.

Because of this, it can be more appropriate to view security in very weak states in terms of the contending groups, organizations and individuals, as the prime objects of security. The concept of national security requires national objects as its points of reference, and in very weak states such as Lebanon, Mozambique, Chad and Uganda, these hardly exist. To view such a state in the same security terms as one would view Sweden or Japan is misleading. When there is almost no idea of the state, and the governing institutions are themselves the main threat to many individuals, national security almost ceases to have content and one must look to individuals and sub-state units for the most meaningful security referents. Foreign intervention becomes much harder to assess in national security terms (unless other states are trying to seize parts of the physical base, in which case the threat is clearly on a national scale) because outside powers will be helping factions which are themselves in conflict. Thus, neither Western aid to União Nacional para a Independêcia Total de Angola or UNITA, nor Soviet and Cuban aid to the Movimento Popular de Libertação de Angola or MPLA, during the Angolan civil war can be described as threats to the national security of Angola, because no national socio-political entity existed to threaten. Who should be classed enemy and who ally simply depends on one's point of view, or, in the longer term, on which side wins.

This distinction between states with serious domestic security problems and those whose primary security concerns are external is crucial to the understanding of national security. The weaker a state is, the more ambiguous the concept of national security becomes in relation to it. To use the term in relation to a very weak state, as if such a state represented the same type of object as a strong state, simply paves the way for the wholesale importation of national security imperatives into the domestic political arena, with all the dangers of legitimized violence that this implies. The security of governments becomes confused with the security of states, and factional interests are provided with a legitimacy which they do not merit. In a strong state, one might expect a considerable, though by no means total, correlation between the government's view of national security and the array of referent objects discussed in this chapter. In weaker states this correlation declines, and one needs to be more suspicious of the assumption that national security is what the government deems it to be. There will almost always be useful grounds, in either weak or strong states, for testing government assertions about national security against suspicions that more sectional interests are being promoted.

To suggest this type of distinction between weak and strong states runs against the grain of orthodoxy in International Relations. The illusion that all states are basically the same type of object springs not only from their common possession of sovereignty, but also from the habit of looking at them from an external, system-level, perspective. When looked at from outside, states appear to be much more definite and similar objects than when they are viewed from within. From outside, they nearly all appear as sovereign entities in which governments exercise control over territories and populations which are, for the most part, neither ruled nor claimed by other states. Most of these states either recognize, or treat with, one another as sovereign equals, and even the weakest states can usually exercise their right to vote in international bodies like the UN General Assembly.

This external perspective distorts the view in relation to national security by covering over the domestic security dimension. National security cannot be considered apart from the internal structure of the state, and the view from within not infrequently explodes the superficial image of the state as a coherent object of security. A strong state defines itself from within and fills the gap between its neighbours with a solid socio-political presence. A very weak state may be defined more *as* the gap between its neighbours, with little of political substance underlying the façade of internationally recognized statehood. Since the object itself is so tenuous, the concept of national security lacks coherent referents.

National security most easily refers to the relationship of the state to its environment, and becomes profoundly confused to the extent that the state is insecure within itself. In other words, the concept of national security can only be applied sensibly to the external side of the state's Hobbesian security functions. Unless the internal dimension is relatively stable as a prior condition, the image of the state as a referent object for security fades until it becomes a nearly meaningless blur. There is thus no doubt that the concept is easiest to apply to the strong states which it was originally coined. Strong states provide a relatively clear referent object for national security. They have a single source of authority which commands a broad legitimacy among the population. Because state and society are closely linked together, indigenous domestic issues play a relatively minor role in national security concerns. Even a strong state must guard against subversive penetration of its political and military fabric by foreign agents and interests, but for a strong state the concept of national security is primarily about protecting its independence, political identity and way of life from external threats, rather than from threats arising within its own fabric.

Within the externally oriented conception of national security appropriate to strong states there is still vast room for argument and contradiction about the ends and means of national security. Should protection of the government and ideology have priority over protection of the population? Are nuclear threats a reasonable way to pursue military security when they might lead to national suicide? How, indeed, does one pursue national security in an age when states are increasingly interdependent in economic and environmental terms, and when the power of military technology makes them utterly dependent on the restraint of others for their survival? Can national security be pursued by individual state action or does it require cooperation? An argument can be made that even strong states cultivate external threats as a means of maintaining their high levels of internal cohesion.[37] But despite the ambiguity of the concept in its specific applications, when the referent object is a strong state, it is at least clear that national security is primarily about defining and dealing with external threats to a socio-political entity that is in itself more or less freestanding and stable.

As we move down the spectrum towards the weak end, the referent object for national security gets harder to define, and the primarily external orientation of the concept gives way to an increasingly domestic agenda of threats. When governments rule more by power than by consensus, and when their authority is seriously contested internally by forceful means, then much of the socio-political meaning begins to drain out of the concept of national security. When political power and ideology within the state do not command broad legitimacy, or are contested by force, there is no clear content to such central elements of national security as political style, ideology and institutions. Even the notion of self-government can be questioned in cases where a minority dominates the majority by force. The political conditions of weak states often propel the military into government as the only organization possessing the power and/or the national legitimacy to hold the state together. Strong governments (in the sense of being dictatorial and repressive), especially military ones, usually indicate a weak state. In Latin America, such governments have articulated a whole philosophy of national security specifically oriented towards the domestic conditions of weak states.[38] As one moves towards the weak end of the spectrum, much of the core political content of national security therefore becomes effectively void.

In practical terms, this void leads to some extremely difficult questions about the boundaries of national security as a concept. By definition, governments in weak states will have serious concerns about domestic threats to their own authority. These threats can take many forms including military coups, guerrilla movements, secessionist movements, mass uprisings and political factionalism. Domestic threats are to a considerable extent endemic to states with no clear machinery for political succession. But are such threats to be considered part of the national security problem? Are they really threats to the state or to the nation, or are they just threats to the narrower interest of the incumbent ruling group? Should they be seen merely as a form of domestic political process – a chaotic and bloody substitute for more orderly means of succession – and therefore as an expression of the sovereign right of self-rule rather than as a threat to that right?

Firm answers to these questions lead to awkward dilemmas either way. If domestic threats are accepted as a national security problem, then the government is provided with a powerful tool to legitimize the use of force against its political opposition. In practice, this is often what happens. As well as posing obvious moral issues, the opening up of national security to include domestic threats raises serious logical criticisms about the distinction between the security of the government and the security of the state or nation. There is an important linkage between the two, as indicated by the fact that strong states will often fight major wars to protect their system of government. But in weak states this linkage is very problematic because of the narrowness of the government's political base in relation to the state as a whole. Is it really correct to see opposition to unpopular dictators as part of the national security problems of countries like Nicaragua and Haiti?

But if domestic threats are not accepted as part of the national security problem other equally serious difficulties arise. The fate of the government cannot be wholly separated from the issue of national security even in a weak state. The government is both an important symbol and a major manifestation of the state. The fate of particular governments may not be of much account to the state as a whole, but congenital weakness of government brings into question the integrity, and even the existence, of the state, and therefore has to be regarded as a national security issue. But how does one distinguish between the sectional interests of any particular government's claim that its own security is a national security issue, and the broader national security problem raised by the overall fact of weak sociopolitical cohesion? The case of Lebanon since the mid-1970s illustrates this problem clearly. Is it any longer reasonable to consider Lebanon a state?

Domestic political fragmentation also makes the state exceptionally vulnerable to penetration by external political interests. In weak states, domestic threats to the government can almost never be wholly separated from the influence of outside powers, and in this sense, the domestic security problems of weak states are often hopelessly entangled with their external relations. Almost by definition, weak states will be chronically insecure.

In terms of measures designed to improve long-term nation security conditions, this analysis points to the conclusion that the creation of stronger states is a necessary condition for both individual and national security. The existence of stronger states will not by itself guarantee security, but their continued absence will certainly sustain insecurity. Both national security and international security for the system as a whole, will remain problematic so long as the structure of anarchy is flawed by the presence of many weak states. Although weak states may serve some short-term economic, political and military interests of the great powers, those gains have to be weighed against the risk that conflict within and between weak states poses to international security. For weak states themselves, the idea of national security borders on nonsense unless they can make the transformation to strong state structures. Weak states simply define the conditions of insecurity for most of their citizens. In the regional context, as will be explored in Chapter 5, groups of weak states can make the formation of security communities extremely difficult because of the way in which they export their domestic instabilities to each other.[39] Alas, the building of strong states is only a necessary, and not a sufficient, condition for improved international security. As the European states proved twice during this century, strong states are no guarantee of peace. Building strong states may also have negative consequences for the security of many individuals and groups caught up in the process. Like development, the state-nation process is seldom benign. All that can be said is that without strong states, there will be no security, national or otherwise. The magnitude of this task has been interestingly explored by Migdal, who is not optimistic. He argues that only the massive disruptions of war, revolution or mass migration can create the flexibility necessary to break weak states out of the social and political structures that constrain their development.[40]

NOTES

1. Joel S. Migdal, *Strong Societies and Weak States: State-society relations and state capabilities in the Third World* (Princeton, NJ: Princeton University Press, 1988), pp. xiii, 19; J. P. Nettl, 'The state as a conceptual variable', *World Politics*, p. 591. See also Fred Halliday, 'State and society in international relations: a second agenda', *Millennium*, 16:2 (1987); Hidemi Suganami, 'Halliday's two concepts of state', *Millennium*, 17:1 (1988); Fred Halliday, 'States, discourses, classes: a rejoinder to Suganami, Palan, Forbes', *Millennium*, 17: I (1988); Peter B. Evans, Dietrich Rueschemeyer, Theda Skocpol (eds), *Bringing the State Back In* (Cambridge: Cambridge University Press, 1985).

2. Migdal, *ibid.*, p. 19.

3. Nettl, *op. cit.* (note 1), pp. 561–2.

4. Anthony Jarvis, 'Societies, states and geopolitics: challenges from historical sociology', *Review of International Studies*, 15:3 (1989), pp. 281–2. See also Halliday, *op. cit.* (note 1).

5. Richard Little, 'Understanding units', in Barry Buzan, Charles Jones and Richard Little, *The Logic of Anarchy*, (forthcoming).

6. Alexander E. Wendt, 'The agent-structure problem in international relations theory', *International Organization*, 41:3 (1987).

7. William H. McNeill, *The Rise of the West* (Chicago: University of Chicago Press, 1963).

8. Migdal, *op. cit.*, (note 1), pp. 21, 23.

9. For discussions on the problem of the individual-state analogy, see Hedley Bull, *The Anarchical Society* (London: Macmillan, 1977), pp. 47–52; Robert E. Osgood and Robert W. Tucker, *Force, Order and Justice* (Baltimore: Johns Hopkins University Press, 1967), pp. 270–84; and Hidemi Suganami, 'Reflections on the domestic analogy: the case of Bull, Beitz and Linklater', *Review of International Studies*, 12:2 (1986), pp. 145–58.

10. On idiosyncratic versus role variables, see James N. Rosenau, 'Pre-theories and theories of foreign policy', in R. Barry Farrell (ed.), *Approaches to Comparative and International Politics*, (Evanston: Northwestern University Press, 1966), pp. 27–92.

11. Ralph Miliband, *The State in Capitalist Society* (London: Quartet Books, 1973), p. 46.

12. An exercise partly parallel in form to this model, though rather different in intent, is undertaken by R. W. Cox, 'Social forces, state and world orders', *Millennium*, 10:2 (1981), who notes (p. 127) that, 'there has been little attempt within the bounds of international relations theory to consider the state/society complex as the basic entity of international relations'. Jarvis, *op. cit.* (note 4), p. 283 argues that 'International Relations...is now required...to be a theory of the fit between societies, states and geopolitics.'

13. Peter Willetts, 'The United Nations and the transformation of the inter-state system', in

Barry Buzan and R. J. Barry Jones (eds) *Change and the Study of International Relations* (London: Pinter, 1981) pp. 112–14.

14. Kenneth N. Waltz, *Theory of International Politics* (Reading, Mass.: Addison-Wesley, 1979), pp. 96–7.

15. For discussions of states as a class of objects, see *ibid*, pp. 95–7; and P. A. Reynolds, *An Introduction to International Relations* (London: Longman, 1980, 2nd edn.), pp. 262–3.

16. Waltz, *ibid.*, p. 96.

17. For opposing views on the trend towards more equality among states, see R. W. Tucker, *The Inequality of Nations* (London: Martin Robertson, 1977); and R. P. Anand, 'On the equality of states', in F. A. Sonderman, W. C. Olson and D. S. McLellan, *The Theory and Practice of International Relations* (Englewood Cliffs, NJ: Prentice Hall, 1970), pp. 23–9.

18. For examples of this approach, see Ian Bellany, 'Towards a theory of international security', *Political Studies*, 29:1 (1981); and M. Olson and R. Zeckhauser, 'An economic theory of alliances', *Review of Economics and Statistics*, 48 (1966):

19. Nettl, *op. cit.* (note 1), p. 564.

20 Kenneth H. F. Dyson, *The State Tradition in Western Europe* (Oxford: Martin Robertson, 1980), p. 3. Dyson goes on to explore the intellectual history of the idea of the state in great depth. His purpose is not, as mine is here, to find referents for a concept like security. Instead, he charts the development of ideas about the fundamental character of the state as a collective entity, and tries to relate these developments to the conditions of their times. I am trying to sketch a contemporary cross-section of the idea of the state, whereas Dyson shows how we arrived here. One cannot, of course, understand the current idea of any particular state without understanding the historical development through which it has evolved. Those interested in either the dynamic of the idea of the state, or its character at various points in the past, should consult this work.

21. On nations and states, see Leonard Tivey (ed.), *The Nation-State* (Oxford: Martin Robertson, 1981); and Ralph Pettman, *State and Class* (London: Croom Helm, 1979), ch. 4; Ivo D. Duchacek, *Nations and Men* (Hinsdale, Ill.: Dryden Press, 1975, 3rd edn), chs. 1–3; Hugh Seton-Watson, *Nations and States* (London: Methuen, 1977); M. Rejai and C. H. Enloc, 'Nation-states and state-nations', in Michael Smith, Richard Little and Michael Shackleton (eds), *Perspectives on World Politics* (London: Croom Helm/Open University Press, 1981); Ernest Gellner, *Nations and Nationalism* (Oxford: Blackwell, 1983); Anthony D. Smith, *Nationalism in the Twentieth Century* (Oxford: Blackwell, 1979). For a useful discussion of nations as minority ethnic groups within states, see Vernon Van Dyke, 'The individual, the state and ethnic communities in political theory', *World Politics*, 29:3 (1977).

22. Michael Howard, 'Ideology and international relations', *Review of International Studies*, 15:1 (1989), p. 9.

23. Rejai and Enlock, *op. cit.* (note 21), use this term in relation to the nation-building attempts of many Third World states.

24. See Cornelia Navari, 'The origins of the nation-state', in Tivey (ed.), *op. cit.* (note 21), ch. 1; and Dyson, *op. cit.* (note 20), p. 245. A development view of this type would raise interesting questions about intervening variables. Could one, for example, find any uniform impact on the state-nation process arising from the difference between self-generated states

and states created through the agency of an external colonizing power?

25. See P. J. Vatikiotis, *Islam and the Nation-State* (London: Croom Helm, 1987).

26. On shared hates as a factor, see Duchacek, *op. cit.* (note 21), pp. 53ff.

27. W. Hinckle and W. W. Turner, *The Fish is Red: The story of the secret war against Castro* (New York: Harper & Row, 1981).

28. B. Wolfram Hanrieder, 'Dissolving international politics: reflections on the nation-state', *American Political Science Review*, 72:4 (1978).

29. Milton Viorst, 'These are not my people, this is not my Israel', *The Guardian Weekly* (15 August 1982), p. 17.

30. Alan J. Day (ed.), *Border and Territorial Disputes* (Harlow: Longman, 1982).

31. See Barry Buzan 'A sea of troubles? Sources of dispute in the new ocean regime', *Adelphi Papers*, no. 143 (London: IISS, 1978).

32. Barry Buzan, 'Maritime issues in North-east Asia', *Marine Policy* 3:3 (1979), pp. 194–8.

33. Waltz, *op. cit.* (note 14), pp. 95–7.

34. It does not seem possible to avoid some terminological confusion here on two fronts. The first arises from the use of 'states' and 'powers' as synonyms in the literature. My usage requires that they be kept distinct, which would mean, for example, Michael Handel's book, *Weak States in the International System* (London: Croom Helm, 1981), should be titled *Weak Powers....* My usage of weak and strong states also differs from the meanings used by all of those using state in its narrow institutional sense. These include: Nettl, *op. cit.* (note 1); Migdal, *op. cit.* (note 1); Y. Cohen, B. R. Brown and A. F. K. Organski, 'The paradoxical nature of state-making: the violent creation of order', *American Political Science Review*, 75:4 (1981), pp. 905–7; and Stephen D. Krasner, *Defending the National Interest: Raw materials investments and US foreign policy* (Princeton, NJ: Princeton University Press, 1978), ch. 3. Cohen *et al.* define the spectrum of weak to strong states by using the measure of tax receipts as a proportion of GNP. This useful measure gives them insight into the relative strength of governing institutions as compared to the societies they are trying to rule. Krasner focuses on the degree to which decision-making power is diffused as opposed to centralized. Both these approaches provide very helpful insights, though they give rather different results. Krasner is concerned to argue that the United States is a weak state because the decision-making power of its governing institutions cannot dominate its strong society. Cohen *et al.* produce a view of the weak-strong state spectrum which correlates with the spectrum of underdeveloped-developed states. In my view, both arguments are based on Kenneth Dyson's 'category error' of conflating the idea of state with its apparatus, noted on p. 70. My proposal is to confine the use of the term 'states' to be the more comprehensive conception outlined in this chapter which includes, but is not confined to, the governing institutions. One author who comes close to my usage is David Wilsford, 'Tactical advantages versus administrative heterogeneity: the strengths and limits of the French state', in James A. Caporaso (ed.), *The Elusive State: International and comparative perspectives* (Newbury Park: Sage, 1989), pp. 136–7. See also note 12 above.

35. I am grateful to Gowher Rizvi for this point. Much of what follows in the section is closely derived from my chapter in Edward Azar and Chung-in Moon (eds), *National Security in the Third World: The management of internal and external threats* (Aldershot: Edward Elgar, 1988), pp. 19–26, 40.

36. Cohen *et al.* (note 34), pp. 901–10. If they are correct, then the process of state-building necessarily involves a phase of internal conflict during which contradictions between individual and national security will be extreme.

37. John Burton, *Global Conflict: The domestic sources of international crisis* (Hemel Hempstead: Harvester Wheatsheaf, 1984).

38. Robert Calvo, 'The church and the doctrine of national security', *Journal of Inter-American Studies and World Affairs,* 21:1 (1979).

39. There are some cases where the reverse is true. Both ASEAN and the GCC have sub-regional security regimes based on understandings by a group of weak states that their regime securities are better served by cooperation among them than by conflict with each other. See Amitav Acharya, 'Regionalism and regime security in the Third World: a comparative study of the association of Southeast Asian Nations (ASEAN) and the Gulf Cooperation Council (GCC)', presented to the Symposium on 'The insecurity dilemma: national security of Third World states', University of British Columbia, Vancouver, March 1990.

40. Migdal, *op. cit.,* (note 1), ch.8.

chapter three | national insecurity: threats and vulnerabilities

THREATS AND VULNERABILITIES

The enquiry in the previous chapter addressed several aspects of threat and vulnerability, but it is useful to examine this difficult topic in its own right. Only when one has a reasonable idea of both the nature of threats, and the vulnerabilities of the objects towards which they are directed, can one begin to make sense of national security as a policy problem. Insecurity reflects a combination of threats and vulnerabilities, and the two cannot meaningfully be separated. If Poland is thought to be historically insecure, then not only must its vulnerabilities in terms of size, economic underdevelopment, political instability and indefensible boundaries be taken into account but also the threats posed to it by powerful, expansionist neighbours on either side. If Germany and Russia had been empty lands, Poland's vulnerabilities would have been of little historical consequence. And if Poland had been a stronger state and power, and possessed defensible mountain borders, the threats from Germany and Russia would have been less serious.

This distinction between threats and vulnerabilities points to a key divide in security policy, namely, that states can seek to reduce their insecurity either by reducing their vulnerability or by preventing or lessening threats.[1] These alternatives underline respectively, the ideas of national and international security. In other words national security policy can either focus inward, seeking to reduce the vulnerabilities of the state itself, or outward, seeking to reduce external threat by addressing its sources. I will return to this theme in Chapter 9.

Much of what was said in the previous chapter about the components of the state was to do with their vulnerability. It is clear that vulnerability connects intimately with both weak states and weak powers. Weak powers are a well-understood phenomenon, and require little elaboration. Their weakness is relative to the capabilities commanded by other states in the system, particularly their neighbours and the great powers of the day, and frequently stems from the fact that they are relatively small and/or poorly organized. Although wealth, skill, socio-political cohesion and willpower can compensate for smallness to some extent – as illustrated in different ways by the histories of Prussia, the Netherlands, Israel and

Singapore – they cannot compensate in the long run for the lack of a broader physical base. Weak powers may be able to muster themselves to considerable effect in a single sector, but they cannot make more than a short-term impact in military terms. Even Israel can only deploy its formidable military machine for short periods before the strain on the national fabric becomes too great.[2] Weak powers can usually only prosper by specializing their economies, like many of the smaller European states have done, and this almost by definition produces a host of vulnerabilities arising from dependence on trade.

Weak states, whether or not they are also weak powers, are vulnerable for the political reasons explored in the last chapter. An underdeveloped idea of the state, as in Ethiopia, and/or unstable institutions, as in Uganda, open the state to domestic disruption and foreign intervention. When a state has the misfortune to be both a small power and a weak state, like Mozambique, its vulnerability is almost unlimited. If, additionally, it possesses some attribute of importance to others, be it natural resources like Angola, a vital waterway like Turkey, or a strategic position like Poland, then external pressure on these vulnerabilities is a constant possibility. By contrast, states which are strong both as states and as powers, such as the United States, France and Japan, have far fewer vulnerabilities. Their internal political structures have sufficient mass, momentum and stability to be able to withstand anything but a large-scale intervention. The state commands ample resources in many sectors, and consequently is able to adapt to, absorb or deter many threats which would present overwhelming challenges to countries like the Maldives or Laos. This is not to say that such states are invulnerable, for the oil squeeze and the threat of major war stand as obvious refutations to any such contention. But it is to argue that their vulnerabilities are neither numerous nor easy to exploit, and therefore that they are neither excessively tempting nor particularly cheap to threaten. Even with such states, however, geostrategic factors do make a considerable difference. The flat land frontiers of West Germany and Hungary, for example, are clearly more vulnerable to military threats than are the island territories of Japan and New Zealand.

This discussion can be summed up as in Table 3.1.

Table 3.1: Vulnerabilities and types of state

		Socio-political cohesion	
		Weak	Strong
Power	Weak	Highly vulnerable to most types of threat	Particularly vulnerable to military threats
	Strong	Particularly vulnerable to political threats	Relatively invulnerable to most types of threat

States that are weak in both dimensions, such as Angola and Sri Lanka, will be the most vulnerable to all kinds of threats, and the least capable of dealing with them.

Unless they are fortunate enough to occupy a particularly insulated environment, such as Fiji, their security will depend on the absence of challenges. Conversely, states that are strong in both dimensions will only be vulnerable either to major challenges, or to unstoppable types of threat such as nuclear bombardment or climate change. Weak powers but strong states, such as Singapore and Denmark, will have a particular vulnerability to military threats because of their limited resources. States that combine significant weakness in socio-political cohesion with substantial power, such as India and the Soviet Union have most to fear from political threats.

Vulnerabilities are fairly concrete. But for two reasons threats are much harder to pin down. The first is the subjective/objective problem discussed in relation to individuals in Chapter 1. Actual threats, as well as being impossible to measure, may not be perceived. The threats that dominate perception, may not have much substantive reality. In retrospect, American and Chinese threat perceptions of each other during the 1950s and 1960s seem greatly exaggerated. The question of assessing the Soviet threat to the West was a matter of sharp controversy throughout the Cold War. Attitudes towards the German question during the early 1990s are still strongly affected by memories of previous German bids for power, regardless of whether those memories have any relevance for current developments. How seriously should still uncertain scientific predictions of global warming be taken? Fear is a volatile political commodity, more so for humans in large groups than for individuals. Questions of fear are thus not likely candidates for coolly rational assessment and carefully calculated policy. A further complication is that the fears of leaders may not be shared by much of the population, as the Americans discovered during the Vietnam War.

The second is the difficulty of distinguishing threats serious enough to constitute a threat to national security, from those that arise as normal day-to-day consequences of life in a competitive international environment. Since security has to be defined within the norm of a competitive environment, one cannot take the easy route of defining all threats as national security issues. The difference between normal challenges and threats to national security necessarily occurs on a spectrum of threats that ranges from trivial and routine, through serious but routine, to drastic and unprecedented. Quite where on this spectrum issues begin to get legitimately classified as national security problems is a matter of political choice rather than objective fact. Setting the security trigger too low on the scale risks paranoia, waste of resources, aggressive policies and serious distortions of domestic political life. Setting it too high risks failure to prepare for major assaults until too late. Weak states, and those with narrowly cast ideological orthodoxies, will be impelled by their domestic conditions to push the qualifications for threats to have 'national security problem' status down towards the low end of the threat spectrum. When political threats dominate, the national security agenda can become very wide-ranging indeed.

Wæver's definition of security (page 36) offers a useful insight here because it stresses that the labelling of an issue as a security problem by the government automatically legitimizes the use of exceptional means. The clear inference is that excessive use of security justifications cannot but shift the process of government away from constitutional practices, and towards what are, in effect, authoritarian methods. The political character of this choice has to be assessed against the particular set of threats and vulnerabilities that any given state faces. Threats of invasion, political destabilization and blockade clearly fall within the legitimate national security category for all states. But there is a broad grey area between these obvious threats and the normal difficulties of international relations. Should threats to fish stocks, or uncompetitive industries, or the purity of air and water be considered threats to national security? Should illegal immigration, or restrictions on credit, or the promulgation of radical political views, or the illegal trade in drugs? Unless these questions can be answered with some clarity, one cannot establish a firm basis on which to assess national security policy.[3]

From the analysis of the state in the previous chapter, it is abundantly clear that the range of potential national security issues is wide, stretching across the military, political, economic, societal and ecological sectors. It is worth examining the character of threats within each of these sectors in order to try to get a general sense of the legitimate national security agenda. In this exercise, it is helpful to keep in mind the idea that national security is about the ability of states to maintain their independent identity and their functional integrity. It is also worth remembering that national security is a conservative concept inasmuch as it relates to existing states. Opinions vary strongly about the desirability of some states, and about the viability of others. But national security analysis has at least to start on the level of existing states, whether they are seen as desirable and viable or not.

TYPES OF THREAT BY SECTOR

Military

Military threats occupy the traditional heart of national security concerns. Military action can, and usually does, threaten all the components of the state. It subjects the physical base to strain, damage and dismemberment, and it can deeply disrupt the ecosystem. It can result in the distortion or destruction of institutions, and it can repress, subvert or obliterate the idea of the state. Military actions not only strike at the very essence of the state's basic protective functions, but also threaten damage deep down through the layers of social and individual interest which underlie, and are more permanent than, the state's superstructures. Strong states fear the use of force because it threatens to overthrow a self-created rule by consent, and replace it with an imposed rule by coercion. For weak states, the military threat is harder to judge on a national basis. Certainly the ruling élite will be threatened, but depending on the aims of the invaders, large sections of society may welcome, or be indifferent to, the change. Irrespective of whether the state is weak or strong, the high human and economic costs of military action remain the same.

Because the use of force can wreak major undesired changes swiftly, military threats are traditionally accorded the highest priority in national security concerns. Military action can wreck the work of centuries in all other sectors. Difficult accomplishments in politics, art, industry, culture and all human activities can be undone by the use of force. Human achievements, in other words, can be threatened in terms other than those in which they were created, and the need to prevent such threats from being realized is a major underpinning of the state's military protection function. A defeated society is totally vulnerable to the conqueror's power which can be applied to ends ranging from restructuring the government, through pillage and rape, to massacre of the population and resettlement of the land. The threat of force thus stimulates not only a powerful concern to protect the socio-political heritage of the state, but also a sense of outrage at the use of unfair forms of competition. Images such as the Roman destruction of Carthage, the Ottoman conquest of Byzantium, the European colonizations of the Americas, Africa and Australia, the Nazi occupation of Poland and the devastation likely to result from a nuclear Third World War, all support the high fear attached to military threats. They explain much about how the mutual construction of sovereign states and an anarchic international system occurred. They also show why the existence of external military threats can be an attractive instrument that ruling élites can use to increase socio-political cohesion, and thus ease the task of governing.

The level of military threat varies from harassment of fishing boats, through punishment raids, territorial seizures and full invasions, to assaults on the very existence of the populace by blockade or bombardment. Objectives can range from the relatively minor and specific, as in the American use of warships sailing into coastal waters to indicate non-recognition of expansive territorial sea claims, to the major and general, as in the case of the Brehznev doctrine, where military superiority provided the backdrop to the broad spectrum conditioning of the policies of less powerful neighbours. Military threats also can be indirect, in the sense of not being applied to the state itself, but rather being directed at external interests. Threats to allies, shipping lanes, or strategically placed territories would all come under this heading, and the Western concern over the security of oil supplies is a good illustration.

Military threats occupy a special category precisely because they involve the use of force. The use of force breaches normal peaceful relations, and disrupts diplomatic recognition. In that sense, even the threat of force implies willingness to cross the important threshold that separates the regular competitive interplay of political, economic and societal sectors from the all-out competition of war. The existence of this threshold, and the potentially drastic consequences of crossing it, go a long way towards explaining the disproportionate emphasis given to military security even at a time when threats in other sectors appear to offer greater and more immediate danger. Nearly all states maintain military forces to counter threats, either by defence or retaliation, and the specific issues and dynamics arising from this are considered in Chapters 7 and 8.

Political

Political threats are aimed at the organizational stability of the state. Their purpose may range from pressuring the government on a particular policy, through over-throwing the government, to fomenting secessionism, and disrupting the political fabric of the state so as to weaken it prior to military attack. The idea of state, particularly its national identity and organizing ideology, and the institutions which express it, are the normal target of political threats. Since the state is an essential-ly political entity, political threats may be as much feared as military ones. This is particularly so if the target is a weak state. But even when the state is both strong and powerful, political threats might still be a source of concern. France and Italy in the immediate post-war years were strong on national grounds, but significant-ly divided in terms of organizing ideology. Even the United States feared commu-nist influence in its political life. In both cases, the fear was that successful polit-ical interference might win substantial policy rewards in terms of changed foreign alignment.

Political threats stem from the great diversity of ideas and traditions which is the key underlying justification for the international anarchy. In terms of organiz-ing ideologies, during the twentieth century liberal-democratic, fascist, commu-nist, and more recently Islamic, political ideas have contradicted each other in practice just as much as monarchical and republican ones did in the nineteenth century. Because the contradictions in these ideologies are basic, states of one per-suasion may well feel threatened by the ideas represented by others. Creating an anti-ideology, as the Americans have done with anti-communism and the Soviets did with anti-imperialism, is one answer. But it carries the cost that the cultivation of negatives might begin to override the positive values which they are supposed to protect, as in the case of the McCarthyism episode in the United States, and much more extremely, Stalinism in the Soviet Union.

The competition among ideologies is extraordinarily complex. This fact makes it difficult to define exactly what should be considered a political threat serious enough to justify the national security label. In one sense, the mere existence of a state espousing an opposing ideology constitutes a threat on the grounds of the 'one rotten apple in the basket' principle. To take this seriously, however, would require an interminable and probably impossible military crusade, the costs of which would far outweigh the objectives. Threats to national identity are more straightforward. They involve attempts to heighten the separate ethno-cultural identities of groups within the target state. The purpose could range from increas-ing the difficulty of government in an unfriendly neighbour, as South Africa has done to both Angola and Mozambique, to encouraging secessionism, as in rela-tions between Sudan and Ethiopia, to preparing the ground for annexation by a neighbouring state seeking to incorporate all the components of its nation, as in Hitler's campaigns during the 1930s.

Whether political threats are ideological or national in character, it is impor-tant to distinguish between those that are intentional, and those that arise struc-turally from the impact of foreign alternatives on the legitimacy of states.

Intentional political threats are exemplified by those emanating in many directions from Colonel Qadhafi's Libya, those directed by the United States at various times against radical regimes in Cuba, Chile, Guatemala, Nicaragua and elsewhere, those posed by the Soviet Union's support for communist parties in other countries during the Cold War, and those directed against South Africa because of apartheid. Denial of diplomatic recognition, like that suffered by Taiwan, is also a form of intentional political threat. Specific political interventions by one state in the domestic affairs of another might clearly seem to deserve the national security label, but even here the boundaries are hard to draw. Should propaganda of the Radio Moscow and Voice of America kind be considered a threat to national security, or as part of the general interplay of ideas and information? Propaganda support for political groups of similar persuasion blends upward: into the funding and creation of such groups, and eventually to the quasi-military activities of political assassination and arms aid to rebels. Such activity is clearly a threat to national security, but it can be exceedingly difficult to distinguish from domestically generated dissent, as anyone who follows Islamic politics in the Middle East can testify. How is Iranian support for Shi'ia populations in Arab states to be distinguished from the natural political identity of those populations in their own right? Because of this difficulty, even intentional political threats will almost always involve the confusion between domestic and national security outlined in the previous chapter.

Political threats can also be structural, which is to say that they result more from the nature of the situation than from the particular intentions of one actor towards another. In a broad sense, for example, one might argue that the whole *Zeitgeist* of the twentieth century has posed a political threat to the legitimacy of monarchical rule. The Shah of Iran was but the latest in a long line of autocratic rulers to be swept away by mass-based political movements of various persuasions. Such events cause no puzzlement, although they may cause considerable surprise. The mystery is how such anachronistic forms of government manage to survive at all when the entire socio-political environment of the times acts to corrode their legitimacy. Trying to make such a government secure from political threats must be, in the long run, virtually impossible.

In more specific terms, structural political threats arise when the organizing principles of two states contradict each other in a context where the states cannot ignore each other's existence. Their political systems thus play a zero-sum game with each other whether they will it or not. Relations between South Africa and black-ruled states have this character, as did ideological relations between China and the Soviet Union during the 1960s, and the global rivalry between the United States and the Soviet Union during the Cold War, and as ideological and national relations between the two Koreas still do. During the 1980s the relative success of the Western European pluralist democracies undermined the already shaky legitimacy of communist regimes in Eastern Europe. If the structural threat is ideological, as between Eastern and Western Europe, the fear is that the legitimacy of governing institutions will be corroded. If it is nationality-based, as between

Pakistan and Afghanistan, India and Sri Lanka and the two Koreas, the fear is of territorial dismemberment, or a crippling long-term conflict, or *in extremis*, absorption. The race issue in South Africa is an interesting mixture: partition of the state could be a solution, but so far majority opinion on both sides favours the maintenance of a united South Africa.

Where the achievements and successes of one state automatically erode the political stature of another, this often leads, naturally enough, to more intentional forms of political threat. India and Pakistan offer a particularly tragic case of a structural political threat developing in this way. Their historical, geographical and cultural ties do not allow them to ignore each other. Both came in to existence in 1947 on a tide of antagonism resulting from the failure to maintain the secular political cohesion of the Raj. Their organizing principles pose a permanent threat to each other; a threat amplified by the fact that both states are politically vulnerable. Pakistan is organized on the principle of Islamic unity, and so stands for the definition of the state along exclusively theological lines. India is constituted on secular, federal lines and can only exist by cultivating mutual accommodation among the various large religious groups within its borders, including more than 80 million Muslims. The principle of India thus threatens Pakistan's major *raison d'être*. In the early years this provided grounds for Pakistan to fear absorption by an omnivorous India, though now the threat is more of a debilitating war of attrition that undermines Pakistan's development prospects. The principle of Pakistan likewise threatens India's basic *raison d'être*, raising the spectre of a breakup of the Indian Union in a number of independent, single-religion, successor states. Such a breakdown would solve Pakistan's permanent inferiority to much larger India. The tension between them is neatly institutionalized in their dispute over Kashmir. Since the population of that province mostly adheres to Islam, both states view their claims to it in the light of their national integrity. The political threats posed to each other by India and Pakistan clearly defines a central element in the national security problem of each of them, and illustrate the extensive ground for confusion between internal politics and national security.[4]

Societal
Societal threats can be difficult to disentangle from political ones. In relations between states, significant external threats on the social level amount to attacks on national identity, and thus easily fall within the political realm. Societal threats are often part of a larger package of military and political threats such as that faced by Israel from the Arabs, and that posed by Nazi Germany to the Slavic countries. At lower levels of intensity, even the interplay of ideas and communication can produce politically significant societal and cultural threats, as illustrated by the reaction of Islamic fundamentalists to the penetration of Western ideas. Matters of language, religion and local cultural tradition all play their part in the idea of the state, and may need to be defended or protected against seductive or overbearing cultural imports. If the local culture is weak or small, even the unintended side-effects of casual contact could prove disruptive and politically charged.[5] Even so strong a

nation as the French fear the impact of American fast-food on their culinary her-itage, and the erosion of their language by the incorporation of English words.

The main difficulty with societal threats as a national security issue is that most of them occur within states. If societal security is about the sustainability, within acceptable conditions for evolution, of traditional patterns of language, cul-ture and religious and ethnic identity and custom, then threats to these values come much more frequently from within the state than from outside it. The state-nation process is often aimed at suppressing, or at least homogenizing, sub-state social identities, as countless examples attest. The Bulgarians suppress Turkish identity just as the Turks suppress Armenians and Kurds. The Baltic nationalities fear Russification, the Tibetans Sinification. Iraq massacres and relocates Kurds. Ancient Athenian democracy rested on a large class of slaves. Indonesia encour-ages Javanese migration into less heavily populated islands. Many countries have conducted or allowed programs against Jews or other alien minorities. Delicate ethnic balances, as in Fiji, Malaysia and Sri Lanka, can lead to systematic politi-cal discrimination and even civil war. Internal societal threats are symptomatic of weak states. They cannot really be counted as national security issues, except per-haps where they precipitate conflict between states. It is one of the awful contra-dictions of national security logic that the suppression of sub-national identities might well contribute, in the long run, to the creation of stronger and more viable states.

Economic

Economic threats are without doubt the trickiest and most difficult ones to handle within the framework of national security. The central problem with the idea of economic security is that the normal condition of actors in a market economy is one of risk, aggressive competition and uncertainty. With the virtual collapse of the centrally planned economies as an alternative to market-based ones, the mar-ket stands as the dominant model for sound economic practice. With all of its instabilities and imperfections, it is still the most effective mechanism yet discov-ered by which acceptable levels of production, distribution, innovation and growth can be sustained. In order to function efficiently, markets must impose continuous threats of bankruptcy to inefficient actors. In other words, the actors in a market economy have to be insecure if the system as a whole is to operate in such a way as to deliver wealth and welfare effectively. Herein lies the central paradox: if actors *must* be insecure, what can 'economic security' mean in a market context? A vast range of economic threats fall within the rules of the market game, and therefore cannot, in logic, be seen as exceptional enough to warrant invoking national security. Just where on the spectrum economic threats legitimately become national security issues is an extremely difficult, and highly political question. Invoking national security too frequently would simply mean increasing government intervention in the economy to a point where the market could no longer function.

A further complication is that the state is only one among many types of economic actor. This is especially so in a market economy, where the existence of a variety of independent actors also serves as a vital bulwark for pluralist democracy. But it means that the state's responsibilities and interests are nowhere near so clearly defined in the economic sector as they are in the political and military ones. Whether the government should seek to control the national economy, or steer it, or whether it should try to minimize its own role by maximizing freedom of both action and responsibility for other economic actors under its general aegis, are questions at the centre of many national political debates. Should governments intervene to protect industries that are unable to compete either because they are too new or too old? Should they focus research funding as a way of directing long-term development and enhancing competitiveness? Can they, indeed, do anything about the long-term forces that affect national economic rise and decline? Could the Athenians of classical times have done anything to stop their economic decline once olive and grape cultivation spread beyond Greece and took away their position as dominant supplier of oil and wine? Could any British government have stopped the long decline that arose from the legacy of old industrial plant and practices, plus the spread of industrialization to Germany, the United States and elsewhere?

The national economy is in one sense part of the physical base of the state. But it is also strongly connected to the organizing ideology and institutional components, as would-be reformers in the Council for Mutual Economic Assistance states of Eastern Europe discovered in depth during the late 1980s. Its dynamics are extremely complicated. Its susceptibility to quite dramatic fluctuations in performance is only poorly understood and, the pretensions of finance ministers and economic theorists notwithstanding, neither reliably predictable nor effectively controllable. Because of this, the economy presents a much more ambiguous target for threats than do more concrete elements like territory and government institutions. If one cannot determine the normal condition of something, and does not know exactly what measures help or hinder it, then it is hard to calculate what actions might pose threats to it. What might seem a threat in the short term, like oil embargoes or inflated prices, might turn out to be a boon in stimulating more rational energy-pricing policies and more energy-efficient technological developments over the longer run.

Therefore, within a market system, a huge number and variety of economic threats exist which cannot reasonably be construed as threats to national security. Fierce competition from foreign imports; restrictions against one's own exports; price, currency and interest rate manipulations; difficulties in obtaining credit; default on debts; and a host of other actions may have serious effects on the national economy. These range from balance of payment deficits and reductions of national income, to unwanted pressure on the interest rate and value of the currency and the destruction of long-established industries. But despite the severity of some consequences, these threats all fall within the merciless norms of economic activity within a competitive market. The huge opportunities opened up by participation in the global market can only be seized at the cost of increasing one's own vulnerabilities to the economic actions of others. Inability to compete or adapt is a risk of the game. Economic threats might thus be seen not just as emanating from the iniquitous acts of foreigners, but also as stemming from inept play on the part of those responsible for managing the nation's economic affairs. The negative consequences of participation have to be judged against the loss of stimulus, productivity and wealth that result from adopting autarkic policies.

Within the economic sector, then, economic threats fall very largely within the boundaries of normal conduct, and cannot easily or clearly be linked to the logic of national security. But when the consequences of economic threat reach beyond the strictly economic sector, into the military and political spheres, then three somewhat clearer national security issues can emerge. The linkages involved are between economic capability on the one hand, and military capability, power and socio-political stability on the other.

The link between economic and military capability is quite specific and well understood. A state's military capability rests not only on the supply of key strategic materials, but also on possession of an industrial base capable of supporting the armed forces. For major powers, this means an industrial establishment capable of manufacturing a wide spectrum of up-to-date weapons. When strategic materials must be obtained outside the state, threats to security of supply can be classified as a national security issue. Thus American military industries depend on supplies of manganese and nickel, neither of which is produced in the United States in significant quantities.[6] Concern over the reliability of supply partly underlies American interest in developing technology to obtain these minerals from the deep seabed. Similarly, the Royal Navy became dependent on supplies of various kinds of ship timber from overseas when domestic forests ceased to be able to cope with demand in the later days of sail. Threats to such supplies feed quite quickly through into military capability, and can thus almost be seen in the same light as military threats. Similarly, the economic decline of some basic industries such as steel, shipbuilding and electronics in the face of more efficient foreign producers raises questions about the ability of the state to support an appropriate range of independent military production. Being dependent on others for supplies of warships and fighters has quite different implications for a state than being dependent on external supplies of merchant ships or passenger aircraft. The desire to maintain, or acquire, production capability in key military related industries can easily insert a national security requirement into the management of the national economy.[7] This process can also work in the other direction, as is most conspicuously illustrated by nuclear power, when the pursuit of military research and development skews investment priorities in the civil economy.[8]

The second issue is in some senses just a much broader interpretation of the first. It concerns the link between the economy and not just specific military capabilities, but the overall power of the state within the international system. If the economy declines, then so, inevitably, must the state's power. Decline can occur as much from internal as from external causes. It may be virtually beyond the remedy of government policy, either because of the political inertia of inefficient behaviours within the state, or because of the unstoppable rise of newer powers elsewhere. In one sense, the absence of remedy for such a complex and large scale problem takes it beyond even the national security agenda. All of recorded history is a relentless catalogue of rising and declining powers.[9] The impossibility of any state holding top position for ever makes adjustment inevitable sooner or later. Even a sustained economic decline, like that of Britain, is not normally seen as a national security problem in its own right, though it cuts deeply into the state's military capability.

Nevertheless, economic capability is the crucial foundation on which the relative status of great powers in the system rests. Thus in times of intense power rivalry relative economic performance may come to be perceived as a national security issue regardless of the sense or wisdom of doing so. Britain and France feared the rapid economic expansion of Germany, and Germany feared that of Russia, from the later nineteenth century until the Second World War. Until the 1980s the United States feared the prospect of Soviet economic success providing the Soviet Union with a power base large enough to overawe American influence. Because of its military and political implications, the relative economic expansion of a rival power might have to be seen as a threat to the whole national security position. Doing so raises the danger underlined by Paul Kennedy that increasing military expenditure to offset the rising power of a rival may simply increase the speed with which one's own economic decline occurs.[10]

The third issue is of more recent concern, and involves what might loosely be called economic threats to domestic stability. These occur when states pursue economic strategies based on maximization of wealth through extensive trade. Over time, such policies result in high levels of dependence on trade in order to sustain the social structures that have grown up with increasing prosperity. Some countries become specialized as raw material producers, and depend on sales of their products, while others become industrial centres, and depend both on supplies of raw materials and on markets for their products. Australia, Gabon and Zaire are fairly extreme examples of the former type, while Japan, Singapore and Belgium exemplify the latter. Even countries with large domestic resources and markets, and a relatively small percentage of GNP in external trade, such as the United States, can become significantly locked into the structure of trade. Where such complex patterns of interdependence exist, many states will be vulnerable to disruptions in the flows of trade and finance.[11]

In a crude, direct way, such vulnerabilities give rise to fears of extortion, where states use their economic advantages to extract political concessions. The oil politics of the 1970s raised fear of this type of threat to considerable heights. But such fears are generally offset by the abundant mechanisms of competitive supply that exist in a global market. Except in rare cases, the diversity of the system tends to offer alternative suppliers and markets to undercut attempts to use economic levers for specific political purposes. Even the rather well-placed and well-organized oil cartel was defeated quite quickly in this way. Nevertheless, the risk of such vulnerabilities may create a national security rationale for avoiding excessive or asymmetrical dependencies that might offer political opportunities for the use of economic pressure.

In a much broader sense, the link between economy and political stability generates a set of wide-ranging questions about development that could, not unreasonably, be seen as national security issues. For developed states (i.e. efficient producers by the standards of the day), the concern is that because socio-political structures have come to depend on sustained growth rates and functional specialization, domestic political stability may be undermined by disturbances in the economic system as a whole.

For less developed states, the problem takes a much more immediate form. Because they are less efficient producers, they may find themselves locked into a cycle of poverty and underdevelopment from which there is no obvious escape. Terms of trade favour industrial products over raw materials, and late industrializers face markets already saturated with goods of a higher quality than they can produce for export. Drawing in external finance to support modernizing investments easily leads to insupportable debts, and a net drain of capital, as happened to many Third World countries during the 1970s and 1980s. Participation in the global market economy from such positions of weakness can lead to intolerable domestic pressures. Governments can find themselves having to choose between meeting their debt repayments, or fulfilling conditions for credit-worthiness, at the expense of lowering living standards that are already on the margins of survival for millions of people.

Because of its extreme and wide-ranging consequences, it may not be unreasonable to define this whole situation as a national security problem. Whether there is an advantage to doing so is another question, because there is no known solution to this problem on the national level. Dropping out of the global economy, as Burma did, or pursuing protectionist import substitution policies, as tried by Argentina and India, are just alternative routes to stagnation and unacceptably low levels of welfare. In describing the economic insecurity of economically underdeveloped states there is a kind of horrible truth in the aphorism that 'the only thing worse than being exploited is not being exploited'.

The argument that the whole system is a threat to the national security of less developed states blends into the Marxist critique that capitalism as a system is, in the long run, a threat both to everyone who participates in it, and to those who try to remain outside. But neither grand arguments on this scale, nor the invoking of national security by hard-pressed governments, will make any difference until the problem of development itself is better understood. Putting the whole of the national political economy into national security terms will almost certainly narrow debate. Consequently its principal effect is likely to be to increase the frequency of misguided, wasteful and counterproductive development schemes imposed by force. The experiments of the Khmer Rouge in Cambodia in the late 1970s are an extreme example, and the fruits of many lesser follies can be found rotting in much of Africa and Asia. It is this combination of global scale, deep crisis and theoretical ignorance that motivates attempts like those of the Palme

Brandt Commissions to approach these issues in the planetary terms of common security, rather than on the national security level.[12]

Thus although the case for economic threats to be counted as national security issues is, in some respects, plausible it must be treated with considerable caution. Economic threats do resemble an attack on the state, in the sense that conscious external actions by others results in material loss, strain on various institutions of the state, and even substantial damage to the health and longevity of the population. The parallel with a military attack cannot be sustained, however, because while a military attack crosses a clear boundary between peaceful and aggressive behaviour, an economic 'attack' does not. Aggressive behaviour is normal in economic affairs, and risks of loss are part of the price that has to be paid to gain access to opportunities for gain. From this perspective, economic threats are self-inflicted inasmuch as a choice is made to participate in a pattern of production and exchange in which such risks are endemic, though there is no escape here from the point that many countries have precious little choice about whether to participate or not.

Economic threats also raise once again the dilemma of distinguishing between domestic politics and national security: are other actors, or the economic system as a whole to blame, or do the causes of weak economic performance lie more within societies? If the answer is domestic, then it raises grounds for asking whether organizing ideologies are being improperly implemented, or whether they are in some way themselves basically flawed, a process highly visible in Gorbachev's newly transparent Soviet Union. The continued testing, questioning and modification of organizing ideologies are essentially domestic political matters. Within this process there is a real danger that sub-national vested interests such as declining industries, trade unions and local governments will try to usurp the idea of economic security for their own ends. Only occasionally will specific economic threats deserve to be ranked as a national security problem. Attempts to elevate particular economic issues onto the national security agenda should therefore be treated with suspicion as a matter of routine.[13] I will return to these issues at length in Chapter 6.

Ecological

Ecological threats to national security, like military and economic ones, can damage the physical base of the state, perhaps to a sufficient extent to threaten its idea and institutions. Traditionally, ecological threats have been seen as random, part of the natural conditions of life, and therefore more a matter of fate than an issue for the national security agenda.[14] Earthquakes, storms, plagues, floods, tidal waves, and droughts might inflict war-scale damage on a state, as recently happened in Bangladesh's floods and the Sahel states' droughts. But these were seen as part of the struggle of humans against nature, whereas national security issues arose much more from the struggle of humans with each other.

For most of history, the environment has been a relatively constant background factor rather than an issue in its own right. But with the dramatic increases in the scale, and diversity of human activity during the last century, and with the rapid expansion of knowledge about the planetary ecosystem, the environment is no longer a background factor. The increase in human activity is beginning visibly to affect the conditions for life on the planet. The expansion of knowledge, though still highly imperfect, makes events seem less random and more specifically attributable. The spewers of acids, greenhouse gasses and ozone-eating chlorofluorocarbons (CFCs) are identifiable actors. This steady uncovering of cause-effect relations puts ecological issues more and more into the human, and therefore political, arena.

Some of the smaller-scale ecological threats link activities within one state to effects in another. Trans-frontier pollution such as that between the United States and Canada or that along shared rivers such as the Rhine are one example. Deforestation in Nepal exacerbating floods in Bangladesh is another. Attempts at weather modification is an example which may become of greater importance in the not too distant future. The fact that these threats are unintentional differentiates them from most other kinds of threat, perhaps making them most similar to the structural threats that occur in the political and economic sectors. But their consequences may be serious, and it is not difficult to imagine the issue of allocations of water along rivers such as the Nile, the Mekong and the Indus becoming causes for the use of military force.

Larger-scale ecological threats are more difficult to fit within the national security framework. The weakening of the ozone layer and the greenhouse warming of the atmosphere are global phenomena with global consequences. Should these threats materialize in any substantial way, however, some states would bear the brunt of them. Low-lying countries such as the Netherlands, Bangladesh, the Maldives and some parts of Egypt would face catastrophe from even quite minor rises in sea level. Significant warming would also alter the distribution of rainfall, possibly wiping out some now highly productive agricultural areas, such as those in the United States Midwest, while raising the productive potential of others in Canada and the Soviet Union. This logic leads quite quickly to the possibility of massive transformations in the conditions of human life on the planet. Substantial warming, which means only a few degrees, could drive sea levels up by many tens of metres. Substantial cooling could trigger a return of the ice-age. Either event would totally change the geography of human habitation, and in doing so would sweep away many of the existing social and political structures of the international system.

Very few states have the capability to control these macro-developments by themselves, and so the appeal to national security has no practical logic unless it can be linked to collective action. A collective security approach, however, raises deeply political questions of its own. If the ecosystem is a random variable, then all can accept their part in it as a matter of fate. But if it becomes, as it is doing, a variable subject to human manipulation, then the distribution of costs and benefits becomes an intensely political matter. Some, such as the Soviet Union and Canada, might benefit from a bit of warming, and be seriously threatened by any cooling. For others, such as Mauritania and Mali, the reverse might be true. Add to this volatile situation the errors and imperfections of any early attempts to manipulate climate, and it is easy to see that global consensus is not the obvious response to this problem. With consequences so possibly vast it is not at all impossible to envisage quite near futures in which ecological threats have the same standing as military ones, and in which military and environmental techniques play interactively in relations between states.

This array of military, political, societal, economic and ecological threats does not constitute a static agenda for national security. Indeed, it is the rather dramatic changes in priority among them that are the main driving force behind the shift from the narrow military agenda of Strategic Studies to the broader one of International Security Studies. Military threats still retain a theoretical primacy in security thinking, and so long as international politics is anarchically structured, they will remain of vital interest and importance. But in practice, and especially for the most developed states in the system, their relevance is declining compared to threats in other sectors. Concern about military security traditionally masked underlying issues of political and societal threat.[15] With the nuclear paralysis imposed on the rational use of force among the great powers, political and societal security issues have come more to the foreground in their own right. As the military security agenda has become more static, those for economics and the ecology have become more dynamic and more central to day-to-day concerns. Higher densities of human activity and interaction have increased both practical interdependence and general awareness of events worldwide. The linkage of economic and environmental events throughout the system is becoming increasingly visible, ranging from weather patterns and acid rain to interest rates, currency values and stock market prices.

All of these developments, from the nuclear mightiness-plus-impotence of the superpowers, to the entanglement of Third World debt with both the financial stability of the West and schemes for environmental conservation, point to the centrality of interdependence in security issues. If interdependence is central, then national security policies aimed at reducing vulnerability can by definition be only part of any reasoned response to the issues raised. Dealing with security interdependence in all sectors requires also that the sources of threat be addressed.

THE OPERATION OF THREATS

The question of when a threat becomes a national security issue depends not just on what type of threat it is, and how the recipient state perceives it, but also on the intensity with which the threat operates. The main factors affecting the intensity of a threat are the specificity of its identity, its nearness in space and time, the probability of its occurring, the weight of its consequences and whether or not perceptions of the threat are amplified by historical circumstances. Other things being equal, the more intense a threat, the more legitimate the invoking of national security as a response to it. The problem, of course, is that not all of these variables can be measured, or even estimated, accurately, and that they frequently occur in complex mixtures which make overall weighting on the spectrum of intensity a highly problematic exercise.

Specific threats have a clear focus and source. Examples are that which the British saw in the German navy between the turn of the century and the First World War, and that which the strategic nuclear arsenals of the United States and the Soviet Union have posed to each other since the 1960s. Diffuse threats arise from processes, rather than from a particular actor, object or policy. Thus the spread of communism (or capitalism), nuclear proliferation (both weapons and civil power technology), terrorism, economic depressions and the greenhouse effect are all examples of broad processes which are frequently identified as threats.

The spatial placement of threats can be seen in terms of range. Is the source of threat an immediate neighbour, as for Iran and Iraq, North and South Korea and Greece and Turkey? Is it at some middle distance, as Japan was for the United States during the 1930s, or as communism in Vietnam seemed to many Americans during the 1960s? Or is it remote, as Czechoslovakia seemed to Chamberlain in 1938? Range applies most intensely to military threats, because territorial closeness correlates strongly with ability to undertake effective military action. This correlation has somewhat declined in importance with the development of long-range strike weapons, and policies of state terrorism. It can also be affected by alliance considerations (the Anglo-Japanese alliance of 1902) and concerns about lines of trade and communication (such as major straits). But strategic adjacency is still highly relevant for the small and medium powers that make up the bulk of the international community. Pakistan worries about India, because it is next door, whereas India does not figure at all in Sudan's concerns.

Range is also relevant to political threats, as indicated by uncomfortable juxtapositions such as East and West Germany, North and South Korea, Iran and the Gulf States and India and Pakistan. The relevance of range in the military and political sectors underlines the problems of weak states, where the sources of threat are actually within the territorial boundaries. Range is much less relevant to economic threats, though strong arguments to the contrary might come from those located close to centres of economic power, such as Canada in relation to the United States. For most states, range is a direct function of distance. But for some, especially those great powers who view their security in global terms, range can reflect other priorities as well. In 1938 Britain saw Czechoslovakia as 'a faraway country', at the same time as it placed one frontier of its own security on the Himalayas. Similarly, the Gulf is a high priority for the United States despite its great distance away.

Temporal range concerns distance in time rather than space. Is the threat an immediate one, or will it take some time to develop or be implemented? Some threats are fairly easy to assess in this way, and some are not. The British, for example, could calculate the timing of the naval threat from Germany before 1914 by working out construction rates for dreadnoughts in the German shipyards. Perhaps the most famous example here is the mobilization timetables which played such a large part in the security perceptions of the European great powers before 1914.[16] Other kinds of threat, however, are temporally complex. Nobody really knows how far in the future drastic climate change might be, and neither do we know with any certainty how far in advance responses will have to be prepared in order to be cost-effective. Many threats, especially those of a process kind, display few temporal certainties. Thus threats such as nuclear proliferation, the arms race, pollution, over-population and economic stagnation, tend to be, or to be seen as being, in a constant state of becoming worse. Since there is no reliable way of assessing the risk from these threats, they generate endless arguments about the level of priority and immediacy they should be accorded.

Many threats, including that of a nuclear strike, have two temporal characteristics. The first is precise, in that it is known how many minutes the threat will take to implement once a decision is taken to do so. The second is highly uncertain, in that the threat may remain in being indefinitely, and there is no way of telling at what time, if ever, it will be used. Threats by OPEC to cut off oil supplies fit this pattern, as do most threats of military attack. At this juncture, the logic of temporal range blends into that of probability: what is the chance that any given threat will, in fact, be carried out? Calculating probability for most types of national security threat is a notoriously uncertain business. Was there a high probability that the Soviet Union would invade Western Europe during the forty years following 1945? Is global warming a certainty? Is the world trading and financial system on the verge of collapse? Nobody knows for sure, yet policy decisions have to be made.

In assessing threats, probability has to be weighed against consequences. How serious will the consequences be if the threat is carried out? During the Vietnam War the North Vietnamese had to make calculations of this kind all the time. If they continued, or escalated, their campaign in the South, what would be the probability of an American counter-escalation, and what would be the consequent damage inflicted on the North if such counter-escalation occurred? They must have calculated that the probability of a major escalation, for example to nuclear weapons, was low, and therefore that the risk was worth running even though the consequences would be catastrophic if the Americans did in fact resort to nuclear weapons. Where the probabilities were higher, as with increased levels of conventional bombing, the North Vietnamese calculated that the consequences were acceptable in the light of their larger objectives.

Threat assessments of this type lie at the heart of security policy. Accurate assessment of either risks or probabilities, however, requires an ability to predict that is notoriously lacking in international relations. The universal preparations for a short sharp war in 1914, British and French assessments of the risk from Hitler before 1939, the American conduct of the war in Vietnam and Iraq's attempt at a quick victory over Iran in 1979, illustrate both the weakness of prediction and the lack of progress towards improvement. Even if prediction is possible, the assessment of threat intensity is tricky. Nuclear deterrence logic exemplifies the difficulties with its attempt to weigh the impact of high probabilities of moderate threats against low probabilities of very large threats.[17]

Threats also have an historical dimension which adds further to the complexities of assessment. One aspect of this affects how threats are perceived. A threat which resonates with the historical experience of a state may well be amplified by the heightened sensitivity thus created. The Russians fear land invasions because of their submergence by the Mongols in the thirteenth century, and three major invasions from the west in 1812, 1915 and 1941. The French fear German invasions because of experiences in 1870, 1914 and 1940. The Americans fear surprise attack because of Pearl Harbor. The Japanese share British fears of blockade, in both cases because of the devastation of their merchant fleet by enemy submarines. The British are sensitive to threats from dictators, because of being duped by Hitler at Munich. The Germans fear inflation because of their experience in the 1920s. Greeks fear Turks for reasons going back millennia before even the fall of Byzantium in 1453. Such fears easily cloud rational judgement, and lead to certain kinds of threat being given higher priority than they objectively warrant.

The other historical aspect of threats is that they do not remain constant over time, but change in response to both new developments in the means of threats, and to evolutions in states which alter the nature of their vulnerabilities. Raymond Aron refers to this phenomenon as the 'law of change', which he defined as being that 'the military, demographic or economic value of a territory varies with the techniques of combat and production, with human relations and institutions'.[18] Military technology provides the easiest, but not the only, illustration of this point. Weapons of a certain type are characteristic of any given historical period, and the particular capabilities of these weapons largely defines the nature of military security problems which states face at that time. Unless defences are continuously evolved to meet new capabilities, military security deteriorates rapidly. Fortified castles and cities provided a good measure of military security before the introduction of gunpowder and cannon, but the high, relatively thin walls which served against the pre-gunpowder techniques of siege provided ideal targets for artillery. Similarly, Britain remained secure behind the wooden walls of its ships of the line for several centuries, but by the middle of the nineteenth century, a host of developments in steam power, metal construction and gunnery began to make such vessels obsolete. By 1870, only a fool would have considered venturing out in a wooden-hulled, sail-powered ship to offer serious battle to an enemy equipped with modern naval forces. Changes of this type affect the whole system, because the first to introduce a new military technology holds a possibly decisive advantage over all those who fail to adapt to it.[19]

The character of political and economic threats also changes over time in response to developments in the internal structures of states. In many parts of the world, for example, threats to territory have declined because the historical trend of nationalism has increased the identity between land and people, thereby reducing the political acceptability of annexations. This situation contrasts markedly with that prevailing in the nineteenth, eighteenth and earlier centuries, when boundaries were much more fluid, and the main significance of territorial transfers derived from their impact on the balance of power. Note, for example, Israel's difficulty in establishing the legitimacy of its territorial conquests. Similarly, the shift away from forms of government based on hereditary principles, towards forms based on representation and/or ideology, has changed the prevailing character of political threats. Intrigues over the lineages of succession no longer occupy centre stage as they once did in the murky borderlands between domestic and international politics. Instead, mutual meddling takes place in the broader context of political factions, party politics, elections, insurgency and manipulation of public opinion. The threat has broadened from fear of foreign interference in the affairs of the ruling family to fears of external corruption of mass politics.

Economic threats have changed not only as states have become less self-reliant in being able to maintain their norms of domestic welfare, but also as the nature and source of trade materials have changed according to the economic requirements of the day. Things like oil, mineral ores, computers and automobiles have replaced things like silk, tea, opium and ship timbers as main items of trade, though many things like food, money, weapons and textiles have retained a continuing importance. These changes, plus the continuing evolution in the economic roles and capabilities of states, produce a dynamic pattern of interests and vulnerabilities which requires continuous updates and revisions in the assessment of economic threats. The Soviet Union can, to some extent, be threatened by embargoes on food and high-technology exports, the United States can be threatened by restrictions on oil exports or reversals in the inward flow of foreign capital. Britain, as was demonstrated in the 1956 Suez crisis, has become vulnerable to financial pressure, and many countries, particularly in the Third World, are vulnerable to price manipulations, fluctuations in demand for their export products and squeezes on credit. As interdependence deepens throughout the system, economic threats such as suspensions of credit, exclusion from markets and denial of key imports can begin to take on the swiftness and impact previously associated only with military threats, though rather few states are powerfully enough placed in the international economy to be able to use economic threats in this way.

The effect of these factors on the intensity of threats, and therefore on their legitimacy as national security issues, can be summed up as in Table 3.2.

Table 3.2: The intensity of threats

Low intensity	High intensity
Diffuse	Specific
Distant (space)	Close (space)
Distant (time)	Close (time)
Low probability	High probability
Low consequences	High consequences
Historically neutral	Historically amplified

CONCLUSIONS: THE AMBIGUITY OF THREATS

Most threats in the international arena involve a host of complex factors which make both their direct outcome and their broad consequences highly uncertain. This complexity increases as threats begin to interact with the measures taken to meet them, a process most clearly illustrated by arms racing and trade wars. Even if information was not limited and distorted, as it is, and even if subjective perceptions accorded with reality, which they often do not, the complexities of threats would still defy accurate prediction and assessment. Objectively minor events, like Soviet restrictions on access to West Berlin, can assume major symbolic dimensions in the calculus of Soviet-American rivalry, while objectively enormous threats, like that of global climate change, may get pushed down the priority list because of their diffuse, uncertain and unorthodox character. Bureaucratic traditions, inertia and divisions of labour also impinge on this process. Most states are bureaucratically much better equipped to be sensitive to military threats than they are to environmental ones.

Additional to these problems is the natural propensity of those responsible for national security to hedge their bets by thinking in worst-case terms. Worst-case analyses have the advantage not only of reflecting a prudent distrust of other actors in the system – a position easily justified by reference to history – but also of creating a strong position in the domestic struggle for allocation of resources. The American military establishment, for example, has without doubt been the foremost advocate of the strength and effectiveness of the Soviet armed forces.[20] One might even argue that states need to be threatened. If no threats existed, part of the state's basic Hobbesian function would disappear. Given the mutually constituting character of states and the international system, this logic points either to an anarchic utopia, or to the collapse of government and the rise of civil disorder.

One can conclude that national insecurity is a highly complicated phenomenon. Each state exists, in a sense, at the hub of a whole universe of threats. These threats define its insecurity by the way they interact with its vulnerabilities, and set the agenda for national security as a policy problem. They do not, unfortunately, constitute a clear set of calculable, constant and comparable risks like those faced by players of chess or bridge. Because international threats are so ambiguous, and because knowledge of them is limited, national security policy-making is necessarily a highly imperfect art. It requires constant monitoring and assessment, and the development of criteria for deciding when threats become of sufficient intensity to warrant action. Since threats can be found everywhere, and since national security resources are limited, some cut-off point has to be set below which threats are considered inconsequential or worthy only of monitoring.

The possible range of choice is still huge because, depending on one's resources, and on one's willingness to allocate them to national security, one can choose between a relatively passive policy of waiting until threats loom large, or a relatively active policy of meeting them while they are still small, or merely potential. Since threats increase in number the harder one looks for them, and since there is a tendency to adopt a worst-case view, an active policy has no theoretical limit. It raises the dangers of exhaustion, paranoia, creation of an aggressive appearance to others and unnecessary concern about low-level threats which, left to themselves, might well never develop into larger problems. An excessively passive policy, on the other hand, raises the danger that threats will become too large to deal with except at great cost, although it has the significant advantage of allowing serious threats to separate themselves out from minor ones. US policy offers a partial illustration of these two extremes: excessively passive during the 1920s and 1930s, until bombs were dropping on Pearl Harbor and a massive effort was necessary to turn the tide; excessively active after 1947, finding threats to American security in almost every corner of the globe.[21]

Since threats can only be assessed in relation to a particular state as a target, security policy has to take into account not only the threats themselves, but also the vulnerabilities of the state as an object of security. This is no straightforward matter especially for weak states. Cause-effect relations between threats and vulnerabilities are poorly understood at best, even for relatively calculable forms like military attack. During the Cold War no one knew how a Soviet attack on Western Europe would unfold, just as no one knew that the First World War would end up stalemated in the trenches, or that the Second World War would not be started by aerial gas attacks against cities. For economic and political threats, the problem of distinguishing threats from normal, or at least acceptable activity is much more difficult to begin with. Any sound security policy must, as suggested at the beginning of this chapter, address threats in both these ways: dealing with them as they come, such as reducing vulnerability by preparing defences against invasion; and dealing with their causes, such as seeking peaceful settlement of the dispute. The problems that the profound ambiguity of threats pose for national security policy-making will be taken up in more detail in Chapter 8.

NOTES

1. Kjell Goldmann offers a similar scheme in *Det Intemationella Systemet* (Stockholm: Aldus, 1978), p. 64, quoted in Bengt Sundelius, 'Coping with structural security threats', in Otmar Höll (ed.), *Small States in Europe and Dependence* (Vienna: Austrian Institute for International Affairs, 1983), p. 298.
2. For a useful discussion of the military problems of weak powers, see Michael Handel, *Weak States In The International System* (London: Cass, 1981), pp. 77–94.
3. On threats, see: C. F. Doran, K. Q. Hill and K. Mladenka, 'Threat, status disequilibrium and national power', *British Journal of International Studies*, 5:1 (1979); Kenneth Boulding, 'Toward a theory of peace', in Roger Fisher (ed.), *International Conflict and Behavioural Science* (New York: Basic Books, 1964), ch. 4; Dieter Senghaas, 'Towards an analysis of threat policy in international relations', *German Political Studies*, 1 (1974), pp. 59–103; and Ken Booth 'New challenges and old mind-sets: ten rules for empirical realists', in Carl Jacobson (ed.), *The Uncertain Course: New weapons, strageqies, and mind-sets* (Oxford:

Oxford University Press for SIPRI, 1987) pp. 39–66.

4. See Barry Buzan and Gowher Rizvi, *et al.*, *South Asian Insecurity and the Great Powers* (London: Macmillan, 1986).

5. On this theme, see K. J. Holsti, *Why Nations Realign* (London: Allen and Unwin, 1982).

6. For an argument against excessive emphasis on the security of strategic resources in the American case, see Charles L. Schultz, 'The economic content of national security policy'; *Foreign Affairs,* 51:3 (1973), esp. pp. 522–9.

7. For a fuller exploration of the link between industrial policy and defence concerns, see Gautam Sen, *The Military Origins of Industrialization and International Trade Rivalry* (London: Pinter, 1984).

8. Barry Buzan and Gautam Sen, 'The impact of military research and development priorities on the evolution of the civil economy in capitalist states', *Review of International Studies*, 16:4 (1990).

9. On this theme, see William H. McNeill, *The Rise of the West* (Chicago: University of Chicago Press, 1963) and *The Pursuit of Power* (Chicago: University of Chicago Press, 1982); and Paul Kennedy, *The Rise and Fall of the Great Powers* (London: Fontana, 1988). For an argument against the simple correlation of economic growth with military power, see James R. Schlesinger, 'Economic growth and national security', in F. A. Sonderman, W. C. Olson and T. S. McLellan (eds), *The Theory and Practice of International Relations* (Englewood Cliffs, NJ: Prentice Hall, 1970), pp. 155–64.

10. Kennedy, *ibid.*, pp. xv-xvi.

11. See R. O. Keohane and J. S. Nye, *Power and Interdependence*, (Boston: Little Brown, 1977), esp. chs 1 and 2; Edward L. Morse, 'Interdependence in world affairs', in J. N. Rosenau, K. W. Thompson and G. Boyd (eds), *World Politics* (New York: Free Press, 1976), ch. 28; and 'Crisis diplomacy, interdependence, and the politics of international economic relations', in Raymond Tanter and Richard Ullman (eds), *Theory and Policy in International Relations* (Princeton, NJ: Princeton University Press, 1972); Wolfram F. Hanrieder, 'Dissolving international politics: reflections on the nation-state', *American Political Science Review*, 72:4 (1978); Kenneth N. Waltz, 'The myth of interdependence' in Charles P. Kindleberger, *The International Corporation* (Cambridge, Mass.: MIT Press, 1970); Barry Buzan, 'Interdependence and Britain's external relations' in Lawrence Freedman and Mike Clarke (eds), *Britain in the World* (Cambridge, Cambridge University Press 1991).

12. The Report of the Independent Commission on Disarmament and Security Issues, *Common Security: A programme for disarmament* (London: Pan, 1982); The Reports of the Independent Commission on International Development Issues, *North-South: A programme for survival, and Common Crisis: North-South cooperation for world recovery* (London: Pan, 1980, 1983).

13. For a useful review of this area, see Klaus Knorr and Frank N. Trager (eds), *Economic Issues and National Security* (Lawrence: Regents Press of Kansas, 1977).

14. It is interesting to note, however, that the National Security Council in the United States takes an interest in earthquakes, and even commissioned a study of earthquake risks in California. *Science News*, 119:16 (18 April 1981), p. 254.

15. See Barry Buzan, Morten Kelstrup, Pierre Lemaitre, Elzbieta Tromer and Ole Wæver, *The*

European Security Order Recast: Scenarios for the post-Cold War era (London: Pinter, 1990), chs 1–2.

16. On which, see Maurice Pearton, *The Knowledgeable State* (London: Burnett, 1982), pp. 69–76, 117–39.

17. See Barry Buzan, *An Introduction to Strategic Studies* (London: Macmillan, 1987), ch. 12.

18. Quoted in Frank N. Trager and Philip S. Kronenberg (eds) *National Security and American Society: Theory, process and policy* (Lawrence: University Press of Kansas, 1973), p. 59.

19. For a detailed treatment of this theme, and a guide to sources, see Buzan, *op. cit.* (note 17), chs 2–4.

20. See, for example, *Soviet Military Power*, US Department of Defense annually.

21. Stanley Hoffmann made the interesting argument that the range of security policy expands not only with the growth of power, but also as a result of expanded perceptions of vulnerability and threat. He saw the range of Soviet security policy expanding for the former reason, and that of the United States for the latter. See 'Security in an age of turbulence: means of response', in 'Third World-conflict and international security', Part II *Adelphi Papers*, no. 167 (London: IISS, 1981), pp. 4–5.

chapter four | security and the international political system

The previous three chapters focused on the attributes of the pieces in the great game of international relations. This chapter and the next two will focus more on the nature of the board in terms of the systems that contain and shape the behaviour of states.

THE NATURE OF THE INTERNATIONAL ANARCHY

Because states are essentially political constructs, the international political system is the most important part of the environment of states. Indeed, the political connection between states and system is so intimate that one is at risk of introducing serious misperception even by speaking of states *and* the international system as if they were distinct entities. Although they are distinguishable for some analytical purposes, states and the international system represent opposite ends of a continuous political phenomenon. The international political system is an anarchy, which is to say that its principal defining characteristic is the absence of overarching government. The principal defining feature of states is their sovereignty, or their refusal to acknowledge any political authority higher than themselves. The essential character of states thus defines the nature of the international political system, and the essential character of the political system reflects the nature of states. If units are sovereign, their system of association must be anarchy, and if the system is anarchic, its members must reject overarching government.

This link is much more than a glib tautology. It means that the state and system levels are inextricably associated with each other, and that problems which appear to arise from the anarchic nature of the system cannot be treated purely as systemic matters. If the international anarchy is to be criticized as a system, then one cannot avoid extending the critique to the basic character of the states which comprise the system. If states are thought desirable as the main form of human political organization, then anarchy is the necessary and inevitable systemic consequence. In historical perspective, sovereign states and international anarchy are mutually constitutive in that each generates and shapes the other. By defining and defending themselves, states construct and maintain an anarchic system. The anarchic system in turn sets the structure that defines the competitive, self-help, political environment within which states have to operate. This dynamic interplay begins from the point at which alien human communities first make contact with each other, which is when the idea of system comes into play. It only ends when the international anarchy gives way to a world state, a point still set in the rather remote future. In between these two points, the mutually constitutive dynamic between state and system structure sustains the durability of anarchy.[1]

The alternatives to an anarchic international political system are either no system or a unitary system of some sort, whether a world empire or a world federation. Neither seems likely. Short of some gigantic catastrophe like nuclear war, the human race is unable to go back to pre-anarchic systems where the level of contact among political units is too low to justify the notion of an international political system. In the other direction, neither present conditions nor apparent trends favour a move towards world government. The distribution of power has become more diffuse, and the number of independent states has increased rather than decreased, both trends leading away from any possibility of hegemonic or imperial systemic unification. Nor is there any sign of sufficient political consensus on an organizing ideology around which to base a federative global polity. Nationalism and religion remain potent political fragmenters in most parts of the planet. The pretensions of communism to be a transcendent unifying ideology have collapsed. Capitalism is historically associated with anarchic structure. Anarchy, per-force, remains the dominant international political structure.

Given this fact, one needs to examine the nature of the anarchy in some detail in order to understand its role in the problem of national security. The choice between anarchy and world government (hierarchy) is not a choice between insecurity and security, but one between different types of security problem. Under anarchy, the problem is the threat of violence and intervention between states. The political dynamics are usually oligarchic, the system being dominated by relations among a relatively small group of great powers. Under hierarchy the problems occur within the world state, in the form of disputes over the control and distribution of power, such as those that occurred within the Roman and Chinese 'universal' empires. Anarchy is nevertheless a politically emotive concept. Its basic definition as the absence of government implies that it is a negative condition, along the lines of poverty and illness, which is characterized by a deficiency of some positively valued or normal attribute, in these cases, order, wealth and health. The popular use of anarchy as a synonym for chaos and disorder reinforces its negative image. This prevalent view of anarchy produces a misleading conception of how the international system works.

As argued in the Introduction (p. 39), in relation to the international system anarchy should be used in the strict meaning of absence of central government. This absence describes a structural condition that favours competitive relations, but it contains no necessary inference of chaos or disorder. The association between anarchy and chaos arises from the Hobbesian image of humankind in the state of nature.[2] Under such conditions, and because of the acute vulnerability of individuals, anarchy seems quite likely to result in chaos. But as already argued, the analogy between individuals and states is false in so many respects that it cannot be used to support a parallel set of assumptions about states. An anarchy among states may or may not result in chaos, but certainly does not necessarily, or even probably do so. Because states are much larger, more durable, more easily defended, more self-contained, fewer in number and less mobile than individuals, an anarchic system among them has a much better chance of avoiding chaos than does a similar system among individuals.

The structure of international anarchy does not therefore automatically determine a single overriding quality (chaos) in relations within a system of sovereign states. Instead, it simply sets some basic political characteristics (fragmented, competitive) of such relations. Within the framework set by these characteristics, a vast range of patterns and qualities of international relations might emerge or be built. The fact that a single structural form can be expressed in a wide variety of ways is central to the analysis of security at the system level. It means that the international anarchy is not itself the essence of the security problem. Rather than being seen as the problem to be solved, anarchy can more correctly, and more usefully, be seen as describing the form in which the security problem comes. Because it is only the form, and not the problem, the elimination of anarchy is neither a necessary nor a desirable part of the solution to the problem of insecurity. Indeed, because it is durable, available and diverse, anarchy has much to recommend it as the framework within which to seek solutions to insecurity.

Anarchy sets the form within which nearly all plausible approaches and solutions to the security problem have to be pursued. But while a system may have a single structure, like anarchy, knowledge of that structure alone does not allow one to infer much about the detailed character of security relations within it. Anarchy does not determine outcomes on the spectrum from insecurity to security except to deny the dominance of either extreme over the system as a whole (though not over some parts). Extreme system-wide insecurity is almost impossible within international anarchy because, as discussed in Chapter 1, the state structures protect most people from the terrors of Hobbesian vulnerability most of the time. Extreme security is likewise almost impossible because the political fragmentation of anarchy always contains the possibility that one actor will move against the core interests of another. Absolute security is anyway not achievable, and rarely desired, in human existence. Between these two extremes, all security outcomes are possible under anarchy. This conclusion points to the questions: What factors make the difference? What other conditions or qualities of life in the international system act to increase or decrease levels of security?

Sketching out the beginning of an answer to these questions occupies most of the rest of this book, and requires a tour of many major areas in the literature of International Studies. The short answer is that one cannot understand the security problem without understanding much about the workings and structure of the international system as a whole. The broadly political variables will be dealt with in this chapter, except for the question of regional security which is sufficiently in need of development to warrant a chapter of its own. The economic variables will be considered in Chapter 6, and the military ones in Chapters 7 and 8.

The most basic place to start is with the relationship of anarchy to the idea of system. Waltz's definition of system as comprising units, interactions and structure helps to set this relationship into a clear perspective.[3] Anarchy falls within the structural component of system. It tells us how the parts, or units (in this case states) are ordered, how they stand in relation to each other. All it tells us about the units themselves is that there are at least two of them, and that they recognize no overarching government. All it tells us about interaction is that there is enough of it to give meaning to the idea of system. Clearly, there is already a vast scope for different anarchic systems simply in the range of possibilities for units and interactions. An anarchic system could be composed of 2 or 200 or 2,000 states. A system of two states would almost certainly mean that both were big powers, but as the numbers rise, so too does the probability that political fragmentation will reflect an uneven distribution of power. The present-day system has fewer than 200 states, but by almost any reasonable measure of power the most and least powerful are separated by several orders of magnitude. With higher numbers, both geographical diversity and historical tendency suggest that power is unlikely to be distributed evenly, and more likely to be divided between a few strong and many weak members. Such variations make a very substantial difference to the character of security relations within the system, and the literature on them will be examined below.

Differences in the intensity of interaction are equally important in mediating the security implications of anarchy. The level of interaction necessary to bring a system into being is probably rather low.[4] International systems exist even when the speed and volume of interaction are constrained by the transportation and communication capabilities of horse and sail. The dialectic of threats and vulnerabilities is strongly shaped by the technologies of interaction. Low carrying capacity, limited range and slow and unreliable communication restrict the possibilities for trade and investment, and war. This makes for a strategic environment with many insulating qualities, as illustrated by the long history prior to 1500 of extremely tenuous contact between the major centre of civilization in China, and those in South Asia, the Middle East and Europe.

Compare, for example, the global intensity of economic, societal and military interaction between the fifteenth and late twentieth centuries. In our time, the pattern of interaction has become unprecedentedly dense. Rising density is driven by a combination of increasing population, and increasing technological, organizational and financial capabilities and incentives for action. Density is about more people doing more things. It means that people's activities are more likely to impinge on the conditions of other people's existence, both intentionally (advertising, propaganda, trade, war) and unintentionally (traffic accidents, noise, unemployment, cultural imperialism), and positively (trade, knowledge) as well as negatively (pollution, economic depression).

Rising density is measurable across most of the sectors of security. Military capabilities have reached levels where it is possible for the major powers both to involve the whole planet in conflict, and to inflict levels of destruction that could eliminate the human species. In the political sphere, ideas now circulate globally, many issues are discussed in global or semi-global forums as a matter of routine, and the model of the industrial democracies has emerged as a kind of universal holy grail of development, albeit by very different routes.[5] Economically, the world is increasingly tied into a global market of production, trade and finance, whose circulation system is an ever more efficient transportation network by land, sea and air, and whose nervous system is a world-wide web of electronic communication and data processing facilities. Environmentally, the collective impact of human activity is producing effects of regional and global scale, in the process creating both common fates and a need for collective action.

The pattern of density follows that of power in being unevenly distributed. Both correlate with the distribution of developed and developing states. The difference, however, is that the pattern of density is more embracing and less dividing than the distribution of power. Centres of great power signify separateness, and the reinforcement of political fragmentation. Density is by definition about what ties the centres of power together. Barring major global disasters the pattern of density can be expected to continue its relentless increase.

How does rising density affect the general character of international relations within an anarchic structure? This question defines the central concerns of the liberal (and more recently neoliberal) view of the international system.[6] The principal political impact of rising density is to increase the levels of interdependence among states across a broad spectrum. In the military sphere, states depend for their survival on the restraint of their rivals, nowhere more so than in the context of mutual nuclear deterrence. In the economic sphere, they depend for their prosperity and development on complex patterns of access to external markets, resources and credit. In the environmental sphere, they increasingly depend on each other to adopt restraint towards ecologically damaging activities. Interdependence makes relationships costly to disrupt. It also gives states an expanded repertoire of instruments with which they can influence each other's behaviour. Interdependence is unlikely to reduce conflict, and may increase it by giving states a broader agenda of issues over which their interests and circumstances will differ. But where interdependence is strong, it should reduce incentives to resort to armed force. Such a resort is costly not only in itself, but also in its consequences. In addition, armed force is unlikely to be a well-tuned instrument for many interdependence issues.[7]

This line of reasoning points towards the conclusion that rising density will, other things being equal, tend to lower the salience of military security, and raise the salience of non-military aspects of security on the foreign policy agenda. The natural pressure of rising density is away from the military security-driven imperative of 'look after yourself!', and towards the more economic imperative: 'specialize!'.[8] This logic is apparent in the current diffusion away from advanced industrial countries of basic industries such as steel and shipbuilding, and in the international stratification of production for major goods such as computers, aircraft, cars, and even armaments.[9] I will return to these themes in Chapter 6.

Because anarchic structure is only a part, albeit a very fundamental one, of the international system as a whole, it is not surprising that it provides only one component of security analysis. The structure of the system defines only the general form of the security problem with none of its details. In broad system terms, the security impact of anarchy is strongly mediated by both the pattern of fragmentation and the density of interaction. The idea that the security consequences of anarchy depend on how the raw fact of anarchy is mediated by other variables can be pursued by looking at three relatively well-developed areas of debate about the political constituents of the security problem: the character of states, the effect of the distribution of power and the impact of international society.

THE CHARACTER OF STATES

will complete any review

Waltz has argued that proper systemic theories should not concern themselves with the character of the units which compose the system.[10] But this distinction is based on Waltz's own confusion of system and structure. While it is true that the character of units is excluded from structure, it is by definition not true of system (system = units + interaction + structure).[11] The basic character of the units (sovereignty) and of the system (anarchy) are closely linked. Unit-level explanations for state behaviour (i.e. those based on the internal qualities and dynamics of the state) are self-evidently important to security analysis. They are part of the system level inasmuch as the general character of the states in the system makes a difference to the quality of security relations.

As argued in Chapter 2, the most striking feature of states as a class is their diversity in terms of size, culture, power, political cohesion, ideology, geography and suchlike. This diversity provides one potent justification for maintaining the anarchic international structure. A completely homogeneous state system would have no reason other than the logic of 'small is beautiful' to remain politically fragmented. The potential security consequences of political homogeneity are captured by Marxian, liberal and religious theories that postulate an end to war if only all states would conform to the ideology of preference. While there is some historical evidence to support the theory that liberal democracies do not go to war with each other, advocates for communism, Islam or Christianity are hard put to make their case on empirical grounds. So far, however, the international system has proved remarkably resistant to ideological homogeneity, and remarkably fruitful in generating grounds for political differentiation. If there are any security advantages from ideological homogeneity, they are unlikely to be obtainable.

In thinking about the state-level factors which influence the security environment, two other characteristics are helpful: the difference between *weak* and *strong* states discussed in Chapter 2; and the size of states raised in the discussion of fragmentation above.

As argued in Chapter 2, the building of strong states (those with high levels of socio-political cohesion) is a necessary, though not sufficient, condition for achieving adequate levels of national security. The distinction between weak and strong states affects the political structure of the international political system because the whole idea of anarchy is precisely about the nature and pattern of political fragmentation. Where states are strong, the pattern of fragmentation is clear and provides a firm basis for relations between states. Where they are weak, the pattern is less clear and relations less firmly based. Weak states do not provide adequate security for their citizens. Because their instabilities often threaten neighbours, and their vulnerabilities offer temptations to intervene, they can easily create unstable international security environments in their own regions.[12] Their weaknesses within and without are mutually reinforcing in a cycle of insecurity. Firmness in the pattern of fragmentation is therefore a basic condition for the development of security within anarchy.

The present international system displays a highly mixed picture in this regard. Some regions such as Europe, Northeast Asia and North America contain mostly strong states. Others, most notably Africa and the Middle East, contain a high proportion of weak states. Complicated variations in patterns of historical evolution explain this situation, and its effect is to produce an unevenly developed anarchy in which fragmentation is much better institutionalized in some parts than in others. Since the state system has only quite recently become universal, this situation is hardly surprising. In many ways it can be seen as a linear extension from the era in which states only occupied part of the planetary territory, the rest being occupied by a mixture of empires, colonies and sub-state units such as tribes or clans.

Although these areas are now covered by states, and are thus part of the international system rather than being either outside or subordinate to it, most of the new states are weak as states, however strong they may be as powers. Consequently, they still provide an arena for great power competition in a way that would not be nearly so marked if they were strong states. The universalization of the state system has extended the norms of the older, stronger part of the system to cover the new members, but many of these are so weak as states that they cannot adequately fulfil their role in such a relatively advanced system. System norms now make it much more difficult to occupy and annex territories than it used to be, and international legal and welfare machineries help to prop up states that cannot convincingly fulfil the functions of statehood from their own economic and socio-political resources. Nevertheless, the poorly-developed and divided ideas and institutions in many of the new states provide easy targets for foreign intervention, and an opportunity to continue old patterns of domination in new forms.

Since direct territorial control is no longer the prime target, military threats have declined in utility as between the great powers and the new states. This change partly reflects the fact that even weak states can mount sustained and costly resistance to foreign occupation, a reality confirmed most recently by the Soviet experience in Afghanistan. Among the new states themselves, however, constraints on the use of force are relatively low, and many territorial and political issues remain to be resolved. Even so, the main danger to weak states is their high vulnerability to political threats. Such threats are not, like military invasions, aimed at extinguishing the sovereignty of the country. Instead, they seek to reorient the political behaviour of the state by manipulating the main factional disputes within it. Thus state A does not threaten state B in a simple, direct fashion. Instead, it participates in domestic disputes between factions b1 and b2, backing whichever one seems most likely to pursue policies favourable to A. There are countless possible variations in the style of political intervention. These range from support for legal parties in a relatively stable electoral system, as in the traditional Soviet backing of communist parties, to encouragement of, and military assistance to, armed struggle within the target state, as in United States support for the Contras. Intervention may be aimed at changing the ideological character of the government, or at encouraging secessionist forces with the state. The common theme is the manipulation or destabilization of weak states by foreign powers competing with each other to determine patterns of international power and alignment. Because the state structures of weak states provide such targets of opportunity, governmental security and national security become hopelessly confused, and the development of national political life gets trapped by broader ideological disputes among the powers. Since decolonization, this pattern of competitive intervention has been powerfully driven by the highly divided global competition of the superpowers. The fading of the Cold War and its associated bipolar structure should reduce this source of pressure on weak states. It will not, however, remove their basic political vulnerability, and may increase interventions by neighbouring powers. It remains to be seen whether the incentives for intervention in the emergent multipolar system of the post-Cold War era will ease or exacerbate their insecurity overall.

So long as weak states constitute a significant proportion of the international community, high levels of insecurity in much of the system will be unavoidable. Domestic insecurity in such states will be high by definition. That insecurity will spill over into regional relations. Domestic instability makes stable relations with neighbours difficult. Refugees and guerrillas will cross borders, and unstable elites will seek to bolster their position by cultivating foreign threats. Outside powers will find it difficult not to be drawn into this turbulence, especially if they are competing with each other for spheres of influence, whether ideological, military or economic. The insecurity dynamics of weak states can be seen operating very clearly at all levels (domestic, regional, global) in the Gulf and the Middle East. This region, and others, demonstrate that anarchy cannot provide security unless the units themselves are stable. The security character of the system, and that of the units, cannot be separated. Zbigniew Brzezinski came close to recognizing explicitly this link between national security and the flawed anarchic structure represented by weak states when he ranked 'regional conflict, the fragmentation of wobbly social and political structures in societies incapable of absorbing the political awakening of so many more people' as the second greatest threat to the United States (after Soviet power).[13]

One logical conclusion from this line of argument is support for the underlying drift of the development rhetoric stemming from the North-South debate and the corridors of the United Nations. The UN expresses the weak state problem of the international anarchy very clearly. Its whole purpose is not to replace the anarchy with some transcendent form of world government, but to make it work better by supporting the weaker units. The redistributional pleas and demands that constitute its major output, though frequently distorted by vested interests, can be seen as one way of saying that the anarchy will continue to be unbalanced, unstable and conflict-prone, until its weaker members have become more firmly established as states. Only when they can project a basic solidity into the system, rather than a basic fragility as now, will the system as a whole be stable.

The problem is that we have no firm knowledge about how to instill the process of development in places where it has not happened naturally. Existing strong states are gifts of a long history, and if their development is a model for others, the future holds a large stock of war and upheaval. Strong states can only intervene in the development of weak states up to a limit without being charged with neocolonialism, and since all such intervention is experimental, the risk of negative results is high. Development is not a benign process. It involves massive restructuring of traditional lifestyles, and as such will almost always be resisted, often violently. It is not yet clear whether the momentum of decolonization will tend naturally, if slowly, towards the emergence of stronger states, or whether it will, in some places, result in stagnation or even a collapse of local self-government. The Brandt report and other similar documents are clearly right to argue that international security depends in part on strengthening the political economies of the weak states.[14] Whether their prescriptions on how to do this mark an effective way to proceed is arguable.

A much more speculative angle on the linkage between the character of states and the security qualities of the international system arises from the question of size. Would international security be better served by a more even distribution of power than by the huge inequalities, such as those between the United States and Burundi, that dominate the present system? It can be argued that more equal units might well provide a more manageable anarchy, because each would have difficulty mobilizing sufficient resources to threaten others seriously – assuming all other factors, such as strength as states, to be also roughly equal. This logic can be pursued in two directions: towards an anarchy of small states or towards an anarchy of superstates. The logic of small units is fashionable among much of the Green movement. It offers the virtues of decentralization, and the possibility of eliminating overbearing concentrations of power. But it suffers the liability of diseconomies of scale, and in historical perspective has an arcadian ring.

The historical trend appears to be towards ever larger political aggregates. City-states initially commanded sufficient relative power to build great empires, and over the first four millennia of civilization slowly eroded the domains of barbarian and primitive peoples. More recently, nation-states have provided the model for political aggregation, with the unifications of Italy and Germany in the last century providing clear examples of the transformation from earlier forms.

Most of the current system is based on the nation-state idea, although often inefficiently for the reasons argued in Chapter 2. This is despite the fact that on its European home-ground, the nation-state is widely seen as inadequate in scale to fulfil many economic and defence functions. It is interesting to ponder whether, in addition to their many other troubles, most of the new states may have adopted, or had thrust upon them, a form which is being replaced in the more advanced, or more historically coherent, parts of the system by geographically large 'superstates'. Even in Europe, the home of the nation-state idea, a profound process of integration is pointing towards a substantial abandonment of the old form. The forty-year dominance of the United States and the Soviet Union has provided catalytic models for a further stage of political aggregation, by demonstrating that only states organized on a continental scale can aspire to great power status under contemporary historical conditions.[15] Countries like China, India and Brazil start with an advantage of scale which is already becoming apparent in their regional and global positions, though their development problems should not be underestimated. The integration difficulties of the European Community illustrate the problems of breaking away from familiar, but inadequate, older forms in an attempt to achieve the advantages of scale under conditions of high density. Japan stands in a curious halfway house: it is a big, successful and very cohesive nation-state, but with no prospect of achieving the geographical size of a superstate.

A system composed of relatively large units in relatively small numbers (superstates, but not necessarily or even probably superpowers in the Cold War meaning of that term: more likely powers in the traditional sense) would have some significant security advantages. Such units would better be able to provide the resources and economies of scale for defence and development, and could aggregate international interests more efficiently than is possible under the current degree of fragmentation. As the case of China illustrates, even a relatively underdeveloped superstate can allocate enough resources to defence to create an effective stand-off between itself and more advanced superpowers. The military paralysis engendered by a nuclear balance of terror not only preserves the anarchic structure, but also does much more to preserve the particular pattern of states than is the case under the more fluid regime of a simple balance of power. Aggregation into superstates might thus help to compensate for the differences in economic and industrial strength which appear likely to persist in the international system. A world of superstates might more easily achieve both a multisided deterrence through a balance of nuclear terror, and some degree of insulation from the dominance of more over less-advanced political economies.

These systemic advantages of bigness might, however, also have security costs. Aggregation into superstates almost inevitably undermines the nation-state synthesis which provides such a useful framework for mediating between individuals and the state. The history of the United States demonstrates that a strong state can be constructed on a continental scale, though the peculiar advantage of a mass immigrant population is unlikely to be repeated anywhere else except Brazil. The current nationalist disarray in the Soviet Union shows the dangers and fragilities of multinational construction. Except for natural superstates such as China, great size can only be achieved at the risk of creating a weak state on a gigantic scale, with all its attendant domestic and international security problems. In very different ways, the political experiments in India and the European Community are trying to address the problem of welding diverse national and religious identities into a politically coherent form on their own ground. One of the great security questions for the twenty-first century will be whether a broader civilizational identity can successfully provide the socio-political foundations for strong superstates in Europe and South Asia.

THE USES AND LIMITATIONS OF SYSTEM STRUCTURE IN SECURITY ANALYSIS

Discussion of a world of superstates points to what is perhaps the most common and long-standing approach to analyzing international security in terms of system structure. This involves using the distribution of power, or 'degree of polarity' – in effect the number of major powers in the system – to derive conclusions about system stability in terms of the probability and intensity of war. In Waltz's scheme, the distribution of power counts as the shallowest level of system structure (as compared with the deep structure of anarchy itself).[16] It has none the less attracted the most attention in structural analysis, including from Waltz himself. The reasons for this skewed interest are partly because polarity changes, whereas deep structure is virtually a constant, but mostly because the Second World War generated a very big shift from a multipolar system (the historical norm) to a bipolar one (very rare). Since the United States found itself at the centre of this shift, there was a natural interest among American scholars in exploring its significance.

The first stage was to develop taxonomies for different types of structure. Morton Kaplan, for example, identifies six types of system, not all of them anarchies: balance of power, loose bipolar, tight bipolar, unit veto, universal and hierarchic.[17] The balance-of-power model derives from the European state system up to 1914, the loose and tight bipolar models reflect, respectively, the later and earlier states of the Cold War, and the others constitute theoretical possibilities for which there are no contemporary examples. K. J. Holsti offers four models: hierarchical, diffuse, diffuse bloc and polar; and Richard Rosecrance proposes a more complex scheme based on four variables: stratification, polarity, distribution of power and homogeneity.[18] These efforts generated interesting theoretical debates, such as that resulting from Kaplan's attempt to formulate rules for the balance-of-power system, but they produced no clear conclusions about the security implications of different structures.

Holsti, for example, argues that none of the models he examines produces more security for the independent political units within it than any of the others.[19] While the models produce different styles of international relations, the security risks they pose to their members are merely different, and not demonstrably higher or lower. Some interesting hypotheses do emerge. Rosecrance argues that bipolar systems will have less frequent but more intense international violence, while more diffuse systems will have more frequent but less intense violence. He also argues that more homogeneous systems (that is, those in which differences in organizing ideologies are relatively small) will be less prone to international conflict than those in which ideological divisions are large.[20] On big issues, however, there is no agreement. In relation to the central contemporary issue of the impact of bipolar power structures opinions contradict completely. Rosecrance argues that a tight bipolar system is 'the most intractable' in terms of controlling international conflict,[21] and his view is backed up by the earlier position of John Herz that the bipolar structure produces the most unmitigated form of the security dilemma.[22] Karl Deutsch and David Singer argue that multipolar systems are preferable in security terms to bipolar ones; while Michael Haas disagrees, finding merit and cost in both forms.[23] Against these views, Waltz argues at length that a bipolar power structure is best in terms of international security because it is simpler, more stable and less accident-prone than more diffuse systems.[24] Michael Brecher and others have recently reopened this debate, supporting Waltz's view in favour of bipolarity, but moving away from a purely structural analysis by adding the idea of centres of decision to the distribution of power.[25]

At this high level of generality it is all too clear that one does not find much overall guidance about the impact of system structure on the problem of national security. The system structure approaches do generate useful organizing ideas for thinking about alternative patterns of fragmentation. They also raise the questions about why, when, how and with what consequences, the system structure changes from one form to another, though in the absence of agreement about the significance of the patterns themselves this debate is largely confined to abstract realms. Different structures can themselves be seen as objects of security. If one argues, as Waltz does about bipolar systems, that they tend to produce fewer security problems than do alternative structures, then they would be worth preserving as things in themselves. In a similar way, it can also be argued that system change is likely to generate security problems because old systems represent vested interests that will not give way without a fight. The single transformation in system structure identified by Waltz, for example, occurred through the agency of the Second World War. From this perspective, maintenance of the existing distribution of power can be seen as a type of status quo security interest because of the probability that structural change will be accompanied by increased threats. The search for system stability thus becomes a theme of security analysis.

The problem with this whole attempt to define and compare system structures is that it has been asked to do too much. The fact that polarity has been expected to answer huge questions about peace, war and stability in the international system explains both the lack of clear results and the ease with which the whole exercise can be criticized. Polarity is one-dimensional and ahistorical. That is to say, it attempts to generate knowledge about the conditions for security by looking at the single factor of the distribution of power, and assumes that whatever explanatory power is contained within that factor holds true across different historical periods. To expect this one datum to answer such sweeping questions is unreasonable. Cross-historical comparisons of polarity will necessarily rest on a dangerously narrow base. Can a five-member balance-of-power system be expected to behave in a similar fashion regardless of whether it occurred under the conditions of the eighteenth or of the late twentieth century? The conditions for security depend on a host of variables other than distribution of power, and the variance in these between historical periods weighs heavily against any grand uniformities arising from similarities in system structure.[26]

The kinds of historical variables against which the single variable of polarity has to compete to determine the national security problem include the following:

- The character of the prevailing military technology, particularly its destructive capacity and the range over which force can be projected.
- The availability of effectively empty territory in the system, which is to say, territory which is either uninhabited, or lightly inhabited, or inhabited but not organized to a political level recognized by the major powers in the system.[27]
- The character of the states making up the system, which was discussed in the previous section, and which includes in addition Rosecrance's 'homogeneity' variable in relation to ideologies, and also the matter of whether or not significant powers in the system are revisionist, and what form their revisionism takes, which I will look at in Chapter 8.
- The strength and pattern of war-weariness in the system, which is to say, whether or not the system, or some of its members, are close to a debilitating experience of war, like the European system after the Thirty Years War and after the First World War, and like the United States to a lesser extent, after its experience in Vietnam.[28]
- The legitimacy of war as an instrument of state policy within the system, which, for example, has declined greatly during the present century.[29]
- The levels of enmity between states in the system, which, in the case of Germany and France, can vary greatly with the shift of complex historical conditions.

For all these reasons and more, there exist severe limits on what can be deduced about security from system structure. It simply defies credibility to assume broad similarities between similar system structures when one has nuclear weapons and the other not, or when one is war-weary and the other not. Indeed, one of the problems affecting the debate about bipolarity was how to disentangle its security effects from the impact of nuclear weapons, both phenomena having arrived in the system at the same time. Europe was a balance-of-power system before the First World War as well as after it, but what a difference to the security environment the intervening few years made!

But these criticisms should not be taken as grounds for dismissal. In part, the obsession with polarity has masked the enduring significance of the deep structure of anarchy itself. Ironically, Waltz has been one of those responsible for diverting attention away from his own important insights into deep structure. As this book stresses throughout, it is that deep structure which provides the essential frame-work for the whole security problematique.[30] The deep structure sets the basic conditions for international relations, but it is at much too high a level of generalization to say much about specific outcomes. The distributional structure of polarity is merely a variant within deep structure, and so likewise should not be expected to deliver massive certainties about the whole quality of relations in any specific type of international system.

The balance of power deserves particular mention here, not only because of the important place it has traditionally occupied in the analysis of international relations, but also because it bridges between deep and distributional structure. In one sense, balance of power is just another of the power structure models (usually the multipolar one), and is subject to the same criticisms. As Bull notes, however, 'the term "balance of power" is notorious for the numerous meanings that may be attached to it.'[31] It refers not only to a particular type of power structure, but also to a general principle of state behaviour in an anarchic system. Where the balance of power comes into its own, as Bull argues, is on the system level.[32] On the system level, the balance of power describes a principle which is fundamental to the preservation of the international anarchy, and which is inseparable from it. An anarchic structure can only be maintained by a balance of power, and the two are effectively opposite sides of the same coin. If one accepts Vattel's classic definition of the balance of power as 'a state of affairs such that no one power is in a position where it is preponderant and can lay down the law to others',[33] then it becomes almost another way of describing the basic structure of anarchy. The balance of power will by definition last as long as the international anarchy. This is an important conclusion if one wishes to address the whole anarchic system as an object of security, because the balance of power is essential to the preservation of such a system. The notion of systemic security is, however, pretty esoteric, and far removed from the security problems of individual states. Indeed, with its emphasis on military rivalry and great-power interests, its acknowledgement of the interdependence and uncertainty of security relations, and its open-minded view about the role of war in the system, one can most appropriately see the balance-of-power model as defining the problem of national insecurity.

Both Bull and Hoffmann make the case against the utility of the balance-of-power model in relation to the contemporary international system.[34] Bipolarity, nuclear weapons, economic interdependence, and doubts about the validity of power theories of political behaviour, all militate against it. Even when conditions allow its application, it favours, as Bull argues, the interests of great powers, and can hardly be recommended as a general security policy for all states.[35] Hoffmann argues bluntly that 'the balance of power is not a relevant mechanism in the new arenas of world politics.'[36] While valid against the attempt to load too much into structural analysis, these criticisms go too far, threatening to throw out the polarity baby with the power bathwater. Polarity may not be able to predict the general quality of international relations, but it does provide an extremely useful, and as yet too little exploited, approach to a whole range of more specific questions.[37]

In strategic analysis, for example, polarity is central to the logic of deterrence. It makes a big difference to the whole calculation of deterrence whether the relationship involved is bipolar or multipolar. Similar insights apply to alliance theory, arms racing and arms control. Alliance options under bipolarity are strikingly different from those under multipolarity. In arms racing and arms control, the dynamics of interaction and the availability of parity are both deeply affected by the variable of polarity.[38] Looking forward to Chapter 6, in international political economy, the whole debate about hegemonic actors can be seen as a discussion about polarity within the economic sector of international relations.

The problem with system structure analysis is thus more in the way it has been used than in the idea itself. Properly applied, system structure can offer a wealth of important insights into specific elements of the security problem. By itself, however, it cannot resolve all of the complexities of security analysis. It is simply one of several major variables that shape and mediate the security consequences of anarchy.

INTERNATIONAL SOCIETY

The third of the well-developed literatures that discuss the political determinants of security under anarchy is that on international society. Hedley Bull and Adam Watson define international society as:

> a group of states (or, more generally, a group of independent political communities) which not merely form a system, in the sense that the behaviour of each is a necessary factor in the calculations of the others, but also have established by dialogue and consent common rules and institutions for the conduct of their relations, and recognize their common interest in maintaining these arrangements.[39]

The distinction between system and society is central to this literature. System is the more basic, and prior, idea, being simply a function of significant interaction. Society can be seen as a historical response to the existence of system. As units reorganize the permanence and importance of their interdependence, they begin to work out rules for avoiding unwanted conflicts and for facilitating desired exchanges. As Bull argues, international society is thus closely associated with the idea of international order, where order means: 'an arrangement of social life such that it promotes certain goals or values.'[40]

In historical terms, the development of a global international society has been a function of the expansion of the West. From the fifteenth century onwards, the rise of European power first eroded, and then crushed, the long-standing configuration of four substantially self-contained civilizational areas in Europe, the Middle East, South Asia and East Asia.[41] By the end of the nineteenth century virtually the whole of the international system was either created in the image of

Europe, as in the Americas and Australia, or directly subordinated to Europe, as the African and Asian colonies, or hell-bent on catching up with Europe, as in Japan and Russia. The triumph of European power meant not only that a sharp and apparently permanent rise in the level of interaction (and thus density and interdependence) took place, but also that Western norms and values and institutions dominated the whole system.

Bull and others see this as the high point of international society because the relatively coherent and well-developed international society of the European sub-system briefly held sway over the entire planet. On this basis, they take a rather depressed view of subsequent developments, seeing decolonization, the eclipse of Europe, and the rise of ideologically driven superpowers as unleashing and legitimizing a host of mutually exclusive and competitive social values. This they see as weakening international society by reducing its stock of shared values.[42] In my view, this perspective is not only ethnocentrically narrow and misleadingly gloomy, but also mistaken. To assume that imposed values represent a strong society in the same sense that shared values do is to misunderstand what society (as opposed to power politics) is about. It is certainly true that the European ascendancy created a global imperium, and thus an exceptionally high level of societal homogeneity among the dominant powers. It is also true that this imperium set the conditions for a global international society, both by intensifying the density of the system, and by making all parts of it deeply aware that they were locked into a pattern of interaction powerful enough to shape the major conditions of their societal and political survival. But this imperium can only itself be called a society at risk of ignoring the huge inequalities of power and status between the colonizers and the colonized. The idea of society requires that some substantial perception of equal status exists among its members. On this basis, the late nineteenth century represented not a global international society, but a globalized European international society.

Seen from this perspective, many of the reasons for pessimism about the condition of international society disappear. There has been no decline during the twentieth century because there was no real peak of virtue at the end of the nineteenth. What we have witnessed during the twentieth century is a huge process of transformation in two parts. First, is the collapse of a narrowly based, top-heavy, global imperium. Second is the emergence of an international system that is more truly global in two senses: (a) that the sources of global interaction are now located all through the system rather than being primarily located in one part of it; and (b) that the units in the system relate to each other as legal equals rather than as a hierarchy of states, mandates, dependencies and colonies. This new system was born out of the collapse of the old one, and in many important ways was created by it. The European imperium generated the need for an international society and provided much of the political form within which it took shape. The question is therefore not how much ground has been lost since the heyday of European power, but what legacy was left by the old system for the new? How much of European international society did the non-European states accept, and how much did they reject? What kind of international society has emerged from the first decades of operation of a truly global international system?

The main reason for thinking that international society is in good shape by historical standards is the near universal acceptance of the sovereign territorial state as the fundamental unit of political legitimacy. This can be seen as the great, though unintended, political legacy of the European imperium. So successful was the European state in unleashing human potential that it overwhelmed all other forms of political organization in the system. To escape from European domination it was necessary to adopt European political forms. Some achieved this by copying, others had it imposed on them by the process of decolonization. As even Bull and Watson acknowledge, much of European international society was accepted by the rest of the world when they achieved independence: in particular, the fundamental organizing principle of sovereign states treating each other as juridical equals reigns almost unchallenged as the basic political norm of the system.[43] Except for Islam, all of the universalizing political ideologies from Christianity, through liberalism to socialism and communism, have been firmly nationalized. As the Gulf War demonstrated, even Islam is now heading in that direction. Mutual recognition of claims to territorial sovereignty is the system norm, and the number of serious boundary disputes – perhaps the major source of international insecurity in an anarchic system – is declining as the now universal state system settles down. What this means is that Waltz's two components of deep structure – the ordering principle of anarchy, and the idea that units are not differentiated by function because they all claim the whole spectrum of sovereignty [44] – are in a sense recognized and held as a shared, preferred, value by the international community.

This agreement on political structure is tremendously important. It provides a viable framework for international society despite both the cultural diversity of the post-colonial international system, and the domestic instability of some of the states within it. An anarchic political system is the most obvious depository for the natural diversity of human culture. Provided that there is general agreement on boundaries, the system of sovereign states is well designed to handle the legitimization of relations among diverse social and political cultures. Indeed, given the range and intensity of that diversity as an undeniably dominant historical reality, a system of sovereign states may be the only way of constructing a stable international political order for many decades to come, albeit there may be fighting within weak states about their legitimacy and construction. When sovereign states accept each other as juridical equals, then the keystone to international society is in place, since only when there is some significant element of equality can society properly be said to exist. As Bull notes:

> The system of a plurality of sovereign states gives rise to classic dangers, but these have to be reckoned against the dangers inherent in the attempt to contain disparate communities within the framework of a single government. It may be argued that world order at the present time is best served by living with the former dangers rather than attempting to face the latter.[45]

The carry-over of the state system as a legacy of the European imperium facilitates the carry-over of many of the maintenance mechanisms that Bull identified as supporting the European international society: balance of power, international law, diplomacy, war and great power management.[46] Bull worried that these mechanisms were weakened by the shift to a more cosmopolitan international society. He saw the consensual basis for international law narrowing, respect for diplomacy being violated by radical regimes, and ideological divisions hobbling the possibilities for great power management. All of these observations are correct, but to focus on them puts the weight of analysis in the wrong place. The important thing is that basic agreement exists about the political structure of the system, and very widespread agreement that diplomacy and international law provide the appropriate forms for cooperative behaviour. That so much survived the turbulent transition from a European to a truly global international society is a remarkable and positive development. That violations of these norms have been few in relation to observance of them is nothing short of miraculous, given that the past four decades have been the setting-up and running-in period for a new, substantially untested, and in many places rather poorly constructed, international system. In this perspective, the United Nations (UN) is a major symbol. Though often boring and irrelevant in its day-to-day deliberations, the UN stands as a concrete embodiment of the universal acceptance of sovereignty, legal equality, law and diplomacy as the foundations of contemporary international society. Indeed, the success of the system partly explains why the UN is often boring.

In the late twentieth century we still stand in the formative years of this new international society, and its full quality is difficult to see clearly. Its construction has been a deeply traumatic process involving two world wars, the birth pains of decolonization, a host of revolutions, many ideological experiments aimed at coping with the Western challenge and, latterly, a bitter and divisive Cold War between the ideologically opposed superpowers that inherited power from Europe. This turbulence has masked the solid foundations of international society by highlighting extreme political differences that work to paralyze international law and diplomacy, and to emphasize the disordering rather than ordering qualities of war and the balance of power. But at the time of writing (early 1990) the dust from all of this is beginning to settle enough so that the shape of some common values begins to emerge.

The state system itself is undoubtedly the most universal and important of the shared values of international society, and is defended stoutly even in places such as Africa where its practice has been least successful. Scientific and technological knowledge, and the materialist accomplishments they make possible, are also a nearly universal value, bridging all the major ideologies. Until recently, economics was an area of fierce division, but the failure of the communist experiment with central planning leaves market economics more or less unchallenged as the most effective and efficient way to organize production and distribution of goods. This has taken much of the heat out of the Cold War. The international community – or least the group of major powers at its apex – is beginning to look less ideologically divided than at any time since 1914. As this new norm consolidates, it will weaken and perhaps even eliminate the zero-sum ideological divide that was such a powerful driver of the security dilemma during the Cold War era. As Bull and Watson note, there has also been an internationalization of welfare logic.[47] This operates both privately and through governments, albeit there is still much disagreement about the balance between these two, and about how and to what extent resources should be transferred from the richer to the poorer parts of the system.

A more narrowly based, but no less important, norm is the consensus among the major powers that wars between them are no longer a desirable or fruitful way of settling differences. In some of the great powers – most notably the major sufferers of the last war in Europe and Japan – this norm is quite deeply embedded in their societies. In others, it is more a function of nuclear deterrence, and the fear that victory and defeat will be indistinguishable. This norm has emerged with exceptional strength in some regions, notably North America and Europe, and for rather different reasons in some parts of the periphery, notably among the ASEAN (Association of Southeast Asian Nations) states.[48] In these regions, the existence of security communities offers micro-demonstrations of how a strong international society can moderate the security problems of anarchy by cultivating what Jahn *et al.* have labelled 'non-violent conflict culture'.[49] In this conception, peace does not require harmony. Disagreement and conflict are assumed to be part of the human political condition both within and between states, but war is ruled out as a legitimate instrument of policy except for the purpose of defence against a military attack. If international society is strong enough to support legitimate mechanisms for change, then anarchy can become a framework within which international disputes and conflicts can be both carried on or settled without large-scale violence.

There is a rising prospect that a new norm of international society will develop from increasing concern over ecological issues. Because of the nature of these issues, ranging from wildlife preservation, through pollution, to climate change, this concern carries with it a strong global consciousness. Changes in the planetary atmosphere and biosphere affect everyone in a way that distributes burdens and concerns much more evenly than is the case with the longer-running issue of overpopulation. This is an exceptionally useful counterweight to the deeply ingrained societal parochialness that almost everywhere still dominates the human condition. Ecological, or 'green' consciousness is by no means universal. But its rise has been dramatic, and it looks well set to be ever more widely promoted as the issues on its agenda begin to impact on people everywhere in their daily lives.

Many of these values are the product of Western thought and political practice. It is nevertheless vital that they have become part of the norms of international society not by being imposed on others, but in being adopted by them and made their own. Perhaps the major non-Western input into international society is the formal acceptance of racial equality and the rejection of political doctrines based on racial differentiation. These ideas are inherent in Western humanism, but it seems rather unlikely from the historical record that they would have become politically operational without pressure from an independent non-European world. Note, for example, the failure of the Japanese to get a clause on racial equality into the League of Nations Charter in 1919 because of Western opposition. It seems reasonable to expect that the non-Western countries will continue to write their own interests and perspectives into international law, as happened, for instance, in the massive renegotiation of the law of the sea between 1973 and 1982.

Despite its loss of direct control, the West is still the most powerful and attractive centre in the system. Its primacy makes it a major promoter of potential systemic values ranging from the use of English as an international language, through the crass materialism of brand name consumer 'culture', to controversial sociopolitical norms such as human rights that directly threaten the political practices of many states in the system (and also threaten Bull's distinction between international and world society). It seems likely that the West will continue to dominate international society for the foreseeable future. It has seen off the socio-economic (and military) challenge of communism, and is without serious rivals in the system.

The West itself has been greatly strengthened by the political reconstruction and fuller incorporation of Germany and Japan, an accomplishment for which history will credit the United States. As a consequence, the three major centres of advanced capitalism now form a gigantic security community. Removal of the fear that they will use force in relations among themselves enables them to stand, as it were, back to back, and gives them a huge advantage over those less well placed. This advantage goes a long way to explaining the Western victory in the Cold War. Even a giant like the Soviet Union could not compete against such a coalition, and China can only continue to do so by remaining poor. This capitalist security community represents a quite unprecedented formation among a group of great powers. It will continue to generate what Von Laue calls 'the world revolution of Westernization' in which the West sets the societal standard that others seek to attain, whether by mimicry or reaction.[50]

The condition of international society is an import element of international security. To the extent that an international society exists, it not only makes it easier for states to accept each other's legitimacy, but also facilitates civilized (i.e. non-violent) interaction among them. In this perspective the (mostly British) literature on international society and the (mostly American) one on regimes are talking about the same thing. Anarchical society, in other words, is capable of generating order only if the states within it can adopt norms against which their own and others' behaviour can be communicated, regulated and judged. This is especially so when the density of the system is so high that states cannot escape the consequences of each other's activity. Like strong states, a well-developed international society is a necessary, but not necessarily sufficient, condition for international security. The strong European international society did not prevent catastrophic war, and as McKinlay and Little argue, the norms of international order are inherently ideological and contested.[51] But if anarchy is to remain the framework for security, then the development of international society has a central role in any definition of progress.

CONCLUSIONS: ANARCHY AND SECURITY

The international anarchy does not constitute a single form with relatively fixed features, but rather a single condition within which many variations can be arranged. Some configurations of anarchy heighten the problem of national security, whereas others mitigate it. The systemic perspective enables one to take a broader and more contextual view of national security itself. It helps to identify a number of features, such as density, polarity, the character of states and the nature of international society, which mediate the condition of anarchy. Some of these offer potential targets for national policy in as much as they represent opportunities to manipulate the system into forms more conducive to the enjoyment of national security. The systemic view emphasizes the indivisible side of security (i.e. interdependence) because it highlights relational patterns and general structures. But it also ties this aspect into the divisible side (i.e. national security) by revealing the link between the individual character of states and the character of the system as a whole. It is obvious, for example, that weak states will find it more difficult to generate and support international society than strong ones. State and system are so closely interconnected that security policies based only on the former must be both irrational and inefficient.

One way of dealing with the complexities of the system approach is to hypothesize a spectrum of anarchies which can be labelled *immature* at one end, and *mature* at the other.

An extreme case of immature anarchy would be one in which the units themselves were held together only by the force of élite leadership, with each state recognizing no other legitimate sovereign unit except itself, and where relations among the states took the form of a continuous struggle for dominance. Such a system would approximate chaos. The struggle for dominance would generate endless warfare, and would not be moderated by any sense among the units of the legitimacy or rights of others. The stability of units would depend on their success in the struggle for power. Insecurity would be endemic, and relations among states would be like the automatic and unthinking struggle of natural enemies such as ants and termites. The ethic of such a system would be survival of the fittest, and nothing other than the distribution of power and the level of capability available would prevent the unification of the system under the strongest actor. An anarchy of this sort would be 'immature' because it had not developed any form of international society to moderate the effects of political fragmentation. Its members would share no norms, rules or conventions among themselves, and their relationships would be dominated by fear, distrust, disdain, hatred, envy, contempt and indifference. Order, if it existed at all, would reflect only deference to superior power. In the long run, an immature anarchy would be unstable, both because of the risk of general exhaustion and collapse, and because of the risk of one actor transcending the balance of power and unifying the system under its control.

At the other end of the spectrum, an extremely mature anarchy would have developed as a society to the point where the benefits of fragmentation could be enjoyed without the costs of continuous armed struggle and instability. The mechanisms behind this would be the development of criteria by which states could both consolidate their own identity and legitimacy, and recognize and accept each other's. In a very mature anarchy, all states would have to be strong as states: in other words, the idea of the state, its territory and its institutions would have to be well-developed and stable, regardless of its relative power as a state in the system. On this basis, a strong international society could be built on the foundations of mutual recognition and acceptance. Mutual recognition of sovereign equality and territorial boundaries alone would make a substantial modification to the hazards of immature anarchy.

A mature anarchy requires members that are firm in their own definition, and can project their own inner coherence and stability out into the community of states. Only on that basis can a solid foundation be created for the promulgation and observance of mature anarchic norms based on the mutual respect of units. If all states had developed internally as nation-states or state-nations, then a Wilsonian-type norm of mutual respect for nations as self-determining cultural political entities could easily become part of international society. This would have an enormous moderating impact on fragmentation, in that it would associate the political pattern of states with much deeper and more durable patterns of societal and territorial organization. The state as a purely institutional entity has no natural boundaries, and a system composed of such units is likely to be conflict-prone and power-oriented. But if the notion of the state is broadened to include specified national and territorial criteria, then the state becomes at least potentially a much more fixed and defined object, with fewer grounds for posing threats to its neighbours. John Herz has labelled this idea 'self-limiting nationalism'. He argues for it not only as the view of many of the original proponents of nationalism, but also as the basic ideology of a stable anarchy, in contrast to the 'exclusivist, xenophobic, expansionist, oppressive' nationalism which has caused the world so much suffering and insecurity.[52]

Other norms, like non-interference in internal affairs, respect for different organizing ideologies, avoidance of force in the settlement of disputes and adherence to a variety of international institutions for dealing with problems of a multinational scale, would complete the societal machinery of the mature anarchy. Such a system would still place a high value on political variety and fragmentation, and it would still be as much an anarchy in the structural sense as the immature variant sketched above. But it would none the less be a highly ordered and stable system in which states would enjoy a great deal of security deriving both from their own inner strength and maturity, and from the strength of the institutionalized norms regulating relations among them.[53]

Between these two rather unlikely extremes lie a whole range of possible international anarchies, including our own. The present anarchy lies somewhere in the middle of the spectrum, for if it is obviously a long way from the calm and stable realms of maturity, it is just as obviously well removed from unbridled chaos. Some elements of maturity are quite strongly developed in our system, such as mutual recognition of sovereign equality and its associated baggage of international law. Some are firmly established as principles, like the right of national self-determination and the sanctity of territorial boundaries, but partially respected in practice. And others are accepted as ideals, like not using force to settle disputes and not intervening in the domestic political affairs of others, but are applied only in a limited number of cases and have only a minor restraining effect on state behaviour. The United Nations Charter stands as a model for a more mature anarchy than the one we have, and is a kind of benchmark for the progress which the system has made away from chaos. But the record of disputes, conflicts, weak states and insecurity which the modern era has produced marks the difficulty of the problem, and the distance we still have to go.

These models illustrate further the need to combine the state and system levels in analysing the character of the system. To comment about a mature anarchy is to say things of significance about both the component units and the pattern of relations among them. A mature anarchy must be composed of strong states, because only states well ordered and stable within themselves could generate and support strong common norms for the system as a whole. But once such norms exist, they become a characteristic of the system, enriching, but not transforming, the basic structure of anarchy.

These models imply the idea of progress from immature to mature anarchy. The idea of progress is not strongly developed in International Relations, not least because of reluctance to take risks with normative or deterministic positions. On the national policy level, ideas of progress are commonly either very short-term, or non-existent, excepting those (increasingly few) states governed by forward-looking ideologies. Progress is much easier to define for revisionist than for status quo powers. For the international system as a whole, hazy ideas about a more peaceful world provide almost the only yardstick for a sense of progress.

Progress raises the whole issue of determinism. Can the evolution of international political systems be compared with that of biological organisms or species? If it can, then there will be a strong though not necessarily uniform or inevitable, tendency for the maturity of systems to increase with the passage of time. If it cannot, then movements towards greater maturity can only come about by the direction of collective effort to achieving specific national and systemic objectives. The idea of a temporal imperative behind an evolution toward maturity has considerable appeal, and does not exclude trying to force the pace by more directed measures.

Even within the recent span of our own system one can detect substantial developments towards a more mature anarchy. The idea of national self-determination – the nation as the foundation of the state – for example, was firmly rooted in the system by the middle of the nineteenth century, as exemplified by the legitimacy attaching to the processes of national unification in Germany and Italy. While nationalist developments had a destabilizing side in the power-oriented and expansionist notions of Social Darwinism (the survival of the fittest nation), by the time of the Versailles Treaties in 1919 national self-determination was close to being a system-wide principle. Despite continuing difficulties with it, such as in the partition of Germany, Korea, China, India and Vietnam after the Second World War, it underlay the post-1945 decolonization movement, with its gigantic transfer of political authority from imperial powers to local states.[54] Even an overtly imperial power like the Soviet Union before Gorbachev recognized the nationality principle both in its domestic constitutional structure and in its relations with its satellites.

Similar signs of evolving maturity can be read into the development of international organizations like the League of Nations and the United Nations, and the attempts through them to fix territorial boundaries and to establish norms and principles aimed at restraining the use of force. In addition, the historical development of states themselves seems to add weight to the maturity of the system over time. Long-established states have had time both to develop their own ideas and institutions, as well as to reach accommodation with their neighbours on boundaries. The Western European states, and the United States and Canada, come to mind as examples of relatively mature states among which force has ceased to play a significant role in relations. Younger states, like many of those in the Third World, appear weak as states because of their newness, and there is enough similarity between their situation and the earlier history of the more mature states to support some hopes of evolution. This parallel cannot, however, be pushed too far. Contemporary Third World states face much more serious problems of external intervention by more highly developed states than did the European countries in their state-building phase.[55]

At least two major lines of criticism disturb this pleasing image of historical drift towards greater maturity and security in the international anarchy. The first rests on an extension of the biological analogy in which a phase of maturity is followed by decline and death. This could apply either to states or to the system as a whole, and results in Toynbeean-style historical cycles which interrupt any continuous progress towards harmony. There is, of course, no way of proving that a cyclic pattern will be valid for the future even if it has been for the past, especially given the rapid and fundamental changes in human capabilities and institutions that characterize the modern era. But the image of a system that proceeds by a series of peaks and troughs is made compelling by the retreat of political order in Europe following the collapse of the Roman empire, and by the possibilities for collapse inherent in the capabilities and vulnerabilities of contemporary human social organization.

This last point ties into the second line of criticism, which is that if increase in maturity is a function of time, then that increase does not take place against a static background of threat. Instead, it runs a race against parallel increases in both the scale of threat and the scope of vulnerability. From this perspective, increasing system maturity cannot be seen as a process of steady gain on a problem of fixed dimension. Rather, it must be viewed as part of a larger process in which the forces of order compete endlessly against the ever-mounting capability for chaos. If we now have much better developed international institutions than existed in the nineteenth century, it is not because we are more civilized, but because we have more demanding problems arising from the greater density of the system. Progress towards a more mature form of anarchy is not a cause for congratulation or complacency in its own right, but only if it seems to be outpacing the simultaneous increase in threats. The growth of threats and vulnerabilities stems basically from the increase in human numbers and capabilities, which up to the present has shown the long, steady build-up, and then the rapid growth of a geometrical curve. One has only to think of the risks that increasing human capabilities pose in matters such as the destructiveness of war, the impact of pollution, the potential for mass migration, the fragility of distribution systems on which large numbers of people now depend for meeting their basic human needs, and the dangers of new plagues, to get the flavour and urgency of this race. There are no grounds for feeling sanguine about either the past progress or the future prospects of the international anarchy. Threats and vulnerabilities multiply and evolve at the same time as the system advances towards maturity, making security a highly dynamic problem of uncertain dimensions. There is an ever-present danger that the system will split between an increasingly mature centre, carrying with it substantial parts of the periphery, and a hopeless, isolated outer periphery, unable to cope with the problems of self-government and development, and increasingly crushed by the weight of modern problems.

Progress so far has been much more by evolution than by design. The anarchy we now find ourselves living with is much more an imposition of history on the present generation than it is a matter of conscious, preferred choice. No grand design over the centuries has produced it. Its maker has been a myriad of apparently unconnected decisions, actions and capabilities. But although we did not choose to make the anarchy we have, once conscious of it, we can choose to mould it into more – or less – mature forms. The character of anarchy can take very different forms, from providing an ideal arena for raw power struggles at one extreme, to sustaining diversity with security at the other. From this perspective, international anarchy need not be seen as an obstacle standing in the way of world government and universal peace. Instead, it can be seen as a field of opportunity offering attractions different from, but no less morally appealing than, those which sustained support for world government. Improved anarchies, though by no means within easy reach, are not so far off as world government. They may be seen in one sense as necessary developments on the way to a planetary federation, but they may also be seen as an ideal form of international association, and thus as desirable objectives in their own right.

NOTES

1. On the historical links between state and system, see William McNeill, *The Rise of the West: A history of the human community* (Chicago: University of Chicago Press, 1963). On the durability and variety of international anarchy see Barry Buzan, 'Peace, power and security: contending concepts in the study of international relations', *Journal of Peace Research*, 21:2 (1984). On the theory, see Kenneth Waltz, *Theory of International Politics* (Reading, Mass.: Addison-Wesley, 1979), chs 4–6; and Barry Buzan, Charles Jones and Richard Little, *The Logic of Anarchy* (New York: Columbia University Press, 1993). See also Richard K. Ashley, *The Political Economy of War and Peace* (London: Pinter, 1980), ch. 1, esp. pp. 48–9; and Oran R. Young, 'Anarchy and social choice: reflections on the international polity', *World Politics*, 30:2 (1978). For a very useful discussion of sovereignty and anarchy, see John G. Ruggie, 'Continuity and transformation in the world polity: toward a neo-realist synthesis', *World Politics*, 35:2 (1983). Ruggie explores the medieval system as a form of international anarchy. If accepted, his view precludes the use of the neat formulation that sovereignty defines anarchy, and anarchy defines sovereignty. While the first part of the proposition would still hold, the second would not. Anarchy *might* define a system of discrete sovereign units, but might also express itself in much messier forms, like the medieval system, in which the actors had not aggregated sovereignty into exclusive units. This argument does not disturb my conclusion that sovereignty and anarchy need to be treated as aspects of a single phenomenon. The anarchic structure could not be replaced unless states as currently constituted ceased to exist. The equation is a little less clear in the other direction: states could transform themselves without undoing the anarchic system structure (for example, by reversion to some neo-medieval form of layered, partial sovereignties), but the nature of their transformation could also replace the anarchy (for example, by subordination of states into a world federation). For elaboration on this theme see Buzan in Buzan, Jones and Little, *ibid*.
2. Thomas Hobbes, *Leviathan* (Harmondsworth: Penquin, 1968), ch. 13.
3. Waltz, *op. cit.* (note 1), pp. 79–80; Buzan in Buzan, Jones and Little, *op. cit.* (note 1).
4. See Buzan, *ibid.*
5. Theodore H. Von Laue, *The World Revolution of Westernization: The twentieth century in global perspective* (New York: Oxford University Press, 1987).
6. Robert O. Keohane and Joseph S. Nye, *Power and Interdependence* (Boston: Little Brown, 1977), and 'Power and interdependence revisited', *International Organization*, 41:4 (1987); Joseph S. Nye, 'Neorealism and neoliberalism', *World Politics*, 40:2 (1988).
7. Keohane and Nye (1977), *ibid.*
8. I borrow the two imperatives from Waltz, *op. cit.* (note 1), p. 107.
9. Stephanie G. Neuman, 'International stratification and Third World military industries', *International Organization*, 38:1 (1984).
10. Waltz, *op. cit.* (note 1), ch. 4.
11. For discussion, see Buzan in Buzan, Jones and Little, *op. cit.* (note 1).
12. For discussion, see Barry Buzan, 'People, states and fear: the national security problem in the Third World', in Edward Azar and Chung-in Moon (eds), *National Security in the Third World* (Aldershot: Edward Elgar, 1988), pp. 27–39.

13. Quoted in Larry W. Bowman and Ian Clark (eds), *The Indian Ocean in Global Politics* (Boulder, Col.: Westview Press, 1981), p. 99.

14. The Brandt Commission, *North-South: A programme for survival,* and *Common Crisis – North-South: Cooperation for world recovery* (London: Pan, 1980, 1983).

15. This line of argument extends from earlier attempts like that of John Herz, 'The rise and demise of the territorial state', *World Politics*, 9 (1957), to argue that the territorial state *per se* was being made obsolete because of the collapse of its defence functions in the face of nuclear threats. Developments since then suggest that deterrence is an adequate security policy to sustain the legitimacy of the state, and that superstates have the advantage of being large enough to provide some sense (whether false or not) of both security and defensibility. Superstates additionally dispose of sufficient resources to arm themselves fully with the most modern military technology required for effective deterrence, an option not open to smaller powers. Robert Jervis, 'Cooperation under the security dilemma', *World Politics*, 30:2 (1978), p. 172, argues for the stabilizing effect of large powerful actors. Waltz, *op. cit.* (note 1), ch. 8, and 'The myth of interdependence', in Charles P. Kindleberger, *The International Corporation* (Cambridge: Mass.: MIT Press, 1970), pp. 213–22, can also be interpreted in this light, although their main burdens are to argue, respectively, the merits of bipolarity, and the limits of interdependence in relation to superstates.

16. Waltz, *op. cit.* (note 1), ch. 5. For further discussion see Buzan in Buzan, Jones and Little, *op. cit.* (note 1).

17. Morton A. Kaplan, *System and Process in International Politics* (New York: Wiley, 1964). See also the critique in Kenneth Waltz, *op. cit.* (note 1), pp. 50–9.

18. K. J. Holsti, *International Politics: A framework for analysis* (New Jersey: Prentice Hall, 1967), p. 91; Richard Rosecrance, *International Relations: Peace or war?* (New York: McGraw-Hill, 1973), pp. 107–23.

19. Holsti, *op. cit.* (note 18), pp. 93–4.

20. Rosecrance, *op. cit.* (note 18), pp. 118, 122.

21. *ibid.*, p. 124.

22. John H. Herz, *International Politics in the Atomic Age* (New York: Columbia University Press, 1959), p. 241

23. Karl W. Deutsch and J. David Singer; 'Multipolar power systems and international stability', *World Politics*, 16 (1964); Michael Haas, 'International subsystems: stability and polarity', *American Political Science Review*, 64:1 (1970).

24. Waltz, *op. cit.* (note 1), ch. 8.

25. Patrick James and Michael Brecher, 'Stability and polarity: new paths for inquiry', *Journal of Peace Research*, 25:1 (1988); Michael Brecher, Jonathan Wilkenfeld and Patrick James, 'Polarity and stability: new concepts, indicators and evidence', paper presented at ISA Conference, London, March 1989.

26. On the problem of historical comparisons, see Klaus Knorr 'On the utility of history', in K. Knorr (ed.), *Historical Dimensions of National Security Problems* (Lawrence: University Press of Kansas, 1976), pp. 1–4; Young, *op. cit.* (note 1), p. 245; and Rosecrance, *op. cit.* (note 18), pp. 200–7.

27. Rosecrance, *op. cit.* (note 18), ch. 6, deals with this under the useful concept of environmental supply.

28. For an elaboration of this argument, see Robert E. Osgood and Robert Tucker, *Force Order and Justice* (Baltimore: Johns Hopkins University Press, 1967), pp. 88–120.
29. *ibid.*, p. 195.
30. For discussion, see Buzan, Jones and Little, *op. cit.* (note 1).
31. Hedley Bull, *The Anarchical Society*, (London: Macmillan, 1987), p. 109.
32. Bull, *ibid.*, pp. 106–7.
33. Quoted *ibid.*, p. 101.
34. *ibid.*, ch. 5; and Stanley Hoffman, *Primacy or World Order* (New York: McGraw-Hill, 1978), pp. 168–77.
35. Bull, *ibid.*, pp. 107–8.
36. Hoffmann, *op. cit.* (note 34), p. 176.
37. See Buzan in Buzan, Jones and Little, *op. cit.* (note 1) for further discussion.
38. Michael Intrilligator and Dagobert Brito, 'Nuclear proliferation and the problem of war', Center for Arms Control and International Security, UCLA, 1979; Barry Buzan, *An Introduction to Strategic Studies: Military technology and international relations* (London: Macmillan, 1987), esp. ch. 12 and pp. 172–7.
39. Hedley Bull and Adam Watson, *The Expansion of International Society* (Oxford: Oxford University Press, 1984), p. 1.
40. Bull, *op. cit.* (note 31), ch. 1, and in Bull and Watson *ibid.*, pp. 117–21. See also earlier writings on international society: E. H. Carr, *The Twenty Years Crisis* (London: Macmillan, 1946) 2nd edn, pp. 162–9; and Martin Wight, *Power Politics* (Harmondsworth: Penguin, 1979), pp. 105–12.
41. Bull and Watson, *op. cit.* (note 39), p. 1. For the detailed history, see McNeill, *op. cit.* (note 1).
42. Bull, *op. cit.* (note 31), pp. 38–40, 257–60, 315–17; E. Kedourie, A. Bozeman, and H. Bull and A. Watson in Bull and Watson, *op. cit.* (note 39), pp. 347–56, 387–406, 425–35.
43. Bull and Watson, *op. cit.* (note 39), pp. 434–5.
44. Waltz, *op. cit.* (note 1), pp. 88–97.
45. Bull, *op. cit.* (note 31), p. 287.
46. *ibid.*, chs 5–9.
47. Bull and Watson, *op. cit.* (note 39), p. 434. See also note 14.
48. Barry Buzan, 'The Southeast Asian security complex', *Contemporary Southeast Asia*, 10:1 (1988), pp. 12–13.
49. Egbert Jahn, Pierre Lemaitre, Ole Wæver, *European Security: Problems of research on non-military aspects*, Copenhagen Papers no. 1, Centre for Peace and Conflict Research, Copenhagen, 1987, p. 55.
50. Von Laue, *op. cit.* (note 5).
51. R. D. McKinlay and R. Little, *Global Problems and World Order* (London: Pinter, 1986), chs 1 and 11.
52. John H. Herz, 'The territorial state revisited', in J. N. Rosenau (ed.), *International Politics and Foreign Policy* (New York: Free Press, 1969), pp. 82, 89.
53. For an interesting attempt to discuss some of the conditions necessary for a mature anarchy, see Stanley Hoffmann, 'Regulating the new international system', in Martin Kilson (ed.), *New States in the Modern World* (Cambridge, Mass.: Harvard University Press, 1975), pp. 188–97.

54. Decolonization, it must be stressed, was a highly distorted and imperfect implementation of national self-determination. States were made independent, but these often reflected arbitrary colonial boundaries rather than nations, leaving the new states with a formidable task of nation-building along state-nation lines.

55. On the modern state, see Joseph R. Strayer, *On the Medieval Origins of the Modern State* (Princeton, NJ: Princeton University Press, 1970); Heinz Lubasz, *The Development of the Modern State* (London: Macmillan, 1964); Leonard Tivey (ed.), *The Nation-State: The formation of modern politics* (Oxford: Martin Robertson, 1981); and Kenneth Dyson, *The State Tradition in Western Europe* (Oxford: Martin Robertson, 1980).

chapter five | regional security

This chapter addresses the level of analysis between individual states and the international political system as a whole. It posits the existence of regional sub-systems as objects of security analysis, and offers an analytical framework for dealing with them. This framework is designed to highlight the relative autonomy of regional security relations, and to set them in the context of the state and system levels. One of its purposes is to provide area specialists with the language and concepts to facilitate comparative studies across regions, which is a notable weakness in the existing literature. Another is to offset the tendency of power theorists to underplay the importance of the regional level in international security affairs.

The chapter starts with a detailed explanation of how regional security subsystems work, and how they are differentiated both from each other and from the great powers. This provides the static part of the framework against which significant change can be identified. The second section goes on to consider the history that produced the current pattern of regional security, to complete a rough global sketch of that pattern and to expand on how the regional and great power dynamics interact with each other. Figure 5.1, at the end of this section, gives my interpretation of the current pattern, and readers may find it useful to refer to this in the discussions of particular cases throughout the chapter. The third section describes how regional patterns can change, and sets out systematic options for capturing the dynamics of change at this level. The concluding section considers the policy utilities of regional security analysis using this method.

FILLING THE GAP BETWEEN STATE AND SYSTEM LEVELS: SECURITY COMPLEXES

Any attempt to study security has to face the problem of the seamless web. Security is a relational phenomenon. Because security is relational, one cannot understand the national security of any given state without understanding the international pattern of security interdependence in which it is embedded. This leads to analysis on the system level as explored in the previous chapter. The trouble with the seamless web is that its logic pushes towards complicated holistic perspectives. If the security of each is related to the security of all, then nothing can be fully understood without understanding everything. Such a tall order threatens to make the study of security unrealistic.

Since the reality of security interdependence is unavoidable, the only hope of defining manageable subjects for study that neither lose nor succumb to the vital sense of the whole, is to find a hierarchy of analytical levels within the international system. Each of these levels must identify durable, significant and substantially self-contained features of the security problem. By self-contained, I do not mean totally free standing, but rather a security dynamic that would exist even if other actors did not impinge on it. Israel and Syria, for example, would be military rivals even if neither of them was supported by a superpower sponsor. No one level will, by itself, be adequate to understand the security problem as a whole, and the full meaning of each will only become clear when it is seen in relation to the others.

The top and bottom levels of this scheme are readily apparent. The system and the state levels of analysis tell us important things about the national security problem, and have been discussed in Chapters 2 and 4. But there is also an important set of security dynamics at the regional level, and this often tends to get lost or discounted. At that middle level, one finds only the hazy notions of regional balances of power and subsystems, or crude media references that use region to describe whatever location currently contains a newsworthy level of political turbulence.

So weak is the sense of regional security patterns that an otherwise excellent 1984 study on security in southern Asia frankly admitted that the choice of a set of countries as a region was 'necessarily arbitrarily defined'.[1] In my view, there are strong grounds, both empirical and theoretical, for rejecting such an intellectual surrender. Comprehensive security analysis requires that one take particular care to investigate how the regional level mediates the interplay between states and the international system as a whole. Unless that level is properly comprehended, neither the position of the local states in relation to each other, nor the character of relations between the great powers and local states can be understood properly.

In security terms, 'region' means that a distinct and significant subsystem of security relations exists among a set of states whose fate is that they have been locked into geographical proximity with each other. This idea of a regional system has historically been very strong in thinking about the European balance of power: Europe was (and is) a regional system because both its power relations and its escalation chains tied all of the states within it together. Denmark and Italy might have almost no direct security interaction, but both of them could easily find themselves caught up in the same pattern of alliance and war. In part, subsystems of regional security stem from the simple mechanism discussed in Chapter 3 by which threats, particularly political and military ones, are most strongly felt when they are at close range. But because the European states came to dominate the world system – and indeed to occupy much of it directly – no similarly strong sense of other local security subsystems has developed within Western thinking about international relations. Even the massive processes of decolonization, which should logically have caused attention to be paid to the re-emergence of local security subsystems, has been overshadowed by the global rivalry between the superpowers.

Giving a firm identity to regional subsystems establishes two intermediate levels of analysis between system and state: the subsystems themselves, and the pattern of relations among them. The only traditional subsystem idea with any potential for the purposes of security analysis is the notion of local or regional balances of power. But this idea has never proved very useful precisely because it was confined to that single dimension – power – on which the great power dynamic most strongly overrode and obscured the local ones. Although local balances of power do operate, and are a significant feature of the security environment, they can be easily upset or distorted by movements in the globe-spanning resources of the great powers. Because of their susceptibility to external influences, balances of power are a much less reliable guide to security relations in the periphery than they are at the centre.

By itself, the idea of subsystem – defined by Haas as 'any subset' of the international system[2] – is too broad to offer any guidance as to how region might be defined. Haas and Brecher both made attempts to devise frameworks for subordinate subsystems based on fairly broad notions of what constitutes a region.[3] Russett pursued this line from the perspective of integration,[4] but his, and others' idealist, functionalist concerns led to a search for regional foundations for integration that not surprisingly proved difficult to find. The most interesting older work is that by Cantori and Spiegel, who undertook an ambitious attempt to devise a whole comparative framework for the study of regional international relations.[5] Many of their concerns motivate the present proposal, especially the need to fill the gap between the state and system levels of analysis. Their scheme is suggestive on several fronts, including the importance of geographical proximity in establishing regions, and the role played by 'intrusive systems' in regional relations. But despite their wealth of suggestive ideas, their attempt to tackle region across the whole agenda of international relations, and to set up a detailed comparative politics framework, proved too complex and cumbersome to establish a generally followed understanding of region. Consequently, none of these approaches resulted in any widely accepted definition of region. A review of the earlier literature on regional subsystems by Thompson sadly catalogues the lack of progress towards development of any coherent theoretical or even descriptive framework.[6]

More recent work by Ayoob, Buzan and Rizvi *et al.*, Little, Väyrynen and Wæver avoids many of these earlier difficulties by focusing on regions in terms of security relations.[7] These provide a narrower and more manageable approach than the total framework of Cantori and Spiegel, and one with firmer roots in the realities of regional relations than that of the integrationists. Security is a broader idea than power, and it has the useful feature of incorporating much of the insight which derives from the analysis of power.[8]

In defining regional security, the principal element that must be added to power relations is the pattern of amity and enmity among states. By amity I mean relationships ranging from genuine friendship to expectations of protection or support. By enmity I mean relationships set by suspicion and fear. Separating these two poles is a broad band of indifference and/or neutrality, in which amity and enmity are either too weak to matter much, or else mixed in a way that produces no clear leaning one way or the other. An extreme view of balance-of-power theory would hold that patterns of amity/enmity are a product of the balance of power, with states shifting their alignments in accordance with the dictates of movements in the distribution of power. The view here is that the historical dynamic of amity and enmity is only partly related to the balance of power, and that where it is related, it is much stickier than the relatively fluid movement of the distribution of power. Enmity can be particularly durable when it acquires a historical character between peoples, as it has between Greeks and Turks, Poles and Russians, Koreans and Japanese and many others. Consequently the two patterns must be considered as distinct factors in the security problematique.

Patterns of amity/enmity arise from a variety of issues that could not be predicted from a simple consideration of the distribution of power. These range from specific things such as border disputes, interests in ethnically related populations, and ideological alignments, to longstanding historical links, whether positive or negative, such as those between Jews and Arabs, British and Americans, and Vietnamese and Chinese. By adding the dimension of amity/enmity to the picture, one gets a clearer sense of the relational pattern and character of insecurity than that provided by the raw abstraction of the balance-of-power view. On this basis, regional security subsystems can be seen in terms of patterns of amity and enmity that are substantially confined within some particular geographical area. I use the term *security complex* to label the resulting formations. A security complex is defined as a group of states whose primary security concerns link together sufficiently closely that their national securities cannot realistically be considered apart from one another.[9] The name has the advantage of indicating both the character of the attribute that defines the set (security), and the notion of intense interdependence that distinguishes any particular set from its neighbours. Security complexes emphasize the interdependence of rivalry as well as that of shared interests.

In one sense, the idea of security complexes is simply an analytical device. As such it serves as a perceptual lens designed to bring the regional level of analysis more clearly into focus. It is a way of making the relative autonomy of regional security dynamics stand out from the local and systemic levels. It helps one to locate and identify specific regional formations, and it provides a language and a framework for comparative security studies of different regions.

In another sense, however, the idea represents more than the arbitrary abstraction implied in the 'any subset' definition of subsystem. Security complexes are an empirical phenomenon with historical and geopolitical roots. In theoretical terms, they can be derived from both the state and the system levels. Looked at from the bottom up, security complexes result from interactions between individual states. They represent the way in which the sphere of concern that any state has about its environment, interacts with the linkage between the intensity of military and political threats, and the shortness of the range over which they are perceived. Because threats operate more potently over short distances, security interactions with neighbours will tend to have first priority. Seen from the top down, security complexes are generated by the interaction of anarchy and geography. The political structure of anarchy confronts all states with the security dilemma, but the otherwise seamless web of security interdependence is powerfully mediated by the effects of geography. Unless capabilities for transportation are very unevenly distributed, as they sometimes are, all states will thus tend to be thrust into closer contact with their neighbours than with those further afield. By either of these routes, security complexes can be seen as characteristic products of an anarchic international system. They represent durable rather than permanent patterns within such a system. Other things being equal, one should expect to find these nodes of distinctively intense security interdependence existing throughout the system.

The empirical side of this argument courts the charge of reification (treating abstractions as objects). But the fact that security complexes are in some sense 'real' is important. It is their reality which explains the mediating effect that they have on relations between the great powers and the local states. The reality of security complexes lies more in the individual lines of amity, enmity and indifference between states, than in the notion of a self-aware subsystem. Like a balance of power, a security complex can exist and function regardless of whether or not the actors involved recognize it. They will, of course, recognize the particular lines of threat which bear on them, for if they did not, the whole idea of security complexes would be void. But they may well not see, or appreciate fully, the whole pattern of which they are a part. Typically, states will be much more aware of the threats others pose to them than they will be of the threat they pose to others. This issue of recognition marks a fairly sharp analytical divide between balance of power models, which generally do not require that actors recognize the patterns that shape their behaviour, and subsystems, which frequently require such awareness as part of the definition of a subsystem.[10] Though recognition of the complex, as with a balance of power, is not a necessary condition for its existence, if recognition occurs, it may well influence the policies of the actors involved by making them more conscious of the larger relational context underlying their specific policy problems.

The dominance of particular amity/enmity relationships over awareness of the whole, complicates the process of identifying security complexes in hard scientific terms. The individual lines of security concern can be traced quite easily by observing how states' fears shape their foreign policy and military behaviour. Pakistan deploys the bulk of its army against India rather than on its borders with China, Afghanistan or Iran. Thailand is much more concerned by threats from Vietnam than from any of its other neighbours. Greece worries more about Turkey than about its other neighbours. But assessing the overall pattern formed by those lines, and particularly finding concentrations of interaction within the pattern which are strong enough to constitute a complex, may be a matter of controversy. The problem of the seamless web is at its most acute in the regional level of analysis.

The task of identifying a security complex involves making judgements about the relative strengths of security interdependencies among different countries. In some places these will be very strong, as between India and Pakistan, in others relatively weak, as between Indonesia and Australia. In some places the interdependencies will be positive, as in the mutually supportive neutralities of Sweden and Finland, in others negative, as in the triangular rivalry among Iran, Iraq and Saudi Arabia. Usually, they will arise from local relationships, but when very large powers are involved a whole group of states can be bound together by a common threat. The squeezing of the Western European states by superpower rivalry during the Cold War provides an example of this kind of interdependence.[11] In some places interdependence will be very low, and these point to boundaries between more intense nodes of interaction. Burma, for example, marks a boundary where the local security dynamics of South and Southeast Asia stand, as it were, back to back.

Within the overall seamless web of interdependence, one can thus expect to find patterns shaped by the different intensities of the lines of amity and enmity. A security complex exists where a set of security relationships stands out from the general background by virtue of its relatively strong, inward-looking character, and the relative weakness of its outward security interactions with its neighbours. Security interdependencies will be more strongly focused among the members of the set than they are between the members and outside states. The boundaries between such sets will thus be defined by the *relative indifference* attending the security perceptions and interactions across them. The strong insecurity links between Iran and Iraq put them clearly within the same complex, while the relatively weak links between Iran and Pakistan, and between Burma and all its neighbours, suggest the existence of boundaries between complexes. Evidence for the existence of security complexes also comes from patterns of war. It is notable, for example, that several substantial wars in South Asia have had virtually no impact on Southeast Asia or the Gulf. Conversely, major wars in Southeast Asia and the Gulf have had relatively little impact on South Asia. This insulation from the upheavals of neighbours points strongly to the existence of distinct nodes of concentration in the pattern of security relations across southern Asia, and suggests the existence of three distinct local security complexes in that area.

The principal factor defining a complex is usually a high level of threat/fear which is felt *mutually* among two or more major states. Unless they are world class powers, these states will usually be close neighbours. In theory, a high level of trust and friendship can also serve as a binding force, as it does among the ASEAN and Nordic groups of states. Security interdependence can be positive as well as negative, though instances of this defining a whole complex are rare. Europe could be moving in this direction, but if the European Community continues to integrate politically it will pass beyond the structure of an anarchic subsystem into the grey zone of semi-statehood. In other words, the pressure from outside on the Community as a single actor will begin to outweigh the internal anarchic dynamics of the subsystem.[12]

More commonly, the existence of sub-regional organizations defines lines of regional rivalry, as in the case of ASEAN, the Gulf Cooperation Council (GCC) and the Southern African Development Coordinating Conference (SADCC).[13] In South Asia, the complex is defined by the Indo-Pakistan rivalry, while in the Gulf, it is defined by a three-sided rivalry among Iran, Iraq and Saudi Arabia, and in Southeast Asia, at least up to the late 1980s, by the rivalry between the ASEAN group and Vietnam. The extent to which neighbouring local dynamics like these are distinct is indicated by the security rhetoric of the states towards each other, by their military deployments and by the record of their conflicts.

One reason for using the criteria of mutuality in defining a security complex is the problem that otherwise exists because of a lopsided security link between two major local states. The relationship between China on the one hand, and India and many of the Southeast Asian states on the other, provides a clear example.[14] China is a major security concern for India, and also for Vietnam, Malaysia and Indonesia: arguably even the principal one. Chinese military strength lies close to India's and Vietnam's main centres of population, and China has fought fierce little border wars with both. This evidence points to a strong insecurity link and therefore possibly to a security complex. But the lack of balance in the relationships points to distinct complexes instead. India and Vietnam are relatively minor security concerns for China, whose main security worries are with the superpowers. Indian and Vietnamese military strength sit far from China's heartlands, and weigh little compared with the other threats to China's interests.

A situation like this typically indicates the existence of a boundary between a *lower*- and a *higher*-level security complex. A lower-level complex is composed of local states whose power does not extend much, if at all, beyond the range of their immediate neighbours. This constraint on power is a key element in the existence of relatively self-contained local security dynamics among sets of neighbouring states. A higher-level complex, by contrast, contains great powers: states like the United States and the Soviet Union, whose power may well extend far beyond their immediate environment, or states like China and the Soviet Union, whose power is sufficient to impinge on several regions of what their enormous physical size makes a vast 'local environment'. Higher-level complexes define the system or global level of analysis. The distinction between lower- and higher-level complexes thus becomes important when all of the levels of security analysis – domestic, regional, super-regional, and global – are reintegrated. Given large power differentials between the higher- and lower- levels, one expects unequal intervention from higher to lower to be a normal feature of the system. The question then becomes not a dispute about the boundaries of a security complex, but about the relative weight of local security dynamics in relation to those pressing on the region from outside. In Southeast Asia for example, the local dynamics have to compete with much more powerful outside pressures on the region than is the case in South Asia. One major advantage of the security complex idea is precisely that it provides an insight into the regional level security dynamics that shape and mediate such intervention.

Because security complexes are in part geographical entities, they will often include by default a number of minor states. Due to their relatively low power in comparison with their neighbours, these states may have little impact on the structure of the complex. Their own securities are intimately bound up in the pattern of the larger states, but they can only become a source of threat to a larger state by virtue of the impact of their alignments on relations among the larger powers. In the Gulf, Kuwait, Bahrain, Qatar and the UAE are in this position. In South Asia, it is occupied by Bangladesh, Bhutan, Nepal, Sri Lanka and the Maldives, nearly all of which are tied closely to India by the dictates of geography and culture. Some of these small states may play buffer roles within the local security dynamics: Switzerland, Belgium, Cambodia, Jordan, Kuwait, and before 1976 Lebanon, are examples.

As already noted, some states occupy insulating positions between neighbouring security complexes. They define and occupy the boundaries of indifference between the self-contained dynamics on either side of them. Burma is a very clear example of this role between South and Southeast Asia, as is Turkey between Europe and the Middle East, Afghanistan between South Asia and the Middle East, and the belt of states stretching across the Sahara from Mauritania to Sudan between the Middle East and black Africa. These insulators may exist in relative isolation from the security dynamics on either side in the case of Burma, or they may, as it were, face both ways on the edges of neighbouring complexes without linking them, as Turkey, Afghanistan and the Sahel states do. A variant on this theme is those states that act as insulators between lower-level complexes and a member of a higher-level one. Finland, Sweden, Austria and Yugoslavia played this role between the Soviet empire and Western Europe during the Cold War, and Nepal plays it between China and India.

The question of whether cultural and racial ties should be a factor in identifying security complexes is an interesting one. It seems not unlikely that shared cultural and racial characteristics among a group of states would cause them both to pay more attention to each other in general, and to legitimize mutual interventions in each other's security affairs in particular. The South Asian complex, for example, coincides with what K. Subrahmanyam has called a 'civilisational area'.[15] It is not difficult to find evidence that Arab, Latin American and Islamic cultural factors likewise facilitate and legitimize security interdependence among a large group of states. A similar line of ethno-cultural thinking underlies much traditional analysis of European history, with its emphasis on the role of Latin Christendom in defining a community of states.

This factor is particularly clear in the Middle East, a vast area stretching from Morocco to Oman, and from Syria to Somalia. Within that area, the idea of an Arab nation, and the transnational political force of Islam, combine to create a potent regional political arena. Arab nationalism and Islam both weaken the identity of the local states, and legitimize an unusually high degree of security interpenetration.[16] They stimulate a marked propensity to establish regional organizations (the

Arab League, the Gulf Cooperation Council, the Arab Cooperation Council, the Maghreb Group), and even to promote (mostly with little success) mergers between states. They also play a major part in defining the main nodes of conflict in the region centred on three non-Arab states embedded within it – Israel, Iran and Ethiopia – two of which are not Islamic, and the third of which is the representative of Islam's principal schism. In defining the shape and structure of security complexes, cultural and racial patterns may well be an important contributing factor, though they come second to the patterns of security perception which are the principal defining factor.

Even using these guidelines, it is an empirical question whether the relative strength of different lines of security interdependence is sufficient to establish the location of boundaries that distinguish one security complex from another. Measuring variables like amity and enmity, is an even less precise business than measuring power or socio-political cohesion, though in all of these cases the main features usually stand out quite clearly even in the absence of scientific scales for comparison. As argued above, security complexes are a natural product of anarchic structure. Other things being equal, one should therefore expect to find a pattern of such complexes covering the entire international system. Sometimes this is a fairly straightforward exercise, as in South Asia. But other things, of course, are not always equal. As a consequence, there are cases where security complexes are hard to find, and cases where the correct placement of boundaries is not obvious.

There are two general conditions that explain why a security complex may be hard to find. The first is that in some areas local states are so weak that their power does not project much, if at all, beyond their own boundaries. These states have domestically directed security perspectives, and there is not enough security interaction between them to generate a local complex. These conditions are characteristic of some parts of Africa, and perhaps also among the small Pacific Ocean island states, where very weak powers are separated by vast insulating distances of water.

The second condition is more complicated. It occurs when the direct presence of outside powers in a region is strong enough to suppress the normal operation of security dynamics among the local states. This condition is called *overlay*. It normally involves extensive stationing of armed forces in the overlain area by the intervening great power(s), and is quite distinct from the normal process of intervention by great powers into the affairs of local security complexes. Intervention usually reinforces the local security dynamics: overlay subordinates them to the larger pattern of major power rivalries, and may even obliterate them. The best examples of it are the period of European colonialism in what is now the Third World, and the submergence of European security dynamics by superpower rivalry after the Second World War.[17] Under overlay, one cannot see with any clarity what the local security dynamics are, and therefore cannot identify a local complex.[18] One knows only what the local dynamics were before overlay. Since overlay is normally a transforming political experience, one can only speculate as to what the local dynamics might be once overlay breaks up. When the colonial overlay lifted, it left behind the more than 100 territorial states that now populate the Third World. As the superpower overlay of Europe breaks up, it is obvious that what is emerging is much changed from the pre-1945 dynamics. Indeed, what the character of the European security complex will be in the twenty-first century is one of the great speculative questions of the day.[19]

Three quite different conditions explain why it can be difficult to locate the boundaries of security complexes whose existence is not in doubt. The first is simply that the boundary between two security complexes is dissolving in a major change in the pattern of regional security dynamics. This will be discussed further below. The second involves the existence of the lopsided security interdependence that occurs when higher and lower level complexes are physically adjacent. As discussed above in relation to China, and India and Vietnam, significant security relationships may exist across these boundaries. The argument here is not that such relationships should be ignored or discounted by being defined out of the security complex, but that the best place to deal with them is when looking at the interaction between the higher-level complex(es) at the system level, and the lower-level ones rooted in particular regions. The issue is then about the relative autonomy and interaction between the dynamics at the two levels. The picture, in other words, comes clear when all of the levels in the security analysis from domestic to global are reassembled into a complete picture.

The third difficulty in identifying the boundaries of complexes is caused by situations in which two or more nodes of security interdependence exist within a group of states which there are also grounds for thinking of as a single complex. South Asia is unproblematic in this regard, having just two major states and one defining rivalry. Southeast Asia, with nine states, including four biggish ones, is more complicated, but still unproblematic, since these are polarized into a single rivalry.[20] The Middle Eastern complex, however, contains two dozen states and three, or possibly four, subcomplexes that have distinct dynamics within the complex overall. The three main subcomplexes are centred on the Gulf, with Iran, Iraq and Saudi Arabia as the principals, the Horn of Africa, with Ethiopia, Sudan and Somalia as the principals, and the Eastern Mediterranean, with Israel, Syria and Egypt as the principals. There is a vaguer node of rivalry in the Maghreb among Algeria, Morocco and Libya. All of these nodes have their own distinctive dynamics, but there is enough crossing of boundaries within the Middle Eastern complex to justify identifying the larger formation as the main regional unit. Syria plays in the Gulf subcomplex by allying with Iran and opposing Iraq, and Egypt does also by supporting Iraq against Iran. Saudi Arabia and Egypt take an interest in the Horn. Nearly all of the Arab states take some part in the opposition to Israel, which returns the favour by stirring up inter-Arab and inter-Islamic rivalries wherever it can. The Arab League provides a legitimizing forum in which the affairs of the different subcomplexes are linked together, and which helps to differentiate Middle Eastern security affairs from those in Asia, Europe and central Africa.

A similar complexity prevails in Europe. The more than two dozen states there contain several distinct sub-regions such as the Nordic area and the Balkans. As yet, regional security analysis in Europe is made difficult by the lack of clarity about local dynamics because of the still substantial presence of overlay. What is clear, is the unique position of Europe over the last forty years during which the threats from superpower rivalry far outweighed any security threats arising from within Europe itself. Despite their different locations, Sweden and Spain and Ireland and Italy all faced the same common threat that Soviet power might over-awe Europe, or that Europe might be destroyed in a war to defend it against Soviet attack. As with the Middle Eastern complex, that in Europe also has some awk-ward boundaries. The Middle East blurs into Africa, and Europe blurs into the Soviet Union. Politics has never been a tidy subject.

Controversy over such issues reflects genuine ambiguities in the real world. What is important for security analysis overall is that *some* coherent sense of the regional security dynamics be interposed between the global and state levels. In my view, it is a much bigger analytical error to have *no* systematic conception of regional security dynamics than it is to have a disputed one. The main issue is rec-ognizing that strong local security dynamics almost always exist in an anarchical-ly structured international system. Once that point is accepted, and integrated into security analysis, disagreements about the location of boundaries within the seam-less web are unlikely to result in major contradictions. Indeed, by providing alter-native perspectives on both intra-regional and global-regional security relations, they could well enrich analysis where genuine ambiguity exists. So long as the logic behind contending positions is made clear, there is no harm in controversy about how security complexes are defined.

Once the regional level is established, then the full range of levels that com-prise a comprehensive analytical framework can be sketched out. At the bottom end lies the domestic security environment of individual states. It is vital to under-stand the internal character of the states concerned, because weak states with unstable socio-political structures clearly have more vulnerabilities, and therefore face different and more complicated security problems, than strong states. Next comes the lower-level, or local, security complexes. One would expect relations to be relatively intense within these complexes, and relatively subdued between them. But in some instances, significant interplay can occur across the boundaries of indifference that mark one complex off from another. Thus relations between security complexes also comprise a layer within the framework, and one that becomes important if major changes in the pattern of security complexes are underway. At the top end, one finds the higher or great power complexes. These define the system level, as discussed above. One would expect security relations among the great powers to be intense, and to penetrate in varying degrees into the affairs of the local complexes. The method of analysis within this framework is first to understand the distinctive security dynamic at each level, and then to see how the patterns at each level interact with each other. (See summary table 5.1 on p. 185.)

One final point concerning the definition of security complexes is the role of economic factors. In looking for the sets of states that constitute security complexes, one is primarily concerned with the military, political and societal dimensions of security. The reason that these sectors are the most relevant to the patterns of threat and amity/enmity that define the set is because economic relations are not nearly so much conditioned by geographical proximity as are military and political ones. Consequently, the problem of economic security is likely to have a quite different relational dynamic from that of military and political security. In the European complex before 1914, for example, major military rivalries ran alongside extensive trading relationships. But in the contemporary superpower rivalry, a strong interdependence in military security is paralleled by a very low level of economic exchange. A pattern similar to that of the superpowers prevails in most Third World regions, where local political and military interdependence is strong, but economic relations follow a much more wide-ranging pattern that has little to do with region. Under such conditions, the economic security of the states concerned does not depend primarily on their relationship with the other states within the complex. Some exceptions do exist. Advanced capitalist countries in Europe and North America combine close politico-military and economic relations. In the Southern African complex, control over workable railways adds a major economic dimension to the defining framework of political rivalry.

Economic factors do play a role in determining both the power of states within their local complex, and their domestic stability and cohesion as actors. They may also play an important role in motivating the patterns of external interest in the local complex, as in the case of the United States and the oil-producing countries of the Gulf. And they can affect the prospects for regional integration, which can influence how a given security complex evolves. South Asia, for example, offers much less prospect for economic cooperation than does Western Europe, because the similarities among the South Asian economies make them more competitive than complementary. So, economic factors need to be taken into account in analysing a security complex, but the framework we are using here is not usually appropriate for examining economic security itself.[21]

A BRIEF HISTORY OF REGIONAL SECURITY

Regional security has had an odd history in the modern international system. From the theory, one would expect a pattern of regional security complexes to be a normal condition of the system. In historical fact, other things have rather seldom been equal over the last few hundred years, and the current pattern of regional security is mostly of quite recent vintage.

For two millennia before the great European rise to global dominance, the international system was structured around four great civilizational areas: Europe, the Middle East, India and China. These were all in a rough balance with each other, and each was as much, and sometimes more, threatened by periodic surges of barbarians from the Eurasian steppe, as it was by attack from its neighbours. At times each of these areas achieved imperial unity, and at times they lapsed into phases of division and warring states. In a slow process of diffusion, civilization seeped steadily outwards from its heartlands in the great river valleys of Mesopotamia, Egypt, India and China, stimulating higher levels of social, political and economic organization in Southeast Asia, Central and Northern Europe, and much later in Africa. Barbarism steadily gave way to more settled, state-like forms of socio-political organization. Minor outliers to this process developed independently in the Americas, but these were of a very primitive type, being similar in construction to the first civilizations that had grown up in the valleys of the Tigris and Euphrates more than 3,000 years earlier.[22]

This essentially Eurasian world system could be analyzed in terms of both great power dynamics and regional security complexes. Sometimes great empires clashed for control of civilizational core areas. Hellenistic and Persian, and later Islamic and Christian empires clashed repeatedly, India largely succumbed to Islamic conquest, and almost everywhere except Western Europe gave way to the short-lived power of the Mongol Khans. At other times, something more like local security complexes operated, as in the warring-states periods in India and China, and the fragmentation of Europe after the collapse of the Western Roman empire. The typical pattern of great power intervention in the affairs of local security complexes did sometimes operate. The Persian empire meddled in the highly divided politics of ancient Greece, and the Chinese empire tried always to keep the steppe barbarians to its north and west divided against themselves. But limits to military and economic power generally prevented the operation of sustained long-distance power projection by great powers into the affairs of lesser states.

The rise of the European powers from the fifteenth century steadily subjected nearly all of this ancient system to overlay. As European empires spread, the pattern of global security became less and less driven by local dynamics, and more and more subordinated to the dynamics of European rivalries. One of the great paradoxes of the European ascent is that the European states became dominatingly powerful in good part because they were divided and competitive among themselves. It was not a united European empire that took over the international system, but an exceptionally vigorous and aggressive local security complex. Having sharpened their capabilities against each other, the European powers quite suddenly found that their superior organization and technology fairly easily enabled them to overawe local power almost everywhere else in the system. As a consequence, the 2,000-year-long quadripolar balance of civilizations in Eurasia, was steadily transformed into a global extension of the European security complex. The primitive Amerindian empires collapsed at the touch of a social and military system three millennia more advanced than themselves. Resistance elsewhere from both barbarians and civilized peoples was more robust, but the power advantage of the Europeans was so great that they had more often to worry about each other than about local opposition.

The overlay of most of the international system by European, and later Japanese and American colonial empires effectively suppressed most of what is understood in this analysis as regional security dynamics. As discussed in Chapter 4, the European complex had moved to a higher-level status, and captured the whole system. The pattern of global security was thus simply an extension of European great power rivalries, with Japan and the United States as late-arriving additions. But although overlay suppressed local security dynamics, it was by no means politically neutral as regards the subject populations. In retrospect, overlay can be seen primarily as a process of state construction. In effect, the Europeans global- ized the form of political organization – the territorial state – that underlay their own success. Sometimes they did this by direct transplanting of population, as in the Americas, Australia and South Africa, sometimes by imperial imposition, as in Asia and Africa. In a few cases, local adaptation to the European model, as in Japan, Thailand, Ethiopia and China, provided a narrow escape from colonization. This operation was most successful either when the local populations were large- ly replaced by European immigrants, or where, as in much of Asia, older civiliza- tional traditions could be fitted into the new political structure. It was least suc- cessful in Africa, where the rather sparse civilizational traditions had shallow roots, and local populations constituted a highly divided social mosaic.

Despite its mixed results, the transplantation of the European territorial state to the rest of the planet, inevitably paved the way for the universalization of the competitive European style of anarchic international relations. When overlay lift- ed, first in the Americas, and then, after the Second World War, in Asia and Africa, it left behind an entire international system organized along sovereignty-anarchy lines. It is from that release of overlay that the contemporary dynamics of region- al security stem. In some places, as in the Americas and parts of Africa, the suc- cessor states to the European empires constituted a wholly new pattern of rela- tions. In other places, as in much of the Middle East and Asia, they released older patterns of relations dressed up in the new form. The relative recentness of these events perhaps goes some way to explaining why great power perspectives still dominate analysis of regional security: for a long time such a perspective reflect- ed reality. For those with a sense of historical irony, there was also some justice in the fact that the principal colonizers in Europe and Japan were themselves over- laid by the superpower rivalry after 1945.

The freeing of the Third World from European and Japanese control did not, of course, give rise to fully formed security complexes. As Walter Little argues from the Latin American case, a 'working out' period is necessary after decolo- nization in order for the new states to find their feet and sort out their relation- ships. For Latin America, that period was more than half a century.[23] The South Asian complex sprang into existence almost fully formed in 1947, but elsewhere in Asia and Africa the process of decolonization itself was strung out over two decades. In addition, the new states did not emerge into a neutral environment. Most of them remained dependent on the ex-metropolitan powers, and all of them, after 1947, were subject to the intense global rivalry of the two superpowers.

The global pattern of security complexes that has resulted from this process is not yet fully formed. In most areas, distinct local dynamics have emerged, and fully fledged regional security complexes are functioning. This is the case in

South Asia, Southeast Asia and the Middle East, all of which have been sketched in the previous section. It is also true in Southern Africa, where the confrontation is between (and within) South Africa and the frontline black states; and, more arguably, in the South Pacific, where the South Pacific Forum binds Australia, New Zealand and many of the small island states into a loose security community. Water acts as a significant damper of the security dilemma between neighbours, and this not only facilitates peaceful relations within the ASEAN group, but also allows Australia to disengage itself from Southeast Asia.

But in some areas, most notably the band of over twenty states sandwiched between the southern side of the Middle Eastern complex and the northern side of the Southern African one, no firm patterns of local security interdependence have yet emerged. Most of these states are too weak both as states and as powers to generate a significant pattern of regional security relations. All of them are more pre-occupied with domestic than with national security problems, and rare exceptions such as the Tanzanian invasion of Amin's Uganda scarcely begin to create a pattern that might indicate the outlines of future regional security complexes.

The Americas are somewhat harder to characterize, not least because of the overwhelmingly powerful presence of the United States. North America, including Central America and the Caribbean, is perhaps best seen as mixture of security community and hegemonic complex. The Central American and Caribbean states are mostly very weak both as states and as powers. They have been so penetrated by the United States, and/or by superpower rivalry, as to make the emergence of any independent security dynamics virtually impossible to discern. The parallel drawn by Cantori and Spiegel between Latin America and Eastern Europe still holds for Central American and Caribbean states in terms of the maintenance of considerable overlay by a superpower on the security relations of states within their immediate back yard.[24]

South America also falls under the shadow of the United States, but much less so than Central America, and decreasingly as the quite substantial powers there consolidate themselves.[25] In some ways, South America still displays residual signs of overlay, most notably in the role of the OAS (Organization of American States), which ties the region's security relations to the United States. In other ways, it displays tendencies towards a security community, with the Latin American Nuclear Weapon Free Zone (Treaty of Tlatelolco) constituting a significant regional regime, indeed one that extends right up the United States border. With its relative civilizational homogeneity, Latin America was long the hope of the regional integrationists. It could be argued that South America, like central Africa, lacked sufficient interaction to form a security complex. Although its states are better developed and more powerful than those in Africa, nearly all of the territorial boundaries run through remote, sparsely populated areas that are either mountainous or covered in dense jungle.

But against this, the region's history does show clear signs of indigenous security dynamics. There have been several substantial wars – Paraguay versus Argentina, Brazil and Uruguay (1865–70); Chile versus Bolivia and Peru

(1879–84); Paraguay versus Bolivia (1928–35) – and one crisis with clear threats of war – Columbia versus Peru (1932–3). All of these concerned territorial disputes, and Bolivia is still not reconciled to the loss of its coastal territory. More recently, Chile and Argentina have been in tension over disputed islands in the south, and Venezuela claims a large chunk of Guyana. Brazil and Argentina have indulged in a general power rivalry since before the First World War, when they competed to buy expensive dreadnoughts from Europe. More recently, their competition has taken the form of military-run 'civil' nuclear power programmes. The Amazon jungles are quickly disappearing, and as the Brazilians continue their road-building plans,[26] many of the continent's territorial boundaries will cease to be insulated by remoteness. Thus all the makings exist for the South American complex to evolve either towards the rivalry dynamics typical of most other Third World regions, or towards a more mature anarchic structure in which the security dynamics of the region are governed by a stable multilateral regime.

All of these regional security dynamics in the Third World are evolving against a background in which the higher-level complex is also entering into a period of transformation. For most of the post-war period, the pattern of intervention from higher to lower levels was structured by the bipolar rivalry between the superpowers. But as the century draws to a close, both the superpowers and their rivalry are weakening in relation to the rest of the international system. China has already established itself as an independent great power in Asia, and India is also headed down that road. More significantly, as overlay is lifted in Europe and Northeast Asia, both Japan and the European Community are in their own odd and hesitant ways beginning to play roles in the system commensurate with their power. Thus the historical abnormality of superpowers and bipolarity is steadily reverting towards the more familiar structure of a system dominated by several great powers.

This shift away from bipolarity towards a more polycentric power structure at the system level cannot but have profound consequences for regional security. Where penetration from higher to lower levels is unipolar, then the result is like overlay, and the consequence is suppression of local conflicts. The American role in Latin America, and the Soviet one in Eastern Europe illustrate this process. Bipolar penetration suppresses local conflict if it takes the form of overlay, as in Europe; but if it is just alignment, as in much of the Third World, then it amplifies them. Väyrynen suggests that the logic of this progression points to multipolar penetration as the worst of all cases,[27] but this may be arguable. Bipolarity encourages peculiarly intense, zero-sum competition, and might thus be thought the most likely to amplify local rivalries. Multipolar penetration, as currently in Southeast Asia, may be messy, but it is less intense, and gives the local states greater latitude in their political relations with outside powers. Thus to the extent that bipolar conflict and the concentration of power in the centre are both presently weakening, the current outlook should be for less competitive intervention by the great powers in regional security affairs.

That trend is supported by the diffusion of power to the regional states, which should extend the process begun by decolonization of increasing the importance of regional security dynamics relative to those of the great powers. Whether a lower weight of intervention will mute or exacerbate regional conflicts very much depends on circumstances. It may, as in the case of the Gulf War, give freer reign to the pursuit of local rivalries. On the other hand, it may, as apparently in Southeast Asia and Southern Africa, provide external support for regional efforts at conflict resolution. Either way, as Kolodziej and Harkavy put it, there is a trend towards the 'decentralization of the international security system'.[28] It seems a safe bet to predict that indigenous patterns of regional security will be increasingly important features of the international system in the twenty-first century, thus closing for ever the brief historical period in which huge differentials in technology and socio-political organization enabled a handful of states to impose their control on the entire international community.

SECURITY COMPLEXES AS STRUCTURES: THE PROCESSES AND OUTCOMES OF CHANGE

Security complexes are not part of the structure of the international system in the meaning established by Waltz.[29] In relation to the international system as a whole, they are action-reaction phenomena, and thus akin to other recurrent patterns such as arms races and trade wars. In Waltz's scheme, which I broadly accept, such phenomena count as part of the unit level of analysis. I have labelled this action-reaction category *process formations*, in order to differentiate it from explanations that stem from the characteristics of the units themselves.[30] It is nevertheless valid to see security complexes as subsystems – miniature anarchies – in their own right. From that perspective, by analogy with full systems, they do have structures of their own. Since security complexes are durable rather than permanent features of the anarchy overall, seeing them as subsystems with their own structures and patterns of interaction provides a useful benchmark against which to identify and assess changes in the patterns of regional security.

In any discussion of change, one faces the core theoretical problem of distinguishing what is significant from what is not. Change is ubiquitous and continuous, and yet one can say with meaning that on some levels some things remain effectively the same over long periods.[31] The South Asian security complex, for example, has displayed a durable bipolar structure for nearly four decades. Its continuity resides in the primacy of India and Pakistan within the subcontinent, in the continuation of their treatment of each other as major rivals and in the absence of any developments within, or external impositions upon, South Asia strong enough to break this pattern. Structure in this sense has endured despite the endless changes within and around the subcontinent. Internal changes, including the partition of Pakistan, have not altered the basic pattern of relations. Neither have external ones, which have so far tended more to reinforce, than to undermine, the existing bipolarity. The more complex internal structures in Southeast Asia and the Middle East have exhibited more mobility, especially in terms of patterns of

Figure 5.1: Security complexes in the Third World

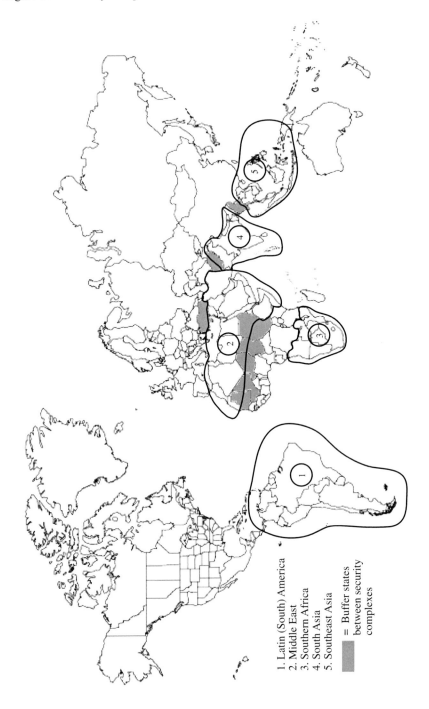

1. Latin (South) America
2. Middle East
3. Southern Africa
4. South Asia
5. Southeast Asia

■ = Buffer states
  between security
  complexes

amity/enmity, though they have not changed their external boundaries.

One can use the idea of *essential structure* as a standard by which to measure significant change in a security complex. The two key components of essential structure in a security complex are first, the patterns of amity and enmity and secondly, the distribution of power among the principal states. Major shifts in either would normally require a redefinition of the complex. This approach allows one to analyse regional security both in static and dynamic terms. If security complexes possess structures, then one can look for outcomes resulting from either structural effects or processes of structural change.

In analysing a security complex in terms of its distribution of power, the logic is the same as that for analysing the polarity of the system as a whole. But unlike in system analysis, shifts in the distribution of power in a subsystem can occur for either internal or external reasons. Power shifts resulting from internal factors can be caused in several ways. Actors can disintegrate, like Pakistan in 1971 and Austria-Hungary after the First World War, or they can merge, like the component parts of Germany and Italy during the nineteenth century. Such events have to be on a large scale to affect the essential structure of the complex. In South Asia, India's absorption of small states like Goa and Sikkim, made no real difference to the distribution of power within the subcontinent. Pakistan's loss of Bangladesh was both absolutely and relatively a much more substantial event, and at first seemed likely to put India into a position of such dominance as to call into question the basic bipolarity of the complex. But although Pakistan was certainly weakened politically by the loss of its pretension to Islamic exclusivity, its military strength was not much affected, and its leaders quickly left behind any inclination they might have had to defer to Indian hegemony. In some ways, the secession of Bangladesh removed a strategic liability from Pakistan and made its military position easier to handle. Despite its many troubles, Pakistan has remained both strong enough and wilful enough to sustain bipolarity. Only if the secession of Bangladesh turns out to be the first stage in a more complex Balkanization of Pakistan will the 1971 events be seen as the start of a major transformation of the South Asian complex.

Power shifts can also result from differences in the rate of development among actors. Japan rose to prominence in Asia because of its ability to modernize faster than its neighbours, and the Shah of Iran clearly had similar hopes for his own country. In the absence of different rates of growth, there is some scope for power shifts in the way countries allocate their existing resources. Major diversions of resources away from investment and civil consumption towards military expenditure can produce a power shift as India demonstrated in the doubling of its military budget after the 1962 war with China. But neither differences in rates of development nor differences in resource allocation have so far eroded the essential structure in South Asia. Rates of growth have not been wildly disparate, and whilst India has not tried to push its advantage of size, Pakistan has shown a willingness to bear a proportionately greater military burden.[32] A variation on this theme is the introduction of new military technology. The acquisition of powerful strike weapons such as nuclear-armed missiles can very quickly change perceptions of power and threat, possibly even sufficiently to redefine security complexes. A major Indian drive towards a nuclear missile arsenal, for example, could transform security relations with China. If Pakistan becomes entangled in the nuclear relations of the Middle Eastern complex, that too could reconstruct the pattern of security relations between South Asia and the Mediterranean.

Power shifts resulting from external factors are similarly diverse. External actors can change the power structure of a local complex in two ways: either by joining it, if they are adjacent, or by making alignments within it, whether they are either adjacent and/or members of a higher-level complex. For new actors to join a complex normally requires a redefinition of more than one complex, and is an infrequent event. The movement of small states may not have much impact on the essential structure. The historical and geographical ties that bind a local complex together are not easily overcome. In South Asia, one can imagine scenarios in which India achieves ascendancy over Pakistan, and extends its influence into the Gulf, or in which some of the Gulf states develop such close ties to Pakistan that the security dynamics of the Gulf and South Asia become entangled into an expanded new complex. But neither of these possibilities has so far developed to the point of overturning the established patterns in South and Southwest Asia.

External actors can impinge upon the local distribution of power in many ways short of actually joining, and thereby redefining, the complex. They can add to the power of local states directly, either by arms supply, or by the direct involvement of their own armed forces. Arms supply has been the characteristic tool of intervening great powers in almost every Third World security complex. Soviet arms supplies to Cuba, Syria, India and Vietnam, and American supplies to Israel, Pakistan, Iran and Saudi Arabia are only the most extreme of many examples. Direct involvement of armed forces is rarer, but the Americans tried it in Vietnam, and the Soviets in Egypt and Afghanistan. Through economic aid, external powers can try to alter the local rates of development to the advantage of one side or the other. American and Japanese support for South Korea is perhaps the most spectacularly successful example of this technique. In the early stages of external penetration the addition of new supporters to one side or the other is likely to be a major source of influence on the affairs of the local complex. Later, the local balance may be affected by the withdrawal of one external actor, like the loosening of American support for Pakistan in the 1960s and 1970s, and its withdrawal from Vietnam in 1973. In *extremis*, external powers can overlay the local power dynamic completely by imposing their own direct presence on the entire complex.

The distribution of power in a security complex shapes the possibilities for alignment. The patterns of amity and enmity shape the whole character of relations within the region. Shifts in the pattern of hostility occur either because an existing dispute has been resolved, or because new disputes have developed. In bipolar South Asia, there is only room for one major dispute and therefore a change in the pattern of hostility can only come from some form of resolution between India and Pakistan. Either the two countries can weary of their rivalry, and negotiate an agreement, as has been done by France and Germany, and Egypt and Israel, or else one side, most probably India, can effectively win the rivalry by overawing the other in some way. Alternatively, if the membership of a complex changes because of the break-up or merger of existing members, then a new pattern of amity and enmity occurs by definition. Some possibility for this exists in South Asia because of the internal fissiparousness of both India and Pakistan.

In complexes with three or more centres of power, like of the subcomplexes within the Middle Eastern complex, is more scope for change in the pattern of hostility. Significant bilateral conflict resolutions, like that between Egypt and Israel, can occur without basically altering the overall pattern, in this case Arab-Israeli enmity. Similarly, new conflicts can emerge to alter the priorities given to old ones. Iraq, for example gyrates among Syria, Iran, Saudi Arabia and Israel as its principal foe.

As a rule, external actors have a much lesser impact on the pattern of local hostilities than they do on the distribution of power. This conclusion is illustrated by the history of great power intervention in the Southeast Asian, South Asian and Middle Eastern complexes. The rule seems to be that external actors tend, whether explicitly or implicitly, to fall into line with the pattern of local hostility. Since external actors are usually pursuing their own interest, acquiescence in the local pattern of hostility is much the easiest way to penetrate a local complex. Local states frequently beg, as Pakistan did, for external support against local rivals. Unless the pattern of intervention is very lopsided, competing external powers will therefore normally reinforce rather than change the existing pattern of local hostility. They may attempt to mediate in the local disputes, as the Soviet Union has done in South Asia, the United States tries periodically to do in the Middle East, and both are trying to do in Cambodia. But attempts by external powers to go against the grain of local alignments do not have a good record, especially when the external powers are highly divided among themselves. As Cantori and Spiegel observe: 'In general, the experience of intrusive powers has been that it is easier to impose conflict than cooperation upon members of a subordinate system.'[33]

The major exception to this rule is when external powers resort to direct overlay of the local complex. The evidence indicates that external actors can only have any hope of changing local patterns of hostility when they impose their own presence on the countries concerned. The American role in the peace between Israel and Egypt provides a minor example. Other than the colonial period, the principal illustration is the complete overlaying of the European security complex by the larger pattern of hostility between the United States and the Soviet Union after the Second World War. The direct presence of the superpowers effectively suppressed virtually all of the previously existing local patterns of hostility for more than four decades. Only the hostility between Greece and Turkey managed to prevail openly against it, though as this overlay began to break up during the 1980s, other long suppressed disputes in East-Central Europe began to re-emerge. The process of overlay, however, requires exceptional historical circumstances, and after bitter and costly experiences, both superpowers are now nervous about committing their own forces abroad.

The generally low impact of external actors on local hostilities is indicated by the fact that the superpowers can switch sides without affecting them as happened between Ethiopia and Somalia during the late 1970s. The only other way in which external actors can change the local pattern of hostility is by joining the complex. The logic of this is the same as that for power discussed above. Although it might be possible for external actors to affect local hostilities by manipulating changes of government in local actors, this course is uncertain in the extreme. Iran is only the most recent example of cases where even revolutionary changes in government do not result in alterations of the basic patterns of local security perceptions, though as the Iranian case illustrates, the rhetoric and the detail of those perceptions may change substantially. Indeed, it has been a notable feature of post-war superpower interventions in the domestic politics of Third World countries that the superpowers were much more interested in manipulating Third World attitudes towards the East-West divide, than in reconditioning the attitudes of Third World states towards each other.

The internal and external changes bearing on any given local security complex are usually both numerous and continuous. Power relativities are in constant motion, and even patterns of amity and enmity shift occasionally. The key question is, do such changes work to sustain the essential structure or do they push it towards some kind of transformation? Four broad structural options for assessing the impact of change on a security complex are available; maintenance of the status quo, internal transformation, external transformation and overlay.

Maintenance of the status quo means that the essential structure of the local complex – its distribution of power, and pattern of hostility – remains fundamentally intact. For this outcome to occur does not mean that no change has taken place. Rather, it means that the changes which have occurred have tended, in aggregate, either to support, or else not seriously to undermine, the structure. South Asia is a good example of a local complex in which the status quo has been maintained. The complex was born abruptly when the unifying overlay of British rule was replaced by a set of independent states. Since then, the continuity of the complex's essential structure has been demonstrated by a series of wars. None of these has been decisive or destructive enough either to break the power of one side, or else to convince both that their mutual hostility is self-defeating. Consequently, the South Asian wars have served more to reinforce existing hostility than either to eliminate it, or to break the bipolar power structure.

Several powerful external actors have brought their influence to bear on the complex, but again, the sum of their impacts has been to sustain the existing structure. It might be argued that this external support has become a vital prop to the status quo. If the subcontinent had been left to its own devices, the greater weight of India and the greater political fragility of Pakistan might already have produced a transformation. But with military and economic support from the United States, China and several Middle Eastern states, Pakistan has been able to sustain what might otherwise well have been a hopeless rivalry with its giant neighbour.

Pakistan's nuclear weapon programme is obviously aimed at creating a great equalizer between the two rivals. If the essential structure of the complex rests more on external than on internal sources of power, then its durability lays hostage to continued involvement by countries whose main interests lie outside the sub-continent.

Internal transformation of a local complex occurs when its essential structure changes *within* the context of its existing outer boundary. Such change can come about as a result either of decisive shifts in the distribution of power, or of major alterations in the pattern of hostility. The unifications of Germany and Italy during the nineteenth century, for example, constituted an internal transformation of the European security complex. So did the consolidation of the ASEAN group within the Southeast Asian complex. ASEAN not only reduced sharply threat perceptions among its members, but also paved the way for a general polarization of alignment within the region between ASEAN and the Vietnamese-dominated group. The elimination of Israel as a Jewish state would mark an internal transformation of both the Arab-Israel subcomplex and the Middle Eastern complex as a whole. Similarly, the ending of Apartheid in South Africa would mark a transformation in the Southern African complex.[34] Where the process of decolonization left no firm boundaries for the successor states, as in Latin America, a long period of internal transformation occurred as part of the formative process of the complex.

Within a complex, changes in the distribution of power can have the same sort of structural effects as those commonly used for describing the international system as a whole. Whatever the starting number of poles of power within a complex, change can move it either towards greater concentration or towards greater diffusion. At one extreme is the possibility of a monopolar, or hegemonic, complex in which a single power dominates a set of minor powers. The North American complex has this character, and so would the South Asian if Pakistan either lost its external support or disintegrated. When a complex becomes monopolar, the dominant power may well adopt a wider security perspective which could quickly have implications for either the security structure of, or the pattern of intervention into, neighbouring regions. At the other extreme is a diffuse distribution in which several more or less equal powers jostle for influence. The classical balance of power in Europe, and even more so the current power structure of the Middle Eastern complex, both illustrate the multipolar pattern. Where the membership of a complex is large, prospects exist for shifts up and down from, say, tripolar to either bipolar or quadripolar. The smaller the number of principal actors, the more significant will be the shift. A move from seven to six powers might well not constitute a significant transformation, but a move from three to two definitely does.[35]

Changes in the patterns of hostility are trickier to define, not least because amity and enmity are more mobile qualities than power. One country represents only a single pole of power, but it may, as the case of Iraq illustrates, be the focus of several relations of hostility. In South Asia, the pattern of hostility is as simple as it could be, and the only path of internal change is towards resolution. In complexes with higher levels of polarity, there are usually core hostilities, like those centring on Iran, Vietnam, Israel and South Africa, which are essential to the definition of the status quo. Secondary shifts in hostility like that between Iraq and Syria, or between Libya and Egypt, can often occur without disrupting the basic pattern of the complex. Changes in core hostilities constitute an internal transformation.

As Ole Wæver suggests, within any given complex there exists a spectrum of relational possibilities described by the degrees of amity and enmity that define security interdependence.[36] At the two extremes of the spectrum are chaos and security community. In chaos, all relations are defined by enmity, each actor being the enemy of all the others. Lebanon provides a microcosmic example of this condition. One step up from chaos is what Raimo Väyrynen calls 'regional conflict formations'[37] in which conflictual relations dominate, but amity is also possible. Southeast Asia and the Middle East display this pattern. Next would come what Robert Jervis calls 'security regimes' in which a group of states cooperate to manage their disputes and avoid war by seeking to mute the security dilemma both by their own actions and by their assumptions about the behaviour of others.[38] He gives the Concert of Europe as the strongest example of this. Opposite from chaos is a security community, in which disputes among all the members are resolved to such an extent that none fears, or prepares for, either political assault or military attack by any of the others.[39] The United States and Canada, the Nordic countries and the European Community are examples. Beyond security community lies regional integration, which ends anarchy and therefore moves the regional security issue from the national and international, to the domestic realm.

External transformation occurs when the essential structure of a complex is altered by either expansion or contraction of its existing outer boundary. Minor adjustments to the boundary may not affect the essential structure significantly. The addition or deletion of major states, however, is certain to have a substantial impact on both the distribution of power and the pattern of amity and enmity. Where the decolonization process was extended over time, as in Africa and the Middle East, the local security complexes underwent several external transformations as newly independent states joined them. The changing of the Portuguese colonies into independent states during the mid-1970s marked the last major event in this process.

Once a security complex is established, external transformations will be infrequent, and mark very large changes in regional security dynamics. As yet, there are no contemporary examples of external transformation. Even the transformation of the great power complex at the system level is best seen as internal, with first China, and more slowly Western Europe and Japan, emerging from within the area of superpower overlay to challenge the global bipolarity of the United States and the Soviet Union. Three areas where visible potential for external transformation already exists are in relations between South Asia and the Gulf, South Asia and China, and Australasia and Southeast Asia.[40] Both Pakistan and Afghanistan have some military and Islamic ties to the Gulf states which cross the existing boundary between the two complexes. Should those ties grow to become alliances directed at India, then the existing boundary would disintegrate, and a whole new pattern of security relations would take shape. Similarly, there is a possibility in the middle-distance future for Sino-Indian rivalry to become a major axis, bearing particularly on Southeast Asia. That scenario, however, has implications for the higher level complex, and depends on movements in other major powers, particularly Japan. The boundary between Indonesia and Australia would collapse if Australian fears of an expansionist threat from overcrowded Indonesia grew strong enough to dominate its national security policy.

Overlay means that one or more external powers move directly into the local complex with the effect of suppressing the indigenous security dynamic. As argued earlier, it is quite distinct from the normal process of intervention by great powers into the affairs of local security complexes. Overlay can be imperial in character, and during the height of European empire, most of what is now the Third World was overlaid by direct political and military control. With decolonization, imperial overlay has become unfashionable. Even its sole remaining practitioner, the Soviet Union, has now had to abandon it. It has been replaced by more voluntary forms of submission, like that of Western Europe and Japan to the United States.[41] Under this arrangement, overlay takes the form of unequal alliance. Local security concerns are subordinated to the security orientation of the dominating power, and this orientation is reinforced by the stationing of that power's military forces directly within the local complex. The local states acquiesce in their own subordination either because they collectively fear some other outside power, or because they fear the further unrestrained operation of their own local security dynamic. In the case of Western Europe, both reasons apply.

The likely result of overlay is that the suppression of the local security dynamic, and/or protection against another external power, is gained at some, perhaps considerable, cost in entanglement with the larger security dynamic of external powers. Thus in Europe, overlay gained four decades of relief from the local dynamic which focused mainly on the position of Germany. But in return, the old continent was polarized into a front line in the rivalry between the United States and the Soviet Union. As the history of the NATO alliance attested, many tensions arose between the Western Europeans and the Americans about the nature and purpose of their joint rivalry with the Soviet Union.

In the post-colonial era, it is fair to assume that the overlay option requires exceptional circumstances to come into being. The post-war conditions in Europe and Japan provided such circumstances. The enormous upheaval of the Second World War produced not only exhaustion and weakness resulting from the self-destructive operation of the local security dynamics, but also the physical and political dominance of the United States and the Soviet Union in both areas. To be feasible, overlay requires either or both of a massive, locally applicable, military superiority by the external power(s), and a strong will on the part of the local states to invite a large and sustained external presence. It also requires a strong enough interest on the part of external power(s) to justify the costs of extended presence. Given the strength of feeling about national independence in the Third World, the geographical remoteness of most of it from the centres of American and Soviet power and the decline in the relative predominance of the superpowers, such conditions are difficult, if not impossible, to find in the contemporary world. The Americans discovered the cost of attempting overlay against the grain of local conditions in Vietnam. On a smaller scale, the Soviets learnt the same lesson in Afghanistan.

CONCLUSIONS: SECURITY COMPLEXES AND POLICY ANALYSIS

Security complexes are a typical product of an anarchic international structure. Yet they come much closer to reflecting the operating environment of most national security policymakers than do system-level abstractions about the distribution of power in the system. They also have the advantage of avoiding the critique of ahistoricism to which higher-level system theories are subject. Almost every country can relate its security perspectives to one or more complexes, and the concept provides a useful tool for organizing patterns of relations, and for arranging them into lateral (complex to complex) and hierarchical (higher to lower) categories. By positing a defined structure of relations at the regional level, the security complex framework raises a number of general questions. How durable are the complexes in question, and what is the relationship between their internal dynamic, and their interaction with other complexes? What role does penetration from high-level complexes play in the security of local complexes? How do the trends within the structure of security complexes influence the foreign policy options available to the states concerned? And how, in turn, do the foreign policies of individual states feed into the structure of relationships defined by the security complexes? Are all of the states concerned essentially locked into patterns of relationships over which they have little control, or do some of them have real leverage over the structure of events, and therefore real choices to make in the directions of their foreign policies?

As nodes in the system, security complexes not only define intense and relatively durable local patterns, but also serve to guide and shape the impact of larger external powers on these local patterns. The local and external patterns tend to reinforce each other's rivalries through the addition of resources and allies. The impact of this higher-lower level relationship is normally greater on the local pattern because of the disproportion in resources. The local states do have considerable influence over how external powers impinge on their affairs. But they have little ability to control external penetration unless they are able to resolve the local rivalries which generate the demand for external support. Conversely, the external powers cannot easily moderate or control the local security dynamic because they depend on it for access to the region. The process of rivalry among the great powers automatically reinforces the existing local rivalries in a pattern that is difficult to break.

Security complexes offer a systemic approach to security analysis which requires attention to the macro level of great power impact on the system, the middle level of local state relations, and the micro level of domestic affairs. In forcing attention to all three levels, security complexes emphasize the mutuality of impact among them, with external influences tending to amplify local problems, and local problems shaping and constraining external entanglements and influences. As a tool for analysis, security complexes encompass traditional power priorities by allowing for linked hierarchies of complexes. At the same time, they stress the importance of patterns of relations and sources of insecurity at all levels through which power relations are mediated.

Security complexes go rather against the grain of the Anglo-American analytical tradition in International Relations. Both because of their relative geographical isolation, and because of their status as 'top dog' states in the power leagues, Britain and the United States have tended to view the world in terms of the highest level security complex among the reigning great powers. These special factors insulated both countries from any constant, intense experience of their own local complex, and encouraged a rather detached view of international relations. Their experience does not, for the most part, bear comparison with that of countries like Russia, Germany, Egypt, Cambodia, Greece and Iran, whose entire histories have been sharply conditioned by inescapable pressures from intense local security complexes. Add to this the natural propensity towards ethnocentrism in security thinking explored by Booth,[42] and the predictable result is a rather self-centred view of national security.

This rather insular perspective has its uses, and must obviously be part of any comprehensive analysis. It may even be the most efficient perspective in a system within which the differentials in power and status between the top and the bottom of the hierarchy of actors are very large. In such a system, like that of the nineteenth century, the great powers could almost treat the world as their stage, not bothering to pay much regard to local actors and patterns of relations. Their political and military power was so great in relation to the non-industrial, often substate entities which they encountered, that they could override or distort local patterns without even thinking about it, as was done in Africa, and earlier in the Americas. Their only concern needed to be their immediate neighbours, if any, and the other major powers.

Such conditions no longer exist. Decolonization has filled the world with states, and in the process has created much higher levels of political and military mobilization outside the great powers than existed before. Many of these new states may be weak both as states and as powers, but they nevertheless constitute an order-of-magnitude improvement, particularly as regards consciousness of the rights and potentials of political self-organization. The spread of modern weapons to the Third World also carries military significance for relations between major and minor powers, and is an important part of the trend towards a diffusion of effective power.

The significance of the diffusion of power in the contemporary system is that it raises the importance of the actors at the bottom of the power hierarchy for the functioning of the system as a whole. If, because of their relative weakness, they still serve as the objects of great power rivalry, at least they now have some durable features of their own, and create patterns within and among themselves which to some extent condition the behaviour of the great powers. As Hoffmann argues, 'it is a mistake to treat issues in which third parties are embroiled as if these countries were pawns in a global balancing game, instead of dealing with the issues' intrinsic merits and the nations' interests.'[43] It is these features and patterns that the idea of security complexes aims to capture and bring into the field of analysis.[44] If security complexes are accepted as basic features of the international anarchy, then they automatically provide a major counterweight to the pressures for ethnocentrism in national security analysis. The single state, self-help view of national security derives from assumptions of a relatively immature anarchy, and tends to focus attention on what the state itself can do to improve its security. National security in this approach gets treated as a good that is largely produced by the efforts of the actor concerned.

An approach based on security complexes focuses attention on sets of states whose security problems are closely interconnected. Security is viewed as only partly divisible, a substantial portion of it residing in essentially indivisible relational patterns among states. Ethnocentrism is avoided, because one not only has to view one's own state in the context of the complexes of which it is a member, but has also to apply the same logic to other states, be they friend or foe. Although such a procedure by no means avoids all sources of bias, it does at least ensure that all states are viewed in a relational context larger than themselves. An extreme ethnocentric perspective centred on Pakistan, for example, might tend to see India as the problem and a more powerful Pakistan with more allies as the answer. The same problem viewed through the security complex lens produces a quite different analysis, which centres on the whole relationship between India and Pakistan as the problem, and emphasizes the way in which increased strength and the pursuit of external alliances amplify the problem rather than solving it. From the point of view of the analyst, this broader perspective almost ensures better insight. It could be used, for example, to offset some of the wilder hypotheses about 'chains' of nuclear proliferation in the Third World. Should consciousness of regional security dynamics grow in the minds of policy-makers, it might well inspire better-focused efforts to deal both with local conflicts and great power penetration.

Because security complexes provide a useful framework within which to consider policy issues, they can also be used to evaluate policy proposals. Some of the sillier, though serious, debates and proposals now in the policy realm might be more difficult to sustain if the notion of security complexes was more firmly established in people's minds. For example, the perennial debate about whether the Israeli-Palestinian conflict or the threat from the Soviet Union is the key issue in the Middle East looks completely different if viewed through the lens of a Middle Eastern security complex. The Israeli-Palestinian issue then emerges clearly as a defining dispute, one of several, within the complex, along the same lines as the India-Pakistan conflict within South Asia. The Soviet threat occurs as part of a higher-level complex, and cannot be analysed without bringing in the rest of the higher complex, including the United States, as it impacts on affairs within the Middle East. The two complexes have quite separate dynamics, and the point is not to confuse them, but to sort out how they interact with each other. On this basis, security complexes can be treated as objects for policy in the sense that problems can only be resolved within the context of the relevant complex as a whole. Following on from this, it would become more difficult to float and defend misguided ideas like the Indian Ocean as a Zone of Peace (IOZP). Since the Indian Ocean in no sense forms a security complex, the idea suffers from a remarkably bad fit with the pattern of security relations in the international system. It cuts across five regional security complexes, and could never hope to contain all the divergent interests within and across its notional boundaries.[45] Failure to accord with the pattern of local security complexes also explains some of the difficulties of the Organization of African Unity (OAU).

APPENDIX (TABLE 5.1): THE COMPREHENSIVE FRAMEWORK FOR SECURITY ANALYSIS

Levels	Analytical focus	Issues	Examples
Domestic	Weak/strong state	-Degree of socio-political cohesion -Domestic political violence	-Strong states = Japan, Sweden -Weak states = Sri Lanka, Lebanon
Regional	Local/regional security complexes	-Security interdependence -Amity/enmity -Polarity -Civilizational area -Subcomplexes -Domestic spillover	-India/Pakistan Iran/Iraq/Saudi Arabia -Israel/Arabs -Mono/bi/tri/multi -South Asia, Arabs -Gulf, Balkans, Horn -Kurds, Tamils, Palestinians
Inter-regional	Boundaries of indifference	-Cross-boundary links -Boundary change?	-Pakistan/Saudi Arabia -Gulf/Saudi Arabia
Global	Higher level, global security complex	-Great power polarity, rivalry -Penetration: -to domestic level -to regional level -Overlay -Adjacency to local security complex	-Cold war -US and Panama -Superpowers and Middle East -Colonial period -Europe 1945–90 -China/S.E. Asia China/S. Asia

Key questions: What are the security dynamics at each level for any given case?
How do these dynamics interact with each other?
What is the relative weight of each level in determining the security situation as a whole?

NOTES

1. Zalmay Khalilzad, *Security in Southern Asia 1: The security of Southwest Asia* (Aldershot: Gower, 1984); and Timothy George, Robert Litwak and Shahram Chubin, *Security in Southern Asia 2: India and the great powers* (Aldershot: Gower, 1984) unpaginated preface, both volumes.

2. Michael Haas, 'International subsystems: stability and polarity', *American Political Science Review*, 64: 1 (1970), p. 100.

3. *ibid.*, pp. 98–123; Michael Haas, *International Conflict* (Indianapolis: Bobbs-Merrill, 1974); and Michael Brecher, 'International relations and Asian studies: the subordinate state system of Southern Asia', *World Politics*, 15:2 (1963).

4. Bruce M. Russett, *International Regions and the International System* (Chicago: University of Chicago Press, 1967); Brecher, with his broader concept of 'subordinate state systems' was also concerned to tackle the analytical gulf between area and system specialists that is part of my concern here. For a critique of the integrationist approach to regions, see Louis J. Cantori and Steven L. Spiegel, 'The analysis of regional international politics: the integration versus the empirical systems approach', *International Organization*, 27:4 (1973).

5. Louis J. Cantori and Steven L. Spiegel, *The International Politics of Regions: A comparative approach* (Englewood Cliffs, NJ: Prentice Hall, 1970).

6. William R. Thompson, 'The regional subsystem: a conceptual explication and a propositional inventory', *International Studies Quarterly*, 17:1 (1973).

7. Mohammed Ayoob (ed.), *Regional Security in the Third World: Case studies from Southeast Asia and the Middle East* (London: Croom Helm, 1986); and 'Security in the Third World: the worm about to turn?', *International Affairs*, 60:1 (1983/4); and 'The Third World in the system of states: acute schizophrenia or growing pains?', *International Studies Quarterly*, 33: 1 (1989); Barry Buzan and Gowher Rizvi *et al.*, *South Asian Insecurity and the Great Powers* (London: Macmillan, 1986); Walter Little, 'International conflict in Latin America', *International Affairs*, 63:4 (1987); Raimo Väyrynen, 'Regional conflict formations: an intractable problem of international relations', *Journal of Peace Research*, 21:4 (1984); and 'Collective violence in a discontinuous world: regional realities and global fallacies', *International Social Science Journal*, 38:4 (1986); Ole Wæver, 'The interplay of some regional and subregional dynamics of security', unpublished paper, Centre for Peace and Conflict Research, Copenhagen, November 1987; and 'Conflicts of vision: visions of conflict', in Ole Wæver, Pierre Lemaitre and Elzbieta Tromer (eds), *European Polyphony: Perspectives beyond East-West confrontation* (London: Macmillan, 1989).

8. On this point, see Barry Buzan, 'Peace, power, and security: contending concepts in the study of international relations', *Journal of Peace Research*, 21:2 (1984).

9. The idea of security complexes is, I think, original, though shadows of it can be found in earlier writings about local balances of power and subsystems. Michael Haas seemed to be moving towards the idea with his notion of 'international military-strategic subsystems', (*op. cit.* (note 2), pp. 100–1), but I am not aware that this notion was ever developed along similar lines. My own earlier attempts to develop the idea of security complexes can be found in the first edition of *People, States and Fear* (1983) pp. 105–15; 'Regional security as a policy objective: the case of South and Southwest Asia', in A. Z. Rubinstein (ed.), *The*

Great Game (New York: Praeger, 1983), ch. 10; and 'A framework for regional security analysis', in Buzan and Rizvi, *op. cit.* (note 7), ch. 1. These should now be considered less authoritative than the presentation given here, though some parts of this chapter are drawn from the 1986 work. See also Wæver *et al., op. cit.* (note 7) p. 309.

10. Thompson, *op. cit.* (note 6), pp. 93–101.

11. Barry Buzan, 'The future of Western European Security', in Wæver *et al., op. cit.* (note 7), ch. 1.

12. Barry Buzan, Morten Kelstrup, Pierre Lemaitre, Elzbieta Tromer and Ole Wæver, *The European Security Order Recast: Scenarios for the post-Cold War era* (London: Pinter, 1990).

13. Raimo Väyrynen, 'Domestic stability, state terrorism, and regional integration in the ASEAN and the GCC', in Michael Stohl and George Lopez (eds), *Terrible Beyond Endurance* (New York: Greenwood Press, 1988), pp. 194–7.

14. Buzan and Rizvi, *op. cit.* (note 7), ch. 7; Barry Buzan, 'The Southeast Asian security complex', *Contemporary Southeast Asia*, 10:1 (1988).

15. In discussion at a conference on South Asian security, St Antony's College, Oxford, October 1984.

16. Michael Mandelbaum, *The Fate of Nations: The search for national security in the 19th and 20th centuries* (Cambridge: Cambridge University Press, 1988), pp. 268–71.

17. Buzan *et al., op. cit.* (note 12), ch. 3.

18. Wæver, *op. cit.* (note 7), pp. 4–5, takes a different view, arguing that a security complex should be defined by the regional specificity of security dynamics and not by the degree of autonomy of endogenous security dynamics. This would mean that security complexes always existed, though it is not clear by what logic their boundaries could be drawn.

19. Wæver *et al., op. cit.* (note 7), pp. 296–7.

20. Buzan, *op. cit.* (note 14), pp. 4–6.

21. For some useful perspectives on the significance of economic factors in defining regions, see Väyrynen, *op. cit.* (note 7), pp. 337–44.

22. This argument draws heavily on themes in W. H. McNeill, *The Rise of the West* (Chicago: University of Chicago Press, 1963).

23. Walter Little, 'International conflict in Latin America', *International Affairs*, 63:4 (1987), pp. 593–4.

24. Cantori and Spiegel, *op. cit.* (note 4), p. 484.

25. See Little, *op. cit.* (note 21).

26. *The Economist* (11 March 1989), pp. 62, 65.

27. Raimo Väyrynen, 'East-West rivalry and regional conflicts in the Third World: cause and consequence', unpublished conference paper, Stadt Schlaining, United Nations University, May 1985. See also Cantori and Spiegel, *op. cit.* (note 5), pp. 33–7.

28. Edward A. Kolodziej and Robert Harkavy, 'Developing states and the international security system', *Journal of International Affairs*, 34:1 (1980), p. 59. See also Väyrynen, *op. cit.* (note 27), pp. 22–8.

29. Kenneth N. Waltz, *Theory of International Politics* (Reading, Mass.: Addison-Wesley, 1979), ch. 5.

30. See Barry Buzan 'Rethinking structure', in Barry Buzan, Charles Jones and Richard Little,

The Logic of Anarchy (New York: Columbia University Press, 1993).

31. For discussion, see R. J. Barry Jones, 'Concepts and models of change in international relations', in Barry Buzan and R. J. Barry Jones (eds), *Change and the Study of International Relations* (London: Pinter, 1981), ch. 1.

32. Pakistan's defence expenditure has ranged between 6 and 7 per cent of its GNP since 1975, whereas India's has been between 3 and 4 per cent. See *The Military Balance 1982–3 and 1983–4, 1988–9* (London: IISS) respectively pp. 125, 127, 226.

33. Cantori and Spiegel, *op. cit.* (note 5), pp. 30–3.

34. B. Buzan and H. O. Nazareth, 'South Africa versus Azania: the implications of who rules', *International Affairs*, 62: 1 (1985–6).

35. Waltz, *op. cit.* (note 29), p. 163.

36. Wæver, *op. cit.* (note 7), pp. 5–8.

37. Väyrynen, *op. cit.* (note 7).

38. Robert Jervis, 'Security regimes', *International Organization*, 36:2 (1982); and 'From balance to concert: a study of international security cooperation', *World Politics*, 38: 1 (1985).

39. On security communities, see: K. J. Holsti, *International Politics: A framework for analysis* (Englewood Cliffs, NJ: Prentice Hall, 1967), ch. 16; and Karl Deutsch and S. A. Burrell, *Political Community and the North Atlantic Area* (Princeton, NJ: Princeton University Press, 1957).

40. For elaboration of the first two of these, see Buzan and Rizvi, *op. cit.* (note 7), ch. 9.

41. A. W. DePorte, *Europe Between the Superpowers: The enduring balance* (New Haven: Yale University Press, 1979).

42. Ken Booth, *Strategy and Ethnocentrism* (London: Croom Helm, 1979).

43. Stanley Hoffmann, *Primacy or World Order* (New York: McGrawHill, 1978), p. 175.

44. On this theme see Väyrynen, *op. cit.* (note 7), pp. 337–9.

45. Barry Buzan, 'Naval power, the law of the sea, and the Indian Ocean as a zone of peace', *Marine Policy*, 5:3 (1981).

chapter six | economic security

The international economy, and in particular the way in which it interacts with the state structure of the system, is one of the major mediating factors that shapes the security consequences of anarchic structure. This chapter opens with a look at the nature of the international political economy in terms of the relationship between anarchy and market. It continues with an examination of the extremely difficult idea of economic security, considering first its central contradictions, and then tracing the logic of its application to individuals, firms, classes, states and the international system as a whole. The chapter ends with a return to the idea of mature anarchy, and an attempt to sketch out how conditions in the contemporary international political economy might move in that direction.

THE NATURE OF THE INTERNATIONAL POLITICAL ECONOMY

The political structure of the international system is characterized much more by what divides it than by what binds it together. Anarchy emphasizes the parts over the whole, and although international society can make a substantial difference to the security consequences of anarchy, it does not affect the basic division of the system into separate sovereign units. The international economic system by contrast, presents a more balanced structure in which substantial elements of division are matched by powerful forces of integration. Although economic activity generates many fragmentations – for example, into classes, firms and national economies – the international economy as a whole is also powerfully tied together by patterns of trade, production, finance, communication and transportation. Cheaper, more efficient production of computer chips in Japan affects the ability of others to pursue similar activity elsewhere. Interest rates in the United States affect debt burdens in Latin America. Technological innovations create powerful pressures for emulation elsewhere, both by their impact on production costs, and by their effect on consumer preferences. Stock market jitters, interest rate fluctuations, and flows of 'hot' money quickly make their impact throughout the system. If trade is pursued as a means of increasing efficiency and welfare, then complicated patterns of dependency arise in which economic activity in one place depends on a host of external conditions, and market pressures permeate the whole system. The international economy is in one sense the main component, and in another the main consequence, of the rising density and interdependence of the international system discussed in Chapter 4.

The problem in characterizing the international economy is that from one view it appears to be a system in its own right, and from another, to be so heavily entangled with the international political system as to be nearly indistinguishable from it.

Taken as a separate system, the international economy appears to have a structure and dynamic of its own. Individuals and firms are its units, trade and finance constitute its interactions, and the market provides its fundamental structure. The economic system has an identifiable historical momentum, its energies being fed by population growth, technological innovation, increasing capacity for organization, class struggle and the development of explicit economic theories. Over time, economic dynamics have generated a powerful trend towards increasing wealth and ever larger conglomerations of activity which have in some senses paralleled, and in other senses outstripped, the simultaneous aggregation process in the political sphere. Their end result to date has been the progressive expansion of locally rooted economies, and an increase in the level of exchange among them. This, in turn, has led to a global economy in which many patterns of production, consumption, finance and class operate on, and can only be understood in the context of, a planetary scale. This world scale contrasts with, and creates an important environment for, the more persistent fragmentation of the international political system. In this view, the international economy has grown up through, and transcended, the state system so that, as Robin Murray argues, international capital is becoming increasingly independent of state interests.[1]

If the international economy is taken not as a separate system, but as subordinate to a dominant international political system, then a very different picture emerges. Although much of the dynamics and structure outlined above remain the same, national economies stand out as the critical level for analysis. The international economy becomes less a thing in itself, and more a part of the complex pattern of interaction among states. Emphasis is placed on the growing economic role and power of governments, on national definitions of economic priorities, on states as economic units and on the numerous links between state power and economic activity. From this perspective, the class structure appears to be more important within states than above them. Economic activity becomes interesting because it forces states to interact with each other, and thus provides a major behavioural force within the international political system.

Arguments over whether the political or the economic system should be given primacy need not detain us here. Both systems clearly possess main structures and dynamics which are strong enough to be identified independently. Just as clearly, however, the two systems are so closely intertwined that neither can be understood in the absence of the other. The international economy is just as thoroughly penetrated by state structures and the dynamics of power and security, as the state system is cut through by patterns of production, consumption and class, and by the dynamics of the market. Because of this, both systems can only dance partly to their own tune, the rest of their movement being prompted or constrained by ties to the partner system. Each state contains a slice of the global economy and class structure, which becomes to some extent differentiated from the global economic patterns precisely because it is contained within a particular state structure. These state structures are more than simply convenient units for rivalries among different national capitalist élites, which was how crude Marxists saw them. They spring from deep historical roots of their own which certainly constrain, and may surpass, the influence of economic and class divisions as a basis for action.

Many writers have dwelt in various ways upon the interaction between the international economic and political systems.[2] Literature on political economy before the middle of the nineteenth century tended naturally to treat the two together because they were seen as one subject, the disciplinary gulf between politics and economics having not yet opened. The literature on imperialism is also premised on the juncture of the two systems.[3] The more recent literatures on interdependence and contemporary international political economy are a conscious attempt to redefine the agenda of International Relations in a way that puts the interplay between political authority and markets at the centre of analysis.[4] Writers such as Wallerstein, Galtung and Ashley have attempted to build general theories of international relations which are rooted firmly in both systems, and the interaction between them,[5] while Tivey pursues the matter on the state level, looking at the political economy of nation-building.[6]

Some analysts link anarchic political structures and capitalist economic ones.[7] Their argument is that the fragmentation of political authority in a system of states is a necessary condition for the emergence of capitalism, and/or the natural political expression of an operating capitalist world economy. Suggestive historical evidence for this view can be drawn from comparisons of Europe and China. The fragmented and anarchical European political experience successfully defied all attempts at imperial unification and generated capitalism. The more centralized, hierarchic tradition of China, in which imperial unity was the norm, and 'warring state' periods the exception, did not, despite similar, and for some centuries superior, levels of science and technology on the Chinese side. Only the relative freedom from central political control created by anarchic structure allowed market behaviour to become a dominant social and economic practice.

This perspective explains much about the inherently competitive character of anarchic relations. If anarchy and market relations are so closely related as to be mutually constitutive phenomena, then competition under anarchy is inherently double-edged. On the economic side, international political fragmentation permits the competition of the market, in which producers are forced to vie with each other in terms of innovation, quality and price in order to pursue their own welfare. The political structure of anarchy creates more freedom for economic actors both because they can move from less to more congenial governments, and because at least some governments will come to see the power advantages of hosting them. Insulated imperiums like that in China can more easily decide to suppress the disruptive challenge from rising economic classes. On the political side, international anarchy, especially when pressured by differential rates of economic development, creates the pervasive unease of the power-security dilemma (see Chapter 8). Rising and declining powers threaten each other's security, and the economic and military measures states take to preserve their security are easily, and often rightly, seen by others as threatening. Competition for strength in the qualities of survival thus has to be added to competition for wealth in the market. Both types of competition stimulate technological innovation, which in turn continuously redefines the requirements for successful (and unsuccessful) economic and strategic behaviour. It was the synergistic effect of these two modes of competition that made the European states into the centre of a world-spanning series of empires, and laid the basis for the present global dominance of the capitalist/anarchic structure.

Powerful insights of this type underline the centrality of economic factors in understanding what anarchy means for international security. They point to the idea of economic security as a major component of the international security problematique. Unfortunately, this idea turns out to be one of the most attractive yet intractable concepts in the whole discourse about security.

THE IDEA OF ECONOMIC SECURITY

In the post-1945 world, the idea of economic security has acquired a firm place on the political agenda. In the West, governments are called upon to provide it for their citizens and to pursue it for the state as a whole. Many Third World countries employ a rhetoric based on it as a way of trying to redress their disadvantaged position in the system. Communist countries long claimed to have solved the problem, but the shortcomings of this posturing have been cruelly revealed by the events of 1989–90. Economic security is talked about as if the words referred to some concrete (usually unspecified) condition, a state of being that could actually be achieved, and which therefore represents a realistic and rational political goal. But with the exception of the basic requisites for individual survival, this perception is false. The idea that economic security represents an absolute value with wide application is an illusion, and the pursuit of it is the pursuit of a chimera. The reality of economic security is a slippery relativity combined with a peculiarly intense nexus of contradictions and trade-offs. Almost nothing can be gained without something of comparable importance being lost. Distinctions between threatening and normal behaviour are exceptionally difficult to draw, and the possibilities for political misuse of the idea are legion.

The elusive quality of economic security becomes apparent immediately one tries to apply the idea to the dominant mode of economic organization in the system: capitalism. As argued in Chapter 3, capitalism is by definition a competitive system, the whole dynamic of which depends on the interplay of threats, vulnerabilities and opportunities within the market. How can any units within such an environment ever be meaningfully secure when competition implies an ever-present danger of becoming a loser? Relative security is possible (some units do better than others), but absolute security is not. A capitalist economy only works if market competition is allowed to shape behaviour. Individuals and firms within it prosper only if they can compete, and the stick of bankruptcy is as important as the carrot of profit in spurring efficient behaviour. The overall productivity and prosperity of the system depends on the less efficient and less innovative units being driven out of business by the more efficient and more innovative ones.

Competitive capitalism is thus founded on a considerable degree of permanent insecurity for all the units within it (individuals, firms, states), making the idea of economic security within capitalism seem a contradiction in terms. Without a substantial level of insecurity, the system does not work. But although security for the units is elusive, capitalism does offer some important systemic security benefits. With all its faults and problems, it can claim in practice to be the most effective generator of wealth and innovation, to distribute these fruits more widely than other systems, and to be the most reliable guarantor of political pluralism (both internally and internationally). To the extent that growth alleviates both the economic and the political problems of shortage and uneven distribution, capitalism can be seen to offer a grand trade-off in which a measure of insecurity on the unit level is endured in return for a measure of security on the level of the politico-economic system as a whole.

Given the predominance of capitalism in the international system, this massive contradiction is already at the core of any practical attempt to think about economic security. The only escape from it is to argue that economic security is incompatible with capitalism. But such an escape is itself utopian, quickly running into contradictions of no lesser magnitude. Because of the effects of scale and specialization on economic activity, no sophisticated, large-scale economic system can escape the basic choice labelled by Luciani as between vulnerability and cost-effectiveness, and by Gill and Law as between security and interdependence.[8] In the economic domain, the most obvious way for actors to increase their security is to decrease the interdependencies that make them vulnerable. But the resultant self-reliance is only achieved by threatening the division of labour and economies of scale that make production efficient. Larger units can evade this contradiction for longer than small ones, but as the fate of the Soviet Union illustrates, under modern conditions even the biggest units become inefficient if they pursue too great a degree of self-reliance. Following this logic to its extreme, Luciani wryly observes that 'poverty may be a virtue from the point of view of security' because it minimizes the difficulty of defending a given lifestyle. But this virtue also has a negative trade-off, because poverty means that the economic base for military strength is small, making the whole system vulnerable to the military capabilities of those who took the economic risks of vulnerability and interdependence.[9]

The tension between vulnerability and efficiency occurs again and again at almost all the levels of economic security from the individual, through firm, class and state to the system as a whole. Not only does this range of referent objects for economic security illustrate the pervasiveness of this fundamental contradiction, it also raises other contradictions both within and between levels. It is worth exploring the idea at each of these levels.

At the individual level, a basic definition of economic security is in terms of ready access to the means necessary to meet basic human needs (food, water, shelter, education). Beyond that minimum, the idea of economic security becomes awkwardly entangled with a range of highly politicized debates about employment, income distribution and welfare. Should individual economic security be restricted to basic conditions for survival, or should it be defined in terms of maintaining a given standard of living? If a right to employment or a right to a minimum income are taken as necessary conditions for economic security, then major inroads into the operation of the market result. If these reduce efficiency too much, then the danger is of a Soviet-type result in which individual security is achieved at the cost of a generally low standard of living, or a British-type result of relative economic decline and increasing difficulty in maintaining full employment and adequate growth. A persistent paradox here is the dual identity of the individual as both consumer and producer. As consumers, individuals should logically favour the market, since that guarantees them the best choice of product and price. As producers, they may well oppose the market if its operation threatens their income or employment. At the extremes of this logic, there is no point in having consumer choice if one has no job and no money, and no point in having a job and money if there is nothing worth buying in the shops. Economic success provides a relative security by allowing individuals to escape these extremes.

If economic security is seen in terms of the right to a particular job, or to a rising income (or protection against a falling one), then the demand is almost impossible to meet. Except in extraordinarily favourable circumstances, governments simply cannot control economic performance in this way, and more often than not the attempt to do so will undermine their ability to stay economically competitive. Even the rich are not completely secure, for they have the problem of maintaining their wealth (and thus taking investment risks), and of protecting it, and themselves, from those made envious or indignant by the resultant inequalities. The more individuals seek to reduce their economic vulnerability, the greater the risk that they will collectively impair the overall efficiency of the economy that sustains them. But if they pay too little attention to their economic security, they risk either exploitation by those better placed, or finding themselves on the street as one of the casualties of market efficiency. Trying to keep these macro and micro insecurities in some sort of balance is a perpetual problem for both individuals and governments. Relative success makes the balancing act easier, relative failure makes it more difficult.

The next referent level for economic security is the business firm. Firms are the most purely economic actors, and therefore the least able to escape the fundamental contradictions of economic security. Firms can seek security by staying on top of the market through superior adaptivity and innovation, or by establishing either a monopoly or a politically protected market share. It is important to note here that firms have no natural love of the market. As profit-driven entities, their natural preference is to escape from (and weaken) the market by seeking monopoly or oligopoly. Within the prison of the market, the pursuit of security through superior adaptivity and innovation only creates a security contradiction between successful firms and those unable to compete. But this is not a serious security issue except for the firms concerned, and any attempt to elevate it to national security status should be treated with suspicion.

In essence, firms are creatures of functional convenience. Unlike states, they carry no deeply rooted sense of permanence and no compelling imperative for survival about them. The ever-shifting environment of economic activity does not encourage or require great longevity in its collective players. The ever-changing conditions of market competition favour organizational flexibility over permanence. Most firms can fail, be dismantled or be absorbed, with much less consequence than states, and such practice is a normal part of economic activity. It creates no general disturbance to the economic system, though it may, of course, have a considerable impact on employees. The major exception to this rule is when firms are large enough and/or occupy such a key position in the economy (like some banks) that their collapse would have massive and widespread consequences. Since bigness is not always efficient, the security choice here may take the form of large, short-term adjustment costs versus sustained economic inefficiency.[10]

But when firms pursue their security by monopoly or protection, there is a high probability of a contradiction between their security interest and the welfare interests of consumers. Both monopoly and protection raise prices to consumers, and protection may also require subsidy out of taxation. Firms pursuing security in this way may claim that their own survival is a national security issue because otherwise areas of strategically significant productive capacity (such as steel, shipbuilding, food, aircraft, energy) might be lost to the national economy. This case has to be weighed against the higher costs, and often inferior products, that result when firms are shielded from the pressures of market competition.

Another possible economic referent object for security is class, but it is exceedingly difficult to apply a concept like security to an object like a class. Class is a more amorphous group of entities than states, so much so that it is hard even to identify its physical boundaries. Classes have no behavioural unity in the physical and political senses that enable states and individuals to be identified as actors. They have structurally shaped interests and attitudes which can be identified, but which are not necessarily held consciously in any individual or collective sense. They seldom have sufficient organizational coherence to produce policies, and so cannot easily be seen as 'actors' capable of providing for their own security. Although a class might have coherent interests, intra-class conflicts of interest are commonplace, and competition within a class may not exclude the use of force. The barons of industry are not less combative among themselves than were the nobility of feudal Europe, even if the dominant forms of struggle have altered somewhat. For those still following Marxism, the problem of Marx's determinist argument about class struggle and historical progress makes a nonsense of class security, If a class like the bourgeoisie is destined to bring about its own destruction through the mechanism of its own success, how can one apply a notion like security to it at all?

Because economic actors are mostly ephemeral amorphous, the concept of security is generally more useful when applied to more durable political structures than to economic ones. To some extent, one can assume that the security interests of classes and firms are largely vested in the states with which they are associated. This assumption tends in the direction of a now rather old-fashioned Marxist view that states are instruments of the dominant class, and therefore naturally oriented towards securing the interests of that class. But as argued in Chapter 2, the state has roots and dynamics of its own, additional to those of its ruling class. Acceptance of 'the relative autonomy of the state' is now common even among Marxist thinkers, and national security must therefore be seen as combining the interests of state and class without necessarily being wholly dominated by either.[11]

Galtung offers a particularly clear attempt to integrate the structures and the dynamics of state and class. He argues that while class structures divide states domestically, they also correlate significantly with the overall pattern of relations among states. Thus the 'centre' versus 'periphery' (élites versus masses) class divide within states is reproduced globally in the 'centre' versus 'periphery' relations between the industrialized states and the Third World countries. Élites within the periphery states share many interests with élites at the centre. But while both sets of élites are at odds with their domestic peripheries, those in the Third World are more so than those at the centre, because they have fewer resources to distribute (because they are the periphery in the system overall). There is no harmony of interests between the periphery of the centre and the periphery of the periphery, because the relative advantage of the former depends on the maintenance of the system which exploits the latter.

There are risks of over-simplification in a sweeping analysis of this type. It underplays conflicts between the élites of North and South that are as diverse as the territorial issue of the Falkland Islands, and the ecological one of the Brazilian forests. But it does have the considerable merit of clarifying how class interests permeate state behaviour, as in the case of North-South economic issues, and how the fragmented political structure of anarchy contributes to international class conflicts, as in the protectionist empire-building of the interwar years. It also enriches understanding of the security problems of weak states developed in Chapter 2.

Domestic class structure, particularly the extent and intensity of disaffection between élites and masses, is an obvious factor in accessing the strength or weakness of a state. When added to the nationality factor, class divisions suggest the kind of political threats, whether domestically or externally mounted, to which specified states will be particularly sensitive. States that are highly divided along both class and nationality lines will be vulnerable to both nationalist and leftist political attack, whereas those divided along one dimension, but relatively harmonious along the other, may be able to employ the strong side to mask or mute the weak one. In some places, such as South Africa and Brazil, there may be substantial correlations between ethnic and class divisions that serve to multiply the political vulnerability of the state.

These arguments open up the question of how economic security might be applied to states and to the international system. On these levels of analysis, the contradictions of economic security, particularly the central one between vulnerability and efficiency, become acute and complicated enough to require separate discussion at some length.

ECONOMIC SECURITY AND THE STATE

If the state is taken as the referent object, then economic security becomes part of the national security agenda. Applying the idea of economic security to the state raises many similar questions to those arising if the referent object is the individual. The simplest view is to equate security with the economic conditions necessary for survival. If the economic criteria for security are raised beyond that, then complex issues arise about the impact of reduced vulnerability on economic efficiency, and thus in the longer term about the state's ability to improve, or even to hold, its position in the international system.

The national equivalent of 'basic human needs' has two elements. The first is that like individuals, states require ready access to the means necessary for their survival. Unlike individuals, states may contain much or even all of what they need to sustain themselves in terms of agricultural production sufficient to feed the population, and resource production sufficient to supply essential industry. If, like Japan and Egypt, they do not encompass sufficient resources, then access to trade becomes an essential part of their basic economic security. Like individuals, their survival depends on interaction with a wider environment. Under these circumstances, disruption of supply threatens the power, welfare and possibly the political stability of the state. The logical security strategies are to ensure continuity of supply (by expanding the state to incorporate the necessary resources, or by cultivating stable trading systems), and to buffer vulnerabilities by stockpiling essential goods.[12]

The second element has no parallel with individuals because it has to do with the internal construction of the national economy. The internal physical construction of individuals is more or less fixed, but that of states is highly variable and continuously changing. The 'health' and even the survival of a state depend not on sustaining a static condition, but on adapting towards the most advanced and successful practices elsewhere in the international system. Failure to adapt, or even relative slowness at doing so, means a steady loss of power, and a steady rise in vulnerability for those that have been more successful. It was differentials in internal performance that enabled Europe progressively to dominate the other ancient centres of civilization after 1500.[13] On a smaller scale, the same phenomena explains the shift in balance between China versus Japan, North versus South Korea, and North versus Latin America. Relative economic growth, in the argument made famous by Paul Kennedy,[14] plays a major role in determining the power of states in the system, and is thus a key element in national security concerns.

It is relatively easy to sketch the economic security problematique of states in these terms, but deep contradictions arise as soon as one opens the question of what strategies states should adopt in order to pursue economic security. This question leads quickly back to the long-standing opposition between liberal and mercantilist positions. Liberals tend to view the economic system through the eyes of consumers. They want to maximize production possibilities, and are prepared to discount vulnerability issues in order to pursue efficiency and abundance. Mercantilists tend to view the economic system through the eyes of producers, and are prepared to sacrifice supposed efficiencies in order to maintain a strong element of self-reliance. The security element in the liberal argument is that a relatively unencumbered operation of the market either solves or eliminates many problems of resources and development. Compared with centrally planned economies, it also takes many economic issues off the political agenda. Under a liberal regime, states can trade for what they need, and so have no reason to fear restrictions on supply. This both encourages economic efficiency, and allows states to avoid going to war over control of resources and markets. It also maximizes the flow of capital, technology and ideas throughout the system, so providing the means by which less-developed states can adapt themselves to the standards and practices of the most advanced. Underpinning the liberal argument is the assumption that large gains in overall economic efficiency will provide the resources necessary to deal with the inequalities, hardships and problems of adjustment that the operation of the market inevitably generates.

The mercantilist argument puts national security interests to the fore, finding the vulnerability consequences of a surrender to the market quite unacceptable. At the core of the mercantilist case is an argument about military security that even liberals accept up to a point: namely, Adam Smith's much quoted remark about defence being more important than opulence. To the extent that states fear being attacked, they are attracted towards industrialization not only for economic reasons, but in order to provide the financial, technological and production foundations for military strength. Because war is an instrument of last resort, the maximum possible degree of self-reliance is a desirable attribute of military strength. Not to command the sources of one's own military power is to endure vulnerabilities that could be fatal in the highly uncertain environment of war. As Sen argues, there are consequently compelling non-economic reasons for states to establish and sustain the range of industries necessary to support modern armed forces. These reasons remain regardless of the fact that such industries may be relatively uncompetitive, and that the cumulative effect of this practice is to generate surplus capacity, and consequently trade friction, in the international economy.[15]

As suggested in Chapter 3, at least three lines of argument offer clear opportunities for building a mercantilist position onto this quite firm military foundation. The first route is simply to extend the military security argument directly. The logical extreme of this is a warfare state such as Nazi Germany or Stalin's

Soviet Union, in which expectation of war (whether offensive or defensive) is very high, and the whole economy is geared towards military strength. Between this extreme and some minimal military industrial requirement, lies a host of possibilities for promoting economic nationalism. As Gill and Law argue, 'the military-industrial complex can be seen as at the centre of a national-capitalist coalition to rival that of internationally mobile capital in any given nation.'[16] The valid linkage between economic and military security can be spun out in such a way as to bring much of the economy under the command of a national security imperative. By assuming the possibility of lengthy, all-out, siege warfare, arguments can be made for maintaining substantial levels of self-reliance in most major manufacturing, extractive and agricultural industries. On this basis, uncompetitive firms ranging from coal miners and wheat farmers, through shoe manufacturers and shipbuilders, to chip-makers and aerospace industries, can all attach their self-interested pleas for protection to the supportive framework of national security. In this way, what starts as a caveat on free trade can be built into a quasi-mercantilist economic nationalist position in which economic logic is subordinated to assumed military security requirements.

This process may reflect genuine military concerns, but it can also be used as a disguise for preferred economic policies. As Luciani concludes:

> much of the tendency to broaden the economic content of security depends on a confusion…between economic risk that may be addressed through appropriate economic measures, and true security implications, that impose a burden on the military capabilities of the nation…while one cannot altogether discard the significance of broadening the economic content of security, it appears that in most cases the security implications of dependence on outside sources of supply are little more than rhetorical expedients, and one should more appropriately speak of simple economic or commercial risk.[17]

A variant on this kind of mercantilism is reactions against foreign ownership of key industries. Such reactions may simply reflect xenophobia or resentment at loss of status to foreigners, but they can easily be dressed up in security concerns about loss of control over military essential industries.

The second route is not to extend the military logic, but to add to it by analogy other areas in which the legitimate responsibilities of governments can be defined in national security terms. As Mayall argues, truly liberal systems require a very narrow conception of security, but the spread of government functions into social and economic areas provides an endless supply of wider security commitments whose logic can be used to undermine liberal economic practice.[18] The logic that liberal systems require a narrow conception of security rests firmly in the argument made above about the inescapable insecurities of market-based relations. The counter logic stems from government commitments to welfare ('social security'), and more broadly to the management of the economy in order to optimize welfare and economic security for the electorate as a whole. This line of reasoning links the more ambitious notions of individual and corporate security to the state level. If 'social security' broadly conceived means maintaining jobs, high incomes and traditional industries and patterns of employment, then welfare logic becomes a rationale for protecting the economy from the pressures of market competition. In an environment in which economic threats have the highest profile for many citizens, this conflation of social and national security logic can be electorally persuasive.

The third route to mercantilism is to attack the liberal assumptions as they apply to the state in question, by pointing out the specific malign and inequitable consequences of letting the market rule. A nationalist line of argument takes a stand on societal security grounds, arguing against both the homogenizing cosmopolitanism of a global market economy and the surrender of economic control to foreign ownership. Participation in a liberal economy exposes the country and its culture to relentless and continuous pressure to make painful adaptations to the endlessly evolving demands of market efficiency. The net effect of this process is to undermine both the moral values of religion and the distinctiveness of national cultures. At best it produces the bland universal culture of brand-name materialism, at worst, decadence and moral decay, and subservience to foreigners. At its strongest, as in post-1979 Iran, and post-1989 China, this is a case for opposing liberalism as a matter of principle.

A less extreme rejection of liberalism is available for late industrializing countries, whose industries are forced to make their way in a system already heavily populated with well-established producers. States in this position can argue that unless they protect their infant industries, as even second-round industrializers such as Germany and the United States did, they have no chance of breaking into the world economy. Without such protection, their industries will be unable to compete against the more powerful firms already in the market. This logic points to the inherent inequity of the liberal market which favours established strength over new entrants. The freedom of the liberal system in fact favours the strong, so that mercantilism becomes a strategy not against the liberal logic itself, but against the self-interested use of that logic by those already in a strong position within the system. This argument still has attraction, despite the failure of most import substitution strategies to work in the several Third World countries that tried them.[19] Liberals answer by pointing to the strictly limited application of this argument, and to the advantages of newer technology and lower development costs that late entrants have over those who first opened up the market. The Japanese were quite easily able to beat long-established car and motorcycle industries in Britain and America despite being latecomers.

A more far-reaching condemnation of the inequities between weak and strong in a liberal system is opened up implicitly in the theories of Wallerstein and Galtung, and explicitly in the work of the *dependencia* school.[20] Their argument is that the relative strengths and weaknesses of state structures vary according to the state's position in the capitalist world economy. States at the centre will tend to have strong structures, and those at the periphery weak ones.[21] Since a centre-periphery structure is widely seen as an inescapable result of uneven development in the capitalist system, one is confronted with a significant intrusion of economic dynamics into the structure of the international political system. Even if Wallerstein, Galtung and the *dependencia* writers have overstated their case, they have uncovered a point that is important to the analysis of immature and mature anarchies.

Using this perspective, when the economic and political systems are considered simultaneously, weak states appear not only as a result of different levels of development, but also as a product of a powerful economic dynamic. If weak states were only a product of a different pace of development, then time plus some external assistance would be sufficient to ensure that they caught up. An assumption along these lines underlay the discussion in Chapter 4 about the prospects for evolution towards a more mature form of international anarchy. If, however, weak states also reflect an economic dynamic, then they will tend to be maintained rather than eroded over time. The mechanisms for maintaining the structure of weak states in the periphery include the unequal terms of trade between primary and industrial producers, and the net outflow of capital from poor to rich.

These are very large-scale arguments which cannot be resolved here. They raise many points of controversy, and probably exaggerate the significance of the central point they make. Nevertheless, they do point to the interesting suggestion that a competition exists between basic political and economic dynamics. In pure form, the competitive political dynamic of anarchy should eventually lead to a world of strong states along the lines of the successful European leaders. In this analysis, the pure economic dynamic would lead to a world divided between strong states at the centre and weak ones at the periphery, with a gradation of semi-periphery states in between. Economic factors would act as a brake on the political dynamic, especially at the periphery, because the emergence of strong states there would tend to increase the disruptive penetration of national divisions into the international economy. The potential of large states such as the Soviet Union, China and to a lesser extent, India, to drop out of the international economy for long periods illustrates the economic problem posed by such political developments. As Gill and Law argue, capital is most advantaged when dealing with smaller and weaker political units.[22] And as Calleo and Rowland put it: 'The elaborate economic interdependence of free-trade imperialism is obviously not without its political implications. It often promotes… political units lacking political or economic viability except as tributaries of the imperial power.'[23]

These arguments posit a significant tension between economic interests and the development of a more mature international anarchy. If centre states define their security in reference to a pattern of global dominance, then weak peripheral states can identify their domestic security problems as part of a wider systemic phenomenon. Their insecurity would be defined, in part, by their position in the structure of the international political economy. The key riposte to this view lies in the long-term mobility of the centre. The centre is not fixed on a particular set of states but shifts over time, as the economic forces at play migrate in search of optimum profit in response to shifting social, technological and political conditions.[24] The mobility of the centre in turn favours different parts of the system, and as it does so it does not necessarily, or even probably, ruin the old centres. There are now three major centres of capitalism, where there was only one not much more than a century ago. Since the planet is fixed in size, the centre (and the semi-periphery) can only expand if the periphery shrinks. By this logic there may not, in the long term, be a contradiction between economic and political forces in the development of a more mature anarchy.

ECONOMIC SECURITY AND THE INTERNATIONAL SYSTEM

Two elements in the discussion so far have already pointed to the importance of the system level: first, the tension between liberal and mercantilist strategies, which has a powerful effect on the market and production structures of the international political economy; and second, the idea of a centre-periphery structure, with its consequence for states in terms of their position within it. If the key to economic security on the state level is the position of the state within the international networks of trade, production and finance, then the key at the system level is the stability of the whole network of market relations itself. This network comprises a complicated interlacing of transportation, communication, credit, and contracts. When it functions smoothly, some actors will do well, and others badly, depending on what leverage their assets give them, and how efficiently they play their hand. But if the market network itself is disrupted, then nearly all the actors in the system end up worse off, as happened during the 1930s.

Part of the international economic security problem arises because of the disjuncture between the global operation of the market, and the fragmented structure of political authority under anarchy. Baldly put, the scale of the international economy far outreaches both the capability and the legitimacy of any national political authority to manage it. Only a global government could do this, but that is the one thing that the international political system in its anarchic form cannot provide. As a consequence, the network of the global market has to function in the shifting, uncertain and relatively thinly managed political environment above the state level, where only regimes and international society can tackle the functions of governing. It can be argued quite convincingly that it is this disjuncture between political authority and global market that makes the international political economy vulnerable to episodes of disarray or even collapse. This argument must, however, be set against the equally convincing one made earlier that capitalism (and thus the dominance of the global market) is so closely associated with anarchic structure that the two can be seen in some important respects as mutually constitutive. In this perspective, anarchy is the optimal political environment for the market. The danger is that an all-encompassing government would either mismanage the economy, or suppress the social forces that drive the market economy, as in the case of imperial China. Although the global market may be unstable because it is unmanaged, that instability may be a lesser evil than the consequences of management, which might kill the market completely. As stated earlier, the contradictions in the idea of economic security are many, deep and intractable!

The secure operation of the global market networks can be threatened in two ways: either by external forces attacking the interaction flows of trade, investment and finance; or by internal instabilities arising from the operation of the market itself. The main external threats are piracy and war. Nature, in the form of stormy seas and impenetrable geographies, used to count as a threat, but has been reduced to a marginal nuisance by advances in technology. It could once again become a factor if the global operation of that self-same technology causes major environmental changes. Piracy has likewise been reduced from being a major parasite to a peripheral problem. War only wrecks the global market when it is a system-wide phenomenon like the Second World War, engaging most or all of the great powers. This threat has also receded since 1945, when the nuclear terror made war irrational as a means by which the great powers could pursue their rivalries with each other. External threats have thus faded somewhat into the background, and are anyway rather straightforward and easy to understand.

Internal threats, however, are far from straightforward, and if anything have grown rather than receded. To consider them takes the discussion back to the grand dialectic between anarchy and high density interdependence raised in Chapter 4. The global market is without question a main generator of rising density, and probably the main generator of interdependence. Some states, notably those with communist and/or extreme nationalist governments, will see the global market as a threat on ideological grounds, regardless of how well or badly it functions. Others will hang their legitimacy on it, as several post-Cold War governments in Eastern Europe have done. But taken as a system in its own right, the global market has a number of inbuilt tensions and operating dilemmas which can, if they become severe, cause states otherwise favourably disposed towards it to see the system itself as a threat. This link between the functional effects of the global market, and the responses that states make to the costs and benefits that flow from it, quickly forms a closed circle. To the extent that states open themselves to the market, they increase the scope of market functions and impacts in the system as a whole. To the extent that they close themselves to it, the opposite occurs, the extreme situation being total closure and the virtual elimination of the global market as a factor in the international system. States thus not only respond to the market, but in a real sense control the taps whose flow allows the market to exist. This control works both ways, however, for states are divided among themselves. As the Soviet Union and China have discovered, those that drop out or attack the market risk weakening themselves in relation to those that do not.

States can thus be classified according to their attitude to the market along two dimensions: whether they oppose or support it in their domestic political economy, and whether they open or close themselves to it internationally. This can be represented as in Table 6.1. As a rule, one would expect market states to support open relations, as Britain and the United States have done, and command states to opt for closure, as the communist states traditionally did. But this rule has many exceptions. As was argued in the previous section, there are lots of reasons why market states might want to protect themselves from global competition, and some

Table 6.1: The relationship of states and markets

		Relations with the system	
		Open	Closed
Domestic political economy	Market		
	Command		

command states might see advantages in access to the global market.

One way of looking at this relationship between states and the global market is in terms of the degree of harmony or discord between the economic and the political systems taken separately. That is to say, the security quality of the anarchy (and not just its economic security) will vary according to whether the structures and dynamics of its economic and political sides fit together reasonably well, or are chained together at cross-purposes. The simplest way to conceptualize this linkage is in terms of the opposition between mercantilist and liberal approaches to structuring the international economy.[25] I do not use these terms to describe the two strictly defined and highly polarized alternatives of economic theory, but to indicate the broadly opposed tendencies of free trade versus protectionism. To avoid unnecessary complications I use the term mercantilist to include both the classical and the neomercantilist perspectives.

Put crudely, mercantilists seek to make the international economy fit with the pattern of fragmentation in the political system by reducing the scope of the global market. They emphasize the integrity of the national economy and the primacy of state goals (military, welfare, societal). They advocate protection as a means of preserving this integrity, but may be attracted to the construction of economic spheres with their own economy dominating at the centre. By contrast, liberals seek to create a more unified, larger-scale, more interdependent global economy which transcends the fragmentation of the international anarchy by encouraging trade in a world-wide market.

Before looking at the theories of liberalism and mercantilism, it is necessary first to consider the attractions and the difficulties that condition state responses to the global market. The attraction of the global market is simple and powerful, and can be summed up in the idea of economic efficiency. To those who participate in it, the market offers open access to a range of buyers and sellers and lenders and borrowers far larger than that available within any state. This larger range opens opportunities to exploit both economies of scale and strategies of specialization that are not available within a closed economy. It offers quick access to finance and technology that could not be generated easily, or even at all, within the state, and it guarantees a steady inflow of stimulating contacts and information. At its best, the global market holds out the promise that states can make the most of their comparative advantages. In so doing they can make themselves richer than they would otherwise be, and also more secure because of the elimination of the need for military rivalries over territory that arise when the pursuit of wealth is tied to direct control over markets and resources.

The operating difficulties of the global market are more complicated, and limitations of space permit only a sketch. Some of them arise from the responsive impact of state policies, and these will be considered in the discussion of liberalism and mercantilism further below. Others concern the dynamics of the market itself. Prominent among these are the provision of money and credit, the tendency for competition to become more fierce, the inevitability of uneven development and the deterioration of the planetary environment.[26] All of these problems are exacerbated as the density of the system rises.

Money and credit
As Susan Strange argues, the financial structure is a mixture of state and market elements. A developed monetary system confers many advantages of growth, flexibility, fluidity and freedom to economic management, but also poses risks of instability, inequality, political abuse and occasional collapse of the system.[27] Part of the attraction of a developed monetary system is the way that it provides escape from local resource constraints through the provision of credit. So important is credit that one could almost interpret the history of economics in terms of advancement of understanding about it. The problem is in finding the optimal amount of credit that a financial system can sustain. Underutilizing credit potential risks at best underachieving possibilities for welfare, growth and power, and at worst economic contraction and recession. Over utilizing credit potential risks straining the management capacity of the system beyond its limits, and causing a massive and extremely damaging collapse of credit. In a complex financial system neither the optimal level of credit nor the management capacity of the system are known with any precision. Both tend to expand in a healthy economy, albeit with the added confusion of complex cyclical fluctuations. Strong economic and political pressures exist not to risk underutilization, which causes the system continuously to push at the limits of its capability. As in the case of the great crash of 1929, and the crushing debt burdens of the 1980s, those limits are often only discovered once the damage is done. States engaged in the global market have to calculate their economic security in terms of the benefits that such linkage brings, against the vulnerabilities and costs of being caught in one of these crises.

Fiercer competition
Competition is what makes the market work efficiently, and in that sense it is a valuable stimulant. But when a market becomes intensely competitive, the costs of competition may rise, and the prospects of being successful fall, to such an extent as to make participation unattractive. Classical economics developed during a period in which industrial capacity was concentrated in Britain, and competition in industrial manufactures was low. By the late nineteenth century, industrialization had spread to Germany and the United States, with France, Russia and Japan not too far behind. By the late twentieth century, it had spread to Brazil, India, China, the Asian newly industrializing countries (NICs), and several other parts of the Third World. With so many manufacturing states in the field, surplus capacities emerge in many areas where the technology is mature, notably steel-

making, shipbuilding and automobiles, not to mention textiles and televisions. Countries once prominent in these areas, such as Britain, find themselves unable to compete with those either better equipped and organized, or having cheaper labour. At the very least, intense competition imposes severe adjustment costs. It forces states continuously to reconstruct their domestic economies, with resultant hardship for displaced workers, and threats to overall levels of national welfare. Such costs promote the formation of protectionist constituencies easily able to blame 'unfair foreign competition' for these hardships without having to address the more difficult question of how welfare levels can be sustained in the long run outside the market mainstream. By reducing the return on investment, intense competition also makes it increasingly difficult for new entrants to break into the high value end of the market. Intensifying competition thus politicizes trade relations and feeds protectionist political forces. Given the continuing spread of industrialization, this problem can only get worse, creating more pressure to restrict the free operation of the market. The main force working against it is the interest of large multinational corporations, whose internal trade now accounts for a substantial proportion of world trade.

Uneven development
Uneven development refers to the way in which the market distributes wealth, and in a broader sense development, unevenly throughout the system. Within states, and even more so between them, the operation of the market creates patterns of wealth and poverty, or advantage and disadvantage, and of growth and stagnation. The centre-periphery model of the international political economy is a way of formulating the problem of uneven development. Within states, the tensions caused by these inequalities are addressed by welfare and redistribution mechanisms, or sometimes by repression; between states, the mechanisms of welfare and redistribution are much weaker, and the use of force much more costly and dangerous. In two ways, the international tensions of uneven development are self-regulating. First, the advantaged areas tend by definition to be more powerful than the disadvantaged ones, and can therefore maintain order. Second, the operation of the market ensures that the locus of advantage is continuously mobile. A century and a half ago, Britain was at the apex of world power, while Japan was barely emerging from feudalism and was in danger of falling into semi-colonial status. British warships bombarded Kagoshima in 1863 as part of the 'opening' of Japan by the West. Today Britain is a marginal power on the fringes of Europe, and Japanese companies steadily colonize the remnants of its industry.

The mobility of the 'centre' makes uneven development more tolerable than it would be if positions in the centre and the periphery were permanently fixed, creating a kind of international caste system. Because the centre migrates, even the most downcast sections of the periphery can aspire to improve their status. But this relentless shifting of advantage also creates problems. On the domestic front it feeds excess demand, which in turn pressures governments to seek immediate gains over long-term management objectives, and to try to export the burdens of adjustment.[28] In a high density system, as the communist giants discovered, not even a totalitarian government can keep from its people the corrosive knowledge that higher standards of living exist elsewhere. Where higher standards have been achieved, the electoral survival of governments depends on their ability to maintain what citizens come to see as a norm, or even a right.

On the international front, the mobility of power feeds inter-state rivalries, and means that the leading states in the system cannot hold their position indefinitely. Since these states play a major role in providing the degree of international order necessary for the market to function, there is a permanent instability of management at the heart of the international political economy. The leading hegemonic states will inevitably face crises of decline, and the system as a whole will have to make periodic adjustments to new configurations of power. Such adjustments have in the past frequently been an occasion for major wars. This is the problem recently given wide prominence by Paul Kennedy in *The Rise and Fall of the Great Powers*. Both the domestic and the international effects of uneven development eventually push states towards protectionist policies, an outcome that perfectly illustrates the centrality of the dialectic between anarchy and interdependence. As Gilpin argues: 'Economic nationalism is likely to be a significant influence in international relations as long as the state system exists.'[29] In their attempts to control the effects of uneven development, states will be hard put to resist the temptation to try to shape the global market to their own advantage, rather than continuously bearing the costs of reshaping their own societies and economies to conform to market demands. In so doing, the temptation to try to cast economic security as a national security issue is strong.

Environmental deterioration
The problems of cyclic instabilities in the global market arising from the operation of financial, competitive and development issues are long established, and are internal to the dynamics of the market system. The problem of environmental deterioration is of more recent vintage, and reflects the fact, already sketched out in Chapter 3, that the rising density of human occupation of the planet has begun seriously to disrupt the natural operation of the ecosphere. Because the market is a main force driving the expansion of human activity, its continued operation becomes part of the environmental problem. The threat is that polluting externalities (smoke, acid, fertilizer, heavy metals, oil, gasses, etc.) or direct assaults on parts of the ecosphere (forestry, mining, farming, fishing, etc.) resulting from economic activity will eventually, and perhaps soon, precipitate a major environmental disaster that will significantly degrade the conditions of human tenure on the planet. Diminution of species diversity may make the ecosystem more vulnerable to collapse. Thinning of the ozone layer may sharply raise the level of solar radiation reaching the surface of the planet. The greenhouse effects of carbon dioxide and other gaseous emissions from industrial society may change the temperature of the ecosystem.

At a very minimum it would seem to be necessary to factor environmental consequences into the cost calculations of the market. But how a highly decentralized and competitive market can adjust adequately to the new constraint posed by environmental limits is not at all clear. Large uncertainties of information about the vulnerability of the environment make political action difficult. So too does narrowly self-interested action by states seeking to improve their position in the market. The Brazilians claim the right to destroy their forests as part of their development process just as the British and Americans did before them. Why should they carry the burden of restraint, so disadvantaging themselves in the development competition, just because their process of industrialization happens to coincide with the rise of global environmental problems? To the Brazilians, such calls for restraint simply look like another strategy by the centre to keep their state in the periphery. Similar arguments could be made about a host of other economic activities from CFC production to the general right to have polluting industries. The conflict of interest they create can only get worse, posing an increasingly difficult problem for global management. In some places, such as South Asia and the Middle East, environmental issues such as the linkage of upstream deforestation (or damming) and downstream flooding (or drought) are possibly serious enough to threaten a resort to force at some point in the future. As Mathews argues, there is certainly a place on the security agenda for environmental issues.[30]

These attractions and repulsions of the global market feed into the choices that states have to make about whether to adopt liberal or mercantilist policies. In turn, the responses that states make massively condition the character of the global market in the manner sketched above, with liberal responses tending to strengthen the market against the state, and mercantilist ones weakening the global market and strengthening the state. These doctrines contain theories of security that go well beyond merely economic security to embrace larger questions about the causes of war and peace. The argument is a structural one, resting on the impact of the distribution of liberal and mercantilist states in the system. When liberal states predominate, the market gains power, and the system itself can be described as liberal. When mercantilist states dominate, the system effect of the global market is weak, and the system can be described as mercantilist. I have discussed these security theories at length elsewhere,[31] and the argument can be summarized as follows.

The liberal case is that mercantilist systems are both economically inefficient and increase the likelihood of force being used, while liberal systems increase welfare and decrease the likelihood of force being used. The core of the argument is that mercantilist systems associate the pursuit of wealth with the control of territory, so creating incentives for imperial rivalries as the major powers seek to capture the markets and resources necessary to sustain their own industrial power. The 1930s are cited as supporting this theory, which bears some resemblance to Lenin's argument about the inevitability of intra-capitalist conflict as the expansion of industrial capitalism first occupied the planet, and then fell into warfare over the redivision of the spoils. Liberal systems, by contrast, delink the pursuit of wealth from the control of territory. In so doing they reduce the number of issues over which states might go to war, and, by linking the economic interests of states together in networks of interdependence, raise the costs to states of using force against each other. The relatively restrained use of force in the international system since 1945 is offered as evidence of the benign effects of a liberal system.

Although not without considerable logical power, the problem is that this argument provides only a very partial explanation for the observed phenomena. The war-proneness of the 1930s can be ascribed to several other factors particular to the time which did not operate in the post-1945 world. Military means offered a real possibility of victory during the 1930s, and thus were an attractive instrument of great power policy. But since 1945 the use of force between great powers has been massively constrained by the fear that nuclear weapons would make victory indistinguishable from defeat. During the 1930s, American and Soviet isolationism made the balance of power weak, and tenuously held European empires offered numerous temptations in the periphery. But since 1945 the balance of power has operated exceptionally vigorously, and the periphery has benefited from a steady gain in political and military strength which makes it no longer attractive for old-fashioned empire building. These military and political arguments weigh more heavily in the scale than economic ones. It can more convincingly be argued that the liberal system required politically and militarily generated restraints on the use of force as a precondition for its own existence, than that the liberal system itself created those constraints.

In addition, the rise of continental states and economic blocs, and the dismantling of empires, mean that there are no longer the same economic incentives for imperialism now that there were for the Axis powers during the 1930s. Domestic economies of scale are more readily available, and the Third World is not closed to trade by imperial preference. It can also be argued that the domestic conditions for the rise of warfare mercantilism that fed fascism during the 1930s no longer exist. Fascism represented a kind of alliance between national capital and government, and required economic conditions in which national capital could see advantages for itself in a belligerent state policy. Such an alliance can only work if national capital identifies its own interest as lying largely within the state, and such conditions still existed during the 1930s. But since 1945, the interests of capital have expanded well beyond the confines of any single state. Elements of national capital still exist, but they are no longer dominant. International capital would have much more to lose than to gain by supporting fascism in the major industrial powers, and so is no longer available to support political movements in that direction. In this sense, the 1930s represented a particular historical phase in the relationship between state and capital that has now passed, at least in the advanced industrial countries.

Not only is the historical evidence for the liberal case against mercantilism contestable, there are also strong arguments that the liberal system itself is not benign, but can also operate to increase the likelihood of the use of force. The unequal development logic of the centre-periphery model points to a whole array of domestic and international violence in the periphery. More serious is the problem of hegemonic instability, which seems to condemn liberal systems to periodic crises precipitated by the decline of the leading state that generates the order necessary to sustain the operation of the global market. There are now well-developed arguments, of which Paul Kennedy's is merely the latest, demonstrating that the operation of a hegemonic power in support of a liberal system creates potent and diverse forces that systematically erode the hegemon's ability to hold its leading position.[32] The extent to which these arguments apply to the current position of the United States is still hotly contested. Hegemonic decline poses the threat of periods of weak management under declining hegemons, and transitional turbulence when a rising hegemon replaces a declining one. Gilpin, for example, unblushingly remarks that: 'Unfortunately, the world had to suffer two world conflicts before an American-centred liberal world economy was substituted for a British-centred one.'[33] This argument turns the 1930s case on its head, making the conflict of that decade look like the result of a collapsing liberal system, rather than a consequence of mercantilism. At worst, the threat is that the declining hegemon will have no successor, as appeared to be the case going into the 1990s. In such a case the management of the liberal economy would depend on the untried and theoretically contested possibility of collective management by a group of leading powers, or diffuse management by way of consensual regimes built around liberal rules and norms.[34]

The conclusion to this argument was that in security terms liberalism was not unequivocally benign, and mercantilism was not unequivocally malign. Neither economic structure determined the probability of the use of force. Liberalism could turn malign when its management mechanism either collapsed or became too weak to contain the operating difficulties of the global market. Mercantilism was malign if the motive for it was to increase the state's military and economic power at the conspicuous expense of other states. But it need not be malign when the motive for economic nationalism was conspicuously concerned with maintaining reasonable standards of economic welfare and socio-political stability within the state. The danger arose when malign economic structures of either kind occurred in tandem with other political and military elements of strategic instability, as happened during the 1930s. Conversely, benign economic structures of either sort could powerfully reinforce political and military configurations that tended towards strategic stability.

CONCLUSIONS: PROSPECTS FOR THE POLITICAL ECONOMY OF A MATURE ANARCHY

Several conditions in the international system point towards an attractive middle-ground synthesis between benign versions of liberalism and mercantilism. Recent developments have strengthened this prospect. The hybrid might be called 'protected liberalism' or 'liberal protectionism', and bears considerable resemblance to the Realist understanding of international economic relations outlined by McKinlay and Little.[35] The international system already has strategic stability because of the restraining effect of nuclear weapons. The collapse of the Cold War in the late 1980s immeasurably strengthened this stability by taking the ideological heat out of great power relations. When added to the existence of a solidly founded security community among the major centres of capitalist power in North America, Europe and East Asia, it augurs well for the continuance of this stability.

Among other things, the winding down of the Cold War strengthens the predominance of welfare over warfare motives for economic nationalism, a development particularly to be welcomed in the case of the Soviet Union, and with considerable scope also in the United States. The Japanese have been either exceptionally lucky, or exceptionally clever, to have avoided remilitarizing their economy for long enough so that it no longer becomes necessary to do so on the scale called for in a system dominated by great power military confrontation. Post-Cold War levels of military spending may well fall somewhat above the Japanese average of just over 1 per cent, but they will be massively below the double-digit Soviet levels, well below the 5–6 per cent of the United States, and probably below the 3–4 per cent of the Europeans. The prospect that the capitalist security community will be able to form what Jervis[36] calls a security regime with the Soviet Union could conceivably create conditions that would break the logic of Paul Kennedy's argument about the pursuit of military greatness leading to economic stress and decline of power.[37] If great powers no longer compete seriously in offensive warfighting capability, confining themselves instead to minimum deterrence, territorial defence and limited force projection capabilities, then they may not undermine their own mechanisms of economic renewal so quickly as in the past. If international order is maintained more by political consensus and a strong international society than by hegemonic military capability, then the demands of hegemonic leadership need not be so burdensome.

Another factor supporting a liberal-protectionist synthesis is the predominance of large actors and well-established economic blocs in the system including: the North American free trade area, the European Community (EC), the group of East Asian states coalescing around Japan (some of which are grouped within ASEAN) and semi-continental states such as the Soviet Union, China, India and Brazil. It may well be impossible to sustain the attempt to bring all of these together within a liberal economy on a global scale. The hegemonic strength does not exist in any single power to accomplish it. Collective management or rule-governed regimes are unlikely to be strong enough to sustain high liberal standards in the whole system, particularly given the severe operating conditions of such a system discussed above, which show no signs of getting any easier. The gloom of writers such as Gilpin at this prospect stems from an all-or-nothing view of liberalism, as if the benefits of liberalism disappear altogether if they cannot be sustained on a global scale.[38]

But the diffusion of power to these big actors and groups offers the makings of a middle ground in which quite high levels of liberalism are pursued within them. Instead of trying to maintain an unmanageable and increasingly crisis-prone global liberal system, the image is one of blocs sufficiently large to generate substantial liberal economies of scale within themselves, but not so large as to be politically unstable. Relations between these blocs would be managed so as to retain some of the virtues of global economies of scale and inter-bloc competition without creating the demanding management problems of a full-scale global liberal order. Indeed, the core capitalist blocs have already sufficiently integrated their economies to make extremes of self-reliant bloc mercantilism unthinkable. A more restricted global market might well be sustainable using the collective management and regime machineries that would not be strong enough to support a full liberal order. Since more of the management would be decentralized to the bloc level, as for example in the creation of a European monetary system, there would be less strain on management at the global level. Considerable trade would be necessary and desirable in order to sustain the efficiencies of competition. Some technologies would require global collaboration to achieve economies of scale in their development and marketing: one thinks of nuclear fusion, space infrastructures, big science (physics, astronomy), and perhaps some forms of high-speed transportation. Any attempt to manage the global environment would also require extensive global cooperation.

The central trade-off in such an arrangement would be the loss of some efficiencies from a global market in exchange for reduction of the threat from an unstable or collapsing liberal order. The loss of efficiency is to be regretted, but unsustainable efficiency is no blessing if its downswings create massive disruptions and dangers of war. A fully blown liberal order also has the disadvantage of putting states and societies under considerable pressure from the continuous necessity to adjust to market changes. This has its constructive side, but at too high a level it adversely affects both the hegemonic power and many of the states in the periphery. Excessive levels of adaptation can also erode domestic political support for open economies. A more decentralized system might ease these problems by lessening the pressure and devolving more control to regions. The fate of weak states in the periphery might improve as a result of association with a regional bloc, but it might equally well simply narrow the centre to which they are subordinate without improving their prospects. Weak states are a problem in any economic structure, especially so when the sources of their weakness have deep domestic roots in the nature of the states and societies concerned.

A scenario along these lines displays many of the characteristics associated with the *mature anarchy* mooted in Chapter 4. Such an arrangement would attempt to escape from the unsustainable contradiction between anarchy and the market that a full liberal system poses. It would seek to bring market and anarchy into a more balanced arrangement appropriate to the technological and density conditions of the late twentieth century, and making full use of an increasingly mature international society. Its big units would have sufficient economies of scale, command of capital and technology and political decentralization so as not to be pushed into rival imperialisms. Many of them would be linked together in security communities or security regimes, and all would continue to benefit from the paralysis on the use of force created by nuclear weapons. Trade and investment would continue to tie them together, and the need for economic and environmental management would engage them all in the construction and maintenance of economic regimes. To the extent that a consensus emerges on market economies and pluralist political structures, collective leadership and regime management at the global level would be supported and facilitated by the existence of a strong international society.

One advantage of market-based political economies is that their very operation generates high levels of transparency across all the sectors that affect security relations. Extensive trade, financial links and investment naturally make societies relatively open to each other, not least by forcing adherence to standard units of account. In market-based political economies, reliable and comparable statistics are readily available on a wide variety of activities within and between states as a matter of course. Without them, the operation of a market economy would suffer sharply reduced efficiency. This socio-economic interoperability avoids serious problems of opacity like those that the West has had in trying to estimate Soviet and Chinese defence expenditure, or to assess the true performance of their economies, or even to get information about environmental threats. The lack of tradable currencies in the communist powers, added to their governments' more than usually self-serving way with statistics, was an impediment to broadly based transparency, and thus an obstacle to international security. The apparent triumph of market over centrally planned economies in the late twentieth century will be a powerful stimulus to greater transparency, and therefore to the easier achievement of international security.

NOTES

1. Robin Murray, 'The internationalization of capital and the nation state', *New Left Review*, 67 (1971), pp. 104–9.

2. For a compact tour of the literature see Stephen Gill and David Law, *The Global Political Economy: Perspectives, problems and policies*, (Hemel Hempstead: Harvester Wheatsheaf, 1988), ch. 1.

3. On imperialism see, for example, J. A. Hobson, *Imperialism: A study* (London: Nisbet, 1902); V. I. Lenin, *Imperialism: The highest stage of capitalism* (Moscow: Foreign Languages Publishing House, n.d.); David K. Fieldhouse (ed.), *The Theory of Capital Imperialism* (London: Longman, 1967); David K. Fieldhouse, *Economics and Empire* (London: Weidenfeld & Nicolson, 1973); E. M. Winslow, *The Pattern of Imperialism* (New York: Columbia University Press, 1948); and Paul Sweezy (ed.) *Imperialism and Social Classes* (Oxford: Blackwell, 1951).

4. On interdependence see, for example, R. O. Keohane and J. S. Nye, *Power and Interdependence* (Boston: Little Brown, 1977); R. Rosecrance and A. Stein, 'Interdependence: myth or reality', *World Politics*, 26:1 (1974); Richard Rosecrance, A. Alexandroff, W. Koehler, J. Kroll, S. Laqueur, J. Stocker, 'Whither interdependence?', *International Organization*, 31:3 (1977); David Baldwin, 'Interdependence and power', *International Organization*, 34:4 (1980); J. N. Rosenau, *The Study of Global Interdependence* (London: Pinter, 1980); R. J. Barry Jones and Peter Willetts (eds),

Interdependence on Trial (London: Pinter, 1984). On contemporary international political economy see, for example, Charles P. Kindleberger, *Power and Money* (London: Macmillan, 1970); David P. Calleo and Benjamin Rowland, *America and the World Political Economy* (Bloomington: Indiana University Press, 1973); Gill and Law, *op. cit.* (note 2); Robert O. Keohane, *After Hegemony: Cooperation and discord in the world political economy* (Princeton, NJ: Princeton University Press, 1984); R. J. Barry Jones (ed.), *Perspectives on Political Economy* (London: Pinter, 1983); R. J. Barry Jones, *The Worlds of Political Economy: Alternative approaches to the study of contemporary political economy* (London: Pinter, 1988); Susan Strange, *States and Markets: An introduction to international political economy* (London: Pinter, 1988); Robert Gilpin, *The Political Economy of International Relations* (Princeton, NJ: Princeton University Press, 1987); Barry Buzan, 'Economic structure and international security: the limits of the liberal case', *International Organization*, 38:4 (1984).

5. Immanual Wallerstein, 'The rise and future demise of the world capitalist system', *Comparative Studies in Society and History*, 16.4 (1974); and Christopher Chase-Dunn, 'Interstate system and capitalist world economy: one logic or two?', *International Studies Quarterly*, 25:1 (1981). For a critique of Wallerstein, see Aristide R. Zolberg, 'Origins of the modern world system: a missing link', *World Politics*, 33:2 (1981); Johan Galtung, 'A structural theory of imperialism', *Journal of Peace Research*, 8:2 (1971); and Richard K. Ashley, *The Political Economy of War and Peace* (London: Pinter, 1980), which is based on the earlier work by Nazli Choucri and Robert C. North, *Nations in Conflict: National growth and international violence* (San Francisco: W. H. Freeman, 1975).

6. Leonard Tivey, 'States, nations and economies', in L. Tivey (ed.), *The Nation-State* (Oxford: Martin Robertson, 1981), ch. 3.

7. Chase-Dunn, *op. cit.* (note 5); Paul Kennedy, *The Rise and Fall of the Great Powers: Economic change and military conflict from 1500-2000* (London: Fontana, 1989 (1988)), p. xvii; Strange, *op. cit.* (note 4), pp. 63–9; Wallerstein, *op. cit.* (note 5); William H. McNeill, *The Rise of the West: A history of the human community* (Chicago: University of Chicago Press, 1963), pp. 467–9; William H. McNeill, *The Pursuit of Power* (Chicago: University of Chicago Press, 1982), pp. 40–1, 69–70, 98, 112–16, 257–8.

8. Giacomo Luciani, 'The economic content of security', *Journal of Public Policy*, 8:2 (1989), p. 164; Gill and Law, *op. cit.* (note 2), pp. 4–5.

9. Luciani, *ibid.*

10. For one view of corporate security strategies, see John K. Galbraith, *The New Industrial State* (Boston: Houghton Mifflin, 1967). See also Robert Skidelsky, 'Prophet of the liberal state', *Times Literary Supplement* (7 August 1981); and Calleo and Rowland, *op. cit.* (note 4), ch. 7.

11. Fred Block, 'Marxist theories of the state in world system analysis', in Barbara H. Kaplan (ed.), *Social Change in the Capitalist World Economy* (Beverly Hills: Sage, 1978), pp. 27–8. Few Marxists, I suspect, would accept the separate political dynamic which I have argued here as the source of the relative autonomy of the state. According to Block (pp. 33–6) their shift of view away from direct class control is more in response to the structural complexities of the pluralist politics which underlie state behaviour. This line of argument ties into the preoccupation of liberal thinkers during the eighteenth and nineteenth

centuries with the existence of a militaristic aristocracy which controlled the state and was seen to be responsible for the malaise of war. Much liberal argument was devoted to removing this class, not least by encouraging free trade so as to undermine its economic base. Notions that the character of the ruling class was responsible for war continued in the socialist tradition, but have now largely been replaced by more diffuse structural explanations for war. For an excellent review of these ideas and their development, see Michael Howard, *War and the Liberal Conscience* (Oxford: Oxford University Press, 1981 (1978)).

12. On stockpiling arguments, see Richard H. Ullman, 'Redefining security', *International Security*, 8:1 (1983), pp. 139–50; Luciani, *op. cit.* (note 8), p. 165.

13. McNeill, *op. cit.* (note 7, 1963); E. L. Jones, *The European Miracle: Environments, economies and geopolitics in the history of Europe and Asia* (Cambridge: Cambridge University Press, 1981).

14. Kennedy, *op. cit.* (note 7).

15. Gautam Sen, *The Military Origins of Industrialization and International Trade Rivalry* (London: Pinter, 1984).

16. Gill and Law, *op. cit.* (note 2), p. 367 and ch. 8.

17. Luciani, *op. cit.* (note 8), pp. 171–2.

18. James Mayall, 'Reflections on the "new" economic nationalism', *Review of International Studies*, 10:4 (1984).

19. Gilpin, *op. cit.* (note 4), pp. 291–2.

20. Wallerstein, *op. cit.* (note 5), pp. 390–412; Galtung, *op. cit.* (note 5), pp. 85–91. From and on the dependencia school, see Gilpin, *op. cit.* (note 4), pp. 273–90; André Gunder Frank, *On Capitalist Underdevelopment* (Bombay: Oxford University Press, 1975); André Gunder Frank, *Dependent Accumulation and Underdevelopment* (London: Macmillan, 1978); *International Organization*, 32: 1 (1978) special issue on 'Dependence and dependency in the global system'; Tony Smith, 'The underdevelopment of development literature'; *World Politics*, 21:2 (1979); André Gunder Frank, 'The development of underdevelopment', *Monthly Review*, 18:4 (1966). For a critique of these literatures, see R. Brenner, 'The Origins of Capitalist Development', *New Left Review*, 104 (July-August 1977).

21. For a critique of this view, see Peter Gourevitch, 'International system and regime formation: a critical review of Anderson and Wallerstein', *Comparative Politics*, 10:3 (1978).

22. Gill and Law, *op. cit.* (note 2), pp. 98–9.

23. Calleo and Rowland, *op. cit.* (note 4), p. 11; see also ch. 9.

24. Gilpin, *op. cit.* (note 4), pp. 18–21, 92–111. Johan Galtung, 'A structural theory of imperialism – ten years later', *Millennium*, 9:3 (1980–1), pp. 186–7, argues that the centre of capitalism is now in the process of shifting towards East Asia.

25. For a general outline of the mercantilist versus liberal arguments, see Robert Gilpin, 'Three models of the future', in his *U.S. Power and the Multinational Corporation* (London: Macmillan, 1976/New York: Basic Books, 1975), ch. 9; also in *International Organization*, 29:1 (1975); and *op. cit.* (note 4), ch. 2.

26. The first three of these derive principally from my reading of Gilpin, *op. cit.* (note 4), but he does not necessarily feature them in the way I do here.

27. Strange, *op. cit.* (note 4), pp. 88–96; and more generally Gilpin, *ibid.*, ch. 4.

28. Gilpin, *ibid.*, pp. 360–63.

29. *ibid.*, p. 34.
30. Jessica Tuchman Mathews, 'Redefining security', *Foreign Affairs*, 68:2 (1989).
31. Buzan, *op. cit.* (note 4), which see for the full range of sources on this topic. An earlier version appeared in Chapter 5 of the first edition of this book.
32. *ibid.*, pp. 621–2; also Keohane, *op. cit.* (note 4); Gilpin, *op. cit*, (note 4), chs 9, 10; Gill and Law, *op. cit.* (note 2), ch. 16.
33. Gilpin, *op. cit.* (note 25, 'Three models...'), p. 259.
34. Keohane, *op. cit.* (note 4), makes the case that regimes are a viable successor to hegemonic stability.
35. R. D. McKinlay and R. Little, *Global Problems and World Order* (London: Pinter, 1986), pp. 147–68.
36. Robert Jervis, 'Security regimes', *International Organization*, 36:2 (1982); and 'From balance to concert: a study security cooperation', *World Politics*, 38: 1 (1985).
37. Kennedy, *op. cit.* (note 7), pp. xv-xxviii.
38. Gilpin, *op. cit.* (note 4), chs 9, 10.

chapter seven | the defence dilemma

This chapter and the next consider the specifically military interaction dynamics among states. Part of their purpose is thus to sketch out the place that Strategic Studies occupies in the agenda of International Security Studies. As I have argued at length elsewhere, Strategic Studies is essentially about the impact of military technology on relations between states – or at least this definition is one of the few meaningful and appropriate ways of differentiating Strategic Studies as a sub-field from the broader realms of International Relations.[1] Military technology as an independent variable thus becomes another of the key factors that mediate the security consequences of anarchy.

The use and threat of force are well understood to be a deeply embedded feature of anarchic international relations. In the international system, as Robert Osgood points out, 'the primary instrument of order – armed force – is also the primary threat to security.'[2] This paradox underpins the widely held view that military power lies at the heart of the national security problem. States in an anarchy require military power both for their own defence and for the broader security purposes of system management. But once acquired, such power generates a counter-security dynamic of its own which threatens both individual states and the order of the system as a whole. Osgood argues that 'force must be as essential to international politics in an anarchy as elections are to domestic politics in an organized democracy.'[3] Hedley Bull supports this view from a different angle by arguing that 'the international order is notoriously lacking in mechanisms of peaceful change, notoriously dependent on war as the agent of just change.'[4] Michael Howard draws the bottom line on the matter, arguing that 'force is an ineluctable element in international relations, not because of any inherent tendency on the part of man to use it, but because the *possibility* of its use exists. It has thus to be deterred, controlled, and if all else fails, used with discrimination and restraint.'[5] He goes on to identify one of the basic engines of the whole military problem in international relations, which is that 'those who renounce the use of force find themselves at the mercy of those who do not.'[6]

The deployment of military instruments by states gives rise to two types of threat: those from the weapons themselves, and those from the fact that weapons are in the hands of other actors in the system.[7] The first threat is mostly one of destruction, though it also has a significant element of opportunity cost even if the weapons are not used. It gives rise to the *defence dilemma*[8] – contradictions between the pursuit of military defence and national security – which is the subject of this chapter. The second threat is of defeat. It gives rise to the *power-security dilemma*, which is the subject of Chapter 8. These two dilemmas, and the interaction between them, express the essence of the military dimension of the national security problem.

THE DEFENCE DILEMMA DEFINED

The defence dilemma arises primarily from the nature of military means as they are developed and deployed by states, and only secondarily from the dynamics of relations among states. The development of military means follows a technological logic which is separate from the patterns of amity and enmity among states. Although such relational patterns may accelerate military developments, as during wars or arms races, they do not fundamentally determine the scientific, technological and organizational imperatives which drive the creation of ever more powerful and expensive weapons. Those imperatives stem from the general advance in human understanding of the natural world. Scientific knowledge and technological virtuosity increase regardless of the particularities of international relations. Although specific defence concerns do shape this technological imperative, they are not responsible for it.

Scientific and technological improvements come as much from civil as from military sources. Except for specialized items such as high-performance jet fighters, military and civil technology are so closely linked as to make the distinction between them questionable. The technology for civil aviation makes bombers possible, that for bulldozers makes tanks possible, that for nuclear power stations makes atomic bombs possible, that for space exploration makes strategic missiles possible, that for air traffic control makes military early warning possible, that for television makes precision-guided bombs possible and so forth. All of these propositions, and many more could be stated in reverse. Because of these links, industrialized societies cannot escape the military implications of technological progress. Even a militarily unprepared industrial society can quickly turn its skills to making weapons, as illustrated by the rapid mobilization of the United States during the Second World War. The military implications of new technology will be much starker and more compelling when international tensions are high than when they are low. But they will be a continuing factor, operating on their own logic, and feeding into international relations independently of the other factors that shape the amity and enmity of states. The military potential of the prevailing technology plays a major role in defining the strategic environment of the day.[9]

The defence dilemma arises from contradictions that exist between military defence and national security. Armed forces are justified principally by their necessity for national security, and it is therefore politically expedient to assume that military might is positively correlated with national security. Since neither concept is amenable to quantification, the proposition cannot be tested. But there are nevertheless two obvious ways in which defence and security can work against each other: because the cost of defence compromises other security objectives, or because the risks of defence appear to outweigh the threats that defence is designed to deter. It is useful to distinguish between the defence dilemma, where defence and security are in some sense at odds, and cases where defence measures are simply inappropriate or irrelevant to security. Where states have major economic and political stakes in the maintenance of an international economy, for example, many of their core interests cannot be effectively protected by military power. The European states cannot use military means either to enhance their benefits from, or protect their vulnerabilities to, contact with the Japanese economy. Similarly, military means are inappropriate where the issue is environmental security.

Defence dilemmas of cost involve straight trade-offs between resources devoted to defence, and resources available to meet other security objectives. One version is the armament versus development debate, which is now firmly institutionalized in United Nations rhetoric. Here the argument is that military spending reduces the resources available for Third World development, both in the Third World countries themselves, and by reducing potential aid resources from North to South. The case is that more serious economic, political and ecological security issues are not dealt with because too many resources are put into dealing with less serious military threats. A similar linkage across security sectors is being developed to support calls for giving increased resources to environmental issues. These campaigns make valid attempts to apply a wider logic of security. They are flawed in their assumption that money not spent on defence would be transferred to their preferred objectives. By linking two sectors together, they also risk paralysis in their preferred sector if they fail to achieve reduction in military expenditure.

The most spectacular example of a cost-defence dilemma is currently unfolding in the Soviet Union, where the success of *perestroika* hangs, among other things, on massive transfers of resources from the military to the civil sector. By chronic overspending on military security, combined with the bureaucratic inefficiencies of central planning, the Soviet Union has created an economic and political crisis so massive as to put its entire domestic structure and international position at risk. Forty years of Cold War have left the United States in a similar though much less severe condition. High military spending has both weakened the commercial competitiveness of American industry and burdened the economy with a chronic deficit. Its main concern is the loss of its technological and financial competitiveness with Japan, which even on a generous estimate spends only one-quarter as much of its GNP on defence as does the United States. The astronomical cost of next generation weapons systems such as the stealth bomber and space-based strategic defence, only serve to underline the Americans' dilemma, though the cracking of the Soviet Union may well save them from having to make the choice. Whether the ending of the Cold War will enable the United States to escape from its defence dilemma of cost, or whether the military-industrial lobby will find ways of sustaining its hold on the economy is one of the interesting questions for the 1990s.

Much more serious defence dilemmas occur when military preparations in the name of defence themselves pose threats to the state's survival. The most obvious form is the threat of unacceptable damage, either self-inflicted, or risked as part of an explicit policy involving relations with other states. An example of self-inflicted damage would be a ballistic missile defence (BMD) system which itself involved low-altitude nuclear bursts over the territory to be defended. Such a system might defend specified targets, such as missile silos, only at the cost of inflicting substantial damage on softer targets. An example of defence risking the destruction of what is to be defended was NATO's policy of flexible response in Europe. The likelihood that much of Germany would have survived a major conflict on its territory is pretty remote.

The system of nuclear deterrence is perhaps the clearest example of a defence dilemma arising from the risk assumed in an overall defence policy. The serious contradiction between defence and security posed by nuclear deterrence arises because of technological developments which have given offensive weapons a marked advantage over the defensive weapons available against them. The marriage of missiles and nuclear weapons continues a twentieth-century trend begun by aircraft and bombs which has seriously undermined the traditional ability of the territorial state to defend itself against military attack.[10] These weapons mean that a state can be severely damaged or punished without being defeated in a full-scale war, and consequently that traditional defence postures no longer carry the same significance as previously.

When two states are armed with nuclear weapons and disposed to treat each other as enemies, their only logical military option is to rest their 'defence' on policies of assured retaliation. Under such circumstances, a convincing case can be made that the interests of both are served by remaining vulnerable to the other's strike (to ensure that incentives to strike first remain minimal on both sides) – the famous policy of 'mutually assured destruction' or MAD.[11] In effect, this means that each side offers its own physical base to the other as a hostage. To make themselves militarily secure, each threatens to use means that might even extinguish human life on the planet. Whatever its merits, and under nuclear conditions they are considerable, deterrence policy basically proposes to defend the state by a strategy which threatens to destroy it. The war-preventing objective of deterrence policy is linked by a horrible logic to credible threats of apocalyptic destruction. Not surprisingly, many people see themselves as potential victims of this arrangement. They find unacceptable as a national security policy an idea that puts both their personal and their collective national (or species) existence at such risk. Some of them are also concerned by the way in which a high technology defence such as nuclear deterrence centralizes command and control in a narrow élite, in the process detaching military security from the mass of the population. When defence depends on mass armies, the population have some control over the state's resort to force. High-technology defence gives more discretion to the leadership, and this can be seen as an undesirable development.

With nuclear weapons, one's perception of security no longer depends, as traditionally, at which end of the weapon one is standing. The defence dilemma arises because technological developments have inflated military means to such an extent that a general threat of destruction is the only militarily logical means of providing national defence. Given the uncertainties involved in the possession and control of such weapons, many individuals conclude that the weapons themselves, and the system of relations they create, detract more than they contribute to the pursuit of security. One such is Richard Barnet, who argues that

> There is no objective, including the survival of the United States as a political entity, that merits destroying millions or jeopardizing the future of man. The pretence that it is legitimate to threaten nuclear war for political ends creates as international climate of fear in which Americans will continue to have less security, not more.[12]

Since force appears to be a necessary feature of an anarchic international system, and since both the anarchy and the technological imperative appear to be durable factors, the defence dilemma poses a major conundrum for national security policy over the foreseeable future. For these reasons, it is worth probing into the historical momentum which underlies the defence dilemma. In particular, one needs to get some sense of whether the defence dilemma can be resolved, or at least muted, in some way, or whether the forces which drive it are so deep and strong that it is likely to remain a permanent feature on the security landscape.

THE HISTORICAL DEVELOPMENT OF THE DEFENCE DILEMMA

For reasons argued in Chapter 3, military threats traditionally take pride of place in the hierarchy of national security priorities. Political philosophies based on the state of nature image place the function of protection against violence at the very foundations of the state. In the real world, military threats pose the most direct immediate and visible danger to state security, and military means have frequently proved useful against both military and non-military threats. The political, economic and societal sectors of the nation's life must be strong enough to survive the rigours of competition within their own sectors and on their own terms, but none of them can reasonably be expected to be strong enough to withstand coercive pressure or violent disruption. The historic failure of pacifism to win mass support reflects widespread recognition of this fact. State military forces provide protection for these sectors against 'unfair' threats of force, and, in the process, maintenance of an adequate military establishment becomes itself a national security interest.

History is full of heroic examples of military force being used to save cultural, political and economic values from violent overthrow – the Ancient Greeks turning the Persian tide at Marathon and Salamis, the Franks stemming the Muslim conquest of Western Europe at Tours (732), the raising of the Ottoman siege of Vienna (1683) and the defeat of fascism in Europe in 1945, to name just a few. The fact that these examples are offset by as many defeats and occupations – the destruction of the Incas by Spanish *conquistadores*, the obliteration of Carthage by Rome, China's annexation of Tibet, several partitions of Poland, colonial conquests too numerous to mention – merely underlines the prudence of being well armed. For all these reasons, military factors have dominated national security considerations and national defence has, at least until recently, been almost synonymous with national security.

National defence has its conceptual foundations in the largely bygone days when most important state interests could be protected by military force. A monarchical state with a largely self-contained, mercantilist economy, like France during the early eighteenth century, suggests an ideal type of state for national defence. Domestic security could be enforced by the army and the local nobility. Trade was not crucial to national survival, and to a considerable extent could be protected by military means and by the structure of empire. External threats were primarily military in nature, and the available technology meant that they were slow moving. Military strength depended largely on domestic resources and could be used to seize, as well as defend, most things held to be of national value. War was a usable, if sometimes expensive and frequently uncertain, instrument of state policy. Ideology and economic interdependence scarcely existed as issues of political significance.

The classical image of national defence thus rests on an essentially autarkic notion of the state as a unit self-contained and self-reliant in all the major political, economic and cultural elements of life. Its principal military need was to defend its domestic universe from disruption by external military attack or internal disorder. Although pristine models of this sort are rare in reality, the ideal type is a useful reference when considering national defence. Tokugawa Japan (1600–1868) illustrates an extreme case in which the Shoguns restricted contact with the outside world to a small, tightly controlled trade outlet. The United States during the first half of the twentieth century also fits the model in many respects: it had no neighbours of military consequence, dominated military and economic relations in its hemisphere, was nearly beyond the reach of major military action by other powers, at least on its continental territories, and enjoyed substantial economic self-reliance within its sphere.

If we set aside for the time being the realm of military aggression in the Napoleonic, Hitlerian and empire-building senses, national defence implies a self-contained, self-reliant and rather passive outlook. The state provides itself with means of defence according to the threats it perceives and the resources at its disposal, and relies on these to deter the threats, or else to meet them should they materialize. War is not desired, but neither is it feared excessively. Defences are adjusted to meet variations in tension and changes in the pattern of threat. Although conditions may necessitate defensive alliances, self-reliance in the tradition of British, American, Chinese and Japanese splendid isolation is the preferred mode. In the national defence orientation, the emphasis is primarily on the state and its military capabilities, taking into account both likely rivals and the balance-of-power dynamics of the international system.

In Europe the supporting conditions for the idea of national defence were deteriorating rapidly by the end of the nineteenth century. Economic activity had expanded beyond national and empire boundaries to such an extent that military means could no longer protect all the main elements of the national economic interest. The First World War devalued the concept mightily. Not only did it reveal the extent of economic interdependence, but aerial bombing and maritime blockade shook the idea that the state could be protected behind the military lines. The new military technologies revealed a terrifying amplification of the hazards and uncertainties of the military instrument, and seriously devalued the notion that war could be a useful or casual tool of state policy. This explains the attraction of collective security policy, the League of Nations, and other idealist approaches to security during the interwar years. Collective security sought to replace national defence, and reflected European disillusionment with war and defence. It is significant that the United States did not participate in the League, because for the Americans the supporting conditions for national defence remained largely unimpaired.

Collective security began to gain favour over national defence during the interwar years because the experience of the First World War had gravely weakened one of the conditions on which national defence was based: that war is an acceptable instrument of policy. If war is feared as a major threat in its own right, then defence is devalued as a posture, but military insecurity is not eliminated as a problem. This is the heart of the defence dilemma. Most traditional military threats remained alive, and in addition all actors were threatened by the process of war itself, which had become so violent and costly that it could easily destroy, or at least damage seriously, the fabric of the state. Even the winners might well be so badly damaged and depleted as to seriously blur the distinction between victory and defeat. Because of the experience of the First World War, fear of war began to rival fear of defeat as the prime concern of national security policy.[13] Fear of war among the masses expressed itself in peace movements and opinion polls, and became politically significant enough to threaten traditional policies aimed at meeting fear of defeat. Some form of collective security arrangement was an obvious response when doubt was cast on the self-help tradition of national defence.

War-weariness and fear of war are recurrent in international relations, usually appearing after a bout of prolonged, wide-spread and destructive warfare, like the Thirty Years War (1618–48), the French Revolutionary and Napoleonic Wars (1792–1815), the First World War and the Second World War. After such wars, war prevention assumes a high priority, and something more than a self-reliant defence policy is required. The favoured technique is to institute measures of cooperation and consultation among the larger powers, with a view to preventing war by moderating and restraining the free-for-all operation of the balance of power. The Congress system set up in 1815, the League of Nations and the United Nations all illustrate this conceptual shift from national defence to collective security.[14] Unfortunately, none of these attempts endured as a major controlling element in international security relations.

This continued failure is surprising in as much as there has been a strong tendency, especially since the First World War, for the fear of war to increase, though not surprising in its affirmation of the ongoing potency of anarchic political logic. Whereas after the Napoleonic Wars the fear of war faded along with the generational memory of those who experienced it, after 1918 the fear of war was nurtured and strengthened by rapid and obvious increases in the destructiveness of new weapons. The First World War inflicted a greater shock on European civilization than any previous upheaval, threatening not only revolutions in the social structure of states and the composition of the state system, but also posing a real prospect that European civilization itself would be heavily damaged, if not destroyed, by a repeat performance. The war proved to be an unpredictable and largely uncontrollable process. Once started, it seemed to gather a momentum of its own, grinding up life and wealth at stupendous rates, making a nonsense of centuries of military doctrine and wisdom, and forcing social mobilization on such a scale that governments could neither control all the forces they had unleashed, nor maintain the traditional separation between foreign policy and domestic mass politics.

Under such conditions, the 'war to end war' propaganda that some governments had used as a mobilizing tool took root in the post-war environment, feeding on new fears of apocalypse arising from the combination of gas warfare and long-rang bombing aircraft. The Second World War proved the exaggeration of these fears, but ended with the appalling detonation over Hiroshima, which demonstrated that the error was merely one of timing, and not of analysis. After such a demonstration, few could question the rationality of the fear that the next major war would devastate its participants to such an extent as to render victory indistinguishable from defeat. What could national defence mean under such circumstances?

By 1945, advances in military technology had undercut the idea of national defence in several ways. The domestic sanctity of the state could be neither protected nor preserved. Total mobilization required massive and not necessarily reversible changes in social and political values, making war more an instrument of societal transformation than of preservation. New weapons dissolved the distinction between the home front and the war front, meaning that defence in the literal sense of keeping the enemy's armed forces away from one's own societal fabric was no longer possible. The destructiveness of weapons reduced the idea of national defence to an absurdity, since the state would be destroyed by the measures required for its defence. As Neville Brown put it,

> For thousands of years before [1945], firepower had been so scarce a resource that the supreme test of generalship lay in conserving it for application at the crucial time and place. Suddenly, it promised to become so abundant that it would be madness ever to release more than the tiniest fraction of the total quantity available.[15]

When added to the difficulties created for defence by the increasing scope of state interests, particularly economic and ideological interests which were not so amenable to protection by military means, these conditions created a demand for a broader concept than defence with which to think about protecting the state. Thus was born the concept of national security.

Because of its peculiar geographical position, the United States, as noted above, adhered longer to national defence than the European powers, as, in a rather different way, did the Soviet Union. It took the experience of the Second World War to break American belief in isolationist national defence, and force the country into a more outward-looking security perspective. In a sense, this put the United States nearly three decades behind Europe in the transition of attitudes from defence to security. It provides a case study of the domestic process by which defence attitudes transformed into security ones.[16] The national defence strategy of the 1920s and 1930s had clearly proved totally inadequate for the United States. A passive, self-protecting outlook had allowed massive threats to build up in both Europe and Asia, eventually forcing the country to fight a huge war at a dangerous starting disadvantage. The lesson here was that security policy needed to be outward- and forward-looking, with the United States playing an active global role to ensure that no such unfavourable conditions would arise again.

The declining viability of national defence as a solution to the problem of national security thus produced very different experiences in Europe and America. Because of the marked contrast in their geostrategic attributes, the European countries and the United States faced quite different orders of threat from military action by their enemies. In Europe, the growing contradiction between national defence and national security had been made apparent by the First World War, and became increasingly obvious with new weapons developments. Not only were the European states more vulnerable to war because of their close proximity to each other, but also their limited geographic size and economic strength made them subject to devastation and depletion on a national scale even before the advent of nuclear weapons.[17] The United States had no military problems comparable to this. In modern times it has never, and still does not, face threats of invasion and occupation. Not until the advent of Soviet intercontinental ballistic missiles (ICBM) in the late 1950s did Americans even confront the prospect of the large-scale military bombardment which had haunted Europe for the previous four decades. For Americans, war was always 'over there'. The Second World War demonstrated that America's ocean buffers no longer sufficed to keep the military reach of enemies at bay, a lesson immortalized in the burning symbol of Pearl Harbor.

But even though this experience caused the United States to move away from a national defence orientation, it did not compare in intensity with circumstances in Europe. For the European states, the defence dilemma simply precluded all-out war. Any serious attempt to defend Europe in the traditional military sense would almost inevitably destroy all the values for which the defence had been mounted in the first place. Ever since the First World War, it has been obvious that security in Europe could only be approached collectively, and that preventing war from occurring must be the prime objective of security, a lesson rammed home by the continent-wide devastation and bankruptcy caused by the Second World War.

These themes underpinned the League of Nations with its hopes for collective security machinery and its attempt to abolish war. They also underlay the gathering together of the by then even weaker western European states into the North Atlantic Treaty Organization (NATO) after the Second World War.

For the United States, the contradiction between defence and security remained much more muted than in Europe. The country was strained, but not damaged, by the Second World War, and emerged at the end of it into a position of enormous relative strength in the international system. Defence was discredited in the United States mostly because a passive outlook had allowed war to creep too close to home. The national security doctrine which replaced it had only a little of European-style collective security and anti-war emphasis, for neither of these had anything like the relevance to American experience that they had in the European context. The principal problem for American national security was to make sure that war, if it occurred at all, stayed 'over there'. The national security doctrine which emerged during the late 1940s amounted more to forward defence than anything else, the prime objective being to take early preventative action to forestall a 1930s-type build-up of threats to the United States.

Despite these basic differences in American and European perceptions of the defence dilemma, at least two common themes united them. The first was that both identified the Soviet Union as the prime foreign threat. The second was that both, albeit in rather different ways, acknowledged that national security could only be pursued jointly with other states. In Europe, the NATO structure symbolized the inability of individual states to defend themselves. But American involvement all along the periphery of the Soviet sphere merely staked out the boundaries for the forward defence of the United States. The United States, despite its initial hesitancy about getting involved, needed to defend Europe (and many other lynchpins of containment) in order to defend itself. Europe was unable at the time to defend itself against the Soviet Union, and more than ever needed to avoid war. The link with America seemed to solve both problems for Europe: the United States could, and would, provide defence, and the American nuclear monopoly appeared to offer a stable, one-way threat of such magnitude as to reduce the probability of war to vanishing point.

At this juncture, the issue of nuclear weapons raises some essential paradoxes in relation to the European defence dilemma. On the one hand, nuclear weapons appear to crown the demise of defence by raising prospective levels of destruction in major military engagements to heights well beyond the limits of rational policy. On the other hand, a one-way nuclear threat such as that wielded by the United States up until the late 1950s offered almost perfect security against attack. Even mutual deterrence, if properly managed, offered a good prospect of avoiding war by balancing a risk of incredibly massive destruction against a very low probability that anyone would resort to war under such circumstances. This paralysing quality of nuclear deterrence alleviated much of the contradiction between defence and security, but only so long as the probability of war remained close to zero. As was subsequently demonstrated by the bellicose rhetoric of the Reagan

Administration, and the mass campaigns against the deployment of cruise and *Pershing* II missiles, even a small rise in the likelihood of war under nuclear conditions revived the defence dilemma at a pitch far higher than that reached with conventional weapons.

Since the defence dilemma was much stronger in Europe than in the United States, both relief at its solution and concern about the failure of deterrence naturally ran stronger on the eastern side of the North Atlantic. This difference in perspective on defence explains the persistent tension within NATO on matters of nuclear policy. Europe wanted effective defence without war, and therefore favoured a posture which maximized deterrence. From the European perspective, the one-way American massive retaliation policy of the late 1940s and early 1950s was ideal, because it emphasized war prevention and enabled problematic questions of defence to be largely side-stepped. Even under conditions of mutual deterrence, it made sense for Europe to favour doomsday-like policies of massive retaliation, because in the European context the risk of defensive war fighting in more gradual, phased 'flexible response' policies was little different from the risk of doomsday anyway. Massive retaliation appeared better tailored to keeping the probability of war close to zero.

The United States, by contrast, favoured flexible response policies designed to increase its strategic options and minimize its risks in conducting the defence of its worldwide strategic perimeter. The threat to fight a phased, limited nuclear war in Europe made eminent good sense from an American security perspective, but except in as much as the threat of it can be argued to serve deterrence, ran contrary to the most basic security need of Europe. This problem has plagued NATO ever since the Soviet Union began to erode America's nuclear monopoly; it underlay French motives in leaving the integrated military structure of the Alliance in 1967. Flexible response policies threatened to re-open for Western Europe the dilemma posed by the contradiction between defence and security. Occasionally this tension became open, as over the cruise and *Pershing* II deployments which ironically were originally requested by West Germany as a way of strengthening NATO's linkage to the American strategic deterrent. But since Western Europe chose to solve its security problem by making itself dependent on the United States, the European states had little room for manoeuvre in relation to American policy. Without the United States, they would still face a whole complex of difficult defence and security issues, and anyway, so long as the Americans remained committed to security through forward defence, it was not at all clear that Europe could simply ask them to leave.

In summary, then, it is clear that nuclear weapons stimulated a quantum leap in the historical trend towards greater fear of war. In so doing, they exacerbated an already serious contradiction between defence and security. This contradiction was historically strongest in Europe, but nuclear weapons also imposed it on the superpowers, who quickly found that their vast military machines were largely stalemated in an uncomfortable and expensive balance of terror. Particularly for the more powerful and advanced states in their relations with each other, military means in themselves now threatened to defeat the objectives of security, both because of their cost, and because of the risks they posed. Almost by definition, the defence dilemma occurs much more acutely in the affairs of advanced industrial powers than it does in the affairs of Third World states, though some are beginning to catch up. Few Third World countries have experienced modern war on anything like the scale of Europe, though Iran and Iraq spent the 1980s replaying their own version of the First World War. Few of them either command or face sufficient military means to raise their fear of war to the same levels as their fear of defeat, though the spread of nuclear-threshold states, chemical weapons and missiles will soon reverse this condition for some states in the Middle East and South Asia. Kolodziej and Harkavy argue that Third World states are still 'rooted in Clausewitzian thought', and are not suffering any of the doubts about the utility of force which affect the major powers of both East and West.[18] In making this argument, however, they also catalogue the massive diffusion of arms to the Third World.[19] This trend, and particularly its nuclear dimension, indicates that the conditions for encouraging the defence dilemma to spread its grip are already well in the making. Although their lower level of development may insulate them for a time from fearing war over defeat, the weak economies of most Third World states will pose them with acute defence dilemmas of cost in relation to the expense of both maintaining and using modern armed forces.

THE DURABILITY OF THE DEFENCE DILEMMA

In the first edition of this work I argued at this point that the defence dilemma was durable. The arguments in support were that defence continued to be necessary because the threats that made it so remained in force, that the technological imperative rolled on regardless, that the institutional momentum of military establishments and armament industries constituted a major obstacle to disarmament, and that the continuing primacy of anarchic structure meant that no coordinated or centrally controlled alternative to national defence was realistically on offer. For many countries in the international system these arguments still hold. One thinks, for example, of the swathe of states defined by a rectangle whose corners are Libya, Turkey, Pakistan and Somalia, and of North and South Korea. The technological imperative argument is still valid for all: weapons continue to get more expensive and more destructive. But the dramatic winding down of the Cold War during the late 1980s clearly blows a major hole in any easy assumption that the threats which make defence necessary have not changed.

The two main dangers of writing from the middle of such a massive and central transformation in relationships as the ending of the Cold War are: first, that things are still too fluid for any new pattern to have set firmly and second, that the found delight in these astonishing developments may cloud one's view of difficulties and tensions lying ahead. As things stand, however, there seems to be a very good chance that a large and permanent reduction in hostility between the United States and the Soviet Union has taken place. The immediate causes of this are the sharp changes of direction in Soviet policy under Gorbachev. Moves towards a more pluralist, market-based, political economy, substantial unilateral and multilateral arms reduction initiatives and the virtual release of the Eastern European empire, have drawn much of the heat out of the superpower confrontation. Many of these changes have gone too far to be easily reversed, and they are based not just on Gorbachev, but on a deep structural crisis in Soviet-type political economies.

In the longer term, a much reduced level of Soviet-American hostility will be supported by the shift in the distributional structure of the international system from bipolarity to multipolarity. The two superpowers are declining into mere great powers. Both are visibly overextended, beset with domestic problems, and increasingly short of both willpower and resources to sustain their global rivalry. Japan, China and India are all in their different ways heading towards great power status (it helps to remember that great powers do not have to be equal: Italy, Austria-Hungary and the Ottoman empire all had great power status before the First World War). The European Community is still *sui generis* as an international actor, but has clearly reached a level of core cohesion sufficient to insert a powerful political, economic, societal and military presence between the declining superpowers. The insecurity of Japan and Western Europe in relation to the Soviet Union that first drew the United States into a global engagement is fading. Both are now economically stronger than the Soviet Union, and the Soviet threat to them is also fading as Moscow retreats from empire.

This diminution of the central confrontation that has dominated international relations for nearly half a century opens major opportunities for reducing the defence dilemma, particularly in East-West relations. It is too early to see what kind of military security arrangements will emerge in Europe.[20] At one extreme is the (in my view rather unlikely) possibility that the Soviet Union joins the European security community, becoming an associate member of the European Community (EC). Such an arrangement would virtually dissolve the need for military security within Europe. In the middle is a sustained detente scenario, in which a significant divide remains between Europe and the Soviet Union, but is cooperatively managed. This would involve much-reduced military deployments, a shift to non-provocative defence strategies and Eastern Europe becoming a kind of permeable buffer between the EC and the Soviet Union. Even a reaction in the Soviet Union, and a return to military tension, would probably be at a much lower level than that of the Cold War, not least because of the probably irreversible detachment of Eastern Europe from Soviet control. All of these scenarios offer scope for some shrinkage in the military-industrial complexes of both superpowers. Although there is no sign that collective international security arrangements will become possible, it seems quite likely that security communities will play an increasing role in reducing the scope of military threat. As mentioned above, a security community among the major capitalist powers has already begun to play a major role in the international system. It is not impossible that a reformed Soviet Union might become a peripheral member of this community.

In the Third World, the impact of this transformation at the centre is rather more mixed. Conflict resolution among the great powers will have hardly any influence on the issues that drive many locally generated conflicts. It will not make Arabs and Israelis, Indians and Pakistanis, or blacks and whites in Southern Africa hate each other any less. It might take some of the steam out of the resort to war, both by reducing the competitive political supply of weapons, and by making easier the provision of international mediation. But the patterns and styles of multipolar interventions in the periphery from the centre remain to be seen. Even if the North takes a more benign role towards the South, this may simply give more scope for Third World states to pursue their own conflicts, as Iran and Iraq did during the 1980s. In some places Third World security regimes might be viable. ASEAN provides the model for a group of weak states forming a security regime because they realized that such an arrangement would strengthen the domestic legitimacy of their regimes, whereas pursuing conflicts among themselves was likely to exacerbate divisions within their fragile domestic structures.

CONCLUSIONS: THE DEFENCE DILEMMA AND SECURITY

In the first edition, I concluded this chapter with the following argument, which is reproduced verbatim.

The defence dilemma has established itself as a durable feature of the security problem, and even though it now operates strongly over only a limited area, the trend in conditions worldwide favours its further spread. Much energy is poured into lamenting the proliferation of weapons, but it is not at all clear that the resultant defence dilemma is a cause for regret. Indeed, the nuclear defence dilemma which lies at the heart of the present international system might well be providing a fundamentally important stepping-stone towards a more mature anarchy. F. H. Hinsley argues that the fear of nuclear war, and the consequent ending of the legitimacy of war as a major instrument of relations among the great powers, amounts to a desirable transformation in the nature of the international system.[21] The defence dilemma, in other words, has paralysed military relations among the nuclear powers, thereby forcing them to find ways other than war to manage their rivalries. On a parallel track to the same conclusion Rober Tucker argues that:

> The peace of deterrence is a peace that rests on the possibility of thermonuclear war. Once men were persuaded that they could with confidence remove that possibility from their calculations, one of the principal inducements to restraint would thereby disappear. With its disappearance would also disappear one of the principal causes of such order as international society presently enjoys.[22]

In other words, the nuclear defence dilemma is providing the international system with an unprecedented service. Because war can no longer act as the midwife of major system change – except change involving the destruction of the system and most of its components – both an opportunity and a necessity to move towards the creation of a more mature anarchy have been created, at least among the great powers. Not only do they have high incentives to prevent tensions among themselves from rising to an excessive pitch, but also they must create stable foundations for relations among themselves over the long term. These relations need not, and most probably will not, end the substantial deployment of armed force by the great powers against each other. Indeed, it could be argued that the maintenance of considerable military power is a necessary condition for maintaining the restraint on war. But such forces will necessarily be oriented primarily towards preserving the paralysis because, in a nuclear-armed system, a philosophy of live-and-let-live among the great powers becomes the only practical alternative to a high risk of annihilation.[23]

Defence, then, remains an important component of security even if it no longer serves as a coverall for security policy in the way it once did. The decline of defence, and its partial shift from being most of the solution to being part of the problem, opens up many questions about the scope and boundaries of national security policy. What issues and problems should be included? And what kinds of policies are appropriate?

The substance of this argument still seems to me to be valid, though the movement of history requires that it be viewed from a different angle. What is happening among the great powers would seem to vindicate the point that the defence dilemma acts as a constructive pressure towards the development of more mature anarchy. What we are seeing as the Cold War ends can be interpreted in part as a recognition by the great powers of the permanence of the defence dilemma, both of its costs, and of the primacy of the fear of war over the fear of defeat. The new arrangements coming into being among them will almost certainly reflect their adjustment to the inescapability of the defence dilemma. These arrangements should involve lower levels of military deployment, more non-provocative strategies, and a maintenance of minimum nuclear deterrence. The underderlying logic of the defence dilemma is that if force cannot rationally be used, and if pretending that it can requires levels of expenditure that cripple other important security objectives, then it should play a smaller role in security relations.

In much of the Third World, the picture is quite different. There the logic of the defence dilemma has not yet permeated societies in anything like the same way that it has done in the North. The relentless spread of modern weapons of mass destruction, and the willingness to use such weapons in war, must eventually bring the defence dilemma to the same pitch for the South as it has already reached in the North. This process will not happen quickly or without much bloodshed. The decadelong battering that Iran and Iraq inflicted on each other has apparently not cooled their willingness to resort to force in any permanent way. To understand this apparently irrational resilience to the lessons of the defence dilemma, one has only to remember the centuries of European warfare, culminating in the apocalyptic destructions of the Second World War, that constituted the learning process for the North.

NOTES

1. Barry Buzan, *An Introduction to Strategic Studies: Military technology and international relations* (London: Macmillan, 1987); Gerald Segal (ed.), *New Directions in Strategic Studies: A Chatham House debate*, RIIA Discussion Papers no. 17 (London: RIIA, 1989).

2. Robert E. Osgood and Robert W. Tucker, *Force, Order and Justice* (Baltimore: Johns Hopkins University Press, 1967), p. 32.

3. *ibid.*, p. 13.

4. Hedley Bull, *The Anarchical Society* (London: Macmillan, 1977), p. 189.

5. Michael Howard, *Studies in War and Peace* (London: Temple Smith, 1970), p. 11.

6. *ibid.*, p. 17.

7. Buzan, *op. cit.* (note 1) is organized around this theme. The arms dynamic and defence/deterrence are considered as responses to military means in the hands of others. Disarmament, arms control and non-provocative defence are considered as responses to military means as a problem in themselves. Those wanting detailed treatment of these topics should refer to that source.

8. This term is used in a narrower sense by Gert Krell, 'The development of the concept of security', *Arbeitspapier* 3/1979, Peace Research Institute, Frankfurt (PRIF). He uses it in the context of nuclear weapons, and alongside companion terms like 'arms race dilemmas' and 'deterrence dilemmas'. My intention is to offer it as a basic concept in security thinking which encompasses a discrete, durable and broad phenomenon, stretching well beyond the confines of the nuclear weapon problem.

9. On these themes see Buzan, *op. cit.* (note 1), chs 2, 3, 8; and Barry Buzan and Gautam Sen, *The Impact of Military Research and Development Priorities on the Evolution of the Civil Economy in Capitalist States*, Discussion Paper no. 339 (London: Centre for Economic Policy Research, 1989).

10. For a full elaboration of this argument, see John Herz, *International Politics in the Atomic Age* (New York: Columbia University Press, 1959), chs 1, 6; and 'The rise and demise of the territorial state', *World Politics*, 9 (1957). See also Buzan, *op. cit.* (note 1), ch. 2.

11. For discussion, see Buzan, *op. cit.* (note 1), chs 10–13.

12. Richard J. Barnet, 'The illusion of security', in Charles R. Beitz and Theodore Herman (eds), *Peace and War* (San Francisco: W.H. Freeman, 1973), p. 276.

13. This distinction between the threat of war and the threat of defeat is drawn by Hedley Bull, *The Control of the Arms Race* (London: Weidenfeld & Nicolson, 1961), pp. 25–9.

14. On this theme, see Osgood and Tucker, *op. cit.* (note 2), pp. 88–120; Richard Rosecrance, *International Relations: Peace or war?* (New York: McGraw-Hill, 1973), p. 36; and Robert Jervis, 'Security regimes', *International Organization*, 36:2 (1982).

15. Neville Brown, *The Future Global Challenge: A predictive study of world security 1977–1990* (London: RUSI, 1977), p. 153.

16. See Daniel Yergin, *Shattered Peace* (Boston: Houghton-Mifflin, 1978); and Franz Schurmann, *The Logic of World Power* (New York: Pantheon, 1974) for assessments of this transformation in the United States.

17. Michael Howard, 'Military power and international order' *International Affairs*, 40:3 (1964), p. 403.

18. Edward A. Kolodziej and Robert Harkavy, 'Developing states and the international security system', *Journal of International Affairs*, 34:1 (1980), p. 64.

19. See also Buzan, *op. cit.* (note 1), chs 3–4.

20. For one attempt, see Barry Buzan, Morten Kelstrup, Pierre Lemaitre, Elzbieta Tromer and Ole Wæver, *The European Security Order Recast: Scenarios for a post-Cold War era* (London: Pinter, 1990).

21. F. H. Hinsley, 'The rise and fall of the modern international system', *Review of International Studies*, 8: 1 (1982).

22. Osgood and Tucker, *op. cit.* (note 2), p. 352.

23. For a very useful discussion of the utility of military power in conditions of paralysis, see Robert J. Art, 'To what ends military power', *International Security*, 4:4 (1980).

chapter eight | the power-security dilemma

This chapter is about the struggles for power and security that are the hallmark of life in an anarchic system. It continues the military theme from the previous chapter, but focuses on the security problem caused by military means in the hands of others rather than on weapons as a problem in themselves. The first section distinguishes the logic of the power struggle versus the security struggle as models of life in the international anarchy, and makes the case that they constitute a dilemma because of the difficulty of distinguishing between them in practice. The next three sections investigate two reasons for this difficulty: complexities and uncertainties in the distinction between status quo and revisionist powers, and ambiguities in interpreting the military postures of other states. The last section considers whether the power-security dilemma can be resolved, and looks at how this dilemma interacts with the defence dilemma discussed in Chapter 7.

THE POWER AND SECURITY STRUGGLES

Explanations of how anarchy promotes insecurity all stress the self-help imperative that a fragmented political structure forces on its constituent units. Under anarchy, states have to look after themselves to ensure both their welfare and the continued survival of their political and societal values. States that fail to look after themselves risk at best loss of power, and at worst loss of independence, or sometimes loss of existence. But taking measures to prevent these things risks conflict with other states as all jostle together in an unregulated environment seeking their own advantage. This structural imperative lies at the core of the power-security dilemma, which is itself the key statement of the security problematique under anarchy. In seeking power and security for themselves, states can easily threaten the power and security aspirations of other states. As the defence dilemma arose from the fear of war stimulated by the nature of military means, so the power-security dilemma arises from the fear of defeat stimulated by the potential uses of military means in the hands of other actors.

Within this overall structural problematique, explanations focus on the behaviour of states, and so add interaction and unit levels of analysis to the structural

one. These explanatory theories divide into two general types: those that emphasize direct, conscious competition and hostility among states as the prime source
of conflict, and those that emphasize the conflict-producing behaviours of states,
or patterns of relations in the system, where 'hostility' is unintended. The first type
leans towards the right-wing (and also Marxist-Leninist) view of the international system as a struggle for power. Actors are assumed to be at best opportunist, and
at worst systematically aggressive, and consequently the immature anarchy features of the system are stressed. The causes of aggressive behaviour are sought in
the domestic political characteristics of states, in historical grievances, in the personalities of leaders, and in patterns of power distribution which provide opportunity and/or provoke revisionist ambitions. I refer to this type of explanation for
conflict and insecurity as the *power struggle*.

The second type of theory fits the liberal or social democratic view of the international system as a struggle for security. Actors are assumed to be self-con-
cerned, but nevertheless generally well-intentioned, or at least indifferent, towards
others. The prospects for a mature international anarchy are given prominence.
The causes of insecurity are sought in the structural and relational dynamics of
states and the system, such as fragmented and incremental decision-making procedures, misunderstandings and misperceptions, arms racing, and the sheer complexity of cross-cutting interests and attitudes in a system of high-density interdependence. I refer to this mode of analysis as the *security struggle*. The interaction
of these two struggles, and particularly the practical difficulty telling them apart,
creates the *power-security dilemma* which is central to any understanding of the
national security problem.[1] To complete the political spectrum it is worth noting
that the left wing tend to concentrate on the defence dilemma in their analysis of
international relations, so exposing themselves to the criticism that they fail to
take the broader structural consequences of anarchy into account.[2]

The distinction between the power and security struggles is important both
because it points to fundamentally different explanations for insecurity under
anarchy, and because it captures different political positions on the issue. Despite
the fact that the idea of the security struggle originated from Realist writers, it
opens up crucial middle ground between the excessively and in my view fruitless-
ly polarized views of Realists and Idealists which have long divided the field of
International Relations.[3] Idealists have mostly chosen not to orient their thinking
around the idea of security, preferring instead the broader and more popular idea
of peace, which follows easily and logically from a preoccupation with the
defence dilemma. Realists have tended to subsume security under their preferred
idea of power, in the process largely masking its distinctive meaning. By discount-
ing security, both sides have weakened their analysis.

Despite the fact that Idealists have neglected it, however, the security struggle
fits closely with their predisposition to see conflict more as a structural, perceptual and resolvable problem. At its most extreme, the choice is between two cosmic
views of international relations: on the one hand, as a ceaseless struggle for survival and dominance among states motivated by the pursuit of power; and on the

other hand, as a tragic struggle for security by states trapped in a system which distorts their legitimate efforts at self-protection into a seamless web of insecurity and conflict. Taken at their extremes, they represent completely different conceptualizations of the security problematique under anarchy,[4] though they are in part connected by power. Relative power is zero-sum by definition (X can get stronger only by making Y weaker). To the extent that security requires relative power, it is also subject to zero-sum logic.

Their difference necessitates trying to treat the two struggles separately in relation to the central problem of national security. But what is clearly distinct in theory, can be difficult to disentangle in practice. In the case of the power and security struggles, both the political and the military factors that might enable one to distinguish between them, in fact often work to blur and confuse their boundary. Because the two struggles are entangled in this way, it is appropriate to consider them as a single dilemma with two layers: the first comprising the zero-sum dilemmas within the two struggles taken individually; the second, the difficulty of distinguishing between them.

The key political factor in the power-security dilemma concerns the motivation of actors, and revolves around the traditional distinction between status quo and revisionist states. The power struggle emphasizes the continuous tension between revisionist and status quo powers, and assumes it to be a permanent feature of the international anarchy. The security struggle emphasizes the tensions that arise even if all states are in some sense status quo. Neither struggle would exist recognizably in the absence of military forces, but both models take as given that states possess armed forces, and go on from there to concentrate on the political dynamics which lead to conflict under those conditions. The problem is how to tell the difference between status quo and revisionist actors.

The military factor concerns not the political motives of states, but the problems arising from the impact that their military measures have on each other. A desire for defence underlies both struggles, the problem being that 'defence' can cover a very wide range of military policies. At a minimum, defence implies preparation for a responsive action which occurs only after a clear attack has started, as when military factors are moved to meet enemy forces which have crossed the border. At maximum, it can involve preparation for forward or pre-emptive action designed either to meet threats which are still remote in time, space or magnitude, or to eliminate all significant sources of opposition or threat. Maximum defence may still be seen by its perpetrators as fitting within the security struggle mould, though in practice, and as seen by others, such behaviour fits more appropriately into the power model. The problem is that the ambiguity of military means often makes it difficult to distinguish between defensive and offensive intentions. Because of the continuous pressure of the technological imperative, the status quo behaviour of maintaining military strength is frequently hard to separate from the challenging behaviour of arms racing.

These problems in distinguishing between the political and military characteristics of power and security struggles are compounded by the fact that the international system as a whole can seldom be characterized purely in terms of one or the other. Some relations within it will fit the power model, others the security model. While the evidence may go quite clearly one way or the other in some cases, as for example, Nazi Germany during the later 1930s, it may be sufficiently uncertain in others so as to defy reliable interpretation. The whole rivalry between the United States and the Soviet Union since the end of the Second World War has suffered from this ambiguity. Some observers stress the power rivalry aspects of the relationship, and others, the baseless mutual terrorizing of actors locked into a security struggle. The resulting uncertainty leads to endless clashes over policy along appeasement versus containment lines, like those which typified debate about responses to Nazi Germany in the mid-1930s. To confuse matters, there is no reason why both struggles cannot be operating simultaneously within a single case. A relatively mild power rivalry could easily generate an acute and overriding security struggle – this might be one view of the Cold War as it unfolded during the 1970s and early 1980s. Because the international system cannot be characterized purely in terms of either the power struggle or the security struggle, neither model can safely be used to generate assumptions which are sound enough to serve as a basis for policy in terms of the system as a whole.

Because this problem of distinguishing between power and security struggles is so central to policy-making, it is worth considering in more detail just why the necessary political and military distinctions are so difficult to make.

REVISIONISM VERSUS STATUS QUO

The process of distinguishing between status quo and revisionist (or, in Morgenthau's terms, 'imperialist') powers has a long tradition in the study of international relations. It goes back at least to the seminal work of E. H. Carr, and played a central in Hans Morgenthau's writing, which provided a backbone for the influential school of post-war Realists.[5] The strong link with Realism underlines the fact that this approach has its roots in the power model of international relations. By implication, an implacable, zero-sum struggle both determines and dominates the issue of security in the system. If this model presents an accurate picture, if revisionist states do push insistently against the dominance of status quo powers, then the power struggle emerges as the central challenge to national security. The security struggle model loses much of its interest if this is the case. Although it would retain some use as an additional mechanism to add onto the power struggle, it would lose most of its utility as an alternative way of viewing the problem of conflict in the international system as a whole. The security struggle comes into its own as an explanation for conflict in a system in which the major powers are essentially status quo in outlook. If some major powers are revisionist then no further explanation for conflict is required.[6] By implication, revisionists raise the level of threat in the system, and push it toward a power struggle, whereas status quo states lower the level of threat and engender only security struggles.

The association of revisionism with high levels of threat, much helped by Hitler, has resulted in revisionism carrying a negative connotation similar to that which burdens anarchy. In other words, revisionist states are identified as the problem instead of being seen as one component in a problem of larger dimensions. If there were no revisionist states, there would be no power struggle. Some kind of natural harmony of the status quo would reign, and national security policy-makers would need only to concern themselves with the relatively muted structural problems of the security struggle. Klaus Knorr provides a good example of this mentality by defining a use of force as 'aggressive' when 'military power is employed towards altering the relevant status quo by force or its threat'.[7] This tendency to sanctify the status quo relates strongly, of course, to the fact that most of the literature on international relations which this book addresses, and is part of, has been written within the confines of two pre-eminent status quo powers, Britain and the United States. As such, a bias towards the status quo is part of the ethnocentrism problem which Ken Booth has explored in relation to Strategic Studies.[8] This bias is, in fact, a legacy of the whole field of International Relations, which is still predominantly an Anglo-Saxon enterprise. In addition, a strong status quo attracts favour on the technical grounds that system management is thought to be easier when power is sufficiently concentrated to generate order by hegemonic means,[9] a point which connects to the arguments about economic management in Chapter 6.

But as Carr points out with such force, the status quo does not represent a neutral position: it constitutes a set of interests which have acquired, and seek to maintain, an advantageous position in the system.[10] This self-interest follows directly from the self-help logic of anarchy. As Carr notes: 'Every doctrine of a natural harmony of interests, identifies the good of the whole with the security of those in possession', and (more polemically) 'the English-speaking peoples are past masters in the art of concealing their selfish national interests in the guise of the general good... this kind of hypocrisy is a special and characteristic peculiarity of the Anglo-Saxon mind.'[11] From this perspective, the clash between status quo and revisionist powers ceases to be a moral problem with clearly demarcated 'good' and 'bad' sides. Although participants in the struggle may choose to see it in that way, as exemplified in the anti-imperialist and anti-communist rhetoric of the Cold War, from a more detached, systemic perspective, the rivalry between status quo and revisionist powers can be seen as a way of describing political orientations towards an existing pattern of relations. Status quo states set, benefit from and support the existing pattern, while revisionist ones feel alienated from it, threatened by it and oppose its continuation.

Moral judgements can be made on the respective cases, but these should be kept separate from assessment of the general propensity of the anarchic system to produce tension between status quo and revisionist powers. That propensity defines an important aspect of the national security problem for all states. The system will normally tend to be divided on some grounds between status quo and revisionist interests. If revisionist powers are assumed to be morally wrong or aggressive by definition, then they simply get dismissed as 'the problem', without having their case considered as a legitimate and persistent part of the security dynamic of the system as a whole. The point is that revisionist states also have legitimate national security interests. For them, the prevailing system is a threat to their security, and sometimes even to their domestic legitimacy. They are as much a part of the anarchy as the status quo states, and it helps to set aside prior moral judgements on them in order to get a clearer view of the security dynamics of the system as a whole.[12]

All states, whether status quo or revisionist in relation to the prevailing international order, share some minimum status quo objectives. It can safely be assumed that the vast majority will give a high priority to protecting all, or at least part, of the domains, rights and powers that they hold. In other words, all states will tend to have a core of status quo objectives in relation to themselves which serve as a bottom line for security policy regardless of their attitude towards the rest of the system. Exceptions occur when states become willing to dissolve themselves into a larger entity, as was done in the creation of the United States, Germany and Italy, or when they become willing to give up colonial possessions, as the European states did after the Second World War. But these exceptions reflect identifiable special conditions which do not detract from the utility of the general rule. The logic of this bottom line is clear and compelling, for even the most rabid revisionist state cannot pursue its larger objectives if it cannot secure its home base. At a minimum, one can say that all states will seek to maintain their territory and their economic, political and societal sectors so that they are viable in their own right, and so that undesired changes are not imposed on them by the use or threat of force, or by political or economic threats.

Where status quo and revisionist states differ primarily is in their outlook on relations with the rest of the system. The compulsion to interact with the rest of the system has grown in intensity as the system has become increasingly dense. Much interaction has been forced, like the colonial 'opening up' of the Americas, Africa and Asia. Much has stemmed from the dynamics of the international economy, with its restless search for resources, markets and profits. And much has occurred through the instrument of communications media and technology, which have made it increasingly difficult not to know what is going on all over the planet. The spreading webs of economic, political and environmental interdependence have made it more difficult for any state to separate its domestic affairs from its relations with the rest of the system. As the 1989 events in China and Eastern Europe demonstrate, even very large and relatively self-contained states such as the Soviet Union and China have found it impossible to insulate themselves successfully from the system for any great length of time. Because of this trend, relations with the rest of the system have become increasingly important to the maintenance of domestic welfare, stability and security in all states. Increasing interdependence puts a premium on the maintenance of international order, and so exacerbates the differences between status quo and revisionist perspectives on the system.

Status quo states are those whose domestic values and structures are, on the whole, supported by the pattern of relations in the system. This does not necessarily mean that they are in harmony with the rest of the system, for the relationship may be exploitative, as argued about centre-periphery relations in Chapter 6. Nor does it necessarily mean that the state as a whole benefits in some clearly defined economic or political terms. A state may be status quo because the international system supports a pattern of relations which serves the interests of an elite which controls the government. Thus a country like Zaïre (at least up to 1990) might be classed as status quo in relation to its alignment with Western interests, even though political and economic arguments could be made that this alignment did not serve the interests of the country and people as a whole. The important point about status quo states is that their dominant domestic structures are compatible with (and thereby dependent on) the prevailing pattern of relations in the system.

Such compatibility ties into the point made in Chapter 6 about the constraints on domestic political choice which result from participation in (and addiction to) a liberal international economy. This compatibility may arise because the status quo state in question is playing the role of hegemon, and has thus organized international relations to suit its own interests, as the United States did to a considerable extent after the Second World War. The leading status quo power may adopt styles of leadership ranging from the domineering and aggressive to the consensual, cooperative and contractual. Hirsch and Doyle hint in this direction with their characterization of leadership as 'cooperative', 'hegemonic' or 'imperial',[13] and such variations offer interesting possibilities for refining hypotheses about relations between status quo and revisionist powers.

Status quo states can also be differentiated according to the power hierarchy among them. Depending on its power, a state which is in sympathy with the system may become an associate, a client or a vassal of the hegemon. Status quo states thus have security interests not only in preserving the system, but also in maintaining their position within it. As Carr notes, security is the 'watchword' of the status quo powers,[14] usually expressed in terms of preserving stability. This could mean attempting to suppress all change in order to capture a current advantage in perpetuity, but as Carr argued, no power has the resources to make such a policy lastingly successful.[15] Richard Barnet also observes that 'To set as a national security goal the enforcement "stability" in a world in convulsion, a world in which radical change is as inevitable as it is necessary, is as practical as King Canute's attempt to command the tides.'[16] A better approach is to try to maintain the existing *pattern* of relations, in terms of the distribution of power, wealth, productive capacity, knowledge, status and ideology. Susan Strange captures this with her notion of 'structural power'.[17] This could be done by using a present advantage to create conditions for superior adaptation and development in the future. The status quo thus becomes dynamic, inasmuch as it rides the wave of change rather than resisting it, but static in its attempt to hold on to the existing pattern of relations.[18] The static image is that of someone holding a fixed position, such as a hilltop. The dynamic image is that of a surfer, who seeks to hold position within a highly mobile environment. Either way, as argued in Chapter 6, serious doubts exist about the ability of status quo hegemons to succeed in this act in perpetuity.

THE NATURE OF REVISIONISM

If stability is the security goal of the status quo, then change is the banner of revisionism. The basic condition for revisionism, as argued by Arnold Wolfers, is that the state is 'denied the enjoyment of any of its national core values'.[19] Revisionist states, in other words, are those that find their domestic structures significantly out of tune with the prevailing pattern of relations, and which therefore feel threatened by, or at least hard done by, the existing status quo. Because of this, revisionist states tend to view security in terms of changing the system, and/or improving their position within it. Although they may, for tactical reasons, give temporary or specifically limited support to policies of stability (for purposes like covering for a period of weakness, preventing all-destroying events like nuclear war, curbing unnecessary arms racing, or gaining some desired trade items), they have no long-term or general commitment to it. Whereas stability is the preferred security solution for status quo states, it defines the essence of the problem for revisionists. That said, it is obvious that system change in general is largely an independent variable. A host of factors ranging from technology through economics to religion may push the system into directions not controlled, not anticipated, and not desired by either status quo or revision states.

Like status quo states, revisionist ones can be differentiated in terms of power. Since membership of the international system has expanded greatly since 1945, there is now much more room for revisionism in the less desirable parts of the power hierarchy. It clearly makes a big difference to the system whether the revisionist states are strong or weak powers. Albania, for example, is highly revisionist, but so weak that its opinion counts for little. While weak revisionists may have low influence in their own right, they can make a substantial impact if their revisionism can be aligned with that of a larger power. This is a point that Waltz misses in his eagerness to argue the merits of a bipolar system structure. While he is right to say that lesser states make little difference to the balance of power in a bipolar system,[20] he ignores the impact which they can make as the spoils of the political competition between the superpowers. Thus small powers, like Afghanistan, Nicaragua, Cuba, Iran and Vietnam, can make a substantial impact on the system by symbolizing the fortunes of a struggle much larger than themselves. Weak revisionists also cannot be entirely discounted because, as the case of the Middle East oil states shows, they may quite rapidly acquire elements of strength which greatly increase their power within the system. This is particularly true in conditions of high interdependence, where otherwise weak powers can exploit sectoral strengths that bear on particular issues.[21] Level of power may correlate with whether or not the revisionist is active or passive in pursuit of its case. China and Japan, for example, could not seriously pursue their territorial claims against the Soviet Union during the Cold War because they lacked the military means to induce Soviet compliance.

But relative powerlessness does not necessarily muzzle the revisionist urge, as demonstrated by states like Tanzania, India, Cuba and Libya which have in their very different ways pursued their views to notable effect. If, as Carr suggests, the status quo represents a sectional interest disguising itself as the common good, then it is vulnerable to verbal and intellectual assaults on the foundations of its international legitimacy. The intensity with which revisionist views are held, the skill with which they are argued, the excess of self over common interest in the status quo order and the availability of global public forums such as the United Nations, can to some extent compensate for deficiencies of revisionist power.

The fact that impulses towards change and stability cover two dimensions – place in the power hierarchy and attitude towards the dominant norms in the system – creates some confusion in trying to differentiate between status quo and revisionism. Some of the cruder Realist models see revisionism simply in power terms, rather along the lines of pecking orders in animal hierarchies in which the dominant male retains its rights to the female herd by defeating challengers in trials of strength. The status quo power dominates the system and gains advantage from it on the grounds of previously demonstrated superior power. Challengers test their strength against the holder until one is able to unseat it and reap the fruits of the system to its own benefit. This model does capture some important elements of revisionism, but it ignores the issue of what attitude revisionist actors have towards the prevailing norms in the system, and therefore of what motives other than power drive their challenge to the status quo. The necessity to consider both the power and ideology motives of revisionism suggests a three-tier classification for revisionist states as: *orthodox, radical* and *revolutionary*.

Orthodox revisionism is purely about power and status. It involves no major challenge to the principles of the prevailing order, but centres on a struggle within the existing order aimed at producing a redistribution of power, status, influence and/or resources. Such challenges are an inevitable feature of any status quo, in as much as the inherent mobility of the distribution of power will always generate a pattern of rising and declining powers.[22] When a system is ideologically homogeneous, as Europe was during the eighteenth century, revisionism will by definition be orthodox. The numerous wars among the European monarchies prior to the French Revolution, excluding those concerned with the Christian schism, were simply about power. The organizing principles of the system remained unaltered regardless of the outcome. Orthodox revisionism can produce massive conflict and insecurity, as happened in the decade leading up to 1914. But the importance of distinguishing orthodox from other types of revisionism is that at least in principle it offers more scope for accommodation and peaceful settlement. Shifts in power need not necessarily result in conflict between the principals to effect appropriate shifts in status and influence, as illustrated by the passing of the torch from Britain to America as hegemon in the international economy. The shift of the Soviet Union towards Western norms, and the consequent dramatic drop in tension between East and West during 1989, also illustrates the less threatening quality of orthodox as opposed to revolutionary revisionism.

Revolutionary revisionism combines a struggle for power within the system with a basic challenge to the organizing principles of the dominant status quo. The

Soviet Union presented this sort of challenge to the capitalist West between 1917 and 1989, just as republican France challenged monarchical Europe more than a century previously. The rise of a strong revolutionary revisionist threatens not only the distribution of power, but also the domestic values and structures of all the states associated with the prevailing status quo. Monarchies rightly quaked before the prospect of triumphant republicanism, just as capitalist states feared the spread of communist power and influence. In both cases, a victory for the revisionists threatened major political transformations like those imposed by the Soviet Union on Eastern Europe after the Second World War, or those imposed by the West on Germany and Japan in the purging of fascism. There may well also be economic dimensions to revisionism. If the status quo is liberal, revolutionary revisionists will almost invariably cultivate mercantilism. When this happens, as in the Cold War, each side poses fundamental threats to the economic and political security of the other. If the status quo is mercantilist, revisionism may express itself in competitive empire-building, as during the 1930s.

A revolutionary revisionist challenge almost certainly means that the tidy model of state versus state gets seriously blurred by the transnational intrusions of political ideology. An orthodox revisionist challenge emphasizes nationalist interests, and so fits conveniently into the power-driven, state-centric model of the Realists. A revolutionary challenge projects political ideology into the international arena, thereby cutting across national lines, and carrying the struggle into the domestic arena as well. This makes the conflict much more intractable, and amplifies it into every corner of the system where a local political development can be either interpreted in terms of, or else subverted to, the alignments of the central confrontation. After the French Revolution, domestic republicans became as much of a security threat as foreign ones, just as domestic communists have appeared to be, and in some cases have been, a fifth column against the establishment in the capitalist West. Similarly, communists in power in Cuba made a far bigger impact on American interests than a nationalist government would have done, simply because of the way they reflected, and impinged upon, the fortunes of the larger struggle between the United States and the Soviet Union.

Revolutionary revisionism also creates an acute security problem for the revisionist state itself. Whereas an orthodox revisionist can, to a certain extent, remain quietly within the system until the time is ripe for it to launch its challenge, a revolutionary revisionist is branded by its internal structure for what it is, and is thus exposed to repressive action from the holders of the status quo. The invasion and harassment of the Soviet Union after its Revolution in 1917 illustrates this problem graphically, as in a lesser way does the situation of Iran after 1979. In assessing the overall security picture in a system in which a significant revolutionary revisionist power exists, one must therefore look not only at the threat that it poses to the status quo powers, but also at the threat that they pose to it. Especially in its early days, the revolutionary revisionist is likely to be relatively weak and vulnerable. It is likely to be highly aware of the differences between itself and the rest of the system, and to be acutely sensitive to maintaining its own basic security against what appears to be, and may in fact be, a generally hostile system. Because it is a revolutionary revisionist, it must expect the status quo powers to be deeply opposed to it.

Two developments can follow from this situation which have major significance for the overall security picture. The first is that the revolutionary state may conclude that its only long-term hope for security lies in converting all or part of the rest of the system to its ideology. Iran's propaganda assaults on its neighbours after 1979 showed this tendency. The second is that it may adopt a highly militarized posture primarily for its own defence, in the expectation that the status quo powers are likely to attack it long before it can itself acquire sufficient power to challenge them other than in the political arena. Stalin's response to Lenin's theory (vindicated by Hitler) that the capitalist powers would attack the heartland of socialism, illustrates this case. Both developments work to create a broad spectrum of mutual threats across the political, societal and economic, as well as the military sectors, and in so doing feed neatly into the pattern of an intense power-security dilemma.

The important point here is that where a revolutionary revisionist exists, *both sides* feel highly insecure. The political difference between them amplifies the simple power struggle by adding a deeply threatening ideological dimension to the normal push-and-shove of military and economic power. This amplification effect may open a gulf of hostility and fear between the two sides much deeper than that justified by either their intentions towards each other, or the condition of the power balance between them. If this problem is best illustrated by the case of the Soviet Union, its opposite, in which the status quo powers misguidedly treat a revolutionary revisionist as an orthodox one, is illustrated by the case of Nazi Germany. It is an irony of post-1945 history that the under-reaction and failure of status quo policy in the interwar case should have so directly led to the overreaction of the post-war one. The inability to recognise a power struggle in the first case has produced, by way of overreaction, an intense power-security dilemma in the second.

Radical revisionists fall between orthodox and revolutionary ones. Their objectives extend beyond the simple self-promotion of the orthodox, but fall short of the transformational ambitions of the revolutionary. Radical revisionists seek to reform the system. They want to keep much of the existing structure intact, but to make significant adjustments to its operation. Both self-improvement and ideological motives may underlie this type of revisionism, and yet it may pose no central threat to the basic distribution of power and status in the system.

The best example of radical revisionism can be found in the Third World coalition known as the Group of 77, or its leading exponents such as Tanzania, Algeria, India and Yugoslavia. These countries, and others in the Third World coalition, occupied the international agenda of the 1970s with their call for a new international economic order (NIEO). The NIEO typifies a radical revisionist approach. It did not call for the overthrow of the existing order either in terms of power structure or basic principles, though extremists within the status quo might have viewed it in that light. Instead, it envisaged reforms to the system which would reduce the inequities in centre-periphery relations by allowing a more even distribution of benefits and the creation of stronger states in the periphery. Whether or not the reforms would have produced the effects desired by their pro-posers, and whether or not the existing system can be so reformed without under-mining its basic productive dynamism, are key questions, but not relevant to the present discussion.[23] The important point is that grounds for reformist revisionism exist in the international arena just as much as they do in the domestic one. The example used here is distorted in terms of the normal conventions of revisionism, because the backers of the NIEO represent a weak rather than a strong power base in the system. One could speculate about the character of a powerful radical revi-sionist; or perhaps there is something in the hypothesis that radical revisionism most naturally appeals to weaker actors in the system. Because there is a possibil-ity of negotiation in relation to it, radical revisionism offers opportunities in an interdependent system where even the weak can create some leverage.

The existence of these varieties of revisionism creates a much more complicat-ed pattern of alignments in the international system than that implied by a simple dichotomy between status quo and revisionist states. The status quo powers may be divided against themselves along orthodox revisionist lines.[24] At the same time, they may also be challenged by both radical and revolutionary revisionists, like the West facing both the Group of 77 and the Soviet Union. Possibilities for innu-merable, apparently bizarre, alignments exist in this *mélange*, and help to explain the constant embarrassment of those wedded to more strictly polarized views in the face of developments like the Sino-Soviet split and the Nazi-Soviet Pact. A revisionist state may be so only in relation to certain areas or issues, and may behave more like a status quo power elsewhere. The Soviet Union, for example, was a revolutionary revisionist. But from Eastern Europe it looked like a status quo power, and it took a status quo position on the law of the sea because of its great-power naval interests. Much of the confusion about Nazi Germany during the 1930s arose from uncertainty about whether Hitler's revisionism was local and orthodox, or global and revolutionary. Competing revolutionary revisionists have to decide whether to join forces against the status quo (the Nazi-Soviet Pact), or give first priority to the dispute between them by seeking alignment with the sta-tus quo (the Sino-Soviet split). Similarly, the status quo powers may seek align-ment with one revisionist (the Soviet Union), in order to quash another (Nazi Germany). Radical revisionists may see the dispute between status quo and revo-lutionary powers as a blessing for their cause because of the increased leverage it provides them against the status quo powers, or they may see it as a disaster, wip-ing out the credibility of their middle ground and forcing them to take sides.

The great complexity and uncertainty of alignments which this analysis reveals explains a good measure of the overlap and confusion between the security and power struggles. Not only do several types of revisionism compete among them-selves and with the status quo, but also locally focused revisionisms intermingle with and distort those based on more global ambitions. The business of correctly identifying revisionist actors, the importance of which is rightly stressed by Morgenthau,[25] is revealed to be no simple matter when the exigencies of a complex pattern may require alignment with obvious opponents.

The absence of any easily identified political and relational character among the states in the system explains why the dynamics of the power and security struggles become so entangled. Uncertainty as to the nature of other actors arises both from the intrinsic difficulty of judging their true intentions, and from the peculiarities of alignment that the system generates. This uncertainty is compounded by the general hazard of life in an armed anarchy, and is the driving force behind the confusion of the power-security dilemma. The security struggle, which is a natural dynamic of an armed anarchy, can easily create the self-fulfilling prophecy of a power struggle. Conversely, an actual power challenge may well be disguised in its early stages as a manifestation of the security struggle. Under such conditions, no actor can rely on absolute distinctions between the power and security models in relation to the formulation of its policy. Consequently, all find themselves forced to play with caution, suspecting power motives everywhere. This stance has the ironic result of intensifying the power-security dilemma throughout the system. The resultant uncertainty and insecurity make a powerful input into the domestic politics of national security which will be examined in the next chapter.

THE MILITARY FACTOR

The blurring of political identities as between revisionist and status quo is matched by a similar confusion in the military sector: how to tell the difference between behaviour aimed at changing the military balance (thus indicating a power struggle) and behaviour aimed simply at maintaining the military status quo (pointing more towards a security struggle). I have dealt with technological, strategic and political components of this issue in detail elsewhere,[26] and it will suffice here simply to set out the basic problem.

Two ambiguities in the nature of military power work to complicate the distinction between aggressive and defensive behaviour. The first is the traditional problem of separating offensive from defensive military postures. Because attack is often a militarily efficient form of defence, and because many weapons can be used for both offensive and defensive purposes, states are hard put to calculate each other's intentions from the nature of their military deployments. To the extent that intentions are calculated from capabilities, the profound ambiguity in military means pushes states towards worst-case assessments of each other's behaviour. This is the classical formulation of the security dilemma: the defence measures that states take to defend themselves are seen by others as potentially aggressive, and responded to accordingly. Those responses raise threats, and so trigger further rounds of responsive armaments. Because military means are ambiguous, the measures that states take to make themselves secure result in all becoming less secure.

   The second ambiguity arises because the technological imperative drives a relentless and continuous improvement in the performance of weapons. This means that the military sector possesses an independent dynamic that functions regardless of ups and downs in political relations. Since military capability is common to both power and security struggles, the fact that it is subject to a dynamic which is separate from the intentions which govern those struggles easily confuses the security signals that states try to send to each other. Fear of defeat governs both struggles, driving states to maintain military forces that are somehow proportional to perceived threats of attack. All states must therefore keep a close eye on how their military capability relates to that of others. Because military power is relative, states will be sensitive to changes in the capability of potential rivals. Such changes may occur because a state has decided to try to change the military balance between itself and others, as Germany did in embarking on the construction of a first-class navy before the First World War, and as the Soviet Union did in constructing a nuclear arsenal to match that of the United States. But they may also occur because a state needs to bring its armed forces up to date. Weapons wear out even in peacetime. They become obsolete as technological advances open new opportunities in design and performance. Since newer generations of weapons are invariably more potent in performance than those they replace, outside observers may have difficulty distinguishing between changes designed to maintain military strength, and those designed to increase it. In other words, modernizing changes made in response to the endlessly advancing frontier of the technologically possible may be confused with changes made with a view to shifting the balance of military power. Because the military idiom is similar, the political differences are hard to read, and prudence dictates caution about benign assumptions.
   Robert Jervis has made a notable attempt to explore the consequences of the ambiguity between offensive and defensive military power.[27] Jervis concludes his piece with a discussion of four scenarios which result from a 2 x 2 matrix.[28] Across the top, the variable is whether offensive or defensive weapons have the advantage at the time under consideration. War-proven examples here would be the First World War (defensive-dominant), and the Second World War (offensive-dominant). Down the side, the variables are first, that offensive weapons (and therefore postures) *cannot* be distinguished from defensive ones, and second, that they *can* be distinguished. Although there are some well-tried difficulties in distinguishing between offensive and defensive weapons – as illustrated both by pre-1914 assumptions that the offensive was dominant, as it had been in 1870, and by the lengthy, and eventually fruitless, debates of the 1932 Disarmament Conference on the subject – Jervis's scheme, suggests some powerful insights into the security implications of weapons variables.
   In brief, his argument is that when offensive weapons are dominant, and the difference between offensive and defensive weapons cannot be distinguished, incentives to acquire offensive weapons will be high all round, and the situation will be very unstable, with the power-security dilemma operating at full pitch. When offensive weapons are dominant, but the difference can be distinguished,

the situation is less tense, and aggressive states can be identified as such by the weapons they procure. The spoiler here is that if the offensive advantage is great, a passive defence option will not suffice, and even status quo states will be obliged to procure offensive weapons. When the defence has the advantage and the difference cannot be distinguished, the power-security dilemma operates, but is moderated by the fact that arms acquisitions produce more security for their owners than insecurity for others.

When the defence has the advantage and the difference can be distinguished, the situation is very stable, with aggressors automatically revealing their intentions by the nature of their military deployments, and the uncertainties which produce the security struggle kept to a minimum. This last scenario is the one favoured by contemporary advocates of non-provocative defence. They argue not only that developments in detection and guidance technology are restoring the advantage to the defensive, but also that the distinction between offensive and defensive military configurations is manifest. High-intensity surveillance combined with precision-guided munitions means that the large movements of forces required for invasions become highly vulnerable. Expensive platforms such as aircraft carriers, tanks and manned aircraft are becoming increasingly cost-ineffective against the missiles that can destroy them. Under these conditions, the deployment of forces capable of robust territorial defence, but structurally incapable of large-scale invasions or bombardments of others, offers an attractive way of breaking one key element in the power-security dilemma. Such policies are the logical complement to a non-domineering status quo political posture, and may be exceedingly well suited to post-Cold War relations in Europe and Northeast Asia. They are, however, much less attractive in situations where there is a real power struggle, and/or where aggressors might be content with a standoff bombardment rather than an invasion.[29]

Even when the power-security dilemma is driven by a power struggle, there may still be some scope for resolvable solutions. Arms races are not all of the same intensity. Like any other form of competition, they range on a spectrum from mild to intense. A mild arms race might be hard to distinguish from maintenance of the military status quo. In such a race, military expenditure could remain at a constant and moderate proportion of GNP, perhaps even declining from this on occasion. A high-intensity race, by contrast, would look more like a mobilization for war, with military expenditure either rising as a proportion of GNP, or else hovering around some high proportion, as in the case of Israel.[30]

The analogy of a race conjures up images of a track event in which two or more runners start from a fixed line and strive to reach a finishing tape first. This image is in some ways unfortunate, for it draws attention away from the more mixed conditions and objectives that are likely to attend an arms race. In an arms race, the competitors are unlikely to start from the same line, and they may well not wish to win or lose in the unconditional sense of the 100 metre sprint. If one assumes a two-party arms race (often not the case), that the states do not start the race with equal armaments (which is normal in modern arms racing history) and

Table 8.1: Possible objectives in a two-party arms race

R		Challenger		
e		Partial catch-up	Parity	Superiority
s	Increase lead	U	U	U
p	Maintain existing lead	U	U	U
o				
n	Allow gain short of parity	R	U	U
d	Allow gain of parity	(R)	R	U
e				
r	Accept inferiority	(R)	(R)	(R)

U = Unresolvable objectives
R = Resolvable objectives
() = Unlikely situation

that the weaker state initiates the race (in the real world, the question of initiation may be difficult to answer clearly), then one can derive a model for arms race objectives. At least one party must want to change its relative military capability, otherwise the process is maintenance of the military status quo, not racing. Assuming that the challenger state (C) is behind, and wants to change, it can have three objectives. It can seek a partial catch-up with the respondent state (R), trying to improve its position without changing the direction of the balance between them; it can seek parity, causing an evening out, but not a reversal, of the balance; or it can seek superiority, a reversal in direction of the existing balance. It may hold just one of these; or it may hold all three as a phased plan; or it may hold a lower one, and then take up the others if opportunity seems to warrant a change of mind.

In the face of these challenges, R has five options. It can attempt to increase its lead, hoping thereby to demonstrate to C the futility of the challenge. It can simply maintain its lead, matching C's build-up, and assuming that C will weary of its labour. It can allow C to achieve a partial catch-up, so that the distance between them is narrowed, but the direction of the balance remains the same. In this case, R would be adjusting to a real increase in C's weight in the system. It can allow C to achieve parity, a much larger adjustment. Or it can allow C to win the race, and accept for itself a diminished stature either in its local security complex, or in the system as a whole.[31] If these objectives are arranged into a matrix, some of them appear as conflicts which are irresolvable short of changes in objectives by one side or the other. Some of them do not clash, and indicate that an arms race need not necessarily ensue. Some combinations are unlikely to occur.

The disputes summarized in Table 8.1 get more serious as one moves towards the top right corner of the matrix, and more resolvable as one moves towards the lower left corner. This exercise obviously begs a number of important questions. The objectives are assumed to be known to both sides, and to be honest, neither of which may be the case. One or both sides may not have their objectives formulated explicitly even to themselves, or if they are clear, they may be kept secret from the other side. Attempts by one deliberately to mislead the other as to its objectives may occur. Even attempts at full and honest communication by both sides are unlikely to prevent misunderstanding and suspicion. Furthermore, the matrix infers that real military strength can be measured with considerable accuracy, which is not the case, and it ignores differences in arms-racing style resulting from the weapons characteristics sketched above by Jervis.

Despite these difficulties, the matrix serves to indicate that a more tractable range of objectives exists for arms racing than would at first appear to be the case in the light of a strict race analogy. It illustrates a set of resolvable combinations, and in so doing moderates the notion of an arms race as being a stark zero-sum game. The matrix also leads one back to the larger concern with the security and power struggles. The more extreme objectives on both sides fit easily into the assumptions of the power struggle, with its emphasis on intense zero-sum competition. If a power struggle is operating, then the arms race it generates is most likely to be resolved short of one side reducing its objectives. The band of resolvable combinations fits more easily into the assumptions of the security struggle. In a security struggle, neither side wishes to threaten the other, but each sees the other as a threat. The mutual, but incorrect, imputation of extreme objectives can lead to an arms race which is indistinguishable from one attending a power struggle, except that it is amenable to resolution if the falseness of the imputed objectives can be demonstrated. In either the power-struggle or the security-struggle case the independent cycle of weapons improvement can act both to spur the racing dynamic and to complicate the calculation of relative strength.

The idea of parity features in the resolvable combinations in Table 8.1, and is often offered as a way of resolving the military ambiguities that help to drive the power-security dilemma. But parity is unfortunately a much trickier, and much less straightforward, idea than it might appear to be at first glance. Aside from the formidable technical difficulties of calculating what parity might look like,[32] the principle of parity itself can be faulted on two grounds as a basis for stabilizing military relations. The first fault is that even if parity of military forces could be reliably and visibly achieved, the nature of military action is such that equality of security would not result. All other things being equal, military action rewards those who strike first. The aggressor gets to choose the time, place and conditions for his attack, and if offensive weapons are dominant, as they generally have been since the Second World War, he may be able to achieve a significant reduction in his opponent's force by mounting a Pearl Harbor-type counterforce strike. The first-strike factor undermines any simple notion of parity based on a balance of military means. Indeed, it seems quite possible that an explicit and visible parity based on offensive means would amplify insecurity. Where force calculations are uncertain, ambiguity acts as a restraint on the first-strike option, but if the balance is known, the calculation can be made with greater certainty.

The second fault is more subtle, and hinges on the instability of relative status in a regime of parity. A case can be made that relations between two states will be most stable when the disparity in power between them is large. The greater power will feel no vital threat and the smaller will, of necessity, learn to accommodate itself. When the difference in power is large, both sides are secure in the knowledge that their relative status will not change quickly. Although the lesser power may not like it, and although the situation generates incentives to arms race, in the short term a large disparity in power is relatively stable (assuming that the dominant power is status quo). By contrast, a situation of parity leaves neither side secure in the knowledge of a comfortable margin of strength, and provides incentives to make an effort to tip the balance. When powers are equal, a small increase by one serves to change their relative status from equals, to superior and inferior, in a way that does not occur when relative status is protected by larger differentials in power.[33] Arms races become much more sensitive when the race is close, because a prospect of winning or losing presents itself. Status instability in an arms race is not a new phenomenon. The Duke of Buckingham, in a letter to Sir Thomas Osborn in 1672, argued that: 'We ought not to suffer any other Nation to be our *Equals at Sea*, because when they are once our *Equals*, it is but an even *Lay*, whether they or we shall be the Superiors.'[34] The same problem occurred in 1906, when the launching of HMS *Dreadnought* precipitated a fierce stage in the Anglo-German naval race by giving the Germans a chance to compete on fairly even terms in the new class of warship.

Status instability is affected by both military and political factors. On the political side, one would expect status instability to be most delicate under the acute zero-sum conditions of bipolarity, and least delicate in the more mobile, varied and less hostile environment of multipolarity. On the military side, one would expect the existence of nuclear sufficiency to mute status instability. In confrontations of conventional forces, superiority and inferiority make a big difference to outcomes, and force calculations are important. But with nuclear sufficiency, both sides have a surplus capacity of destructive power, and logically should not attach much importance to differences in numbers of weapons. As F. H. Hinsley put it, 'These states have passed so far beyond a threshold of absolute power that changes in relative power can no longer erode their ability to uphold the equilibrium which resides in the ability of each to destroy all.'[35]

The case of the United States nevertheless shows the pressure created by status instability. The United States found its decline from superiority over the Soviet Union very difficult to live with despite the presence of nuclear sufficiency, and perhaps because of the persistence of bipolarity. Up to the late 1980s the cost of parity was a recurrent American angst that the Soviet Union was getting ahead – in other words, that the status between the two was shifting towards Soviet superiority. One still heard official statements that nuclear superiority had some political meaning equivalent to the traditional power significance of having more dreadnoughts or more army divisions. While nuclear superiority above sufficiency may have some political effects, particularly in the way nuclear powers see each other and are seen by third parties, the new conditions of the defence dilemma mean that the old political and military meaning of superiority can never return. Perhaps only military forces that are structurally incapable of offence, as advocated by proponents of non-provocative defence, have the potential for solving the status-instability problem of parity.

CONCLUSIONS: CAN THE POWER-SECURITY DILEMMA
BE RESOLVED?

For virtually all of modern history, the power-security dilemma has been an exceptionally durable feature of international relations. It has been sustained by the tensions between status quo and revisionist interests, by the independent technological momentum of the arms dynamic and by the ambiguities in both of these factors that make it difficult to distinguish between benign and aggressive behaviour. Because the power and security struggles could not be distinguished reliably, national security policy could not rest on the relatively clear and straightforward principles that can be derived from either in isolation. The dynamics of both struggles had to be assumed to be in play, leading, in consequence, to the self-maintaining problems and policies with which we are all too familiar.

In general terms, there is no reason to expect the conditions that have supported the power-security dilemma to disappear. The anarchic political structure is robust, and there are no grounds for expecting that the process of rising and declining powers that feeds the tension between status quo and revisionism will cease to operate. Indeed, at the beginning of the 1990s that process is operating in spectacular fashion, as old superpowers decline, and new great powers rise. Similarly, there is no reason to expect that the technological imperative underlying the arms dynamic will weaken. New technologies will continue to open up new military possibilities regardless of whether military applications are intended or not. Since states will remain responsible for their defence for the foreseeable future, they cannot escape from the pressure that these options create. There is therefore no question about whether the power-security dilemma will continue to exist: it will. The question is how important it will be given the impact of other factors on the security problem under anarchy. Here there are some grounds for optimism.

As suggested in the conclusions to Chapter 7, the defence dilemma can provide a significant countervailing force to the power-security one. The two dilemmas are linked together by the arms dynamic. As a consequence, both cannot continue to get worse without strengthening a contradiction which is already very much in evidence between them. This contradiction arises from the independence of the arms dynamic. As the defence dilemma spreads and intensifies, it erodes the traditional conditions which have allowed, and even encouraged, the struggle for power to occur. When the costs and risks of armed struggle rise to the point where massive destruction is certain to be inflicted on both victor and vanquished, then armed struggle ceases to be a useful way of pursuing competitive political objectives. Military forces still need to be maintained and upgraded in order to preserve the paralysis, but notions of inferiority and superiority no longer have the same clear political implications that they had as recently as the Second World War. Once this threshold is passed, military force ceases to be a competitive variable in the traditional sense of arms racing, and becomes more of a constant which rests on the notion of sufficiency. Sufficiency, however, still has to be maintained in the light of technical advance. The same logic of sufficiency should also mute the security struggle, although it would not remove the uncertainties and fears associated with maintaining one's forces at an adequate level.

In the present international system, this contradiction made a considerable impact on military relations among the major powers even during the Cold War. The ending of the Cold War may in part be attributed to it. But many areas still exist where the defence dilemma is weak enough to allow both local conflicts and external interventions by the powers to occur more or less under the old rules. Here, the power-security dilemma operates undiminished, and war remains a feasible instrument of policy.

The defence dilemma certainly has not cured the present system of its security problem, and it is not intended to argue here that it can do so. It is not offered as a preferred solution, but as a visible and powerful trend in the mainstream of events which has major implications for the international security environment. Carried to its logical conclusion, the defence dilemma could produce not Armageddon, as might be feared from the unrestrained operation of a power-security dilemma pressed by an open-ended arms dynamic, but an effectively paralysed international system in which major military force played no role other than ensuring its own non-use.

This path, however, is hardly a safe one. Very high risks must be run to get to the point at which the defence dilemma produces paralysis, as illustrated by the courses of the First and Second World Wars, and by the evidence from current highly armed, but not paralysed, areas like the Middle East and South Asia. It would seem, for example, necessary to take a benign view of some (not all) proliferation of nuclear weapons in pursuit of this scenario, a position that can hardly be described as popular, or in line with mainstream views on what is desirable.[36] Even within the confines of a fully developed defence dilemma, there are still risks of accident and miscalculation which many find unacceptable, not to mention the high costs and moral effects of a permanently militarized system.

Fortunately, the defence dilemma is not the only countervailing force in play against the power-security one. On the military side, the key development is the greatly enhanced transparency to observation that now conditions military relations among all the major powers. In this area, dramatic improvements in space-based surveillance technologies since the early 1960s have worked a remarkable and under-recognized transformation on the dynamics of military security relations. Using national technical means, states can now observe each other's military dispositions and behaviours much more accurately and continuously than ever before. These capabilities make surprise attacks, especially those requiring the mass mobilization and movement of military and naval forces, much more difficult to achieve than in the past. They also support the possibility of non-provocative defence strategies discussed above. Where there is the political will, these national technical means can be bolstered by agreed confidence-building measures (CBMs). CBMs of the kind that have been developed in Europe increase transparency by a system of agreed reporting and inspection measures that give each side the ability to reassure itself about the other's military deployments. The technologies and arrangements that support greater transparency do not eliminate the power-security dilemma. But by reducing uncertainties and increasing warning times, they do reduce the intensity and fear of the military threats that states pose to each other. In so doing they lower the salience of the power-security dilemma in international relations.

On the political side, the ending of the Cold War seems almost certain to bring about a substantial net reduction in the influence of the power-security dilemma. At a minimum, the ending of the Cold War means that the major source of revolutionary revisionism in the system has either transformed itself into an orthodox or radical revisionist, or possibly even joined the status quo. All of these options, but especially the latter, greatly reduce the power struggle in the international system, in the process both easing the dilemma of distinguishing between the power and security struggles and bringing to the fore the inherently more tractable dynamics of a simple security dilemma. In the context of a strengthening international society resting on a consensus about political and economic structure, this development marks a profound improvement in the security conditions of the international system.

The ending of the Cold War also generates another security benefit in terms of transparency. Transparency has a broad political-economy dimension that parallels, and interacts with, the military one. The Soviet Union, for example, traditionally sought advantage in its vigorously promoted non-transparency. Being a closed state enabled the Soviet leadership to hide everything from the size of its nuclear forces to the extent of its military budget. This closedness greatly exacerbated the power-security dilemma for the West, and therefore subsequently for the Soviet Union, by forcing NATO to react to worst-case assessments about Soviet military capability. Gorbachev's policy of *glasnost* has by itself considerably eased this problem. If, as seems possible, *perestroika* means that the Soviet Union will follow Eastern Europe into more market-based economics, then even greater transparency gains will occur, as discussed in Chapter 6.

As also discussed in Chapter 6, there is good reason to think that military force plays a decreasing role in relations among market-based political economies as those relations become increasingly dense and interdependent. The creation of common markets and security communities in Europe and North America, and the emergence of a globe-spanning security community among the three main centres of capitalist power, both support this hypothesis. The existence of these security communities also points towards a further way in which states can improve their security without stimulating the destructive military dynamics of the power-security dilemma. Nearly all of the successful security communities in the system are composed strong states, whereas the great majority of the conflict-wracked parts are composed of weak states. The building of strong states increases domestic security by definition, and is a necessary if not sufficient condition for achieving international security. Unlike the creation of strong powers, the building of strong states does not act directly to stimulate the power-security dilemma. It therefore offers an escape from the self-defeating contradictions that usually attend the efforts of states to increase their own security.

These developments and possibilities, and others discussed above, all point towards the evolution of a more mature anarchy. The more mature the anarchy, the less the importance of the power-security dilemma to the states within it. So long as anarchy remains the political structure, the potential for a power-security dilemma will persist, as will some of its reality. But as anarchy matures, its positive security attributes begin to override its negative ones, pushing them into an increasingly residual role in international relations. Some of the necessary developments towards a mature anarchy are already well underway. Others, particularly the building of strong states, stand as opportunities for security improvement that are still a long way from being fully exploited, in part because they are not yet properly understood.

NOTES

1. The security struggle comes out of Realist thinking – see John H. Herz, *International Politics in the Atomic Age* (New York: Columbia University Press, 1959) pp. 231–43 – but is, in a sense, more in line with Idealist thinking in that it puts emphasis on weapons as a source of tension. It is usually discussed in the context of the 'security dilemma', for example by Herz, and by Robert Jervis, *Perception and Misperception in International Politics* (Princeton: Princeton University Press, 1976), ch. 3; and 'Cooperation under the security dilemma', *World Politics*, 30:2 (1978). These writers use the term security dilemma to refer to much the same phenomenon as I refer to with the term power-security dilemma. I prefer the longer expression because it emphasizes the opposed theses which constitute the dilemma. The simpler term does not do this, and tends therefore to perpetuate the blurring of the distinction between power and security. It is a main theme of this book that understanding of international relations can be improved by distinguishing the concept of security from that of power.

2. I am grateful to Morten Kelstrup for this observation about how the defence dilemma and the power-security dilemma fit with the preoccupations of the political discourse about defence.

3. For the full argument, see Barry Buzan, 'Peace, power and security: contending concepts in the study of international relations', *Journal of Peace Research*, 21:2 (1984).

4. These two views are set out at length in Robert Jervis, *op. cit.* (note 1, 1976), ch. 3.

5. E. H. Carr, *The Twenty Years Crisis* (London: Macmillan, 1946, 2nd edn.); Hans Morgenthau, *Politics Among Nations* (New York: Knopf, 1973, 5th edn.). See also, Paul Seabury, 'The idea of the status quo', in Seabury (ed.), *Balance of Power* (San Francisco: Chandler, 1965), ch. 22; and Richard W. Cottam, *Foreign Policy Motivation* (n.p.: University of Pittsburgh Press, 1977), ch. 2.

6. For general analysis focused on the system dynamic of status quo versus revisionist powers, see Robert Gilpin, *War and Change in World Politics* (Cambridge: Cambridge University Press, 1981); and Richard K. Ashley, *The Political Economy of War and Peace* (London: Pinter, 1980).

7. Klaus Knorr, *Power and Wealth* (London: Macmillan, 1973), p. 106.
8. Ken Booth, *Strategy and Ethnocentrism* (London: Croom Helm, 1979).
9. Carr, *op. cit.* (note 5), p. 84; Knorr, *op. cit,* (note 7), pp. 12, 195; and David Calleo, 'The historiography of the interwar period: reconsiderations', in Benjamin Rowland (ed.), *Balance of Power or Hegemony: The interwar monetary system* (New York: New York University Press, 1976), pp. 228–9.
10. Carr, *ibid.*, pp. 93–222.
11. *ibid.*, pp. 79, 167.
12. Much of the argument in this section is based on Barry Buzan, 'Change and insecurity: a critique of strategic studies', in Barry Buzan and R. J. Barry Jones (eds), *Change and the Study of International Politics* (London: Pinter, 1981), pp. 160–6.
13. Fred Hirsch and Michael Doyle, 'Politicization in the world Economy: necessary conditions for an international economic order' in F. Hirsch, M. Doyle and E. L. Morse, *Alternatives to Monetary Disorder* (New York: McGraw-Hill, 1977), p. 27.
14. Carr, *op. cit.* (note 5), p. 105.
15. *ibid.*, p. 222.
16. Richard J. Barnet, 'The illusion of security', in C. R. Beitz and T. Herman (eds), *Peace and War* (San Francisco: W. H. Freeman, 973), p. 285.
17. Susan Strange, *States and Markets: An introduction political economy* (London: Pinter, 1988), chs 2–6.
18. This approach to the status quo is based on the structure of relations in the system. It implicitly rejects the approach used by Seabury, *op. cit.* (note 5), which relates the status quo to the existence of semi-constitutional international orders like those established by the Congress of Vienna and the Treaty of Versailles. While Seabury's constitutional approach has obvious merits, it forces him to the unhelpful conclusion that the concept of the status quo is 'virtually meaningless' (p. 212) in the contemporary international system.
19. Arnold Wolfers, *Discord and Collaboration* (Baltimore: Johns Hopkins University Press, 1962), p. 18.
20. Kenneth N. Waltz, *Theory of International Politics* (Reading, Mass.: Addison-Wesley, 1979), pp. 168–71.
21. Robert O. Keohane and Joseph S. Nye, *Power and Interdependence* (Boston: Little Brown, 1977), esp. chs 2–3.
22. On this theme, see Gilpin, *op. cit.* (note 6); and Paul Kennedy, *The Rise and Fall of the Great Powers* (London: Fontana, 1988).
23. For some critical evaluations of the NIEO along these lines, see W. M. Corden, 'The NIEO proposals: a cool look', *Thames Essays* no. 21, (London: Trade Policy Research Centre, 1979); Nathaniel Leff, 'The new international economic order – bad economic worse politics', *Foreign Policy*, 24 (1976); M. E. Kreinin and J. M Finger, 'A critical survey of the new international economic order', *Journal of World Trade Law*, 10:6 (1976).
24. An example of this argument is Mary Kaldor, *The Disintegrating West* (Harmondsworth: Penguin, 1979).
25. Morgenthau, *op. cit.* (note 5), pp. 67–8.
26. Barry Buzan, *An Introduction to Strategic Studies: Military technology and international relations* (London: Macmillan, 1987).

27. Robert Jervis, 'Cooperation under the security dilemma', *World Politics,* 30:2 (1978). See also Richard Rosecrance, *International Relations: Peace or war?* (New York: McGraw-Hill, 1973), pp. 65, 300.

28. Jervis, *ibid.,* pp. 211–14.

29. See Buzan, *op. cit.* (note 26), ch. 17. For a comprehensive review of the literature on non-offensive defence (NOD), see *NOD: International Research Newsletter*, edited by Bjørn Møller and available from the Centre for Peace and Conflict Research, Copenhagen.

30. In 1981 Israel spent approximately one-third of its GNP on defence, though by 1987 this was down to a still large 15 per cent. *The Military Balance 1981–82 and 1989–90* (London: IISS, 1981, 1989), pp. 52 and 209.

31. These objectives are an elaboration from a simpler set given by P. Kodzic, 'Armaments and development', in D. Carlton and C. Shaerf (eds), *The Dynamics of the Arms Race* (London: Croom Helm, 1975), pp. 204–5.

32. Buzan, *op. cit.* (note 26), pp. 264–7.

33. For some other angles on status instability, see Richard Rosecrance, 'Deterrence and vulnerability in the pre-nuclear era', in 'The future of strategic deterrence', *Adelphi Papers*, no. 160 (London: IISS, 1980).

34. Quoted in Philip W. Buck, *The Politics of Mercantilism* (New York: Octagon, 1974 (1942)), pp. 116–17.

35. F. H. Hinsley, 'The rise and fall of the modern international system', *Review of International Studies*, 8:1 (1982), p. 8.

36. One courageous advocate of this view is Kenneth N. Waltz, 'The spread of nuclear weapons: more may be better', *Adelphi Papers*, no. 171, (London: IISS, 1981).

chapter nine | national and international security: the policy problem

The preceding chapters have examined different aspects and levels of the security problem at considerable length. The emphasis throughout has been on the logical and objective dimensions of the problem at the level of individuals, states and the system as a whole. Regardless of these neat and rather abstract enquiries, however, at the end of the day national security policy still has to be made by states. Because security policy-making is very largely an activity of states, there is an important practical sense in which national security subsumes all of the other security considerations found at the individual and systemic levels. This is captured by Wæver's 'hourglass' model:

Figure 9.1: Wæver's 'hourglass' model of security

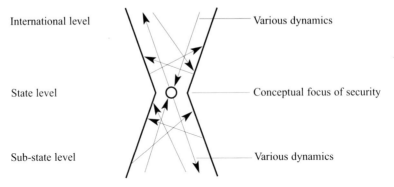

As he explains it:

> the only meaningful way to speak about 'security' is to relate to the classical meaning (national security) and broaden the understanding of relevant *dynamics*: not only state to state, but also the quality of international politics and sub-state dynamics. The concept of security is posited at the level of 'state'. At the other levels developments cannot be summed up in a similar way. We have various interactions at all three levels. But the issue of 'security' has to be read through the lense of 'national security'.[1]

In other words, governments stand at the interface between the internal dynamics of the state, and the external ones of the system. It is the job of government, indeed almost the definition of its function, to find ways of reconciling these two sets of forces. The fact that no other agency exists for this task is what justifies the primacy of national security.

However much one might regret the narrowness of the policy-making base in relation to the scope of the problem, state actors nevertheless have to cope with the whole security problem in real time, and in the light of their very different experiences and capabilities. Among other things, this means that the policy-making process itself is a vital part of the security problematique. In the best of all possible worlds, all the actors in international relations would possess perfect information, would understand the positions and motives of others, and also the workings of the system as a whole, would be capable of making rational decisions based on this information and understanding, and would be free to make, and to implement, these decisions. Such a situation would greatly ease the job both of foreign policy decision-makers and of academic analysts. But we do not live in this perfect world. In the real world, policy-makers are only partially informed, do not fully understand other actors or the system (or themselves), are capable of only limited rationality and are highly constrained in what they can do. As a consequence, many factors within the policy-making process have little directly to do with the security problem, but none the less have a considerable influence on policies produced in the name of national security. Because policy has a powerful impact on security problems, as illustrated by the feedback effects in arms racing and trade wars, the policy-making process itself becomes a major factor in the overall character of the security problem.

The general question of domestic variables in the policy-making process has been extensively analyzed in the large literature on foreign policy,[2] and there is no need to repeat that exercise here. Instead, this chapter will survey the major intervening variables that affect national security policy in particular, and draw some conclusions about how these variables affect the security problem as a whole. Three kinds of problems arising in the domestic arena affect the rationality and quality of security policy: logical dilemmas, perceptual distortions and cross-cutting interests in the political domain. Every country has security relations whether it wants them or not. Most would like to have a coherent and reliable security policy. But such a policy is much harder to acquire than are the problems that give rise to the need for it.

LOGICAL PROBLEMS

The making of national security policy requires choices about both the objectives of policy (ends), and the techniques, resources, instruments and actions which will be used to implement it (means). Even if one assumes that neither political nor perceptual problems interfere with the process, these choices are not straightforward.

As has been demonstrated in the preceding chapters, many complex logical diffi-culties arise which, because they reflect the fundamental character of the national security problem itself, will always impinge on policy choices. These difficulties spring from the essentially contested nature of security as a concept, which was the starting point of this enquiry.

The most obvious logical problem is that if national security is taken as an end, one runs immediately into the problem that it can never be achieved. Complete security cannot be obtained in an anarchic system, and therefore to hold that goal as an aspiration is to condemn oneself to pursuit of an operationally impossible objective. President Reagan's Strategic Defense Initiative, with its hope of break-ing out of the mutual threat structure of deterrence, exemplified this fallacy. If national security is a relative end, then complicated and objectively unanswerable questions arise about how much security is enough, and about how to make adjust-ments to the ceaseless changes in the many criteria by which relative security must be defined. Relative security is a permanently unsatisfactory condition. It can always be criticized as imperfect, because on logical grounds it must be so. It can never serve as a stable resting place, because the factors which define a satisfac-tory relative level at any given moment are themselves ephemeral. The structure of the system and its interaction dynamics complete this dilemma by ensuring that any attempt to acquire, or even move towards, complete security by any actor will stimulate reactions which raise the level of threat in proportion to the measures taken. The arms race, the chase after the chimera of economic security and the defence dilemma give new meaning in this context to Shakespeare's observation that, 'security is mortals' chiefest enemy'.[3]

The logical problems that afflict security policy-making can be grouped under two headings: first, strategic choice, and second, characteristics of the security problem that work against the application of logic.

The problem of strategic choice starts with the tautology that the purpose of national security policy is to make the state secure, or at least *sufficiently* secure if one rejects the possibility of absolute security. The question of how this is to be achieved is the opening point for strategic discussion about the interrelation of ends and means. The whole enquiry assumes that threats exist, and that insecuri-ty is a problem because of vulnerability to those threats. As sketched in Chapter 3, the choice is between taking action to reduce vulnerability, and trying to elim-inate or reduce the threats by addressing their causes at source. The first of these options I call *national security strategy*, because it is largely within the threatened state. The second I call *international security strategy*, because it depends on the adjustment of relations between states either directly, or by making changes in the systemic conditions that influence the way in which states make each other feel more (or less) secure.[4]

If a national security strategy is adopted, then security policy will focus on reducing the vulnerabilities of the state. Vulnerabilities can be reduced by increas-ing self-reliance, or by building up countervailing forces to deal with specific threats. If the threats are military, then they can be met by strengthening one's own military forces, by seeking alliances, or by hardening the country against attack. Economic threats can be met by increasing self-reliance, diversifying sources of supply, or conditioning the population to accept a lower standard of welfare. The whole range of threats surveyed in Chapter 3 is relevant here, for any or all of them might have to be met by countervailing actions to reduce the vulnerabilities against which the threat bears. For example, one of the primary British responses to German naval building programmes in the early years of this century was to increase the strength of the Royal Navy as an offset force. The British made quite clear their intention to match and exceed German construction of dreadnoughts, so that whatever the German effort, they would be allowed to make no gain beyond a ratio of forces (8:5) set by, and favourable to, Britain. In this way, Britain could meet the German threat directly by taking measure within Britain which would counteract or offset the particular type of threat being developed by Germany.

The national security strategy is not without its merits but, almost by definition, it makes less sense for lesser powers. As a rule, only great powers command sufficient resources to carry it off, though some smaller powers (Sweden, Yugoslavia, Switzerland) in favourable geostrategic positions have been able to do so. This great power emphasis is a common bias in thinking about national security. Indeed, the very term 'national security' implies a self-help approach, a fact which is perhaps not surprising given its origins in that most self-sufficient of great powers, the United States. The principal advantages of a national security strategy are that threats can be met specifically as they arise, and that the measures which provide security are largely under the control of the state concerned. In theory, and resources permitting, measures could be taken against all identified threats, so blocking or offsetting all sources of insecurity.

A pleasing certainty attaches to this approach, not only because the state retains firm control over the sources of its own security, but also because it deals with the firm realities of capabilities rather than with the uncertainties of other actors' intentions. For this reason, a national security strategy enables its practitioner to avoid the burden of making difficult distinctions about whether other actors are status quo or revisionist, and whether the security problem reflects a power struggle or a security one. All these distinctions can be ignored to the extent that the state can afford to protect itself against any threats. At its best, this approach would produce a security which was clearly founded, relatively straightforward in operation and indisputably in the hands of each actor in relation to itself. France since 1966 is a good example of a national security strategy in everything from its energy and agriculture policies to its policies on alliance, arms production and nuclear weapons. The Soviet Union, China, Israel, Albania and South Africa also exemplify this approach to security.

The problems with national security strategy are that few countries have the resources to make it work, that its logic operates only on the state level and therefore misses the broader dimensions of the security problem, and that it tends to produce a ruinously expensive and psychologically counterproductive obsession with security. Great powers will be able to make it work to some extent, but even they will not be able to ignore the powerful feedback of security logic on the system level. Because the national security strategy ignores the sources of threats, it risks both an open-ended commitment to expenditure of resources and a failure to deal with the systemic security dynamics examined in Chapters 4–8. The logic of a single-minded national security strategy can easily lead to militarized and security-obsessed societies, of which the best contemporary examples are to be found in the Middle East. On the regional and system levels, it risks generating a highly charged power-security dilemma which will largely, perhaps completely, defeat the strategy by subjecting it to intense negative feedback, as in arms races and trade wars.

The weakness of the national security strategy by itself is that it cannot escape from the interactive consequences of its own effect on the system. Although national security measures may be argued to influence the sources of threat by having a deterrent effect on their perpetrators, any such effect must be balanced against the stimulation that the measures give to a power-security dilemma. Where a defence dilemma is also in operation, the logic of the national security strategy collapses even further, because the fear of war outweighs the fear of defeat. Under these conditions the danger arises of mass popular disaffection undermining the political foundations of the strategy. The national security strategy, then, falls victim both to Booth's critique of strategic ethnocentrism and Ashley's critique of 'technical rationality'.[5]

If the second option – an international security strategy – is adopted, security policy focuses on the sources and causes of threats, the purpose being not to block or offset the threats, but to reduce or eliminate them by political action. The early history of the European Community, for example, represents an international security strategy aimed at solving the rivalry between France and Germany. Similarly, the Conference on Security and Cooperation in Europe (CSCE) is an attempt to reduce the level of threat between East and West, and ASEAN a mechanism for reducing threats among the non-communist states of Southeast Asia. International security strategy has a number of advantages: it addresses the security problem at the regional and system levels squarely, and offers a prospect of a much more cost-efficient security policy than that available with a national security strategy. If threats have been eliminated at source, then resources do not have to be wasted in meeting each of them on its own terms. Such resource economies have a positive feedback effect in as much as they mute the power-security dilemma, and lead to a general lowering of threats all round. They make an attractive alternative to the costly and dangerous competitive security-seeking of uncoordinated national security strategies.

In addition, an international security strategy offers options other than association with a great power to the majority of lesser states whose resources do not permit them to pursue a comprehensive national security strategy on their own. One of the reasons why these lesser powers have posed continuing security problems to the great powers is precisely because they are unable to pursue an effective national security strategy on their own, and therefore need to be protected by a larger power. Pressure from the defence dilemma also makes a very good case for an international security strategy, since the risk of Armageddon in mutual deterrence needs to be offset by sufficient management of relations to ensure that the probabilities of major conflict remain as close to zero as possible.

The international security strategy is also not without its problems. The most obvious is that where a serious power struggle is in operation, the basic conditions for an international security strategy cannot be met. If states actually want to threaten each other, as when a revolutionary revisionist confronts the status quo, or when an orthodox revisionist makes an aggressive bid for hegemony, then there will be severe limits to the scope for threat reduction by negotiation. Those feeling threatened will be forced to adopt a national security approach. Related to this is the disadvantage that states lose considerable control over the factors that provide their security. An international security strategy depends on the management of relations among states, and in historical terms these are notoriously fickle. The instability of intentions as compared with the relative durability of capabilities is one of the longest-standing axioms of Realist international relations. If one rests one's security on restraint by others in offering threats, then one's security is at the mercy of changes of mind by others. This contrasts unfavourably with the self-reliance logic of the national security strategy, for it seems reasonable to argue that if one does not control the conditions that make one secure, then one is secure only in a superficial sense. The remedy for this problem is to follow the international security strategy to its logical conclusion of world government. But this requires the erosion of the state and the dissolution of the state system, eventualities that are quite unreal for the foreseeable future.

Taken by themselves, neither the national security nor the international security strategies are free from serious logical problems as bases for policy. The difficulty is that while national security in general represents a state level objective, this objective cannot be achieved without taking action not only on the state level, but also on the regional and system levels. Action on one level alone cannot work: because of the strain on national resources in the case of the state level, and because of the choice between excessive unreliability and excessive submergence of the state on the regional and system levels. The solution is a policy which mixes elements of a national security strategy with elements of an international security one, but this approach also faces a serious obstacle. While it would be going much too far to suggest that the two strategies are mutually exclusive, there is much between them that makes their simultaneous operation contradictory. The national security imperative of minimizing vulnerabilities sits unhappily with the risks of international agreement, and the prospects for international agreement are weakened by the power-security dilemma effects of a national security strategy.

The power of this contradiction is nicely illustrated by the domestic tensions arising from American attempts to implement deterrence according to the logic of mutually assured destruction (MAD). Although a national security strategy in that it was based on the capability to inflict unacceptable damage on one's opponent,

MAD contained the international security strategy element of remaining vulnerable to one's opponent as a matter of policy. The insecurity caused by this requirement worked against MAD both in public opinion and in the actual policies of the US strategic forces. It was eventually great enough to support the hugely expensive and logically unsound Strategic Defense Initiative promoted by the Reagan Administration as a backlash against MAD. Despite these problems, in the real world security policy eventually must be, and usually is, a mix, if only because the consequences of pursuing either strategy single-mindedly are so obviously counterproductive.

The most common middle ground is alliance policy as part of the balance of power game, as illustrated by Britain's move from splendid isolation to the Triple Entente in the years before 1914. Alliances manipulate the distribution of power by adding national security policies together, and in this sense they represent a step away from the state to the international level. But as the fractious history of NATO illustrates, alliances do not escape the severe tensions between national and international security strategies. More important, however, is that alliances represent much more a variation on the national security theme than a move towards international security. While they may serve some security needs for some states, they do not constitute an attempt to mitigate the basic dynamics of the power-security dilemma. They are more in line with the national security strategy of increasing strength and reducing vulnerability than they are with an international strategy aimed at reducing threats. At best, alliances can serve an international security strategy by creating an aggregated framework for reducing threats. NATO has long served as a structure within which Western European states can reduce the threats they would otherwise exchange among themselves. As a result of the events of 1989, it might also find a role as a multinational unit for negotiating security accommodations with the Soviet Union.

The question that remains is, what kind of mix between national and international strategies is most appropriate? The argument so far is that too much emphasis gets placed on the national security strategy and not enough on the international one, so the implication is that security policy needs a stronger international component. This point will be taken up in the final chapter.

The logical difficulties of choosing between national and international security strategies represent a core element in the national security policy problem, and would do so even if threats, and the means of dealing with them, were clear and understood factors in the equation. In fact, however, neither threats nor policy means are clear factors, and consequently a second, and more basic level of logical problem exists for security policy-makers. The application of logic requires that both clear facts and a reasonable understanding of cause-effect relationships exist. For many aspects of the security problem, neither criteria can be met. Trying to assess vulnerabilities, for example, leads back to the problems inherent in applying the concept of security to intangible referent objects such as the idea of the state. How clear a 'fact' is the idea of the state? How are threats to it caused when the fact itself is inherently changeable? Some facts and causes of a particular threat can be relatively clear (the capability of Soviet missiles to wreak mas-sive damage on the NATO states, the hostility that made such action plausible), while others are clouded in obscurity (the reasons for Soviet force strength, the probability that they would risk a nuclear war). Similarly, a choice of means might appear to strengthen a state's security position (the creation of a powerful German navy between 1898 and 1914), while in fact leading to an aggregate result which worsens it (stimulating a more than proportionate growth in British naval strength, and pushing Britain into an anti-German association with the two powers that had previously been its major rivals, France and Russia).

Similar contradictions disturb the logic of threats. Threats cannot be seen as a uniformly bad thing, no matter how objectively real they may be. Some level of external threat is often politically useful in suppressing domestic political squab-bling, and maintaining the political coherence and identity of the state.[6] Some gov-ernments will even cultivate threats in the hope of making their domestic task eas-ier. While it may be argued that this effect is most useful to repressive govern-ments, it cannot be denied that it plays a significant political role in most states. The history of American domestic politics, for example, would have been quite different in the absence of strong and widespread anti-communist sentiments. Soviet commentators showed themselves aware of this when they teased the United States during 1989 about the Gorbachev revolution having deprived the Americans of the comfortable familiarity of having the 'evil empire' as an enemy. Such unities of negatives are a political fact, and even if they serve mainly the interest of élites, they still leave the puzzle for security policy of 'When is a threat not a threat?' If threats are in some significant sense not threats, then the logical difficulty of security policy-making is compounded.

These problems of unclear facts, poorly understood causes, and possibilities for contradictory interpretation, get worse as one moves away from the highly par-ticular, day-to-day issues of national security, and towards the more general, larg-er-scale and longer-term perspectives that typify the security problem at the sys-tem level. It is relatively easy, though still in an absolute sense difficult, to deal logically with immediate matters such as what to do if another war breaks out in the Middle East. It is much more difficult to handle security questions of a larger scope, such as how to deal with the pressures on sovereignty created by a liberal international economic order, or what to do about the interplay between civil and military technology that proliferates potentialities for nuclear and chemical weapons, and the ballistic missiles with which to deliver them. These questions raise such huge logical complexities that they confound academics, let alone those working at the policymaking level. Yet, as the argument in this book indicates, many of the larger issues have a fundamental importance to the overall problem of national security.

The difficulty of linking these larger ideas to policy is illustrated by the theo-ry that hegemonic powers cannot sustain the role indefinitely, and indeed will be forced into decline by the process of doing so. If true, this theory suggests that, on security grounds, a country should avoid becoming a hegemonic power even if it has the opportunity to do so – a view not without supporters in contemporary Japan. On the other hand, being the hegemonic power has many security benefits and attractions. The theory also argues that the failure of states to take up hegemonic responsibility, as the United States did during the 1930s, destabilizes the system and reduces security for all. How is a logical policy position to be derived from this contradiction?

Another illustration of the logical difficulty of linking larger ideas to the policy level can be taken from the earlier discussion of system structure and process. Even if one finds convincing arguments like Waltz's, that bipolar systems are the safest in security terms, or like the one made in Chapter 4 about the security benefits of a mature anarchy, the question is how such ideals can be addressed in policy terms. No state commands the political resources to create massive systemic effects, and systemic evolution is easily dismissed as a complicated and long-term process that is effectively beyond the reach of individual policy actions. A purposeful move towards a specified system structure would involve not only an unprecedented degree of policy coordination among states, but also a massive political commitment to a largely theoretical proposition. The international economy is often thought about in macro-terms; but only during brief and infrequent watersheds, like that following the Second World War, can major changes in design be implemented by conscious policy. Most of the time, the character of the economic system is determined more by the cumulative impact of many actors pursuing their own interests than it is by the impact of international economic planning. The creation of the European Community (EC) is a rare example of macro-policy in the political domain. Although long in the making, the Community's internal cohesion and momentum had reached a sufficient pitch by the late 1980s to cause other major powers in the system to begin treating it as something like an equal. In this sense, the EC amounts to a major transformation in the international distribution of power, with profound implications for the structure of the system. Little thinking, outside the not unimportant resolution of the Western European security complex which it provides, appears to have been done as to the macro-purposes of this transformation. Those who accept Waltz's argument on the virtues of bipolarity must presumably view its implications with alarm.

National security policy-makers normally have enough difficulty coping with short-term problems without having to think on the grander scale of the system level. From their perspective, it is much easier to leave the system to take care of itself. The system as an entity is too unmanageable for them to deal with, and too poorly understood for them to know what to do about it even if they were so minded. It is beyond their national political mandate in scope, and requires resources of power and time that few if any have at their disposal. Most of them are anyway far too busy dealing with day-to-day crises even to be able to think about the system as a whole. At best the system can be relegated to the background with the hope that its natural development will somehow turn out to be progressive and benign, with factors such as technology, education, experience, interdependence and environmental constraints pushing steadily towards a more sensible arrangement of international relations. Only disarmament, free trade and world government among the grander ideas have actually made it onto their security policy agenda. But none of these is considered realistic. Their function is, at best, to inject a moral and idealist perspective into security policy and at worst, to provide a smokescreen for the practice of short-term, business-as-usual, power politics.

The difficulty of creating a practicable macro-dimension to national security policy tends to confine policy-makers to a narrow, short-term focus. But even at this more restricted level, the logical uncertainties of ends and means cause serious difficulties. Paul Kennedy's hugely successful book has the logical difficulty of security policy as its core theme. His whole argument centres on the difficulty of balancing military expenditure with the maintenance of sufficient productive investment to sustain the economic foundations of great power. Most great powers get it wrong, and in doing so condemn themselves to relative decline, as Kennedy now sees the United States doing. His list of logical policy dilemmas facing the United States is indicative of the shorter-range difficulties:

> how to build a good relationship with the PRC without abandoning Taiwan; how to 'support the stability and independence of friendly countries' while trying to control the flood of their exports to the American market; how to make the Japanese assume a larger share of the defence of the western Pacific without alarming its various neighbours; how to maintain US bases in, for example, the Philippines without provoking local resentments; how to reduce the American military presence in South Korea without sending the wrong 'signal' to the North...[7]

These difficulties are compounded by the lack of clear direction from a well-developed sense of larger objectives, priorities and methods. No benevolent invisible hand operates to ensure that general well-being results from the pursuit of individual national security interests. Indeed, the invisible hand easily operates to reverse effect, amplifying national security-seeking into the generally malign result of the power-security dilemma. Because the large picture is so unclear, even short-range policy can be hard to assess. How, for instance, can policy-makers determine the appropriate range and direction for their policies? If security horizons are set too widely, then resources are wasted unnecessarily, and the countervailing operation of the power-security dilemma is intensified. If they are set too narrowly, then threats will already have become dangerously large before action is taken. The United States again provides an example here, having set its security horizons too narrowly during the interwar years, and, by way of reaction, too widely during the Cold War. Can it be argued in retrospect that either isolationism in the 1930s, or the intervention in Vietnam in the 1960s and 1970s, served the larger purposes of American national security?

Logical conundrums of the kind associated with utilitarian calculus arise from this problem of temporal range. For example, is a policy like nuclear deterrence, which serves short-term interests, but subjects the interests of future generations to grave risks, sound? Was the 1919 Treaty of Versailles a good policy in view of the undeniable short-term security benefits to France and others, as weighed against longer-term outcome in the European security complex with which the Treaty is now associated? Should the United States have backed the Shah of Iran as a regional ally as much as it did during the 1970s, given the consequences of his fall for the 1980s? These questions are unfair in the sense that they apply the easy critical wisdom of hindsight to decisions made under pressure and with virtually no reliable knowledge of future effects. The purpose, however, is not to score debating points, but to illustrate how poorly the normal logic of national security works, even by its own standards. The ultimate example here must be the decision by the German and Austro-Hungarian authorities to facilitate the activities of Lenin and his Bolsheviks during the early years of the twentieth century. Few short-term security ploys aimed at weakening a rival power can have produced such disastrous long-term results as this.

Applying long-term criteria to the judgement of short-term security goals can produce alarming results. In the normal context of security analysis, invasion and occupation rank just below total destruction at the top of the hierarchy of threats to national security. Such a threat is seen to justify extreme measures like those taken by invaded and threatened countries during the Second World War. On the 'better dead than red' principle and its counterparts, occupation might even be resisted by something approaching national suicide – a prospect that faced front-line states in Europe for over forty years. If a long historical view is taken, however, invasion and occupation might be seen as often being no bad thing. Although it might be hard for the generation that experiences it, one could argue that it is seldom worse than war unless the invader is bent on genocide.

Many historical invasions appear in retrospect to have produced a fruitful mixing of cultures. The Roman and Norman invasions of Britain are not now seen as disasters. Much of the Mediterranean world prospered under Roman rule. Japan can hardly be said to have been devastated by American occupation. Even Eastern Europe did not do too badly during the first three decades after 1945 when compared with its previous condition; certainly not so badly that annihilation would seem a responsible alternative if a choice were offered. One can argue that European civilization has been built on the fruits of invasion and cultural mixing. Such thoughts, of course, amount to heresy in relation to conventional security thinking and the political commitment to the independent state on which it rests. They serve not only to illustrate the logical difficulties of security policy, but also to raise core questions about the purposes and priorities of security policy-makers.

PERCEPTUAL PROBLEMS

Logical problems are only part of the difficulty inherent in the national security policy process. In most areas they are reinforced by perceptual uncertainties. The perceptual problem is fundamental because it affects the entire information base on which the decision-making process rests. Perception affects both what things are seen as facts, and what significance these 'facts' carry in security analysis. It has two components, which are the same for individuals as for states: perceptions vary according to where the observer is located in relation to the thing viewed, and according to the internal constitution of the viewer. Positional perspectives vary in time and space. Thus the fall of the Roman Empire looked quite different to a sixth-century citizen of Rome than it did to one living now, and the First World War looked quite different from Japan than it did from France. Constitutional factors reflect the sensory capability, historical memory and psychological make-up of the viewer. As Robert Jervis sums it up, one tends to see what one believes.[8] Perceptions in eighteenth-century Japan were conditioned by the fact that contact with the outside world was deliberately kept very limited. Most Third World countries find their view of the international system heavily conditioned by their colonial experience. Marxist thinkers see the economic troubles of the West quite differently from those trained to liberal economic views. These two components of the perceptual problem apply to all the states in the international system. Each of them has a different positional perspective on the objects and events which make up the information base of the system, and the constitutional structure of each is sufficiently different from that of all the others to ensure that they see any single event or thing differently. The process maintains itself as each state accumulates a distinctive history through which its perception of current events gets filtered.

The mechanisms of perception are rooted in the Byzantine complexities of human psychology, and have already been extensively explored in the context of international politics by Robert Jervis.[9] Perception is distorted initially because information is imperfect. The relevant information for security policy is enormous in extent, covering almost all areas of human activity. It changes and expands constantly. Much of it, such as the depth of political allegiance (a perennial topic in alliances), the quality of military equipment and organization under wartime conditions, the stability of governments and the motives of leaders, is inherently unknowable with any accuracy, even to the actors themselves. Even the greatest powers can gather only a small part of this information as a basis for their security policy. Such information as they get will be distorted by the research process (less will be available from enemies than from friends), and by deliberate deception (attempts at secrecy and bluff, like Khrushchev's cultivation of a missile gap during the late 1950s). Once received, this information will be further distorted by the various processes of deletion, condensation and interpretation which are necessary to reduce it to a form concise enough to be used by those at the business end of policymaking.

Just as in the party game where a message is passed along a chain of people by word of mouth, information going into a government bureaucratic network will emerge at the other end in a scarcely recognizable form. In the process it will encounter the numerous filters of conventional wisdom, each of which will attempt to reconcile incoming data with pre-existing theories, or mental sets. Information which tends to support the conventional wisdom will be amplified and passed on, that which tends to cast doubt on it will be suppressed, devalued or diverted.[10] The aggregate effect of these distortions will be to protect the conventional wisdom against countervailing information up to the point at which the evidence against it becomes overwhelming, either because of its cumulative weight (such as the failure of the Americans to win in Vietnam year after year), or because some highly visible transformational event makes the old view publicly insupportable (such as the collapse of assumptions about a Soviet threat during 1989 as it became clear that Moscow had abandoned its policy of enforcing ideological conformity in Eastern Europe).

This tendency to delay and distort the rationalizing effect of new information has major consequences for the national security problem. The perceptual factor easily feeds into the power-security dilemma by amplifying and perpetuating negative images. Once a pattern of hostility is established, as between the United States and the Soviet Union, each will tend to see the other as an enemy, and assume that worst interpretations of behaviour are correct. Disproportionately large amounts of information will be required to break this cycle. The process is universal, and tends to amplify itself in each of the actors individually, precisely because it feeds back the behaviour of the other actors in the system. Seeing and treating another state as an enemy increases the probability that it will become one, so reinforcing the initial perception. Desirable processes can also benefit from this mechanism. International society can be viewed as a kind of collective mental set involving perceptions of other actors as belonging to the same community as oneself. As Jervis argues, mental sets and simplifying theories of some sort are necessary if any sense is to be made of the huge volume of incoming information.[11] Without some means of ordering and simplifying data, policy-makers would be even more confused and inconsistent than they are with them. Each event would have to be interpreted on its own merits, and no sense of pattern would exist around which to structure policy.

Some of the other perceptual problems identified by Jervis include a tendency to assume that other actors are more centrally in control of themselves than you are, and that your role in and influence on events are greater than they in fact are.[12] Others are assumed to be more centralized because one observes mainly their behavioural output. The outside observer easily imputes all behaviour to conscious central command and control. In observing one's own behaviour, whether individual or state, one is much more aware of the confusion, conflict and error that underlie it. If central control is assumed, then conspiratorial assessments of motive are justified, but if weak central control is assumed, then a more forgiving and less threatening analysis may be appropriate. Enormous differences in analysis and inferences for Western security policy occurred, for example, depending on whether the Soviet invasion of Afghanistan was seen as one more section of a carefully laid, long-term plan for Soviet advancement towards the Arabian Sea and the Persian Gulf, or as a bungled overreaction to events in Iran, combined with traditional Soviet paranoia about the stability of its buffer-states. As a general feature of international relations, a tendency to apply much stricter standards to the behaviour of others than to one's own, feeds directly into the mechanisms which drive and maintain the power-security dilemma.

These and other perceptual mechanisms clearly play an important role in the security policy-making process. They work at all levels, from the generation and influence of public opinion, through the bureaucratic labyrinths of government machinery, to the individual personalities of leaders. They operate constantly, but can be intensified sharply under the pressure of crisis. During a crisis, time for analysis and decision shrinks, the risks and stakes attached to policy behaviour rise, and uncertainties of information inflate. An extensive literature on crises explores both the theoretical and practical effects of these pressures on the psychology of perception and decision-making.[13]

Even under routine conditions of policy, perceptual factors can play a fundamental role. If, for example, one assumes that one's opponent sees things in basically the same way as oneself, then this can serve as a foundation for policy, because one can calculate his reactions to be roughly what one's own would be if the positions were reversed. For many years during the 1950s, 1960s and early 1970s, the conventional wisdom in the West took roughly this view of Soviet strategic doctrine. If the Soviets accepted evolving Western views of nuclear deterrence, albeit with some lag because of their technological inferiority, then policies such as MAD could be pursued with considerable hope that a stable balance of deterrence would result. The falseness of this assumption was revealed during the 1970s, as growing Soviet military strength made its policy more obvious, and this revelation stimulated a reassessment of Western strategic doctrine. Fritz W. Ermarth outlines the historical, geostrategic, doctrinal and military differences in perspective between the two which make it surprising, in retrospect, that any perception of parallel perspectives could have been sustained in the first place.[14]

Instances like this illustrate both the pitfalls which perceptual factors place in the path of the policy process, and the real difficulty of establishing common ground on which to base more orderly relations. Because positional and constitutional differences among states generate different interpretations of the same reality, the natural structure of the system tends to enhance misunderstanding and feed the dynamic of the power-security dilemma. From this perspective, international relations cannot be compared to a chess game, in which a struggle for power and position proceeds according to agreed rules which establish a common perception of the significance of events. Instead, security relations are more like a game in which the players follow somewhat different rules. Each player believes his own rules to be universally valid, and assumes the other player to know this. Enough similarity exists between their rules to enable a game to proceed, but where differences occur, each side assumes that the other is trying to cheat. Not surprisingly, the board is often over-turned in the ensuing squabble.

Logical problems in security analysis are inherent in the nature of the issues, particularly in the weak understanding of cause-effect relations and the conse-quent inability to make reliable predictions. Because of the extraordinary com-plexity and mutability of cause-effect relations in the international system, solu-tions to this problem are unlikely to be developed either quickly or all at once. Perceptual problems are rooted in human psychology, and although some counter-vailing measures can be applied, Jervis concludes that 'no formula will eliminate misperception or reveal what image is correct. Faced with ambiguous and confus-ing evidence, decision-makers must draw inferences that will often prove to be incorrect.'[15] Because neither problem can be easily removed, security analysis is plagued by questions which have either no clear answer, or several equally plau-sible ones. Where such questions exist, the way is clear for politicization of the security policy process, as different interests seek to make their view prevail.

POLITICAL PROBLEMS

The possible rationality of the policy-making process in any state is necessarily limited by the logical and perceptual constraints just discussed. The prospect for rationality is further diminished by the nature of the political process itself. The internal political process of the state is not a routinized, mechanistic, logical, pol-icy-making device, but a dynamic, potentially unstable and normally fractious system of relations among contending interests. This is especially so in pluralist societies, but has its bureaucratic variants even in highly centralized states. As argued in Chapter 5, domestic disputes form the first basic level of enquiry in analysing security problems. One must, then, expect that the national security questions raised by relations between the state and its environment will feed into the pattern of domestic political alignments and disputes. The impact of security policy choices on domestic political interests is seldom neutral, and it would be foolish to assume that domestic interests would allow policy to be made accord-ing to the detached logic of international system analysis alone.

Disputes about security questions concern not only the relations between the state and its international environment, but also relations within the state. As argued in most of the preceding chapters, the state is not a unitary actor. It is per-haps best viewed as a container, or an arena, within which a variety of powers and interests pursue their political life. Disputes and contradictions are the normal stuff of domestic politics. Individual security interests must sometimes clash with national security policy despite the necessary existence of some common ground between the two levels. Domestic contradictions among groups of people with dif-ferent interests exist everywhere. Where these are severe enough to overwhelm, or prevent the creation of, shared norms and legitimate institutions, they create weak states.

The resulting political struggle occurs within and around institutional and normative structures which are unique to each state. In other words, the political process happens everywhere, but is different in style, form, emphasis, organization and procedure from one country to the next. This is the familiar world of comparative politics, with its emphasis on the innumerable paths to political order that have evolved to suit the conditions of different countries. Regardless of these differences, however, it is the domestic political system in each state that actually produces policy. Nowhere does this process allow a detached and rational formulation of security policy. Everywhere, in some form, the dynamic of competing interests intrudes into the security policy process, with the result that extraneous influences become significant determinants of the policy that the state eventually adopts. This is true whether the issue is a narrow one of means, such as whether or not to build a particular weapons system, or a broad one of ends, such as whether to adopt a neutral or aligned policy in the major rivalries of the day. National security policy, in other words, cannot be seen as an unadulterated response to the inputs from the international system. It is skewed and distorted by other interests, and it is worth taking a brief look at what these are.

The purpose here is simply to indicate the scope and character of the problem, without exploring it in detail. Within the state exist many layers of sub-state actors, ranging from the government and its various bureaucratic organs, through the economic, political and media organizations, to the individual citizens, both as individuals and as the amorphous entity known as public opinion. Many of these actors have some interest in national security and involve themselves in varying degrees in the security policy-making process. The problem is that most of them have other interests as well, and these bias their security interests in a variety of ways. This point can be illustrated by glancing at the cross-pressures affecting newspapers, political parties, government bureaucracies and business organizations.

Newspapers are interested in the subject matter of national security, but are constrained in what they report by their need to sell their product to readers and advertisers. Stories of scandal, malice, threat, crisis, mismanagement, conflict and death will sell more newspapers than long-winded and complicated analyses like those in this book. Because of their commercial interest, newspapers distort the public view of what is important in national security, focusing attention on short-term issues and military means while largely ignoring longer-range and more abstract issues. What gets defined as news is to some extent determined by what will sell. Where newspapers are controlled by the state, what gets defined as news is usually what serves the interests of the government.

Political parties suffer from some of the same dual interest pressures as the media. Security policy must be one of their areas of interest, but only one of many, and they must strive to attract a mass following. Complex, or highly unorthodox positions on security policy will both limit their attraction to voters and open them up to attacks from their opponents. Because security policy is so contestable, it can become a useful club with which opposing parties can beat each other regardless of circumstances. Whatever one side advocates, the other can make a plausible case against on grounds of waste, cost, militarism, risk or ideology. Such attacks may occur regardless of what the parties do when in office. In Britain, pro-military Conservatives cut the Navy on economic grounds, while ostensibly anti-military Labour governments allow major nuclear warhead programmes to proceed in secret. Posturing on security issues may have more to do with electoral needs, ideological pretensions, internal party power struggles, and the rituals of party rivalry than with serious thinking about the issues themselves. Considerable domestic political mileage can be wrung from security issues on the principle that a unity of negatives is easier to create and maintain than is a unity of positives. If political cohesion cannot be built on the common ground of what people want, then it can be built on the common ground of what they can be brought to fear or hate. A unity of negatives based on making a bogey out of some foreign power, or out of nuclear weapons, can usefully cover both a lack of constructive ideas and a multitude of domestic disagreements.

More parochially, parties may support certain security policies because they provide employment in politically sensitive areas. Thus weapons might be produced more for reasons to do with the domestic political economy than for reasons deriving from the international situation. These and other interests can all affect the way a political party deals with security policy. This is not to argue that parties have no substantive positions and beliefs on security policy, and that they are therefore totally opportunistic in relation to security issues. Rather, it is to point out that many other considerations affect their position and their ability to act, and that the effect of these is to introduce domestic political considerations into the security policy-making process. The kinds of pressures on parties will vary according to whether the country is a multiparty system or not, but even in one-party states, the party must respond to domestic political interests if it wishes to remain in office. At worst, it will require the armed forces for domestic control, and this need will distort national security policy by importing it into the domestic political arena.

Government bureaucracies of various kinds participate in security policy-making, and each of them brings to the process its own mix of interests. Some will have direct interest in the issues, like those responsible for defence, foreign policy, trade and finance. Others will have the indirect interest of being competitors in the continuous game of resource allocation, in which departments do battle with each other for shares of the budgetary pie. Consequently, security policy will not only be subjected to cross-cutting interests, such as Treasury concerns to limit public spending, or Department of Employment concerns to maintain defence production jobs, but also it will be put through the mill of resource allocation politics, where outcomes may depend as much on political strength and skill as on the merits of the issues. Even within a single department like Defence, many institutional and bureaucratic factors can intervene to skew the logic of security policy. Service traditions and inter-service rivalries are among the more notorious sources of such influence. Different services often develop strong attachments to their own traditions and to the instruments on which those traditions rest. These attachments can lead them to resist technological developments that will undermine their traditions. Thus the Royal Navy was reluctant to abandon wood and sail for iron and steam until the pressure of French technological improvements forced it to. The transition meant the loss of a centuries-long tradition on which British naval superiority and style of naval life had rested. Armies were similarly reluctant to abandon horse cavalry.

In modern times, technological developments threaten even more fundamental changes. Navies still cling to the idea of large surface ships even though they have become increasingly costly and vulnerable, because without them the entire naval tradition is jeopardized. Air forces continue to advocate manned bombers because the whole air force tradition and glamour is based on men flying in planes. Missiles and automated aircraft threaten to eliminate pilots entirely, and with them, the central role and symbol of the air force itself. In addition, the services struggle among themselves to capture functions which will strengthen their case in the scramble for resources. Armies, navies and air forces in various countries have competed for control over strategic nuclear weapons, and the additional resources and status associated with them. In earlier periods, air forces had to fight for a separate existence, while armies and navies tried to hold on to their own air components. These organizational vested interests all feed into the security policy process and play their part in determining its outcome, especially so in that the services are a main supplier of military advice to governments. A good case study of the counter-rational pressures which result can be found in the resistance of the US Air Force to the results of the strategic bombing survey carried out at the end of the Second World War. The Air Force could not (and did not) accept the results of the survey without undermining a major part of the rationale for its existence. Institutional survival demanded that the facts about military effectiveness be ignored, and one consequence of this was the savage and futile aerial campaign against Vietnam two decades later.[16]

Industrial and commercial organizations also have interests in security policy, and again these interests mix with their other concerns to produce distortions in rationality. Such organizations may be more or less closely attached to the government, depending on whether the economy leans towards central planning or towards the market, and this will cause significant differences in their other concerns, particularly on matters such as profit. These organizations can have an interest in security policy either because they produce military equipment, or because, like oil multinationals, they have external interests, such as markets, investments, transportation routes or sources of supply that they wish to see come under the aegis of national security policy.

Arms manufacturers in a market economy will have a number of organizational interests of their own that can affect national security policy.[17] In particular, they will have the normal concerns of business about profit, about creating a reliable demand for their product, and about participating in technological advance in their field. Unless they can ensure these things, their existence as organizations is in jeopardy. Governments, as a rule, will share some objectives with the arms industry. They will wish to ensure that good quality weapons are available for their armed forces, and that research and development is adequate to match the efforts of possible enemies. They may want to keep in being a surplus capacity in the industry in order to allow for a rapidly increased demand in time of crisis or war. Where resources allow, governments will prefer to maintain as much domestic independence in arms manufacture as possible in order to minimize constraints on their freedom of action, though this logic applies mainly to larger powers capable of mounting a significant arms industry in the first place.

This common interest between governments and companies can result in at least two effects which might influence security policy. First, the desire to maintain a sufficient, or surplus, national capacity, combined with the companies' desire to assure markets and make profits, can lead to pressure either to consume more than is objectively required, or to export. For countries like Britain and France, maintenance of a substantial armaments industry requires the cultivation of exports, because domestic demand is too low to support such industry by itself. Larger producers like the United States could maintain their industries on domestic demand, but exports offer a way to reduce costs to the government (by increasing economies of scale in production), to ease the problem of keeping the industry in regular work, to maintain surplus capacity and to increase profits for the companies. An interest in the arms trade, once established, can impinge on security policy in a number of ways. It creates ties to the buyers which affect national security alignments, like those between the United States and Iran under the Shah. It stimulates secondary arms races among purchasers, like those in the Middle East, which can in turn affect the general security of the system. It can create a vested interest in maintaining exports by not being too concerned about the stimulation of rivalries and conflict elsewhere. Similar arguments could be applied to the nuclear power industry, which also illustrates how economic and security dynamics can interact to distort national security policy-making.[18] Economic imperatives work to spread nuclear materials, knowledge and technology to countries like India, Pakistan, Brazil, Argentina, South Africa, Israel, Iraq and others whose interest in nuclear weapons is only thinly disguised.

The second effect concerns the process of technological improvement. Both governments and companies share this interest, but for different reasons. Governments are concerned at least to maintain the quality of their military equipment to the general standard prevailing in the international system, although in some cases (war, planned attack, arms racing) they may also be interested in occupying the leading edge of technological development. Companies may be interested in technological advance for its own sake, with many individuals within them deriving their job satisfaction from pushing forward the state of the art. One has only to look at the number of books published about weapons in order to get some idea of the source and strength of this fascination with the beauty and power of military technology. Companies generally have economic incentives to drive their interest in technology. On simple grounds, better technology gives them a commercial edge in sales. More subtly, sustained pressure for technological improvement increases the pace of obsolescence. If equipment needs to be replaced or upgraded more frequently, then companies can be assured of more regular demand which solves, though at considerable cost, their problem of continuity and the government's problem of assured capacity. A sustained push behind military technology feeds quickly into the arms dynamic, leading both to the self-sustaining rivalry of military competition, and to the self-locking effect in which arms racing becomes internalized in the rivalry between arms manufacturers within a single state. This process can have major implications for national security, even though it derives initially from factors internal to the state and is extraneous to the pattern of external threats which define the national security problem in the first place.

These illustrations underline the point that the structure and character of the domestic political process constitute a major independent variable in national security policy-making. Not only does the domestic political process inject a large number of powerful cross-cutting interests into security policy, but also it subjects that policy to competition with other state policy priorities. In other words, national security policy is disconnected from the rationality of the external security problem not only by domestic intrusions into the policy process, but also by a political market in which even the distorted policy may get bumped or altered while interacting with other policies competing for state attention and resources. Thus the debate in the United States about SDI could not escape links both to the budget deficit, and to pressures for a dose of military Keynesianism to stimulate American industry. Conversely, the Marshall Plan, which would have been impossible to sell politically as an economic policy, gained acceptance in 1947 because of its association with national security interests.[19]

CONCLUSIONS: POLICY-MAKING AS PART OF THE NATIONAL SECURITY PROBLEM

The argument in this chapter has been that the logical and perceptual problems arising from security complicate much of the input into domestic policy-making; that the policy-making process has a limited ability to solve these problems; and that it adds its own dimension of further difficulties to the national security problem overall. The result is that the national security policy which goes out into the international system is as much a product of internal factors, many of them extraneous, as it is of the external ones that provide its principal justification. These arguments could easily be read as a critique of the domestic political process, and in one sense they are. Their inference is that domestic factors get in the way of a rational formulation of national security policy. By doing so, they distort, impede and confuse the process by which the state deals with threats and, by implication, they result in less rational, less effective and possibly even counterproductive policies. One marvels, for example, at the domestic goings-on that resulted in Panama declaring itself to be at war with the United States late in 1989.

Two counter-arguments redress this critique. The first is that no purely detached and rational policy-making process is available in the real world. The logical and perceptual impediments to rationality are to a considerable extent insurmountable, and to assume that an apolitical policy is feasible in a quintessentially political entity like a state, is both naive and contradictory. Domestic political factors will always impinge on national security policy, if only because the whole decision-making apparatus of the state is largely set up in relation to domestic interests. In the case of a large and influential country like the United States it may anyway be difficult to distinguish between domestic and foreign policy. Ostensibly domestic policies on issues as varied as interest rates and decisions about uranium enrichment capacity[20] can have dramatic consequences for other countries.

The second argument reinforces the first, on the grounds that a broad domestic interest in national security policy is justified because of the massive feedback effect that security policy can have on domestic society. Two obvious ways in which security policy can intrude into domestic society are through its costs and through its risks. These considerations alone would justify a major domestic interest in the formulation of such policy. By the late 1980s, the cost of national defence seldom dropped below 1 per cent of Gross National Product (GNP). The norm fell between 2 and 4 per cent. For the United States it was over 6 per cent; for the Soviet Union well over 10 per cent; and for several Middle Eastern states over 20 per cent. The absolute amounts involved are huge. The United States spent $260 billion in 1988, and the major European powers spent over $20 billion each. Forty-three states spent over $1 billion each. Even Japan, which is normally thought to be very lightly armed, spent over $15 billion, outspending China by a factor of three.[21] These sums often amount to a sizeable proportion of public expenditure, and as disarmament enthusiasts never tire of pointing out, their opportunity costs in alternative social goods and services are very great. More schools, more hospitals, cleaner environments, more disposable income, more investment and suchlike all have to be weighed against expenditures on defence. This implies a set of choices about social priorities between defence and other values, and such choices are what the domestic political process is all about. The risks in security policy are more abstract and intermittent than the costs, but pose even graver questions. Bungled policy might lead to the termination of all social values in nuclear obliteration, or to their drastic revision as a result of invasion or revolution. For these reasons, the substance of security policy is clearly a legitimate matter for domestic political concern.

On more subtle grounds, one can increase the strength of this argument by exploring the numerous ways in which security policy can influence the basic structure of political society. Most of these links are well known. Many of them come under the general heading of the militarization of society. They include arguments about conscription, about military influence in government, about the military-industrial complex as a powerful elite interest, about the corruption of higher values by the blatant willingness to use force, about the infringement of civil liberties by the requirements of domestic security and about the self-perpetu-ating logic of security demands on society which arise from the power-security dilemma. These arguments link to those about resources above, for at some point, discussion about the allocation of resources becomes indistinguishable from debate about the value priorities at stake. Commitment to a military establishment creates a new power in domestic politics which will generate organizational imperatives of its own. These imperatives may, in the long run, result in conse-quences which outweigh the original purpose of having a military establishment. Military interests may lead to the self-defeating cycles of an internalized arms race, or to the militarization of national politics which is such a problem in many weak states. As one Latin American observer put it, 'What we are doing is build-ing up armies which weigh nothing in the international scale, but which are Juggernaughts for the internal life of each country. Each country is being occupied by its own army.'[22]

On this level, national security policy has implications which run through the entire structure of the state. An obsession with security can lead to versions of the Spartan-style warfare state in which all political structures and values are subor-dinated to the accumulation of military power. This model has echoes in places like Israel, Syria, Iraq and until recently the Soviet Union, where high levels of mobilization, or readiness to mobilize very quickly, have become a permanent condition rather than a wartime phenomenon, and permeate society with their effects.

The linkage between security and other state structures is obvious in these extreme cases, but it can also be found in more normal circumstances. One might follow Alexis de Tocqueville[23] by arguing that while the political institutions of the United States are excellently designed to contain and manage the numerous and divergent political forces within that vast society, they are, as a direct conse-quence, poorly suited to the conduct of foreign and security policy. Features which serve well in the general political context, such as openness to pressure groups, intricate checks and balances, frequent elections and a politically appointed civil service are ill-designed for the specialized needs of foreign and security policy. They impede continuity of policy where it is most vital (international negotiations, arms policy), and compel it where flexibility might serve better (anti-communism, notions of military superiority, extravagant energy consumption, Middle Eastern policy). They amplify the role of domestic factors and interests in the policymak-ing process, and restrict input from, and sensitivity to, the needs, fears and dynam-ics of other actors in the international system. Such criticisms are not unique to the United States, they are merely more obvious there because of the remarkable openness of the American system and the extent of its impact on the rest of the world. Most states respond more to domestic pressures and interests than to exter-nal ones, but when the United States floats the value of its currency, or subsidizes the price of oil, or raises its interest rates, the effect in the international system is large.

To the extent that domestic forces cause these actions, foreign policy gets made without reference to the rest of the international system. If domestic factors dominate policymaking in most states, then the international system becomes one in which feedback between the units is weak. Behaviour, in other words, is internally generated, and relatively insensitive to the effects which it creates in the system. States cannot be cool, calculating and rational actors in relation to the international dimension of the national security problem. But to the extent that domestic factors dominate decision-making, their behaviour towards each other will be myopic, insensitive and inconsistent. They will be attuned to others as threats and opportunities, and to themselves as possessors of rights and as victims of uncontrollable circumstances. But they will be only dimly aware of how others see them, of the extent to which others are victims of uncontrollable circumstances, of the impact that their own actions make externally and of the sensitivities that drive the domestic politics of others.

Self-centred actors are the key to turning an anarchy into a chaos. In individuals, an excess of internally generated behaviour over behaviour that is rationally responsive to the environment is usually classified as autism or insanity (or occasionally as religious insight or genius). An immature anarchy thus possesses some of the relational qualities of a lunatic asylum. If each actor generates most of its behaviour internally, treating others primarily as sources of threat, then the combined effect is to maximize the power-security dilemma which encompasses them all. The internal dynamics of each will result in policies which others see as threatening and inflexible, and because the policies are internally set, they will be difficult to change. National security strategies will dominate by default, because that is the only level that receives serious policy-making attention. As Rosecrance notes, 'one of the fundamental reasons for tension in the international system is the formulation of objectives and policies on a purely domestic basis.'[24] This political dominance of the state level amplifies the singularity of positional perspective which is the natural geographical and historical heritage of each state. Each tends to interpret the system from the perspective of its own position within it. When domestic political preoccupations intrude as well, the propensity to take a parochial view grows stronger. In as much as each state is governed by parochial views, no strong common view of the system as a whole can develop among them. The absence of such a common view in turn reinforces the parochial impulse, because the system appears to be an unmanageable chaos which leaves no option but to rely on one's own resources.

The inescapable conclusion from this argument is that the structure of domestic politics must be made more sensitive to the international environment. Mature anarchy requires mature states, which is to say states that are stable and developed enough within themselves to be able to take the interests of their neighbours into account in their own policy-making. Outwardly referenced behaviour is difficult to sustain if it loses elections, and so mature states require mature societies that have internalized the understanding that national securities are interdependent, and that excessively self-referenced security policies, whatever their jingoistic attractions, are ultimately self-defeating. The importance of the domestic sphere means that international society cannot develop unless national societies become fundamentally less parochial. The Nordic countries offer one evolutionary model of a group of states that has moved through this maturing process from fierce military rivalry to security community. But historical learning is a slow and uneven process. There is a possibility that we can count on the accelerating pressures of rising density to instil such understanding more swiftly than has occurred in the past. But as the drawn-out difficulties of European integration show, societal and political parochialism is resilient even among strong states. One possible approach to this apparent impasse is to design security policies that work on all four levels – individual, state, region and system – and this idea will be taken up in the last chapter.

NOTES

1. Ole Wæever, 'Security, the speech act: analyzing the politics of a word', second draft, Centre for Peace and Conflict Research, Copenhagen, June 1989, pp, 35–6.
2. See chapter I, note 24.
3. Macbeth, III. v. The speaker is Hecate. The meaning of the quote in its original context is that an excessive feeling of security leads to carelessness in action, and is therefore a cause of weakness and vulnerability. This sense might also be applied to the national security problem, inasmuch as excessive military power, and its accompanying policy orientation, can lead to underestimation of other factors, as illustrated by the American performance in Vietnam and the Soviet one in Afghanistan.
4. For an elaboration along these lines, see Bengt Sundelius, 'Coping with structural security threats', in Otmar Höll (ed.), *Small States in Europe and Dependence* (Vienna: Austrian Institute for International Affairs, 1983), pp. 298–304.
5. Ken Booth, *Strategy and Ethnocentrism* (London: Croom Helm, 1979); Richard K. Ashley *The Political Economy of War and Peace* (London: Pinter, 1980), pp. 205–30.
6. John Burton, *Global Conflict: The domestic sources of international crisis* (Hemel Hempstead: Harvester Wheatsheaf, 1984).
7. Paul Kennedy, *The Rise and Fall of the Great Powers* (London: Fontana, 1988), pp. 669–70.
8. Robert Jervis, *Perception and Misperception in International Politics* (Princeton, NJ: Princeton University Press, 1976), p. 170.
9. *ibid.* See also J. C, Farrell and A. P. Smith, *Image and Reality in World Politics* (New York: Columbia University Press, 1968).
10. Jervis, *op. cit.* (note 8), chs, 4, 5, and 7, Daniel Yergin, *Shattered Peace* (Boston: Houghton Mifflin, 1978), can be read as a case study of the establishment of a major mental-set in American policy-making.
11. Jervis, *op. cit.* (note 8) pp. 160–2, 175–6.
12. *ibid.*, chs 8 and 9.
13. See, *inter alia*, Charles F. Hermann (ed.), *International Crises* (New York: Free Press, 1972); Raymond Cohen, *Threat Perception in International Crises* (Madison: University of Wisconsin Press, 1979); D. Frei (ed.), *International Crisis and Crisis Management*

(Aldershot: Gower, 1978); 'Special issue on international crises', *International Studies Quarterly*, 21:1 (1977); Ole R. Holsti 'The 1914 case', *American Political Science Review*, 59 (1965); Graham T. Allison, *Essence of Decision* (Boston: Little Brown, 1971).

14. Fritz W. Ermarth, 'Contrasts in American and Soviet strategic thought', *International Security*, 3:2 (1978).

15. Jervis, *op. cit.* (note 8), p. 409.

16. John K. Galbraith, *A Life in Our Times* (Boston: Houghton Mifflin, 1981), pp. 195–6, 201, 204–6, 213, 215, 225–37.

17. On the arms industry, see Barry Buzan, *An Introduction to Strategic Studies: Military technology and international relations* (London: Macmillan, 1987), chs 3, 4, 7, 8.

18. Michael J. Brenner, *Nuclear Power and Non-Proliferation* (Cambridge: Cambridge University Press, 1981).

19. L. B. Krause and J. S. Nye, 'Reflections on the economics and politics of international economic organizations', in C. F. Bergsten and L. B. Krause (eds), *World Politics and International Economics* (Washington, DC: Brookings Institution, 1975), pp. 324–5.

20. For an interesting study of this, see Brenner, *op. cit.* (note 18).

21. Figures from *The Military Balance 1989–90* (London: IISS, 1989), pp. 210–11.

22. Edvardo Santoz, quoted in Edwin Lieuwen, *Arms and Politics in Latin America* (New York: Praeger, 1961), pp. 236–8.

23. Alexis de Tocqueville, *Democracy in America* (New York: Vintage Books, 1945), vol. I, pp. 241–4, a theme also taken up Kennedy, *op. cit.* (note 7), pp. 665–92.

24. Richard Rosecrance, *International Relations: Peace or war?* (New York: McGraw-Hill, 1973), p, 186.

chapter ten | concluding thoughts on international security studies

OVERVIEW: THE AGENDA OF SECURITY

If there is one theme that stands out as common to all the preceding chapters it is that understanding the national security problem requires a wide-ranging under-standing of the major levels of analysis and issue sectors that comprise the field of International Studies. Although the term 'national security' suggests a phenom-enon on the state level, the connections between that level and the individual, regional and system levels are too numerous and too strong to deny. Similarly, although 'national security' suggests a focus in the political and military sectors, where the state is most strongly established, the idea cannot be properly compre-hended without bringing in the actors and dynamics from the societal, economic and environmental sectors. The concept of security binds together these levels and sectors so closely that it demands to be treated in an integrative perspective. Some sense can be made of individual, national and international security, and of mili-tary, political, societal, economic and environmental security, as ideas in their own right. But a full understanding of each can only be gained if it is related to the oth-ers. Attempts to treat security as if it was confined to any single level or any sin-gle sector invite serious distortions of understanding.

It might be useful at this point to recapitulate the major linkages and contra-dictions that have emerged in the preceding chapters: starting with levels of analy-sis, and finishing with issue sectors.

The security of individuals is locked into an unbreakable paradox in which it is partly dependent on, and partly threatened by, the state. Individuals can be threatened by their own state in a variety of ways, and they can also be threatened through their state as a result of its interactions with other states in the internation-al system. The question of national security cannot be reduced to the individual level because both the state and system levels have characteristics that make them more than the sum of their parts. For this reason the tension between security on the individual level and on the other levels is a permanent feature.

Much the same is true in practice for ethnic and religious groupings at the soci-etal level, though here the contradiction is more circumstantial than structural. There will always be security contradictions between individuals and states.

Between states and societal groupings such contradictions are common, but not inevitable. They are common because the outcome of history leaves a pattern in which states and societies frequently do not fit together comfortably. In theory, the nation-state ideal offers a possible harmony between state and societal security. But in practice, the state machinery frequently discriminates against some of the societal elements embedded within it: sometimes with discrimination in the distribution of rights and welfare (blacks in South Africa, Palestinians in Israel), sometimes with severe assaults on societal identities (Turks in Bulgaria, Ukrainians in the Soviet Union), sometimes with campaigns of physical obliteration (Jews in Nazi Germany, Kurds in Iraq). These contradictions create threats in both directions. Individuals and societal groups can pose threats to the state as well as being threatened by it, and if these are serious and numerous enough, they can corrode the existence of the state as a meaningful entity, as in Lebanon, Burma and El Salvador.

For some states, clashes with their domestic constituents will define the principal feature of their insecurity, making national security a difficult concept to apply. For most, however, the principal security contradiction is between their own national security and that of other states. The contradiction between states is captured in the idea of the power-security dilemma. This dilemma operates most clearly in the military and economic sectors, where power has a zero-sum quality, where the pursuit of legitimate self-interest easily raises threats to others, and where real possibilities for aggressive behaviour exist. It is no accident that the strategic language used to describe behaviour in these two sectors is strikingly similar: defence and protection, war and trade war, military balances and trade balances, security of supply and so forth.

This contradiction between states is a feature of anarchic structure, but it does not constitute a contradiction between state and system. Since the sovereign structure of states, and the anarchic structure of the international system are the opposite ends of a single political phenomenon, and since the maturity of states is a major factor in the maturity of the system, such a contradiction is hard to envisage. Although both liberal and mercantilist economic structures generate conflict and insecurity, alternative economic orders cannot be created without substantial changes in the policy and internal structure of states. And although the power-security dilemma represents a system-wide phenomenon, the dynamics which create it stem from relations between states. The security problems of states cannot be assessed without reference to the system, and the character and dynamics of the system cannot be understood without reference to states. The system itself only becomes insecure if its structure is threatened. The political structure of anarchy is extremely stable, even though the particular way in which the global sovereignty is divided up is not, leaving states to cope with the shifting vagaries of the balance of power. The economic structure of the global market is less stable, because its freedom to operate can be greatly constrained by widespread adoption of mercantilist policies by states.

Looking at the integrative quality of security in terms of sectors reveals a host of linkages between sectors, but a prevalence of contradictions within rather than between them. The security logic of the political sector has already been covered in the discussion of individual, state and system levels. Its key contradiction lies in conflicting security interests among and between individuals, societies and states. Military policy feeds into the power-security dilemma between states, and also gives rise to the defence dilemma which is a contradiction distinctive to the military sector. Following the arguments of hegemony theory, and Paul Kennedy's historical analysis of great power decline, it is clear that military policy has powerful long-term effects on economic standing. The use of force under modern conditions of warfare has obvious implications for the environment ranging from long-term chemical poisoning to nuclear winter. As illustrated by the effects of the Vietnam and Afghanistan syndromes on the United States and the Soviet Union, and in a quite different way by the First World War, the use of force can also have major societal and political consequences. The Soviet Union, both in the revolution of 1917 and in the reconstruction of 1990, illustrates many of the cross-sectoral consequences of military security policy on the economy, society and politics.

In the economic sector, the distinctive contradiction is between vulnerability and efficiency. Economic policy links to military security in complex ways. Mercantilism serves the goal of self-reliance, but may at the same time weaken the economy overall by denying the benefits of economies of scale and competition. It may also stimulate international conditions that make the use of force more likely. Liberalism may or may not strengthen the economy, depending on the state's position within the global market. It weakens the military self-reliance of states, but also reduces the incentives for states to resort to force within a liberal system. The long-term instability of liberal systems may, on the other hand, trigger periodic crises in the international system as a whole. There is increasing linkage between the economic sector and the environmental one as the requirements of mass production begin to threaten the structure of the planetary ecosystem. Economic policy also has major impacts on the political and societal sectors. Open markets subject societal and political structures to strong and continuous pressures to adjust; closed ones require defensive enclosures of society and polity of the type most extremely associated with communist states.

In the societal sector, the distinctive contradiction is between the deeply parochial quality of the several hundred ethno-cultural societies into which history has divided humankind over the millennia, and the profoundly cosmopolitan quality of the recently emergent international society. The parochial element feeds into the power-security dilemma through its impact on political perceptions and military behaviour. This familiar pattern was given its highest expression in the Social Darwinism of the European powers and the Japanese, but is now perhaps most evident in the contemporary international system in the Arab-Israel dispute, the explosive enmities in the Caucasus, the turbulent relationships in South Asia and the often violent relations both within the Islamic community and between it and all of the other cultures with which it shares boundaries. The particular norms of some societies can create contradictions for them with prevailing patterns of global order. One thinks of the problem posed for Islam by both market behaviour and the idea of the sovereign territorial state, and of the problem that an individualist view of human rights poses for both Islam and China. No more potent symbol of this type of threat could be found than the use of the Statue of Liberty by Chinese students in the spring of 1989 as a symbol of their protest against the communist government.

The cosmopolitan element, by contrast, acts as a significant, and potentially major, mediating factor against the power-security dilemma. In the political, military and the economic sectors a strong international society makes it easier to avoid unintended and unwanted side-effects of national security policy. An international society capable of forming stable regimes not only strengthens itself by so doing, but also facilitates both the pursuit of joint gains, and the avoidance of joint loss in many areas of military, political, economic and environmental policy.

The environmental sector has not yet developed a conspicuous contradiction of its own. The most obvious contradiction that it raises is with the political and economic structures, whose fragmentation obstructs the formation of a policy-making entity big enough to deal with long-term problems of planetary scale. The only offset to this is the impact of environmental consciousness on the development of international society. If major environmental effects manifest themselves more slowly than now anticipated, then this disjuncture may not be serious. The rather slow and incremental measures possible under anarchic management systems may suffice to stave off any catastrophic changes. But if they come more quickly, then they will transform the security environment in all the sectors, and perhaps even at all the levels.

The lesson to be taken from this interplay among the different levels and sectors of the security problem is that the concept of security is a naturally integrative idea. Although individuals, states and the international system all provide valuable starting points for enquiry, none of them, in the end, provide an ultimate basic category of referent objects for the concept of security. The same logic applies to sectors, where the full richness and meaning of security is to be found in the interplay among them rather than the primacy of one. Major security phenomena like terrorism and deterrence, or concepts such as security regime or security complexes, simply cannot be understood properly without a full appreciation of their sources, effects and dynamics at and among all three levels. Neither can military and economic, or political and societal, or economic and environmental security be fully understood apart from each other. The 'national' security problem turns out to be a systemic security problem in which individuals, states and the system all play a part, and in which economic, societal and environmental factors are as important as political and military ones. From this integrative perspective, the levels and sectors appear more useful as viewing platforms from which one can observe the problem from different angles, than as self-contained areas for policy or analysis.

REASONS FOR ADOPTING, AND CONSEQUENCES OF, A BROAD INTERPRETATION OF SECURITY

The case for adapting this broad agenda for security has three elements: the changing priority among security issues caused by rising density; the useful political qualities of the concept; and its integrative intellectual qualities.

The rising density of the international system creates a very powerful interplay between anarchy and interdependence. The linkage between the structure of political fragmentation on the one hand, and the rising tide of mutually consequential activities in several sectors on the other, creates common fates and security interdependencies across a wide range of issues. Under these conditions, narrow views of national security, and the national security strategies that accompany them, are increasingly inappropriate and counterproductive. Rising density changes the profile of threats and vulnerabilities that define the security problem. For many states within the more developed part of the system, the fear of military attack is receding. This is partly to do with nuclear paralysis and a historically conditioned fear of war, and partly because of the rise of security communities, which are themselves complex results of changing social norms, political perceptions, and economic interests. More recently, this trend has been greatly reinforced by the ending of the Cold War.

The fading of military threats naturally causes other types of threat to come more clearly into view, but it is also true that other types of threat are rising in importance regardless of the decline of military concerns. Debt, inflation, capital shortages and trade friction loom large when states have adapted themselves heavily to a liberal economy, and thus made their domestic structures vulnerable to the operating difficulties of the international economy. Societal threats are strongly felt by groups who fear either the overbearing presence of neighbours, or the danger of dissolving in international cosmopolitanism. Political threats are felt by those whose domestic arrangements are either out of step with history (authoritarian monarchies and theocracies), out of step with present trends (communist states), menaced by hostile neighbours (India and Pakistan), or unable to cope with the problems of government (weak states). Environmental threats are increasingly feared by all, though as yet not universally experienced. How will international society react if early rises in sea levels begin to obliterate low-lying states such as the Maldives, Bangladesh and the Netherlands? Rising density drives all of these in three ways. It bathes states in information about each other's activities, thus subjecting them to critical comparison from within and without. It exposes all to the rising levels of absolute power in the system (Britain's absolute power – its wealth, destructive power, technology, etc. – are much larger now than at the height of its relative international power during the nineteenth century). This increase in global capabilities makes it difficult for any state or society or individual to escape from the increasingly large consequences of actions taken by others. And it becomes increasingly difficult to act without coordinating with others. The first reason for adopting a broad conception of security is therefore simply that the realities of the policy environment call for it.

The second reason has to do with the useful political qualities of security. One of these is that, in its broad form, the concept works against the obstructive, and in some ways false, opposition between Idealists and Realists. The notion of security offers much, both to those whose main concern is peace and to those whose main concern is self-protection. It offers little to those whose main concern is to dominate through the accumulation of power, and therefore it divides the aggressive from those genuinely concerned with self-protection. The solid rooting of the concept in both anarchy and interdependence helps to sink a number of unhelpful illusions on both extremes that have clogged up policy debates. These include conceptions of national security based on reducing vulnerability by increasing power, pipe-dreams (and nightmares) of world government, naive assumptions about underlying harmonies of interest and simplistic reductionist assumptions that all politics can be boiled down to the level of individual human beings. None of these ideas can be sustained in a system politically structured as an anarchy, in which density creates conditions of high interdependence.

Another useful, though also potentially dangerous, political quality of security is the action priority that it creates. As Wæver argues (see page 36), to use the word security is to call for exceptional measures to block an undesirable development. The word itself is therefore a powerful tool in claiming attention for priority items in the competition for government attention. It also helps to establish a consciousness of the importance of issues so labelled in the minds of the population at large. The danger is that security will be used to justify measures that are outside the legal framework of government, secretive and narrowly nationalistic. This danger, however, is already with us, arising from the particularly military focus that security has had during the Cold War era. One purpose of a broader conception of security would be to reduce this military tendency by widening the security agenda to other sectors. Another would be to establish the idea that national security in any sector, including the military, is only achievable in an international context. More use of the term international security, or perhaps common security, would help to establish this link. The idea that security is interdependent, and therefore international, has already made headway even in the military sector through both the logic of deterrence (mutually assured destruction), and more broadly in the mass campaigns against excessive militarization.

An integrated conception of security thus serves as an antidote to the political problem of national security as an ambiguous symbol. The logic of national security is seen to lead irresistibly in the direction of international and common security, so much so that the two cannot be separated in relation to achievement of security as a policy objective. Increased awareness of security linkages makes it difficult for domestic vested interests to disguise their own objectives under the cloak of national security. A broader view of security, encompassing its political, societal, environmental and economic as well as its military dimensions serves to raise, rather than to suppress, questions about vested interests and domestic structures. While the military dimension of security traditionally demands, and gets, a considerable measure of secrecy, the non-military dimensions are usually more open to debate. If security is seen to rest on international as much as national factors, and national actions are seen to have a major bearing on the international dynamic of insecurity, then the political utility and mobilizing potency of appeals to purely national and primarily military security will be much diminished.

Nevertheless, the general concept of national security, albeit firmly fixed in an international context, and complemented by international and common security, is a necessary part of this broader agenda. It addresses the interplay of threat and vulnerability for states locked into the context of interdependence that characterizes many contemporary international issues both military and non-military. In my view it is the most appropriate, and perhaps the only, concept able to orientate state policy for the international relations of a mature anarchy. The continuing primacy of the state as policy-maker seems a firm reality for the foreseeable future. Even in Europe, where a large group of states are steadily integrating their political economies, this will simply result in a larger entity forced to play a state-like role in the international system.[1] This means that national security will remain a potent and relevant concept. But because the logic of security contains a strong international and collective dimension, it avoids the destructive zero-sum logic of power. It offers a reasonable prospect that, if properly handled (and here is where the work of grand strategists should play its role), policy can avoid the unstable extremes of power and peace, and find a judicious balance between national and collective security interests.

The third reason for adopting the broad security agenda is the intellectually attractive integrative qualities of the idea itself. This is an academic point, already discussed above. The gist of it is that the concept of security provides a way of linking together many areas of theory and analysis within International Studies that are normally isolated from each other. These include: international relations theory, international political economy, area studies, strategic studies, peace and conflict research, human rights, development studies, international history and some areas of science and technology. This book is itself an attempt to make these links clear, and to demonstrate the attractions of pursuing them. The centrality of security to the study of international relations is underlined by the fact that one can derive from it major concepts and images: security complexes, the defence and power-security dilemmas, weak and strong states and mature and immature anarchy. These ideas stand comparison with those that can be derived from the concept of power, and, on this evidence, security stands available as an organizing idea for International Studies which is at least as effective as power in unifying the subject, and less destructive in its policy consequences.

If these reasons make the case for adapting a broad interpretation of security, then it is the inherent breadth, and natural integrative quality of the concept that underlies the arguments made about Strategic Studies versus International Security Studies in the Introduction (see page 40 ff). The key issue is where to locate grand strategy. Grand strategy is precisely the art of comprehending a diverse but interacting set of factors sufficiently clearly so as to be able to identify lines of action that maximize benefits and minimize costs. It might be defined as the application of strategic vision and analysis to both the structures of the international system, and to the interplay of threats and vulnerabilities within and among states and societies within it. By 'strategic vision' I mean a perspective that is forward-looking, interdisciplinary, multilevel and concerned with policy problems as well as explanatory theory. Since security is so interdependent, grand strategists have not simply to accomplish this for one actor in relation to others. That kind of strategic perspective is only appropriate for zero-sum military conflicts. Where security is interdependent, and especially where it is acknowledged to be so, the grand strategists must work for the system as a whole as well as for individual actors. As Keohane and Nye put it:

> From the foreign policy standpoint, the problem facing individual governments is how to benefit from international exchange while maintaining as much autonomy as possible. From the perspective of the international system, the problem is how to generate and maintain a mutually beneficial pattern of cooperation in the face of competing efforts by governments (and non-governmental actors) to manipulate the system for their own benefit.[2]

Strategic Studies is too narrow in its expertise and outlook to be able to encompass this broad security agenda either comfortably or well. When security and insecurity are seen to rest on much more than military factors, then Strategic Studies will be able to pursue its specialized military agenda unencumbered by distorted images and inflated expectations. Grand strategy must therefore be located in the broader field of International Studies, making International Security Studies, in a sense, an approach to the whole field rather in the same way that McKinlay and Little present Realism, Liberalism and Socialism as perspectives on the international system as a whole.[3] Some might even see International Security Studies as a liberal reformulation of Realism, emphasizing the structural and security-oriented approach of Neorealism, and applying it across a broader agenda. I would support such a view. One benefit from adapting the new label would be to escape from the vast encumbrance of misunderstanding and invective that are now perhaps irretrievably associated with Realism.

Many people who now locate themselves within Peace Conflict Research might also be attracted to the pursuit of grand strategy within the broader context of International Studies. The agenda of Peace and Conflict Research has always been much wider than that of Strategic Studies, so the problems of transition are not large. The main requirement would be abandonment of simple-minded anti-militarism, and acceptance of anarchic structure as the framework of analysis. Developments within Peace and Conflict Research already make these much less formidable obstacles than they might once have been. The normative commitment to address public policy concerns, and to promote a reformist agenda, would be a welcome part of International Security Studies. To the extent that Peace and Conflict Research defines itself as a reaction to Strategic Studies, the rise of

International Security Studies would undermine its *raison d'etre*, or at least confine it to a smaller and more radical constituency than is now the case.[4]

Whether and how International Security Studies should seek to institutionalize itself – by infiltrating existing research institutes and journals or by founding new ones, by setting up new postgraduate courses – is an interesting question.

IMPLICATIONS FOR POLICY

The objective of this book was not to find a definition for national security, but to explore the concept in an attempt to clarify its domain, identify its contradictions and gain some idea of its part in the overall picture of international relations. As a consequence of that mandate, the enquiry has been conducted at a rather high level of abstraction, avoiding the harsh world of specific crises and problems except as illustrations. The purpose of the exercise was not to seek solutions to particular policy problems, but to refine, and hopefully make more accurate, the intellectual lenses through which particular policy problems are viewed. For that purpose, the conclusion about a broader security agenda, a field of International Security Studies and a corps of grand strategists, serves well. But this whole approach is vulnerable to the criticism that it simply reflects the comfortable academic belief that if one can change the way people think about something important, then reality will also be changed: and never mind questions about how many people will read the book and how long the ideas will take to work their supposed alchemy. I can be accused, in other words, of leaving the hard thinking about real policies to others.

I cannot avoid the substance of this charge, and in mitigation can only plead for a division of labour, and point to my few ventures towards the policy realm.[5] I can also show that although the analysis presented here is designed primarily for conceptual purposes, it can be read with policy-making in mind. Two major constraints apply to this exercise. The first is the general rule that understanding something does not necessarily increase one's ability to do anything about it: we know quite a lot about how the solar system works, but that does not give us the ability to alter its functions. Awareness of contradictions is only a preliminary to their resolution, and as demonstrated in Chapter 9, policy-making is itself a heavily politicized activity, bounded by numerous pressures and restrictions. Only in rare circumstances, such as the period immediately following a major war as in 1945–50, or during the collapse of a major political idea as in 1989–90, can one expect the leeway for dramatic reforms to be very wide. The second constraint is the need for a case study with which to bring policy questions into focus. In order to talk sensibly about definitions of national security and the appropriate policy options associated with them, one needs to anchor one's discussion firmly onto some empirical realities. Such a study is beyond the scope of the present volume.

What can one say about security policy in the absence of a case-study? The most obvious potential policy error identified in this book is to base security analysis too narrowly on one level or in one sector. This error is made by all those who argue that the problem is to choose between the national versus international security strategies discussed in Chapter 9. The issue at stake is whether security is essentially divisible in character (i.e. whether a strictly national security is possible), or whether it is essentially indivisible (i.e. security is interdependent). This question has dominated the policy debate about security, and especially military security, and in so doing has perpetuated a largely sterile polarization of mutually exclusive views in such a way as to distract attention from more constructive lines of enquiry. Nationalists broadly assume that security is divisible, and consequently place their policy emphasis on the state. They acknowledge, of course, an element of indivisibility in the balance of power and deterrence, but their policy orientation tends strongly towards national security strategies. Internationalists, with the notable exception of unilateral disarmers, stress the indivisibility of security, and the need to negotiate with the sources of threat.

Both positions represent a logic which is internally correct, but too narrowly based. If it is assumed that the two approaches must be separate, because their logic is mutually exclusive, then each is forced into a more extreme version of itself. In other words, because nationalist policies require the arming of the state, protectionism and a power-struggle analysis of the system, they naturally clash with internationalist policies based on disarmament, international cooperation and a harmony-of-interests model of the system. If that clash is seen as so basic that it precludes a meaningful mix between them, then each alternative must carry alone the whole burden of security. To do this, the national security policy must exaggerate the necessity for a powerful state, and the international security policy must leap all the way into utopias of general and complete disarmament, free trade and world government. When presented in those forms, they appear to confirm the idea that no common ground exists between them, so making the initial distinction self-reinforcing.

The fallacy of this polarization makes the middle ground hard to occupy, as many an advocate of arms control and managed trade has discovered. Broader views lack the appealing simplicity of either extreme. Failures or short-lived successes in middle-ground policies like the SALT negotiations simply justify critics on both wings. There are two well-established intellectual strategies for dealing with this type of polarization on policy strategy. One is E. H. Carr's rather despairing logic of a pendulum relationship. A period dominated by one extreme is followed by a period dominated by the other, the transitions usually being marked by policy failure, crisis or catastrophe, and therefore of reaction in favour of the alternative pole.[6] Repeated trial and failure of inadequate alternate approaches on this model can only lead to cynicism. A more progressive view is Arnold Toynbee's image of a wheel which rotates endlessly in the same pattern.[7] This sustains the cycle of swings between alternative strategies, but adds the element that the wheel moves itself and its burden forward over the ground, thus suggesting improvement in each turn of the cycle. In this view there is a dialectical mechanism by which the two extremes subtly merge into, and moderate, each other. Some comfort can be taken from this view, subject to the caveats about automatic progress argued in Chapter 4, but it does not address the core of the problem, which is that the polarization between the two approaches is false in the first place.

In reality, as I have sought to demonstrate, both the logic and the practice of security policy under contemporary conditions mean that to choose is to begin by making a fundamental error. On practical grounds, there is no choice, because neither alternative can possibly deliver the security objectives desired of it. The very process of choice ensures not only that policy will be self-defeating, but that subsequent policies which result from reactions to it will also be ineffective. On conceptual grounds, there is no choice because individual, society, state and system cannot be disconnected from each other in relation to security.

Instead of alternating between state and system in an endless cycle of frustration, a more appealing logic is to combine and expand the two approaches by seeking integrative security policies that work on all three levels simultaneously, while paying maximal attention to the positive and negative linkages across sectors. This is a tall, but not impossible, order. It is what grand strategists should be paid to do. It requires that simplistic notions of security as deriving either from the power of the state, or from the creation of trust and order in the system, be replaced by more complex appreciations of how state behaviour and system structure interact. It also requires policies that are as sensitive to the vulnerabilities of other actors, and their own legitimate assessments of threat (including threat from the policy-makers' own state), as they are to the vulnerabilities of, and threats to, the state generating them.

This last is the most difficult requirement. As Jervis notes: 'To put oneself in another's skin is terribly hard. But the costs of acting as though the meaning of one's behaviour is self-evident are enormous.'[8] If threats are intended, then they need to be controlled in relation to the desired effect, as in deterrence policy. If they are unintended, then their effect on the system, and by way of feedback on the state concerned, must be assessed in relation to the domestic costs of whatever reforms would be required to remove them. Such assessments might be very difficult to make, requiring acknowledgement of unpleasant facts or contradictions about one's own society. They may also reveal irreconcilable ideological differences, where there is no ground for agreement between the state perceiving a threat and the state which is allegedly generating it. Market economy states, for example, might refuse to acknowledge that their economic practices pose a threat to weak developing states, because to do so would undermine the domestic legitimacy of their own organizing ideology. Communist states (should any remain by the time of publication) might similarly refuse to acknowledge the political threat they constitute to others, on the doctrinal grounds that it applies only to a class, and not to the state as a whole, or that socialism is inherently peaceful and capitalism inherently aggressive. Despite these difficulties, even the exercise of considering one's own state as a source of threat would lead to improved understanding of security dynamics in the system as a whole. The use of security complexes as a framework for analysis offers one useful technique for avoiding the normal excesses of both

ethnocentric policy and utopian prescription, and for moving towards a more integrated view of the national security problem on the regional level.

One policy conclusion from the integrative view of security is that security
cannot be achieved by either individuals or states acting solely on their own
behalf. Some collective measures are necessary among the members of the system
if each is to achieve security. Just as security cannot be created by individual
actors, neither can it be created by concentrating all power and responsibility at
the upper levels. When such concentration happens, as in the case of individuals
in a totalitarian state, the collective institution becomes a major source of threat to
those smaller actors it was supposed to protect. For the same reason, states fear
submergence of their own powers and authorities in larger regional or global entities. If all power were concentrated in a world government, neither nations nor
individuals would control their destinies, and both would feel insecure in relation
to the higher authority that bound them. The sheer scale of larger entities necessarily reduces their sensitivity to the security needs of smaller actors. Thus the
logic of common security does not point towards the replacement of anarchic by
hierarchic political structures. It confirms the utility of anarchy. The more actors
at every level retain some control over their security, the more stable the system
will be, for a collapse at any point will not entail a collapse of the whole security
system.[9]

One idea that exemplifies most of the criteria for an integrative security policy is non-provocative defence (NPD), discussed briefly in Chapter 8. NPD is integrative in that it incorporates elements of both national and international security
strategies. On the national side, it responds to the need for a robust and credible
defence policy that can be achieved by the state using its own resources. It has the
moral appeal of being strictly and obviously defensive, and if militia forces are its
mainstay, it also serves to decentralize organized military power within the state.
Both of these make it plausible to construct a domestic political consensus around
the idea. NPD also requires the maintenance of both skilled armed forces and
high-technology defence industries, and therefore does not defy political practi-
cality by alienating important elements of the domestic military security constituency.

On the international side, it shows sensitivity to the security needs of others
without at the same time appearing weak or lacking in commitment. Because it
involves an explicit and very public attempt to mute the logic of the power-security dilemma, it is unlikely to be counterproductive on the international level in the
way that the normally ambiguous military posture often is, where opponents have
difficulty distinguishing offensive from defensive capability. It is not without risk,
and is probably unwise when the likelihood of war is seen as being high. But it is
no riskier than other defence policies under normal circumstances, and has the
great merit of challenging opponents to reconfigure their own forces in less threatening ways. If they do not do so, they stand exposed for all to see as the source of
aggression. If they do, then defence requirements can be reduced all round. By this
logic NPD offers at least the prospect that the negative link between military and

economic strength can be broken. It would also reduce the military obstructions to trade, since there would be fewer objections to the diffusion of defensive military technology than there are to technology that is potentially useful for military offensive purposes.

Integrative policies such as NPD, or cooperative regimes such as the General Agreement on Tariffs and Trade (GATT), or the Group of 7 meetings, or ASEAN, can form new perceptions of the national security problem. Prevailing narrow images of the security problem constrain new policy approaches both because of their hold on the minds of policy-makers and because they define the political dimension of public opinion on security policy. When public opinion becomes concerned about security issues, it tends to do so in extreme forms. The cry goes up either for power or for peace, and in the end neither is, or can be, delivered. So long as political opinion is dominated by images of anarchy as chaos, order as world government and defence as militarism, it will be difficult to begin the reform of policy.

An integrative security perspective offers several alternative concepts which might be useful in recasting public opinion towards a more realistic and constructive sense of the costs and benefits, and opportunities and constraints, of life in an interdependent international anarchy. Security complexes provide a much more subtle and balanced image of regional relations and crises than does the conventional model of power struggles. A greater sense of the interdependence of regional security subsystems might usefully recondition national security policies in many Third World countries. The defence dilemma and the power-security dilemma also weigh against crude images of power struggle, setting a more systemic perspective than the arms race for discussions about military affairs.

But the most important image is that of the mature anarchy, which offers an alternative ideal image for the political economy of international relations as a whole. The international system has already developed to a point at which the internationalist ideal model has convincingly demonstrated its bankruptcy as a practical alternative. But anarchy is generally perceived as a negative condition, despite the mounting evidence that in its international form it can and does provide an impressive measure of peace and security, and that it can be reformed in ways that increase these results. The image of a mature anarchy opens a possible way forward as a realistic image of what might ideally be strived for. Like the other images, it is simple enough in its basic idea to be easily grasped, but complex enough so that the practical process of working through its logic in the real world would create real change. It has the massive advantage of focusing attention on the structures that actually exist. The trend of events at the beginning of the 1990s offered the prospect of an international environment unusually receptive to positive reform within these structures. Without images that connect aspiration to reality, security policy can only steer aimlessly through immediate crises without any larger sense of direction or purpose.

NOTES

1. Barry Buzan, Morten Kelstrup, Pierre Lemaitre, Elzbieta Tromer, Ole Wæver, *The European Security Order Recast: Scenarios for a post-Cold War era* (London: Pinter, 1990).

2. Robert O. Keohane and Joseph S, Nye, 'Power and interdependence revisited', *International Organization*, 41:4 (1987), p, 730.

3. R. D. McKinlay and R. Little, *Global Problems and World Order* (London: Pinter, 1986).

4. Richard Ned Lebow already uses the term 'Peace and security studies' to define a field: 'Interdisciplinary research and the future of peace and security studies', *Political Psychology*, 9:3 (1988). See also Egbert Jahn, Pierre Lemaitre and Ole Wæver, *European Security – Problems of Research on Non-military Aspects*, Copenhagen Papers 1, Centre for Peace and Conflict Research, Copenhagen, 1987.

5. Buzan *et al., op. cit,* (note 1); 'Japan's future: old history versus new roles' *International Affairs*, 64:4 (1988); 'Common security, non-provocative defence and the future of Western Europe', *Review of International Studies*, 13:4 (1987); and with H. O. Nazareth, 'South Africa versus Azania: the implications of who rules', *International Affairs*, 62:1 (1985/6).

6. E. H. Carr, *The Twenty Years Crisis* (London: Macmillan, 1946, 2nd edn), p, 93.

7. Arnold J. Toynbee, *A Study of History*, abr. D. C. Somervell (New York: Dell, 1965), vol. 1, p. 296.

8. Robert Jervis, *Perception and Misperception in International Politics* (Princeton, NJ: Princeton University Press, 1976), p. 187.

9. On the stability of layered hierarchies, see H. A. Simon, 'The architecture of complexity', *Proceedings of the American Philosophical Society*, 106 (1962).

index

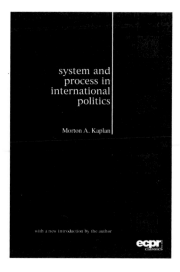

System and Process in International Politics

Morton A. Kaplan

April 2005
234x156 - 142pp
Pb: 978-0-9547966-2-4
£22.00

First published in 1957, *System and Process* broke the mould in political science by combining systems, game, and cybernetic concepts in its theoretical formulations. Since its publication, serious research in international relations has needed to respond to the bold hypotheses that matched equilibrial rules with type of system. Kaplan's life-long interest in finding an objective basis for moral judgments had its scholarly origins in an appendix of this classical book, which incorporated his understanding of philosophy and, in particular, the philosophy of science. A second appendix on 'The Mechanisms of Regulation' explored the cybernetic and recursive nature of knowing.

For this ECPR Classics edition Professor Kaplan has added a new introduction to the original text.

place an order at www.ecprnet.org
ecpr members receive a 10% discount

bringing key texts back into print for the political science community